Research for Effective Social Work Practice

In this book and companion custom website you will find:

- A practice-oriented description of qualitative and quantitative research methods that engages rather than intimidates students
- Illustrations of real-life research and evaluation from different levels of social work practice, encompassing many populations
- Attention to the ethics and the politics of research at each phase of the process, from the identification of an issue through reporting findings
- Exercises that provide hands-on learning opportunities in research and evaluation
- A historical, strengths-based perspective on research and evaluation in social work that teaches empowerment and professionalism
- Six in-depth, interactive, easy-to-access cases, that include data in SPSS and Excel
- A wealth of instructor-only resources available at www.routledgesw.com/research, including sample syllabi, links, and multiple-choice and free-response test items all linked to current EPAS standards, and PowerPoint presentations

Judy L. Krysik is an Associate Professor in Social Work at Arizona State University, Phoenix, and Director of the ASU Center for Child Well-Being. She teaches research methods, evaluation, program planning, and practice with children and families. Her current research pursuits focus on infants and toddlers in out-of-home care and community collaboration in the field of child welfare. She is a member of the NASW National Ethics Committee and she serves on the editorial review boards of the *Journal of Social Work Education*, *Social Work Research*, and the *Journal of Social Work Values and Ethics*.

New Directions in Social Work

Melinda Lewis, University of Kansas, Series Editor

An authentic breakthrough in social work education...

New Directions in Social Work is an innovative, integrated series of texts, Web site, and interactive case studies for generalist courses in the Social Work curriculum at both undergraduate and graduate levels. Instructors will find everything they need to build a comprehensive course that allows students to meet course outcomes and prepare for effective and ethical social work practice. The New Directions series is distinguished by these unique features:

- All texts, interactive cases, and test materials are **linked to the 2015 CSWE Policy and Accreditation Standards (EPAS)**.
- **One Web portal with easy access** for instructors and students from any computer – no codes, no CDs, no restrictions. Go to www.routledgesw. com and discover.
- **The Series is flexible and can be easily adapted for use in online distance-learning courses as well as hybrid/blended and traditional format courses.**
- Each Text and the Web site can be used **individually** or as an **entire Series** to meet the needs of any social work program.

TITLES IN THE SERIES

Social Work and Social Welfare: An Invitation, Fourth Edition by Marla Berg-Weger

Human Behavior in the Social Environment, Fourth Edition by Anissa Taun Rogers

Human Behavior in the Social Environment: Perspectives on Development, the Life Course, and Macro Contexts by Anissa Taun Rogers

Research for Effective Social Work Practice, Fourth Edition by Judy L. Krysik

Social Policy for Effective Practice: A Strengths Approach, Fourth Edition by Rosemary K. Chapin

The Practice of Generalist Social Work, Fourth Edition by Julie Birkenmaier and Marla Berg-Weger

Research for Effective Social Work Practice

Fourth Edition

Judy L. Krysik

Routledge
Taylor & Francis Group

NEW YORK AND LONDON

Fourth edition published 2018
by Routledge
711 Third Avenue, New York, NY 10017

and by Routledge
2 Park Square, Milton Park, Abingdon, Oxon OX14 4RN

Routledge is an imprint of the Taylor & Francis Group, an informa business

First edition published by McGraw-Hill 2007
Second edition published by Routledge 2010
Third edition published by Routledge 2013

Library of Congress Cataloging in Publication Data
A catalog record for this title has been requested

ISBN: 978-1-138-81952-8 (hbk)
ISBN: 978-1-138-81953-5 (pbk)
ISBN: 978-1-315-74438-4 (ebk)

Typeset in ITC Berkeley Oldstyle
by Sunrise Setting Ltd, Brixham, UK

Visit the companion website: Routledgesw.com

This book is dedicated to professional social workers who give of themselves every day to improve the lives of individuals and the hearts of communities.

JK

Brief Contents

Contents

Preface

As with the first edition of *Research for Effective Social Work Practice,* this edition is written with the undergraduate social work student in mind. Our adopters also use the book at the master's level, and some even refer PhD students to it when they need a tool to help students better understand major research concepts. We continue to develop the book from the perspectives of both using research in practice and producing research. The examples in this edition relate to current issues of concern to social work, many populations, micro and macro practice contexts, and span many areas of practice including substance abuse, corrections, gerontology, social work in an international context, child welfare, prevention research, community organizing, social policy, program planning, and evaluation.

The fourth edition of *Research for Effective Social Work Practice* expands on earlier editions to include:

- ■ Current research examples and studies with updated language.
- ■ A greater emphasis on how to conduct literature reviews.
- ■ Questions at the end of each chapter to develop students' skills at integrating research concepts and thinking through ethical and design issues.
- ■ A section on writing and presentation with an emphasis on how research and evaluation are integral in the writing of successful grant proposals.
- ■ Greater integration of qualitative and qualitative research methods with an emphasis on how these methods complement both developing new knowledge and the evaluation of programs.

What most sets this book apart from other social work research books is that it is engaging to social work students. The most frequent comment we receive from our adopters is how much students enjoy the book. Similar to most social work research books, *Research for Effective Social Work Practice* has chapters devoted to basic research topics such as formulating research questions, sampling, research design, measurement, and analysis. Unlike these other texts, however, this book logically links the chapters so that, based on the research question that the social worker selects, the student will be able to (a) make a reasoned judgment about the best research methods to apply, (b) articulate the strengths and weaknesses of different choices, and (c) critique the research methods used. In addition, the critical thinking approach this text promotes and the examples and guidance it provides will help social workers avoid common errors in research and evaluation. Finally, as the name implies, the book will assist social workers in using and producing research that will lead to effective social work practice.

Some authors of social work research books maintain that research is too complex a task for undergraduate and even graduate social work students. Instead, these authors aspire to prepare social work students to read research and to have a greater appreciation of the role of research in social work. *Research for Effective Social Work Practice* goes beyond these limited objectives by helping students to develop their own research skills. We are constantly impressed by the research projects that social work students at all levels are engaged in. Our experience has shown that if students read this book with the intent to learn and engage in the exercises, not only will they be able to access, read, and critically evaluate research, but they will develop valued research skills and will find they actually like research!

ORGANIZATION OF THE BOOK

Each chapter in the book follows a similar format. The chapters begin with an interesting quote to set the stage for the topic. The quote is followed by an introduction to the chapter and a list of learning objectives. Each chapter devotes attention to social work in a culturally diverse context, and it provides guidance to social workers striving for culturally proficient practice. In addition, as research terms are introduced, they are displayed in bold type and are supported by a glossary. Each chapter is summarized by a conclusion and a series of main points.

There are a number of exercises at the end of each chapter that are carefully designed to promote active learning. *Exercises* are intended primarily to apply the concepts in the chapters to small group learning formats and can also be used for independent learning. Many of the exercises draw on case studies that are on the book's web site. Test questions on the web site present additional questions and answers for each chapter that will help assess student learning.

To be consistent with the length of most social work research courses, we organized this book into 13 chapters. Chapters 1 and 2 present an introduction to the context of social work research. Chapters 3–9 represent applications of research in social work and the design phase, and chapters 10–12 discuss the implementation and analysis phases. Finally, Chapter 13 explains how to present research for maximum impact.

- Chapter 1 sets the context for social work research and discusses the importance of research to the social work profession. The chapter presents social work research in its historical context; examining the challenges the profession has overcome and those it continues to face. As you prepare yourself for the job market, Chapter 1 introduces you to a world of opportunities to engage in social work research, both as a complement to practice and as a profession in itself.

- Chapter 2 reflects on the way politics shapes research agendas and the choice of research methods. It emphasizes the need for social workers to commit themselves to ethics in conducting and using research. Similar to the first chapter, Chapter 2 uses a historical approach, reflecting the belief that we should learn from the mistakes of our past.

- Chapter 3 sets out the process of conducting research, and provides a step-by-step approach to framing research problems and questions. After a research problem and question are identified, chapters 4–9 present a "how to" approach to answering the research question using either a quantitative, qualitative, or mixed-methods approach.

- Chapter 4 represents one context in which social workers apply their research skills. The chapter addresses the evaluation of a single case through single subject research.

- Chapter 5 focuses on research strategies used by agencies and community groups to gather information to support, evaluate, and improve social programs. Attention is given to the purposes of evaluation as well as its limitations and political context. The chapter includes types of evaluation, including evaluability assessment, needs assessment, process, outcomes, and cost evaluation.

- Chapter 6 describes a variety of qualitative research methods to answer research questions that focus on gaining an in-depth understanding of social work-related areas of inquiry.

- Chapter 7 provides an approach to determining the best design to answer specific research questions or test hypotheses.

- Chapter 8 deals with sampling, that is, how to make decisions on what or who, and how many to include in a research study.

- Chapter 9 covers the basics of measurement, including how to design your own measures.

- Chapter 10 deals with the mechanics of collecting and safely storing data and preparing the data for analysis.

- Chapter 11 presents a "how to" approach to analyzing quantitative data.

- Chapter 12 examines the analysis of quantitative data, guidelines for selecting statistical tests to analyze the data, and considerations for interpreting them. Statistical tests include Pearson Correlation, Chi-square, three uses of t-tests, and Analysis of Variance (ANOVA).

■   Chapter 13 provides valuable tips on presenting a research study for pub-
    lication, conference presentation, workshops, and grant writing.

Finally, this book is designed to guide students in meeting the Council on Social
Work Education (CSWE) *Educational Policy and Accreditation Standards*
(EPAS) by developing competencies related to the use of research in social work
practice. These competencies can be found on the CSWE web site.

Acknowledgments

We wish to thank the thousands of social work students in our research classes over the years. They have taught us not only how to teach research through their feedback, interest, humor, and occasional anxiety, but also how to KEEP IT REAL in the classroom!

Appreciation goes out to our reviewers for their very thoughtful and candid evaluations and suggestions:

Sik Yin Chan, Concordia University
Megan Lindsey, Arizona State University
Jessica Ritter, Pacific University
Mary Mullins, East Tennessee State University
Kevin Borders, Spalding University
Victoria Anyikwa, Saint Leo University
Rebecca Moore, Tennessee State University
Elizabeth Anthony, Arizona State University
Layne Stormwall, Arizona State University
Sharon Johnson, University of Missouri
Clarence Williams, Grambling State University
Fredi Giesler, University of Wisconsin
Tammy Faux, Watrburg College
Catherine Mancomber, Saginaw Valley State University
John Elliot, Ohio State University
Andrew Zekeri, Tuskegee University

And finally, our enduring thanks go to Sam Barbaro and Athena Bryan of the Taylor and Francis Group; and to our series editors Dr. Alice Lieberman and Melinda Lewis of the School of Social Welfare, University of Kansas.

About the Author

DR. JUDY KRYSIK is an Associate Professor in Social Work at Arizona State University, Phoenix, and Director of the ASU Center for Child Well-Being. She teaches research methods, evaluation, program planning, and practice with children and families. Her current research pursuits focus on infants and toddlers in out-of-home care and community collaboration in the field of child welfare. She is a member of the NASW National Ethics Committee and she serves on the editorial review boards of the *Journal of Social Work Education*, *Social Work Research*, and the *Journal of Social Work Values and Ethics*.

THE CONTEXT OF SOCIAL WORK RESEARCH

For more than a century, social workers have been transforming our society. Social work interventions doubled the number of babies who survived in the early twentieth century, helped millions out of poverty from the Great Depression to today, and assisted people with mental illness through de-institutionalization, aftercare, treatment, and advocacy. Today our society faces urgent, interrelated, and large-scale challenges—violence, substance abuse, environmental degradation, injustice, isolation, and inequality. Today we need social workers' unique blend of scientific knowledge and caring practice more than ever.

American Academy of Social Work & Social Welfare (n.d.)

People generally become social workers because they want to have a positive impact on social conditions in order to improve the lives of others. Impact comes from the commitment to make change, and the knowledge and skills to put that commitment to use. Social work history is rich with examples of committed individuals informed by knowledge and skill.

Dorothea Dix, for example, was a pioneering social worker who used **research** to make an enormous impact in the area of mental health. In 1841, she volunteered to teach a Sunday school class of 20 women inmates at the Cambridge, Massachusetts, jail. After the lesson was over, she went down to the lower level of the building—the dungeon cells. This was where the "insane" were sheltered. She saw miserable, wild, and dazed men and women chained to walls and locked in pens. They were naked, filthy, brutalized, underfed, given no heat, and sleeping on stone floors.

This visit moved Dix to start a campaign to have stoves placed in the cells and to fully clothe the inmates. She also began to study firsthand the conditions for people with mental illness throughout the state. She traveled from county to county, gathering evidence to present to the Massachusetts legislature as the basis for laws to improve conditions. She eventually visited states all over the nation, systematically gathering evidence and making presentations to lobby for the establishment of state-supported institutions for those suffering from mental illness. The first state hospital built as a result of her efforts was located in Trenton, New Jersey. The construction of this hospital was the first step in the development of a national system of "asylums"—places of refuge. Proponents argued that putting people in asylums would be more humane and cost effective than the existing system.

Research continues to impact our society's approach to mental illness. By 1955 there were 560,000 people in mental hospitals throughout the United States. The institutions themselves had become overcrowded, abusive, and in need of reform. Social workers again used research to convince state legislators that mental hospitals were ineffective treatment facilities. They used interviews with patients and family members to document abuses. They argued that releasing people from mental hospitals would be more humane and cost effective than the existing policy of institutionalization.

In 1843 Dorothea Dix made the following plea to the Massachusetts legislature: "I tell what I have seen—painful and shocking as the details often are—that from them you may feel more deeply the imperative obligation which lies upon you to prevent the possibility of a repetition or continuance of such outrages upon humanity."

As a result, beginning in the mid-1960s, many mental hospitals were closed in favor of community treatment models. Although community treatment is promising, it has led to an increase in homelessness and mass incarceration among adults with mental illness. Research continues today on the effectiveness of community-based treatment and enhancements such as peer and family support models, as well as jail diversion programs, have been implemented. Researchers play a major role in our understanding of mental illness and in the improvement of services, and hence outcomes, for this population.

This book was written to help social work students develop the research knowledge and skills needed in order to have a positive impact on social work practice and social conditions. As a social worker, you will need to answer many fundamental questions: Did I help the individual, couple, or family I worked with? What types of interventions are most likely to lead to positive change? Who is not receiving social work services even though he or she is eligible for such services? What interventions are the most cost effective? What evidence do I need in order to obtain or maintain funding for a social program? What information do I need to provide policy makers with so that they might support change that will help people in the community? To answer these questions, you will need knowledge and skills in research. The realization that research is vital to social work practice is not new, and the need for research has been demonstrated over and over again, as illustrated throughout this book.

Before we begin to develop research knowledge and skills, however, we must address the one question that is on the minds of so many beginning social work students: Why? Why do I need to learn research? To address this question we present you with an open letter in Exhibit 1.1. We continue to address this question in this chapter by briefly examining the function of research in social work, the history of research in social work, the struggles the profession has overcome, and the opportunities and challenges that lie ahead. Overall, this chapter is devoted to helping you to achieve an appreciation for the place of research in social work and to increase your knowledge of the infrastructure that has been developed to support social work research. The remaining chapters are geared toward helping you develop the research knowledge and skills that will enable you to fulfill your dream of making an impact.

EXHIBIT 1.1

A Letter to Students from the Authors

According to an old maxim, "What goes around comes around." In fact, this happened to me. I took my first policy class when I was a first-year MSW student. I wanted to be a therapist. After a week I (foolishly) asked my professor, "Why do we need any of this?" He looked pained and proceeded to tell me that policy was "the rules" and that those rules would determine what services I could provide and to whom, as well as what funding and access would be available for my "therapy." I didn't get it at the time.

Now I am teaching research. One evening, one of my MSW students looked frustrated. I asked if there was something she didn't understand. "No," she answered, "I just don't see why I'll ever need this." I am sure I made the same pained expression that my policy professor had made 30 years earlier. For drama, I also clutched my heart. But she was serious and did not mean to induce cardiac arrest. In fact, she wasn't asking a question; she was honestly stating her feelings.

And so, I was sure I had failed her—not her grade, but her education. Hadn't I given the "Why you need research" lecture? Hadn't we examined fascinating research designs and crucial outcome studies? Hadn't we discussed research ethics, literature reviews, critical analyses, statistical testing, and outcome evaluation? We had . . . and yet the question had remained.

I came to realize that the student didn't doubt the importance of research. Rather, she doubted the relevance of research *for her*. She was sure that SHE would never knowingly do research, just as

I was sure 30 years earlier that I would never (knowingly) do policy analysis (or teach research). Foolish me, and probably foolish her.

I guess I need to make my case again. How can you be a clinician, a therapist, an advocate for rape victims, a worker in a domestic violence shelter, a youth counselor, or any other direct service worker without developing research skills? It would be nice to think that we taught you everything you needed to know in the social work program. Too bad—we didn't. When I was a therapist, I was seeing a client for marital counseling. I had learned a lot about family systems and marital counseling. One day my client told me that his father had sexually abused him as a child. My first thought was, "My program never taught me about sexual abuse of boys by their fathers. What should I do?" I needed to know the developmental impact of this kind of sexual abuse. What kinds of treatments were likely to be effective? How great was the risk of suicide? Should I explore and reflect the client's past feelings, or should I teach avoidance and compartmentalization? I was very glad—and relieved—that I knew how to access the research literature. Other people's research made my work a lot less anxiety provoking, for both my client and for me.

Good social workers care about what happens to their clients. Yes, using effective treatments and validating results is part of the NASW Code of Ethics. However, good social workers don't want to be effective just because the Social Work Code of Ethics demands it. Instead, they want to be effective because they CARE. Research helps you and your clients to see what you are accomplishing (or not accomplishing) as a result of services provided.

I recently heard about an exciting new treatment: eye movement desensitization and reprocessing therapy (EMDR). It really works. At least, that's what they tell me. But for whom, and in what context? Does it work equally well for men and women, adolescents and preadolescents, Hispanics and African Americans? Decisions, decisions, decisions . . . so many decisions to make as part of providing services to your clients. Is it better to use it in individual or group treatment? How many sessions does it take? Sometimes the research literature provides answers; sometimes it doesn't. You need to know how to get the evidence you need to make treatment decisions. You can be a "force" for evidence-based practice at your agency. We do things because it has been demonstrated that they work. OK, sometimes we try something innovative if there is enough theory or evidence to suggest it's worth a try. However, we don't continue to do the same thing using up scarce resources if it doesn't work. You have to know one way or another.

Money. Money. Money. Why does it always come down to money? You want money so you can continue your program. You want money so you can expand your services or offer new services. You can get the money, but you have to know how (and who) to ask. These days, funders don't give money easily. You have to get it the old fashioned way, by demonstrating that you need it and will use it wisely. Demonstrate that people want, need, and will use your service. Demonstrate that what you want to provide is effective. Demonstrate that you put the money already given you to good use. You demonstrate these things through program evaluation, a.k.a. research.

Sometimes people say some strange and hurtful things in the name of "truth." Sometimes they do this because they want to stop what you are doing. I'm referring to comments like, "Most people on welfare cheat the system." Going further, in some cases they actually come up with *research* to support their claims. You need to know enough about research to show them (or politicians/funders/your community) the error of their ways, or of their method of obtaining data, or of their statistical procedures, or of their (false) conclusions. First you have to "smell" it, then point it out, then get rid of it.

OK, if you don't want to "walk the walk," at least learn to talk the talk. SOMEONE will do research. Do you want to be able to explain your program and its objectives in a language that a researcher understands, and do you want to understand the language of the researcher to be sure that what is being done in research is appropriate. Bilingual is good.

So, maybe you won't ever have to do research or policy analysis. Or, maybe you will. Maybe you think you'll be a case manager or a therapist for the rest of your life. I thought that. Funny, though, things change. You may become a supervisor, an advocate, an administrator, a program evaluator, or even a *research professor*. Who knows where life leads? In the meantime, I have a hammer in my garage. I rarely use it, but when I need one, it's incredibly handy. We wish you the best with your research tools.

Reprinted with permission, previously published in Finn (2004). To once and future social work students. *The New Social Worker, 11*(4), 12.

By the end of this chapter you should be able to:

■ Articulate the role of research in social work.
■ Discuss the alternatives to knowledge based on research.
■ Describe how research can be used to empower both social workers and the people they endeavor to help.
■ Summarize the positions of social work's professional organizations on the use of research in social work.
■ Describe the concept of evidence-based practice.
■ Identify the types of career opportunities that research skills afford the entry-level social worker.

THE FUNCTIONS OF RESEARCH IN SOCIAL WORK

At this point you may be wondering, "How can research make me a better social worker?" There are several answers to that question, and they all relate to the functions of research in social work. In this section we discuss research both as a method for providing the scientific basis of the social work profession, and as a tool for improving social conditions. We focus on four basic functions of social work research:

■ promoting science as a way of knowing
■ increasing accountability

- improving communication
- enhancing access to scarce resources

Promoting Science as a Way of Knowing

Social workers have many ways of acquiring knowledge (see Exhibit 1.2), and they are all important. One way of knowing is through direct experience. Social work education promotes knowing through experience by requiring students to complete a specific number of hours in an internship or a field practicum. Through observation and direct experience, social workers develop a sense of what works and under what circumstances.

EXHIBIT 1.2

Five Ways of Knowing

Authority: Depression is anger turned against the self. I know because my supervisor told me.

Direct experience: A caseload of 60 cases per worker will cause burnout. I know because I experienced it. I know because I saw, smelled, touched, or tasted it.

Intuition: I think the child is being abused. I don't know why exactly, but my intuition tells me so. I know because I feel it to be so.

Tradition: "There is nothing wrong with spanking a child. My parents spanked me, and my grandparents spanked my parents, and look at me, I'm OK."

Science: In 2014, the estimated number of rapes increased 2.6 % per 100,000 inhabitants from 2013 (United States Department of Justice, Federal Bureau of Investigations, 2015).

Intuition is another way of knowing. As social workers we are told to pay attention to our reactions or our "gut feelings." Sometimes our intuition causes us to explore certain lines of questioning or to make observations that lead to important insights in our work.

We also gain knowledge from authority. From infancy we are programmed to believe that what people in positions of authority tell us is true. For instance, we may seldom question what our parents, teachers, and clergy tell us. In social work practice we gain knowledge from our supervisors and our colleagues. We also acquire knowledge from our clients, who are authorities on their own lives.

Another source of knowledge is tradition. Knowing through tradition involves believing something because that is the way it has always been, because it is a part of who we are. Tradition is an important source of culturally specific knowledge. For instance, many indigenous cultures have folk healers; in Mexico they are sometimes called curanderas (or curanderos, masculine). The curanderos are a cornerstone of Mexican culture. Some people who seek the services of the curanderos are true believers; others are skeptical. In either case, however, participation is a product of knowledge rooted in tradition.

Human service agencies may also have traditions, for instance, traditions about the best ways to deliver social services. The way it is done is because "that's how it has always been done." For example, an agency may pride itself on providing insight-oriented therapy to their clients. However, this "tradition" of service delivery may become outdated as changes within the community bring more people with severe and persistent mental illnesses to the agency.

One particularly important source of knowledge for social workers is **social work research**, a systematic way of developing knowledge that relies on the scientific method. The **scientific method** is a process of accumulating knowledge that involves five distinct steps:

1.   identifying a problem or issue
2.   defining that problem or issue in terms of a question that is capable of study
3.   developing a plan to answer the question
4.   gathering data according to prescribed practices
5.   drawing conclusions from the data

The knowledge and skills we learn in social work research—like those we learn in other social work courses, such as interviewing and assessment—change the ways we see, hear, and understand people and make us more effective social workers. An education in social work research leads us to question the knowledge claims of all sources. One of the most important reasons you are taking this course is to learn to question what you think you know and how you know it – this is the hallmark of **critical thinking**.

Making judgments about what to believe is a part of everyday life for social workers. The danger of basing social work practice decisions on direct experience, intuition, authority, or tradition is that what you think you know may be no more than a few isolated observations, or what we refer to as **anecdotal information.** For example, knowledge based on authority may be based on what feels right or comfortable for a particular person who has the authority. It may be rooted in tradition or may be an untested assumption.

To be effective as social workers, we must critically evaluate our ways of knowing and make judgments based on the best information available. We must learn to question basic values and claims, even those that are made on the basis of published scientific findings that we previously may have taken for granted. This does not mean that social workers discount other ways of knowing or never use them. They are, however, keenly aware that much of their work, from understanding problems and issues to selecting interventions and evaluating their effectiveness, should be based on critical thinking and science.

Increasing Accountability

A second function of social work research is to help us evaluate our own effectiveness. How do we know when our actions are working (or not working)? How will we know if something can be done better, faster, or less expensively? Through social work research we soon learn that our interventions are usually not entirely effective. We use research to help us determine when to stay the course and when to take corrective action. We learn to be curious about and question the effectiveness of what we, as social workers, do.

Through research, we also provide information to others about our effectiveness. We are accountable to those we serve. They have a right to know the extent to which we have been successful in meeting their needs and goals, and the needs and goals of others who have gone before them. In addition, we must be accountable to those who fund social work services, whether that is through public funds, private donations, or fee for service contracting. Indeed, the funding of social programs depends increasingly on providing evidence of success.

Enhancing Communication

A third basic function of social work research is communication. Social workers use research to communicate precisely and with confidence. When social workers use research effectively, they are not just talking; they are talking knowledgeably.

For example, the National Transgender Discrimination Survey of 6,456 transgender and non-gender-conforming adults in the United States found that 41% of respondents had at some point in their life attempted suicide. The likelihood of attempting suicide was the highest among those who had experienced rejection by family and friends, discrimination, victimization, or violence (Haas, Rodgers, & Herman, 2014). The results of this survey suggested that recognition as transgender or gender nonconforming, whether actual or perceived, increased the likelihood of rejection and discrimination. These findings can prepare social workers to speak knowledgeably when debating federal and state policy issues such as transgender access to restrooms. It is important to be able to confidently use data to communicate.

Enhancing Access to Scarce Resources

A fourth basic function of social work research is to gain access to scarce resources. Research can make the difference between losing and maintaining the funding for vital social work services. Failure to engage in research on program effectiveness weakens the ability of social work advocates to garner scarce resources, and ultimately hurts potential recipients of social services.

CASE-IN-POINT: RESEARCH PROVES CRITICAL TO MAINTAINING HOME VISITATION PROGRAMMING

Infancy is a critical and vulnerable period of life. When parents lack the knowledge, skills, and resources to ensure a child's healthy development, the result can be long-term disadvantage, serious harm, and even death. Voluntary home visitation programs were developed to support parents to care for their infants and toddlers in a manner that would promote child and family well-being and improve long-term outcomes. Realizing the potential of home visitation, the majority of states invested in a variety of program models. By fiscal year 2010, annual state expenditures on home visitation totaled almost $1.4 billion, frequently without any requirements that states select program models with an existing track record of success, and with little oversight or accountability. Approximately 119 program models existed across 46 states and the District of Columbia and few tracked even basic performance indicators.

Recognizing the potential of home visitation to improve outcomes for the most vulnerable infants and toddlers, Congress enacted as part of the Affordable Care Act the Maternal, Infant, and Early Childhood Home Visiting Program (MIECHV). To receive funding under this Act, 75 % of the funds had to be used to support the implementation of evidence-based programs that had been rigorously evaluated with documented evidence of success. The remaining 25 % of funds could be used to implement and evaluate promising home visitation approaches, or to pilot significant innovations to existing evidence-based approaches. As the MIECHV legislation was debated, home visitation program advocates scrambled to demonstrate credible evidence of effectiveness. The federal government contracted with a large research firm, Mathematica, to evaluate the evidence and only seven program models emerged as meeting the criteria. In total, $1.5 billion dollars were made available through MIECHV over a five-year-period (2010 to 2014) with 41 states participating. Of the 119 program models, only seven met the litmus test and were granted access to these valuable resources. Why? Not necessarily because the other programs did not work, but because only seven had invested in developing credible research results that could be used to advocate for their continuation.

CONTROVERSIES IN THE HISTORY OF SOCIAL WORK RESEARCH

So far we have taken the position that in order to have an impact, social workers need to acquire knowledge and skills in research. There have been many times since the days of Dorothea Dix, however, that the place of research in social work has been hotly debated. Three of these historical controversies have called into question the status of social work as a profession, the very nature and value of research, and the roles of the social worker in producing and using research. A brief history of these controversies is warranted because it allows us to appreciate where we are today and how we got here. Understanding our professional history is also part of the socialization process to the profession.

Historical Controversy 1: Is Social Work a Profession?

Of course social work is a profession. Isn't it? How do we know? About a century ago, in 1915, the National Conference of Charities and Correction in Baltimore invited an educational reformer named Abraham Flexner to speak. Flexner chose to focus his address on the question of whether social work was a profession. To answer this question, Flexner presented the defining criteria of a profession, applied them to social work, and concluded that social work did not measure up. In fact, Flexner publicly stated that social work was not a profession. Flexner's comments sent shock waves throughout the social work community.

Flexner's criteria to define professional status included the following:

- The work involves personally responsible intellectual activity.
- The work has a practical purpose.
- The work is teachable in a curriculum.
- The work pursues a broader social good.
- The content of the discipline is derived from science and learning and does not employ knowledge that is generally accessible to everyone.
(Kirk & Reid, 2002)

Although there is some controversy with regard to the criteria Flexner used to assign social work a failing grade, social work was most vulnerable to the criticism that it lacked a unique scientific body of knowledge. Does social work have a unique scientific knowledge base? If so, what makes it unique?

The **research methods** that social workers use—that is, the procedures for conducting research studies and gathering and interpreting data to get the most valid findings—are not unique to our profession. The same is true of the theories that social workers draw upon to guide their research. Perhaps the best explanation of what makes social work research unique is based on the idea that the identity of a profession depends more on the uniqueness of its goals than on its **methodology** (Wakefield, 1988).

The ends to which social workers strive are defined in the preamble to the **NASW Code of Ethics**. It defines social work's primary mission as being "to enhance human well-being and help meet the basic human needs of all people, with particular attention to the needs and empowerment of people who are vulnerable, oppressed, and living in poverty" (NASW, 2017, p. 1). Social work research is needed to fulfill this mission. Thus, the purpose of social work research is to create **applied knowledge**; that is, we use research to develop knowledge that will inform social work practice.

Social workers consider not only the usefulness of the research questions they ask to inform practice but also the ways that research findings may be misused. Social workers have been instrumental in expanding research to include problem areas that were little understood and populations that were largely ignored by research in other disciplines. They also study people and problems in a way that challenges stereotypes and focuses on strengths as well as problems. For instance, they tend to examine not only risk factors for problems but also protective factors, that is, factors that reduce the risk of certain problems and that lead to resilience.

Historical Controversy 2: Do Social Workers Use Research?

The next major area of controversy in social work research focused not on the production of research by social workers, or the lack thereof, but on the use of research. Aaron Rosenblatt was the first social work researcher to conduct a study on the use of research by social workers. Almost 50 years ago, Rosenblatt (1968) found that social workers rated research the least used or least valued activity in making treatment decisions. Other early studies of social workers' use of research found similar results. Specifically, they revealed that social workers (a) did not read many research articles, (b) seldom used research studies in their professional work, and (c) had difficulty accepting findings that challenged their beliefs (Casselman, 1972; Kirk & Fischer, 1976).

In response to the question of why social workers did not use research to a greater extent, some researchers offered the following explanations:

■ Social workers were not appreciative of the work that researchers do.
■ Social agencies were barely tolerant hosts of research.
■ Agency administrators were interested only in research that supported the status quo.

(For a discussion of this controversy, see Kirk & Reid, 2002.)

Later research led to optimism that research use in social work was increasing (Reid & Fortune, 1992). The response to the claim that social workers did not use research to inform their practice served to shift the debate away from the shortcomings of the social worker to the nature of the research. If social workers were not using research to inform practice, perhaps it was because they failed to see the utility of much of the research.

Historical Controversy 3: Is Research Relevant to Social Work?

The third controversy in social work research involves the utility of research for social work practice (Kirk & Reid, 2002). Specifically, many social workers questioned whether research could improve their practice, and others insisted that the profession use knowledge that was research based. This issue and the preceding controversy on the use of research illustrate the division that existed between those who saw themselves as social work practitioners and those who saw themselves as social work researchers. To understand how this gap between research and practice occurred, we must briefly comment on the origins of modern-day science.

The Emergence of Logical Positivism

The idea of applying science to the social world grew out of a period of European history known as the Enlightenment. Seventeenth-century thinkers moved away from religious and authoritarian explanations of human behavior toward an empirical analysis that relied on observation and measurement as the way of knowing. This new framework, or paradigm, was called **logical positivism**. It was seen as a way to replace the old ways of knowing with objective rationality.

Essentially, logical positivism argued that scientists could understand the human experience in the same way as they do the physical world. Going further, social scientists who understood the human experience in this way could engineer solutions to individual and social problems just as physical scientists attempted to engineer solutions in the natural world. In order to remain objective, the expert scientist had to distance himself from the subjects of the research. (We use the gender-specific term "himself" because early social science was dominated by men.)

Many social scientists embraced logical positivism as the path that would lead to objectivity and truth. For all its promise, however, logical positivism was not without its problems. For instance, it could consider only a limited number of variables at one time. The idea of being an objective scientist was also criticized because, after all, scientists are human, and, like all humans,

Descartes' idea of how impulses from limbs
reach the brain.

Source: Photos.com Copyright: ©Getty Images

they are socialized to a set of values and beliefs that influence what they see and
how they interpret it. The critics of logical positivism contended that, despite
its claims of objectivity, logical positivism was biased and often served as a form
of power rather than a source of truth. History provides us with numerous
examples to support this position.

One illustration is the following commentary by the late Stephen Jay
Gould, an evolutionary biologist and science historian. In his 1981 book *The
Mismeasure of Man*, Gould presents numerous examples of bad science that
was produced in the name of objectivity and has served to maintain the status
quo. For example, during the 19th century, scientists involved in the field of
craniometry compiled data on skull size to rank people by race and sex. Gould
states that the proponents of craniometry regarded themselves as "servants of
their numbers, apostles of objectivity" (p. 74). As an example he cites Paul
Broca, an eminent French scientist of the time:

> We might ask if the small size of the female brain depends exclusively upon
> the small size of her body. Tiedemann has proposed this explanation. But we
> must not forget that women are, on the average, a little less intelligent than

men, a difference which we should not exaggerate but which is, nonetheless, real. We are therefore permitted to suppose that the relatively small size of the female brain depends in part upon her physical inferiority, and in part upon her intellectual inferiority.

(cited in Gould, 1981, p. 104)

Interestingly, advancements in technology have made the study of the brain relevant to social work research and practice today. For instance, studies that use brain imaging of elderly individuals suffering from Alzheimer's disease and other forms of dementia, as well as studies of children and adults who experience trauma symptoms as the result of traumatic events such as child maltreatment and war, have helped to shape prevention and intervention programming as well as our general approach to such clients.

Interpretivism: The Alternative to Positivism

The claims that (a) research carried out in the tradition of logical positivism leads to the objective truth and (b) knowledge flows one way, from expert to nonexpert, have contributed to the division and distrust between researchers and social work practitioners. In the 1970s and 1980s, the debate in social work focused on the most appropriate paradigm for developing social work knowledge. As a scientific alternative to logical positivism, many researchers came to embrace a paradigm known as **interpretivism**. The interpretivist paradigm is concerned with understanding social conditions through the meaning individuals ascribe to their personal experiences.

In essence, interpretivism maintains that (a) there may be several versions of the truth, and (b) the version that a researcher adopts will depend upon her or his vantage point. Given these assumptions, then, the meaning a researcher ascribes to an event or phenomenon should not be separated from the context in which the event occurs. The researcher's personal perceptions and experiences strongly influence the way she or he sees and interprets the world. This reality should always be acknowledged in the findings of the research.

Entire editions of journals and books have been devoted to arguing the relative merits of positivism and interpretivism for social work research (see, for example, Hudson & Nurius, 1994). The debate has revolved around philosophical questions such as: What is truth? If there is such a thing as truth, how can we know it? Researchers who favor the interpretivist paradigm argue that the positivist paradigm is reductionistic: it oversimplifies life's complexity by reducing it to a set of observations, and it leaves out important aspects of the human experience. Proponents of the positivist framework respond that interpretivist research is subjective and cannot be generalized beyond the individuals or groups studied.

A Comparison of Positivist and Interpretivist Research

The differences in research conducted using either the positivist or the interpretivist paradigm are reflected in the following example, which involves welfare reform. What is the best way to learn the "truth" about women's experiences as a result of welfare reform?

One possibility is to investigate in great depth the experiences of individual women receiving Temporary Assistance for Needy Families (TANF) through interviews with these women, their children, their families, their neighbors, and other community members. We might even stay with a family receiving TANF for a period of time, observing how its members live. We would be interested in their explanations of what led them to apply for TANF, how they view their future, what aspirations they have for their children, and what their everyday life experience is like.

From our observations, we would then develop additional questions and hypotheses that would increase our understanding of their circumstances. Our goal would be to develop insight and perhaps a theory to explain the impact of welfare on a woman's life. We might better understand the forces that lead women either to leave welfare or to remain on it. In-depth research focusing on extensive examination of a limited number of subjects conducted in the interpretivist tradition is known as **qualitative research**. Chapter 6 is devoted to the topic of qualitative research.

Another way to find the "truth" is to "count things" that we believe are important. Again using welfare as an example, how many women receive TANF? How many men are receiving TANF? What are the age, race, education, employment status, income, and number of children of adults receiving TANF? After we have accumulated these data, we can look for relationships in the data. We might learn, for example, that women who never finished high school have a higher likelihood of remaining unemployed than women who have finished high school. This type of research conducted in the positivist tradition, which involves the use of numerical data, is known as **quantitative research**. The latter half of this book focuses on quantitative research. See Exhibit 1.3 for a simple comparison of the two research traditions.

Although both qualitative and quantitative research approaches are valued for their unique contributions to social work research, there is a perceived hierarchy of research approaches. Quantitative research has been referred to as "hard science" and qualitative research as "soft science." There has also been a perception that social workers who wanted their research to be funded and published were better off pursuing a quantitative research approach.

In response to the debate on epistemology—how we know what we know—positivism has evolved considerably. The evolution in positivism includes the recognition that scientists are not immune to values, political pressure, and ideologies, and that objectivity is something to strive for rather than

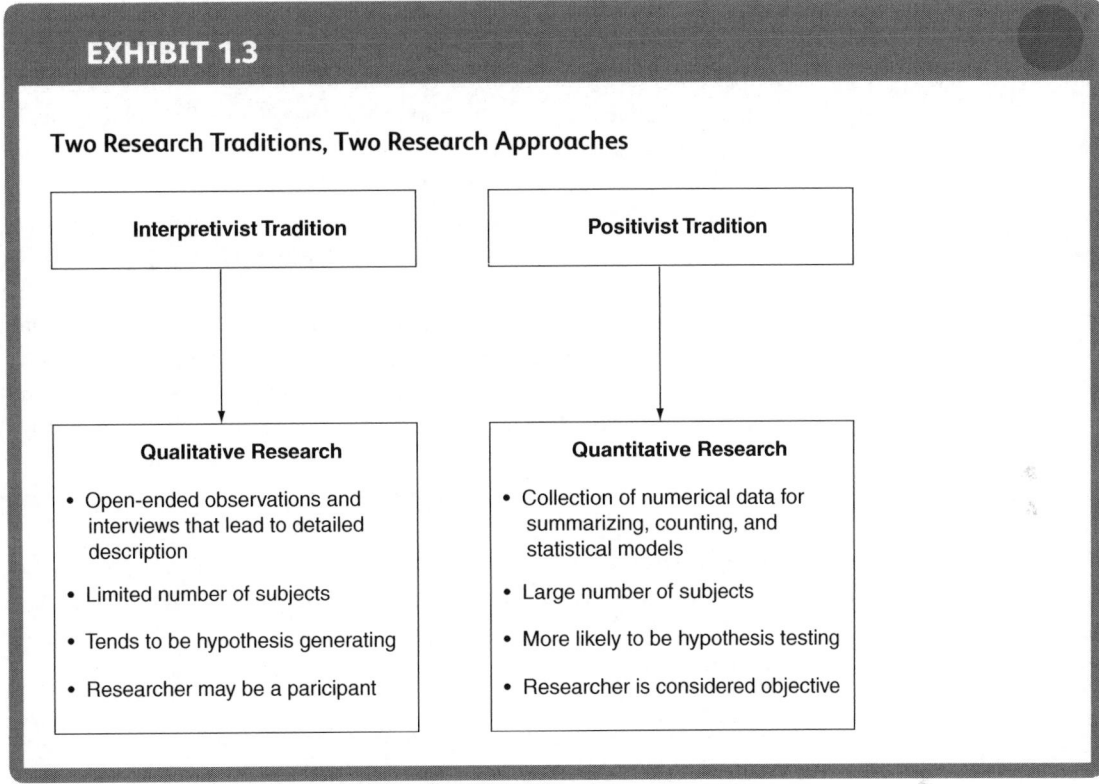

EXHIBIT 1.3

Two Research Traditions, Two Research Approaches

Interpretivist Tradition	Positivist Tradition

Qualitative Research

- Open-ended observations and interviews that lead to detailed description

- Limited number of subjects

- Tends to be hypothesis generating

- Researcher may be a paricipant

Quantitative Research

- Collection of numerical data for summarizing, counting, and statistical models

- Large number of subjects

- More likely to be hypothesis testing

- Researcher is considered objective

a characteristic of a research approach. The contemporary paradigm maintains that knowledge derived from observation is superior to knowledge based on authority, experience, tradition, or other forms of knowing. Through highly structured research methods and controls, positivism seeks to limit the influence of any type of bias that might threaten the validity or truthfulness of the findings. As a result, we no longer use the term logical positivism. We are more likely to use the terms post-positivism or quantitative research. Similarly, we often use the term qualitative research to refer to research conducted in the interpretivist paradigm.

Lessons Learned from the Controversies

Contemporary social workers need not choose one paradigm over the other. As social workers in search of knowledge, we now recognize that each approach provides useful and complementary knowledge and makes a unique contribution.

Moreover, we sometimes combine qualitative and quantitative approaches in which the limitations of one approach are offset by the benefits of the other.

We call this a **mixed-methods approach**. For example, in one mixed-methods study examining young people's experience of service use, a survey was administered to 605 individuals, and was followed-up with interviews of 109 young people and case file reviews (Munford & Sanders, 2016). The survey utilized standardized measures and gathered information on patterns of service use in systems such as child protection and juvenile justice, behaviors such as substance use and delinquency, and resources in problem solving and relationships. Young people with the highest and lowest resilience scores were then invited to be interviewed. Researchers asked the young people questions about their experiences of family relationships, and their views on school and community. The results of the survey found that young people were more satisfied with services when they had a choice about attending services, and when providers were perceived as respectful in their interactions. The results of the interviews revealed that young people were often confused about how they became involved in services, and voiced uncertainty about their future and what would be happening to them next. The data from the qualitative interviews aligned well with the survey data and emphasized that social work practices that were empowering and respectful were related to better outcomes.

Finally, if social workers are going to successfully use research-based knowledge, those producing research need to consider the following priorities:

- Produce research that is relevant for social work practitioners, in part by collaborating with practitioners and those affected.
- Produce focused research in areas we know little about, such as the factors that influence the effectiveness of treatment with different ethnic and racial groups.
- Adopt better methods of disseminating research findings.
- Write for social work practitioners, producing succinct reports that state the core findings understandably and explain how the research can be applied to practice.

The controversies regarding the professional status of social work, research use, and research relevance have moved the profession forward and provided opportunities for professional growth. As social workers have tackled each controversy with passion and debate, the profession has emerged with a stronger position on where research fits into social work and what the nature of that research should be. We examine the result in the next section.

THE PROFESSIONAL MANDATE

The days of questioning the relevance of research to the social work profession are over. To further the goal of widespread use of research, the profession has created an infrastructure to promote social work research and to create opportunities for social workers to engage in research. The current position is clear: Professional social workers are expected to understand and use research.

Our professional organizations have made explicit statements concerning the importance of research to social work. The National Association of Social Workers and the Council on Social Work Education, two bodies that represent and guide the social work profession, strongly support social work research. Quick Guide 1 is an easy-to-reference guide that summarizes how research can be incorporated intelligently and ethically into your social work practice.

QUICK GUIDE 1 GUIDELINES FOR INCORPORATING RESEARCH INTO SOCIAL WORK

- The ends served by our research are as important as the methods we use to conduct our research.
- We must always be critical consumers of research-based knowledge, and we need to evaluate reliably the observations, facts, inferences, and assumptions stated in the research.
- When scientific claims depart radically from our professional experiences, we should not quickly discount our professional knowledge, and we must question the reasons for the discrepancy.
- Research benefits from popular participation, and it works best when knowledge flows in more than one direction—from expert in research to expert in the phenomenon being studied—rather than from expert researcher to nonexpert research object.
- As social workers, we must concern ourselves with the social consequences of our research findings, and we should divorce ourselves from the political and moral passivity that can result when we cloak ourselves in a veil of scientific objectivity.

National Association of Social Workers

The **National Association of Social Workers (NASW)** is the largest organization of professional social workers in the world, having approximately 130,000 members (NASW, 2016). The NASW works to enhance the professional growth and development of its members and to create and maintain professional standards. The NASW Code of Ethics specifically states the following under Section 5, Social Workers' Ethical Responsibilities to the Social Work Profession, 5.02 Evaluation and Research:

(a) Social workers should monitor and evaluate policies, the implementation of programs, and practice interventions.

(b) Social workers should promote and facilitate evaluation and research to contribute to the development of knowledge.

(c) Social workers should critically examine and keep current with emerging knowledge relevant to social work and fully use evaluation and research evidence in their professional practice.

(NASW, 2017).

The responsibility to conduct and use research is considered an ethical obligation of all professional social workers. This expectation has been formalized through its inclusion in the NASW Code of Ethics.

Council on Social Work Education

Another major social work organization, the **Council on Social Work Education (CSWE)**, develops educational policy and accreditation standards for social work programs on the baccalaureate and master's levels. In 2015 the CSWE implemented the most recent Educational Policy and Accreditation Standards (EPAs). Under Competency 4—Engage in practice-informed research and research-informed practice—the CSWE educational policy specifically states the following:

Social workers understand quantitative and qualitative research methods and their respective roles in advancing a science of social work and in evaluating their practice. Social workers know the principles of logic, scientific inquiry, and culturally informed and ethical approaches to building knowledge. Social workers understand that evidence that informs practice derives from multi-disciplinary sources and multiple ways of knowing. They also understand the processes for translating research findings into effective practice. Social workers:

■   use practice experience and theory to inform scientific inquiry and research;

■   apply critical thinking to engage in analysis of quantitative and qualitative research methods and research findings; and

■   use and translate research evidence to inform and improve practice, policy, and service delivery.

(CSWE, 2015, p. 8)

CSWE has given all schools of social work a mandate to educate students in research in order to prepare them to produce and use research to make a positive impact.

TRENDS THAT SUPPORT RESEARCH UTILIZATION

Several trends have also converged to solidify the place of research in the future of social work. For example, the Internet has promoted the development of communication networks such as Listservs and web sites that connect researchers and practitioners who have similar interests and information needs. In addition, information technology has made electronic bibliographic databases, indexing services, and electronic journals widely available, thus making research reports more accessible to social workers.

Greater access to research reports has also given social workers the means to bridge research and practice. This development has been encouraged by legislative changes such as the Government Performance and Results Act, as well as paradigm shifts in social work education such as evidence-based practice. We examine these trends in this section.

The Internet

The widespread use of the Internet supports research utilization in several ways:

- The Internet facilitates a faster and more cost-effective means to share knowledge. Many social work journals have online versions and publish papers as soon as they are accepted. Other knowledge-producing organizations publish newsletters. Publishing online has major cost saving benefits and allows greater access to research.
- The Internet has also facilitated communication between researchers and practitioners and has broken down geographic barriers. Collaborations are easier and less costly to manage than they have been in the past and conference attendance is now including options for virtual participation similar to webinars and online meetings.
- Data collection can also occur via means of Internet enabled devices and is moving from the personal computer to a range of mobile devices including smart phones and tablets.

Government Performance and Results Act

A landmark piece of legislation, the **Government Performance and Results Act** (P.L. 103-62, or GPRA) has forced agencies and organizations receiving federal funds to become more accountable for their results. Enacted in 1993, the GPRA requires all federally funded agencies to become results-oriented by setting program performance targets and reporting annually on the degree to which they met the previous year's targets. The GPRA shifted the federal government away from a focus on process—that is, which services the agency provided, in what context, at what cost, and how well these services matched what was planned—to focus on outcome, or what the agency actually accomplished with the use of resources. Outcome questions pertain to the effects of treatment on participants, the program and individual factors associated with the outcomes, and whether the effects can be maintained over time.

At the local level, the GPRA requires social workers who are applying for federal funds to demonstrate their ability to collect and report data. Moreover, if a worker is awarded a federal grant, the terms and conditions of the grant specify the data to be submitted and the schedule for submission.

Evidence-Based Practice

In the past, social workers were reluctant to use research-based knowledge, in part because it was not widely available and social workers had difficulty understanding how research applied to practice. Another reason for this reluctance, however, was that teaching students how to use research findings or even how to conduct research was not part of the broad culture of social work education in the past.

Perhaps one of the newest and most promising developments in research utilization is the advent of **evidence-based practice (EBP).** In their simplest form, evidence-based practices are interventions that appear to be related to preferred client outcomes based on scientific evidence. For example, scientific studies have shown cognitive behavioral treatments (CBT) to be effective in treating anxiety disorders among adults, although it appears that they are less effective for elderly adults than for younger adults (Gould, Coulson, & Howard, 2012). Thus, the implications are that mental health practitioners should choose these treatments over insight-oriented therapies that have not been supported by evidence of effectiveness, and at the same time should investigate ways to enhance the effectiveness of CBT for the elderly. Increasingly, funding decisions are being tied to the use of EBPs and treatment outcomes as described in the Case-in-Point earlier.

In the context of social work education, EBP is much more than a set of interventions whose effectiveness has been documented by scientific evidence. By adopting EBP as a guiding pedagogical principle, schools of social work are attempting to produce professionals who are lifelong critical thinkers and learners, who draw on practice-related research findings. Because information technology has given social workers greater access to research studies, schools of social work must now teach students the skills to use and produce research.

This task has been made somewhat easier in recent years owing to collaborative efforts such as the Cochrane Collaboration and the Campbell Collaboration. These groups explore the evidence for and against the effectiveness and appropriateness of interventions in specific circumstances and make this information available through systematic reviews that are available to the public.

The challenges inherent in EBP extend the paradigm shift in social work education. How will evidence-based practices move from their establishment in research to broad awareness and wide-scale adoption in the practice community? Much remains to be discovered about the trajectory of EBP in social work.

Another tool that makes the evaluation of scientific evidence easier for the social work student and practitioner is meta-analysis. Meta-analysis is a statistical technique that combines the results of several related studies to address an overall research question, often related to the effectiveness of an intervention. For example, one research team conducted a meta-analysis including 23 studies to evaluate the ability of parent-training programs to reduce parent perpetrated child abuse (Lundahl, Nimer, & Parsons, 2006). Based on the results from the 23 studies, the researchers concluded that parent training conducted in the home, or in a combination of group and in-home services, was more effective than group-only parent training.

RESEARCH IN PROFESSIONAL SOCIAL WORK PRACTICE

What does being a professional social worker mean to you? To answer this question, think for a moment about what you expect from other professionals whom you encounter. One of the first things you might look for is a degree hanging on the office wall. This degree will tell you where and when the individual received her or his professional education. Second, you might expect a certain professional demeanor, dress, and use of language. Third, you probably expect that the individual will act ethically, not violating her or his professional boundaries or your trust and safety. Fourth, you expect a professional to be aware of and use the most effective methods of practice—EBPs. Finally, you might expect a professional to know her or his limitations, to evaluate her or his work, and to be willing to refer you elsewhere if necessary. Empathy, warmth, and genuineness—three characteristics valued in any professional—are of limited value unless they are accompanied by attention to effective practice. There may be no better way to promote the profession of social work than through research that demonstrates our accountability and makes a valued contribution to knowledge development.

Lifelong Learning

The expectations for producing and using research in professional social work practice are clear. The question that remains is: How? Entry-level social work jobs can be demanding, leaving little time for consultation, research, or even reflection. A social worker is more likely to use research if the employing agency or organization has a culture that supports it and if the worker is committed to making it happen.

Will you commit yourself to a career of lifelong learning? If so, the first step is to develop an action plan to make it happen. A few ideas that you might consider adopting are listed in Exhibit 1.4.

EXHIBIT 1.4

Avenues for Lifelong Learning about Social Work Research

- Join the NASW
- Choose a conference that is relevant to your practice area and make a commitment to attend every year
- Ask your manager or supervisor to subscribe to a professional journal(s)
- Join a Listserv dedicated to critiquing knowledge in your area of practice
- Join your local library and spend at least one day a month in professional development reading about the latest research in your area
- Initiate a brownbag lunch session at your workplace at which you and your colleagues discuss research
- Attend research-based trainings and workshops or college whenever possible
- Make a presentation to share your research at a conference
- Evaluate your practice
- Collaborate with others to evaluate the services provided by your agency or organization
- Seek employment in agencies and organizations whose culture supports using research and evaluating practice
- Continue your formal education by taking courses online or at a university

---

Research Opportunities for Entry-Level Social Workers

Virtually all social work positions present opportunities for research, even though research may not be the primary activity. Research opportunities may include assessing a client's situation, deciding on an intervention strategy, evaluating success with a single case, developing a survey to answer a question, conducting a needs assessment, and writing grant proposals. Sometimes research involves helping communities to do their own research while offering guidance and added credibility. All of these activities require social workers to have a working knowledge of research.

Other employment opportunities for social workers have research as their primary focus. Careers in social work research can be personally rewarding. Social workers in research positions enjoy the opportunity to be influential in the creation, continuation, expansion, and sometimes termination of social programs, and in the promotion of EBPs. Research conducted by social workers often influences whether legislative amendments will be made to government-funded programs.

Regardless of whether research is the focus of a social work position or a complement to some other form of social work practice, employing agencies often seek out and highly value graduates who are skilled in research. Marketable research skills include expertise with database development and management, data analysis, and presentation software. The exercises in this book will help you develop these marketable skills. In addition, many universities and colleges offer training workshops on these types of software programs that either are free of charge or cost far less than courses taught off campus. In addition, software programs are often available at great discounts to students through campus bookstores and computing centers.

CONCLUSION

Social workers are employed in areas where difficult and life-changing decisions are made on a daily basis. Many of the problems social workers deal with are multidimensional and complex; some are chronic and relapsing. Some problems, such as post-traumatic stress disorder (PTSD), are major public health issues that affect millions of people and place an enormous social and financial burden on society. To make a positive impact, social workers require knowledge about how best to intervene in these problems. Social workers also need the skills to produce new, scientifically-based knowledge about social problems and the most effective ways to address them.

The bright spot in a social worker's day comes when we know with confidence that something we did had a positive impact. Social workers must be confident in the knowledge they acquire, not only for themselves, but also to demonstrate accountability and to communicate with the people they serve and those who approve of and fund their services. In addition, social workers need to know when they are not effective so that they can either adopt a different approach or refer elsewhere.

Moreover, being able to demonstrate to a client—whether an individual, a couple, a family, an agency, an organization, or a community—that progress is being made is empowering to the client as well as the social worker. For example, to help a community group obtain funding for a teen center by providing accurate information on the impact of the teen center on juvenile delinquency rates is empowering. Social workers also empower organizations and policy makers when they use their knowledge to provide information to inform policy decisions and to understand the costs and benefits of policy changes.

The research skills necessary for effective social work practice do not come naturally; rather, they are cultivated through learning and experience. The remainder of this book is devoted to helping you develop the research knowledge and skills you need to be an effective social worker with a lifelong commitment to learning.

MAIN POINTS

- As professionals, social workers are expected both to use research to inform their practice and to contribute to the production of research.
- The purpose of social work research is to better help those we aim to serve.
- Research helps us to critically evaluate information and make judgments on the best information available; to assess our own effectiveness; to communicate; and to gain additional resources.
- Research is a process that teaches social workers to question how they know what they think they know and to be skeptical of knowledge claims, even those based on the scientific method.
- The struggle over the primacy of qualitative versus quantitative research approaches has been more or less settled by an appreciation of the uniqueness of each approach and in the adoption of mixed-method approaches that recognize the strengths and limitations of each.
- There are many sources of organizational support for social workers engaged in research, including the NASW and CSWE.
- Evidence-based practices (EBPs) are interventions that have shown consistent scientific evidence of being related to preferred client outcomes. A commitment to developing and using EBPs is a commitment to lifelong learning.
- For most social workers, research will be a complement to their career. For those social workers who are interested, there are many employment opportunities with a research focus.

EXERCISES

1. Using The Sanchez Family: Systems, Strengths, and Stressors case, list three ideas for how a quantitative approach to research could be used to inform practice by the social worker, and three ideas of how a qualitative approach could be used.

2. Using the Riverton: A Community Conundrum case, consider how each of the NASW Code of Ethics, Section 5, Social Worker's Ethical Responsibilities to the Profession, 5.02 Evaluation and Research guidelines could apply.

3. Using the Carla Washburn: Loss, Aging, and Social Support case, discuss how you could use EBP literature in your work. What research information would you search for that might help inform your approach to practice with this client?

4. Read the RAINN National Sexual Assault Online Hotline case. Write notes that address:
   a. Your initial thoughts regarding the needs of the clients of RAINN.
   b. Questions that you think should be answered through research in order to help RAINN better serve its clients.

5. Find and read two research based articles on victims of rape and incest. As a staff member of RAINN, how would the articles you read help inform your practice? Are the findings and conclusions of the articles you read consistent with a quantitative, qualitative, or mixed-methods approach? Explain your answer by describing the details of each approach.

6. Review the Hudson City case and familiarize yourself with the details. How might research function to assist the social worker and the community?

7. If you were a member of Brickville youth leadership development group, how might you find research helpful to attaining the goals of the group? In what format do you think the group members would best be able to learn about research, e.g., published research articles, talks, research briefs, news stories, etc?

chapter 2

THE POLITICS AND ETHICS OF SOCIAL WORK RESEARCH

The profession has become increasingly concerned about problems of misuse, whether the source be politics, asking the wrong questions, pressures on internal evaluators to present only positive findings, petty self-interest, or ideology. Misuse, like use, is ultimately situational. Consider, for example, an illustrative case. An administrator blatantly quashes several negative evaluation reports to prevent the results from reaching the general public. On the surface, such an action appears to be a prime case of misutilization. Now consider the same action (i.e., suppressing negative findings) in a situation in which the reports were invalid due to poor data collection. Thus misutilization in one situation may be conceived of as appropriate nonuse in another. Intentional nonuse of poorly conducted studies can be viewed as appropriate and responsible.

Michael Quinn Patton (2005, p. 255)

Research takes place in a social and political context. Unfortunately, terrible and unethical things have been done in the name of research, and individuals and communities have suffered negative consequences as a result. For example, from 1940 to 1944 doctors performed "experiments" to test the effects of poisons and surgeries on prisoners in Nazi concentration camps. In the United States, our own record of research is far from clean. For example, from 1932 to 1972 the U.S. Public Health Service studied 600 African American men, two-thirds of whom had contracted syphilis, in order to observe the long-term effects of the disease. The men were not given penicillin even though the medical profession had known since the end of World War II that the drug could be used to treat syphilis. Forty men died during the experiment known as the Tuskegee Study, and wives and children became infected.

In 1955 the Willowbrook School, a New York institution for children with developmental disabilities, conducted a study that involved more than 700 developmentally delayed children. Without their parents' *informed* and fully *voluntary* consent, some children were intentionally infected with hepatitis so that researchers could follow the course of the disease and test the effectiveness of gamma globulin (Pence, 2000). As we will see in this chapter, these abuses and others have led to the creation of a strict code of ethics related to research procedures, and yet, unethical research practices continue. The NASW Code of Ethics is not merely about responding to these types of abuses, but is also about endowing social work research with a legitimacy that should increase other's faith in research. As suggested by the opening quote, responding ethically requires consideration of the context, and a determination of what is ultimately right and wrong in a given situation.

Social workers are often faced with ethical dilemmas when planning and conducting research. For example, can we pay low-income mothers to participate in a study of childhood sexual abuse experiences? Can we survey middle school students about drug use without getting their parents' permission? Can

The electric fence at Auschwitz concentration camp where medical atrocities were committed in the name of science.

we divide consumers of mental health services into an experimental group that receives a new treatment and a control group that receives no treatment? Can we accept research funding from a pharmaceutical company that may have a vested interest in our study that compares talk therapy with psychotropic drugs as treatments for mild depression? Can we conduct research on a public online self-help group without telling members that we are copying their messages? Can we use research findings from another field to undergird our interventions in a distinct field, even if they may not transfer to the different context? Can we tout promising findings from a study with a very small, nonrepresentative sample, without emphasizing the limitations of the research? In order to answer these questions, we must have a clear understanding of the principles that guide the ethical conduct of research.

Similar to research, the human services delivery system also exists within a social and political context. What services get funded and at what levels is a political issue, meaning that choices must be made, with interest groups advocating for their particular agenda. The research enterprise, starting with whether or not it happens, and towards what ends, is not apolitical. Where should we put our research dollars: the Zika virus or Fetal Alcohol Spectrum Disorders; interventions for child abuse or for elder abuse? These value-laden questions raise issues of the uneasy relationship among power, politics, and resources, as well as where research gets published and the attention it then receives.

A common maxim asserts that "knowledge is power." If this saying is true, research should play a major role in decision making about the funding and organization of human services. However, as seen in the following Case in

Point, sometimes power influences what becomes "known," with significant implications for the profession and those we serve. The social work researcher's role is, in part, to ensure that research findings influence decision making. To perform this role, researchers must consider the ends for which they engage in research and their ethical responsibilities to clients, colleagues, and the broader community. Chapter 1 discussed the context of social work research. This chapter extends that discussion by addressing the politics and ethics of social work research. By the end of this chapter you should be able to:

- Identify the mission and goals of the social work profession.
- Identify the social work skills needed to ensure that social work research is used to achieve the mission and goals of the profession.
- Discuss the interrelationship of politics and research.
- Discuss the implications of applying social work values to research with persons and groups who historically have suffered disadvantage.
- Discuss how the NASW Code of Ethics applies to ethical conduct in the production and utilization of research.

CASE-IN-POINT: DISMISSIVE ATTITUDES TOWARD DATA

As the residents of Flint, Michigan, consumed tap water contaminated with unhealthy levels of lead, multiple communications that had been sent to state officials were dismissed as political wrangling and "data" (Bosman, Davey, & Smith, 2016). Concerns documenting the problem were discounted, despite the fact that at least some included data and were being put forth by concerned health professionals. Almost 300 pages of emailed complaints were later made public as evidence of the administration's desire to be transparent about the crisis. What is now considered a major public health crisis with negative, long-term, health consequences for the predominantly poor and African American affected residents of Flint is but one example of the dismissive attitude of public officials toward data. In the New York Times (Bosman, Davey, & Smith, 2016), President Obama is quoted as stating: "The notion that immediately families were not notified, things were not shut down—that shouldn't happen anywhere." It should not, but it does! The Flint water crisis of today is the new Tuskegee Study and Willowbrook of the past century. Data are not sufficient to make change, it is how data are used that matters.

SOCIAL WORK RESEARCH: THE MEANS TO SOCIAL JUSTICE

To pursue goals such as social justice, research must be used not only to inform direct practice but also to influence and inform policy practice. If we define social justice as access to basic social goods for all individuals and groups, narrowly conceived roles of case manager and therapist fall short of the social justice goal. Rather, progress toward social justice requires social workers to also become directly involved in social action and in developing and modifying social policy (Figueira-McDonough, 1993). To perform these roles, social workers often must conduct research and advocate for the use of data and research that will influence policy makers and the general public to make changes in policies. Failing to attend to policy practice weakens the impact of research, as illustrated in the previous Case-in-Point; pursuing policy change without a strong evidence base can risk wasting resources or, worse, exacerbating the problems we seek to improve.

FUNDING FOR SOCIAL WORK RESEARCH

In most cases, before research can be conducted, it has to be funded. Research expenses include the costs of the researcher's time, materials such as paper, computers and tablets, transportation, telephone charges, and, in some instances, contracted expertise and incentives to participants such as movie tickets, food vouchers, and cash. Sometimes researchers advertise to recruit participants to their studies; other times, researchers must purchase datasets and/or statistical analysis software. Generally, the larger the research study and the longer its duration, the greater the expenses.

Who funds social work research? To begin with, the federal government provides a great deal of funding. The National Institutes of Health (NIH), for instance, has an annual budget of about $31 billion that is divided among competing interests in health and behavioral health. Additional sources of funding include federal, state, and local governments as well as private non-profit and for-profit institutions. Sometimes research funding is provided by a partnership between government and private entities. Many philanthropies have increased their budgets for research and evaluation to inform their approaches to addressing complex social problems. Agencies and organizations that employ social workers also fund research and evaluation. Programs receiving government funds commonly set aside 10% of the program budget for research that is related to evaluation.

To receive funding for research or evaluation, the researcher generally must submit an application in response to a Request for Proposals (RFP). The RFP will typically include questions pertaining to the intent of the research or evaluation, the methods of collecting and analyzing data, a proposed timeline, qualifications of the researcher, and anticipated benefits of the research. In addition, it will specify a submission deadline, as well as any other pertinent instructions for the applicant. Often social workers from the community partner with researchers and evaluators to submit applications for funding. Through this process, social work knowledge advances.

Research Priorities: What's Hot, What's Not

Research and research priorities are strongly influenced by funding, and funding in turn is strongly influenced by politics. As the old saying goes, "The one who pays the piper calls the tunes." Besides the applicant's qualifications and the strength of the proposal, perhaps the key factor that determines the likelihood of being funded is how well the proposal fits with the funder's current priorities. Two factors that can help determine research priorities are the extent of knowledge in the field and the amount of attention focused on a particular issue. Research priorities can also be influenced by what is considered politically popular at a given time as illustrated in the following Case-in-Point.

CASE-IN-POINT: THE POLITICS OF INTERVENING

Zika has quickly become a household word

Source: wildpixel/thinkstock

Microcephaly is a product of the Zika virus and alcohol use during pregnancy

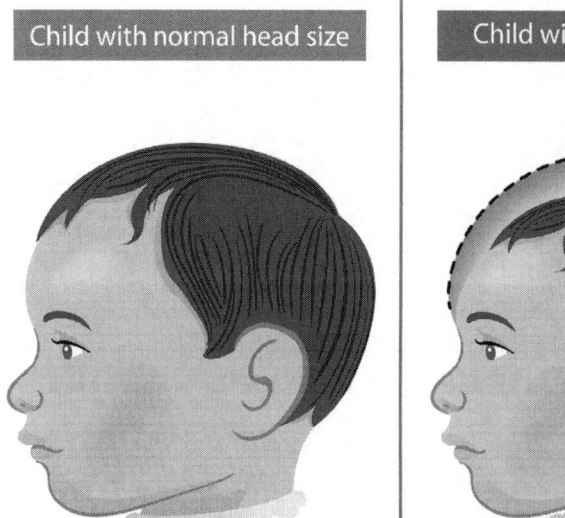

Child with normal head size   Child with microcephaly

Source: LCOSMO/Thinkstock

Recently President Obama requested 1.8 billion dollars to address the harmful effects of the Zika virus (Jenkins, 2016). The Zika virus, transmitted to pregnant women by mosquitos, can cause babies to be born with microcephaly. Microcephaly is a condition that causes small head size and an underdeveloped brain at birth. The condition cannot be treated and impacts the child's physical, mental, behavioral, and cognitive development. It is easy to understand the concern surrounding the Zika virus. However, it is not easy to understand the lack of attention to Fetal Alcohol Spectrum Disorders (FASDs). Pediatrician Dr. Ira Chasnoff, known for his work with maltreated infants and toddlers, has asked, "Where is the outrage over alcohol use in pregnancy that causes lots more brain damage and microcephaly than the Zika Virus?" There are over 40,000 cases of Fetal Alcohol Spectrum Disorders (FASDs) detected in the U.S. each year (NTI Upstream, April 2016). FASDs are 100% preventable; the most preventable form of intellectual disability. In 2004, a national task force coordinated by a number of federal agencies established a "call to action" to confront this serious and widespread public health problem (Olson et al., 2009). In response, the opinion was expressed that it is a woman's right to decide whether or not she wants to drink alcohol during pregnancy and that public agencies should not lay guilt on pregnant women. Social policy and public opinion are not changed by simply presenting scientific information. If these battles are to be won, they must go beyond the facts and address ideology.

THE ETHICS OF RESEARCH

Thus far, we have observed that politics influence the subject matter of research, the amount of attention and funding a particular issue receives, and the likelihood that research will be considered when policies are developed to address a problem. Chapter 1 addressed the production and use of research among social workers as an ethical obligation. Social workers also have an ethical responsibility to ensure that research is conducted and utilized in a way that does not violate the trust or well-being of those involved nor mislead the public or key stakeholders regarding the issues in question.

Due to their life circumstances, some groups of people are particularly vulnerable to abuse by researchers. Vulnerability is not always a result of poverty and disadvantage. It can also stem from age—including both very old and young people—and disability. Groups dealing with a relatively poorly understood problem may also be particularly vulnerable, since their hunger for answers may elevate their risk of exploitation. In addition, ethnic and racial minority groups have often been subject to abuse by researchers. A classic example of this is the Blood Study of the Havasupai Native American tribe as described in the following Case-in-Point.

CASE-IN-POINT: BLOOD VICTORY DAY

Blood Victory Day is celebrated by the Havasupai Native American Tribe of Arizona in the final week of April (NPR, 2014). That is because in April 2010 a long-awaited settlement was reached with Arizona State University agreeing to pay $700,000 to 41 of the tribe's members, to return their blood samples that were used for research that tribal members did not consent to, and to provide other forms of assistance (Harmon, 2010).

In February and March 2004, the Havasupai tribe and some of its members filed two federal lawsuits seeking a total of $75 million in damages from Arizona State University (Fehr-Snyder, Nichols, & Slivka, 2004). The lawsuits claimed that genetic information contained in various blood and handprint samples taken from tribal members was used for studies of which they were not advised and would not have approved. The tribal members claimed that they only gave their consent to participate in a study on diabetes. One of the researchers, however, used the data to study a broader range of issues including population migration. The researcher's findings on migration were in stark contrast to traditional Havasupai cultural beliefs of how the tribe originated.

The alleged breach came to light when tribal members read some of the published findings and recognized that the study was referring to their tribe. This incident is tragic given the fact that American Indians die from chronic liver disease and cirrhosis, diabetes, and tuberculosis at rates that are higher than those of other Americans and therefore could greatly benefit from health-related research (Barnes, Adams, & Powell-Griner, 2005).

There are three ethical approaches that social workers can draw from in considering the ethical conduct and use of research: 1) teleology: the study of behaviors and their ethical consequences also known as consequentialist ethics; 2) deontology: the rightness of action dictated by rules and conformance with those rules, also known referred to as a normative approach; and 3) virtue ethics: focusing on the development of virtuous beings or character states (Barsky, 2010). To date, much of the attention on ethics in social work has been rules-based, consistent with the deontological approach, the origins of which are discussed further in the next section.

Rules of Ethical Conduct

In response to research abuses such as the Nazi experiments in World War II and the Tuskegee Study, the United States and the international community have established rules of ethical conduct specifically for research. Ethics is a set of moral principles or values to guide behavior in certain contexts. The ethical standards for research and evaluation articulated in the NASW Code of Ethics and the Belmont Report—discussed in the next paragraph—represent a proactive attempt to educate researchers concerning their ethical responsibilities to research participants and the broader society.

In 1974 Congress passed the National Research Act, which led to the creation of the National Commission for the Protection of Human Subjects of Biomedical and Behavioral Research. One of the responsibilities of the commission was to identify the basic ethical principles that should underlie the conduct of medical and social research. The document detailing these principles is called the Belmont Report.

The Belmont Report does not make specific recommendations. However, it outlines the three basic ethical principles that should guide ethical decision making in research: (1) respect for persons, (2) beneficence, and (3) justice. The first principle, respect for persons, implies that people should be treated as autonomous individuals, capable of making informed decisions when provided the information to do so. This principle also recognizes that due to some circumstances such as age or disability, some persons have diminished autonomy and therefore require additional protection in research. The extent of this protection should depend on the risk of harm and the likelihood of benefit.

The principle of **beneficence** is reflected in two general rules: (1) do no harm and (2) maximize benefits while minimizing risks. Researchers need to weigh the potential risks and the benefits of the research, including the benefits extended directly to participants. Participants should not be asked to subject themselves to potential harm when they are unlikely to receive any direct benefit from their participation.

The third principle, justice, pertains to who should pay the price for participation and who benefits. The principle of justice implies that it is unfair to expect one group to take the majority of the risk when a different group will likely realize the benefit. For instance, in the Tuskegee Study, the burden of the research fell to poor, rural, African American families, whereas the disease knew no boundaries, including geography, color, or income. In this study, one group assumed all the risk, whereas the entire society would benefit from any knowledge about the disease that emerged from the study.

Being knowledgeable about ethical principles and standards can help social workers avoid hurting the very people they endeavor to help. The current version of the NASW Code of Ethics sets out 16 ethical standards relevant to evaluation and research. All 16 standards are reproduced in Exhibit 2.1. The first three guidelines speak to the conduct, promotion, and use of research as an ethical responsibility—a position consistent with the one we adopted in Chapter 1.

EXHIBIT 2.1

NASW Ethical Guidelines for Research and Evaluation

(a) Social workers should monitor and evaluate policies, the implementation of programs, and practice interventions.

(b) Social workers should promote and facilitate evaluation and research to contribute to the development of knowledge.

(c) Social workers should critically examine and keep current with emerging knowledge relevant to social work and fully use evaluation and research evidence in their professional practice.

(d) Social workers engaged in evaluation or research should carefully consider possible consequences and should follow guidelines developed for the protection of evaluation and research participants. Appropriate institutional review boards should be consulted.

(e) Social workers engaged in evaluation or research should obtain voluntary and written informed consent from participants, when appropriate, without any implied or actual deprivation or penalty for refusal to participate; without undue inducement to participate; and with due regard for participants' well-being, privacy, and dignity. Informed consent should include information about the nature, extent, and duration of the participation requested and disclosure of the risks and benefits of participation in the research.

(f) When using electronic technology to facilitate evaluation or research, social workers should ensure that participants provide informed consent for the use of such technology. Social workers should assess whether participants are able to use the technology and, when appropriate, offer reasonable alternatives to participate in the evaluation or research.

(g) When evaluation or research participants are incapable of giving informed consent, social workers should provide an appropriate explanation to the participants, obtain the participants' assent to the extent they are able, and obtain written consent from an appropriate proxy.

(h) Social workers should never design or conduct evaluation or research that does not use consent procedures, such as certain forms of naturalistic observation and archival research, unless rigorous and responsible review of the research has found it to be justified because of its prospective scientific, educational, or applied value and unless equally effective alternative procedures that do not involve waiver of consent are not feasible.

(i) Social workers should inform participants of their right to withdraw from evaluation and research at any time without penalty.

(j) Social workers should take appropriate steps to ensure that participants in evaluation and research have access to appropriate supportive services.

(k) Social workers engaged in evaluation or research should protect participants from unwarranted physical or mental distress, harm, danger, or deprivation.

(l) Social workers engaged in the evaluation of services should discuss collected information only for professional purposes and only with people professionally concerned with this information.

(m) Social workers engaged in evaluation or research should ensure the anonymity or confidentiality of participants and of the data obtained from them. Social workers should inform participants of any limits of confidentiality, the measures that will be taken to ensure confidentiality, and when any records containing research data will be destroyed.

(n) Social workers who report evaluation and research results should protect participants' confidentiality by omitting identifying information unless proper consent has been obtained authorizing disclosure.

(o) Social workers should report evaluation and research findings accurately. They should not fabricate or falsify results and should take steps to correct any error later found in published data using standard publication methods.

(p) Social workers engaged in evaluation or research should be alert to and avoid conflicts of interest and dual relationships with participants, should inform participants when a real or potential conflict of interest arises, and should take steps to resolve the issue in a manner that makes participants' interests primary.

(q) Social workers should educate themselves, their students, and their colleagues about responsible research practices.

Source: NASW, 2017. Reprinted with permission from NASW.

Institutional Review Boards (IRBs)

The fourth guideline in the NASW Code of Ethics deals with complying with the guidelines developed for protecting evaluation and research participants and consulting appropriate institutional review boards. An **institutional review board (IRB)** is a peer/community review committee of five or more individuals who review research proposals and monitor ongoing research studies to ensure that the people participating in the research are being adequately protected. Participants in research studies are sometimes referred to as **human subjects**.

IRBs may be associated with an academic institution, a hospital, or a social worker's employing or contracting agency or organization. Since 1991 federal law has required all research conducted at institutions receiving federal funds to be reviewed by an IRB. This was the result of several federal agencies that conduct, support, and regulate human research joining together to simultaneously publish a regulation known as the "Common Rule" to regulate the conduct or support of research involving human subjects. The requirements are set forth in Title 45 Part 46 Subpart A – Code of Federal Regulations. The link to this document can be found by searching on the Internet. Although some privately funded agencies and organizations are not required to submit to an IRB process, they may voluntarily do so to protect both themselves and their research participants.

Some research may be exempt from an IRB review or qualify for an expedited review because it poses no more than minimal risk. An example might be a study that asks adults their opinions about various candidates running for local office. In contrast, certain types of research require a full IRB review. For example, research that poses more than minimal risk or that involves vulnerable human participants is never exempt because of the potential for coercion and harm. Vulnerable participants include children under 18 years of age, prisoners, pregnant women, people with mental disabilities, economically disadvantaged people, persons not proficient in the language of the research study, and any participants likely to be vulnerable to coercion or undue influence.

It is usually best either to confirm with the IRB administrator that a proposed study is exempt or to submit an application and then let the IRB committee decide. The process of submitting instruments and consents and clarifying procedures—required for IRB approval—can also help researchers prepare the study. IRB committees typically meet monthly during the regular academic session, and they often are overwhelmed with research proposals. Consequently, the IRB approval process can be a lengthy affair. To minimize the waiting period, most IRB committees have a fast-track review process called "expedited review" that they can apply to research proposals that pose only minimal risk or that involve only minor changes in previously approved research protocols.

The IRB has the power to deny permission for a research study to begin or to stop a study in midstream. IRBs typically are not obstructionist, and they often work with researchers by requesting further details and by providing valuable suggestions on revisions to ensure that research participants are protected. Despite these actions and precautions, however, all of the ethical standards and review boards in the world cannot guarantee that research will be conducted ethically. As illustrated in the following Case-in-Point, IRB approval is a trust, not a guarantee that ethical violations will not survive the IRB. Ultimately, ethical conduct is the responsibility of each individual social work researcher.

CASE-IN-POINT: THE PROBLEM WITH RETRACTIONS

Retracting a paper from a scientific journal means that an error has occurred that significantly distorts the findings, or that scientific misconduct such as plagiarism or fraud have occurred, to the degree that the study should be withdrawn from the scientific literature (Van Noorden, 2011). One of the most high-profile retractions in recent times was the withdrawal of a study on attitudes toward same-sex marriage that was published in 2014 in the top-ranked journal *Science*. The authors, it was discovered, had misrepresented the use of incentives provided to participate in the survey, had falsely identified the sponsors of the study, and had falsified data (Carey, 2015). Although it may be comforting to know that retractions of peer-reviewed articles in scholarly journals are rare, they are on the increase. In the past decade retractions have increased ten times their prior level. Retractions, however, do not mean that studies are no longer used. Research examining 235 retracted articles found that they were cited more than 2,000 times after their withdrawal, with fewer than 8 % of the citations mentioning the retraction (Van Noorden, 2011). The trouble with retractions, beyond the continued use of erroneous findings and misleading conclusions, is the distrust that they bring upon the entire research enterprise. If research is to be used to influence practice and policy, then it must be broadly viewed as trustworthy, or else it can be easily dismissed. Rule-based ethical approaches rely on the ethical conduct of individual researchers.

Informed Consent

NASW guidelines *e* through *i* deal with **informed consent**, a procedure whereby subjects agree in writing, or verbally using audio or video recording, to participate in research under the following conditions:

1. They are informed of the foreseeable risks and potential benefits of participation.
2. Participation is voluntary and does not reflect mere acquiescence.
3. Consent is rendered only by an intellectually competent and mature individual.

Depending on the duration of participation required by the research, informed consent can be an ongoing process. The purpose of informed consent is to ensure that those participating in research are doing so under voluntary and informed circumstances; it is not to protect the researcher. Unfortunately, that is how informed consent is sometimes approached, apologetically and regretfully, and as an unnecessary nuisance that merely involves signing a document.

The words informed consent imply that the potential participant fully understands all of the following:

■ The purpose of the research.
■ Who is funding and who is conducting the research.

- Risks and benefits that may occur as a result of the research.
- Services that will be provided, such as transportation, food, child care, and incentives to participate.
- Procedures in place to deal with any risks that may occur, for instance, emotional distress that may arise as a result of the subject matter.
- The nature of participation, including what is expected, when, and where.
- How and when the data will be recorded, stored, and destroyed.
- Who will have access to the data.
- How the findings from the data will be published and used, including procedures to protect the identity of participants and opportunities for participants to participate in interpreting and applying the findings.

In addition to these safeguards, participants must be assured that (a) they will not be coerced into participating and (b) if they decline to participate at any time, they will not be punished in any way. Moreover, they should know that they may ask for more information at any time. To facilitate this process, they should be given the name and contact information for an appropriate person or persons. Participants must also understand that they can withdraw their consent to participate at any time and for any reason. Finally, informed consent requires an agreement as to what exactly participants are consenting to, in contrast to the practice illustrated in the Case-in-Point above.

NASW guidelines provide a useful outline for developing an informed consent form. When developing such a form, the researcher must make a special effort to avoid jargon and to write at a level that is understandable to the lowest level of reading ability found among potential participants. Researchers can use the checklist in Exhibit 2.2 to evaluate the sample letter of informed consent in Exhibit 2.3.

EXHIBIT 2.2

Checklist for Evaluating Informed Consent

The informed consent letter should include the following information:

- Introduction of the researcher, the research project, and sponsorship.
- Purpose of the research.
- How and why the participant was selected.
- Statement of benefits of the research to the participant and larger community.
- Statement of possible harm or risk and procedures to deal with it.
- Expectations of the participant: time, place, procedures.
- Ways that the researcher will maintain privacy and confidentiality.

- Promise of confidentiality.
- Rights regarding refusal and dropping out of the study.
- An appeal for help/cooperation.
- Name and contact information of the researcher and the person in charge if questions or concerns arise.

EXHIBIT 2.3

Sample Informed Consent Letter

Informed Consent Form—Parent

The Casey Family Services Building Skills–Building Futures Information Technology Pilot Project (BSBF) seeks to evaluate the usefulness of providing information technology resources to foster families. As a current foster family with Casey Family Services, you have been selected to participate in the project and the evaluation. The University of New Hampshire has been chosen to conduct the evaluation of the project. We are requesting your assistance by providing information about foster family needs, foster family learning, and your use of information technology.

   Families agree to participate in the program and the entire evaluation by:

a.   Filling out several information forms at the beginning of the project and at one-year and two-year intervals. These forms will assess your use of information technology, your satisfaction with the program, and the impact of the program on family life.
b.   Participating in a telephone interview about the program after three months.
c.   Participating in a two-hour discussion group at 12-month and 24-month intervals to provide feedback to the program.
d.   Participating in an e-mail survey by answering a monthly e-mail question about your use of and satisfaction with the program.
e.   Reviewing and providing feedback about web sites and other Internet resources related to parenting and foster care.

   The researchers will protect the confidentiality of the information you provide by:

a.   Using code numbers instead of names in keeping or reporting any information.
b.   Reporting the summary of group information rather than any individual responses.
c.   Keeping all information in a secure place.
d.   Having a signed confidentiality oath from all program staff and evaluators.
e.   Assuring that you have the right to see your evaluation information at any time.

Benefits

Families will receive hardware, software, training, and Internet connection. (Please see the Casey Family Service Contract with Families Form for an explanation of resources.) It is expected that this will provide families with greater access to information, greater interaction with staff, and increased social support.

Risks

The risks and/or discomforts of participating in this evaluation are minimal. As with any new experience, learning to use the Internet can, at times, be a frustrating experience. In addition, a very small number of people that use the Internet experience difficulties such as receiving unwanted e-mail, development of inappropriate relationships, loss of privacy, and accessing unwanted web sites (for example, pornography). Casey Family Services will facilitate training and technical support to minimize these risks.

In addition, efforts have been made to reduce the risk of discomfort:

a. No one is required to participate in this evaluation of the project. Your participation is completely voluntary.
b. You may withdraw from the evaluation at any time and continue to receive standard Casey services.
c. No family will be refused or denied standard services at Casey Family Services because they do not participate in this evaluation.
d. You may skip any question at any time, with no penalty.
e. All information collected by the University of New Hampshire is confidential and securely stored as described above.
f. Evaluation information will NOT be available to Casey Family Services for personnel evaluation.

If you have any questions about the evaluation process or your rights as a participant in the project, please call Dr. Jerry Finn, University of New Hampshire, (603) XXX-XXXX (e-mail: research@unh.edu), or Julie Simpson, Office of Sponsored Research, UNH, (603) XXX-XXXX (e-mail: OSR@unh.edu).

I have read and understand this Informed Consent form and agree to participate in the Casey Family Services Building Skills–Building Futures Information Technology Pilot Project.

Signed:

_____ / _____

BSBF Family Participant / Date

_____ / _____

Jerry Finn, Project Evaluator / Date

University of New Hampshire

Assent

Due to age or developmental capacity, some individuals may not be able to legally or reasonably provide informed consent. In such cases a parent or legal guardian may be asked to provide consent on their behalf. Nevertheless, these individuals may be asked to sign an **assent** form stating that they are aware that their parent or guardian has consented to their participation and that they voluntarily agree to participate or, in the case of children too young to give written assent, researchers may record children's verbal assent. This procedure is intended as a sign of respect for their rights as individuals. Exhibit 2.4 presents a sample assent form.

EXHIBIT 2.4

Sample Assent Form

Informed Assent for Minors

If there is something you don't understand on these pages, please ask a parent or guardian for help.

The Casey Family Services Building Skills–Building Futures Information Technology Pilot Project (BSBF) wishes to learn the usefulness of providing computers and Internet to foster families. As a member of a foster family with Casey Family Services, you have been selected to be in the project, if you choose to do so. In this project, you would use the computer and Internet and answer questions about what you are doing.

Children agree to help by:

a. Filling out several information forms at the beginning of the project and at 12-month and 24-month intervals. These forms will ask about how you use computers and how much you like the program.
b. Participating in a two-hour discussion group at 12-month and 24-month intervals to talk about the program.
c. Reviewing and providing information about web sites for foster families.

All of your answers will be private, and your name will never be on any reports. The University of New Hampshire will protect the confidentiality of the information you provide by:

a. Removing your name from any data that are collected or reported.
b. Keeping all information in a secure place.
c. Having a signed confidentiality oath from all program staff and evaluators.
d. Assuring that you have the right to see your evaluation information at any time.

Benefits

Families will receive hardware, software, training, and Internet connection. You will also be able to communicate with others over the Internet.

Risks

There are very few risks in participating in this evaluation. As with any new experience, learning to use the Internet can, at times, be a frustrating experience. In addition, a very small number of people that use the Internet have problems such as receiving unwanted e-mail and meeting people or finding information on the Internet that can upset you. CFS will give you training and help to minimize these risks.

In addition, efforts have been made to reduce the risk of discomfort:

a. No one has to be in the project. Your participation is voluntary.
b. You may leave the evaluation at any time and still receive standard Casey services.
c. No family will be refused or denied standard services at Casey Family Services because they do not participate in this project.
d. You may skip any question at any time, with no penalty.
e. All information collected by the University of New Hampshire is confidential and securely stored as described above.

If you have any questions about the project, please call Dr. Jerry Finn, University of New Hampshire, (603) XXX-XXXX (e-mail: research@unh.edu), or Julie Simpson, Office of Sponsored Research, UNH, (603) XXX-XXXX (e-mail: OSP@unh.edu).

I have read and understand this Informed Assent form and agree to be in the Casey Family Services Building Skills–Building Futures Information Technology Pilot Project.

Signed:

_____ / _____

BSBF Family Youth / Date

_____ / _____

Jerry Finn, Project Evaluator / Date

University of New Hampshire

Researchers who recruit children through schools and communities can face considerable challenges in obtaining parental consent. This challenge becomes particularly acute when only a select group of children who are not representative of the population as a whole return the signed consent forms and, then, may participate in the research. Research has demonstrated that parents from lower socioeconomic backgrounds are less likely to return parental consent forms and are less likely to allow their children to participate when they do return the forms (Spence et al., 2014). This pattern is problematic because successful research requires that the study include participants who are representative of the entire group. Furthermore, if marginalized populations are not included in the research, it becomes less likely that findings will be reflective of their realities and, then, relevant to their particular needs.

To deal with nonparticipation, some researchers have developed passive consent procedures. **Passive consent** requires that parents or legal guardians provide written notice only if they refuse to allow their children to participate. Otherwise, the children decide for themselves whether or not they want to participate at the time the study is conducted. Passive consent differs from **active consent**, which requires the parent or legal guardian to sign an informed consent form under all circumstances. The argument for passive consent is that the failure of parents or legal guardians to respond to active consent procedures does not always indicate a refusal to participate. Rather, it may be due to nonreceipt—that is, the child never took the consent form home—lost or misplaced forms, or confusion regarding the consent procedures. Passive consent procedures typically yield participation rates that far exceed those attained through active consent. However, passive consent may be objectionable to the IRB, as it violates principles of informed consent and may be seen as infringing on parental rights (Fletcher & Hunter, 2003). The Case-in-Point below describes a method of obtaining a high rate of participation using active consent.

CASE-IN-POINT: OBTAINING A HIGH RATE OF PARTICIPATION THROUGH ACTIVE CONSENT

If active consent is required for ethical considerations, methods to maximize participation have been developed. Fletcher and Hunter (2003) outline a tested strategy for obtaining a high participation rate using active parental consent procedures for school-based research. Their study involved children's friendships and parental involvement in these friendships. Potential participants were third-grade students enrolled in nine schools in a single county. Fletcher and Hunter used the following strategy to obtain a return rate of 95 percent for parental consent forms.

1. The researchers engaged the support of key school personnel, beginning with the highest office and working to the classroom level. They asked principals to designate a contact person for the duration of the project to serve as an intermediary between the research staff and the teachers. Often the contact person was the counselor who knew teachers and students and was able to elicit a high level of enthusiasm for the research. In addition, they informed teachers in writing

and via the school contact person about the importance of obtaining the participation of a representative group of children. They further declared that no research would be conducted in any classroom that did not have a 90 % rate of returned forms, regardless of whether consent was granted. Teachers who had a rate of return of 90 % or better received $5 gift certificates from a local educational supply store for each consent form returned. These certificates were given to the teachers on the day of data collection from their class, thereby providing immediate reinforcement.

2. Research assistants were assigned to specific schools and were encouraged to become personally invested in the consent process. Teachers appreciated the consistent communication and attention they received from a familiar research assistant.

3. The informed consent forms were designed to be clear and easy to read and to catch the parents' attention. A cover page with large bold print stated a set of instructions for completing the forms. The instructions informed parents that the child's class would receive a donation for each form returned, regardless of whether they checked yes or no. Areas that had to be filled out were highlighted. Any information that could be filled out in advance, like the school name and address and child's grade, was completed to reduce the burden on the parent. Different colors of paper were used to indicate different schools. Significantly, the researchers discovered that the brightest paper yielded the quickest and most complete responses. Parents commented that they liked receiving the bright paper.

4. The researchers provided consent forms multiple times to those children who had not returned the form on the first round. They gave out the forms one week apart. Moreover, they personalized the second and third waves by writing the child's name on the top of each form. The fourth time the forms were given out, a teacher or school official called the parent to ask if she or he had received the form and, if so, to request her or him to return it the next day.

Privacy

NASW guidelines *l* through *n* deal with protecting participants' privacy by not revealing identifying information. Identifying information goes beyond names and addresses and can include demographic characteristics such as race or ethnicity, age, position or title, membership in various organizations, and details of an event or circumstance. Researchers must be extremely careful not to violate privacy by identifying an individual by his or her demographic information. Some research studies can put a participant at risk of harm through embarrassment, retaliation, penalty, or discrimination if her or his identity is revealed. For example, in a worker satisfaction survey, a social worker who is critical of the administration may worry that providing honest answers could affect his or her relationships with supervisors. As social workers we should always consider privacy from the point of view of the participant, not the researcher. In some cultural groups, certain information is considered sacred, and having that information shared outside the group would be considered a breach of confidentiality. Indeed, our overriding concern as social work researchers is to do no harm.

The perception of possible harm, real or imagined, is a great disincentive to participation and therefore must be dealt with before recruiting participants. For example, in the research with members of the Havasupai Tribe described in Case-in-Point BLOOD VICTORY DAY, the use of data to examine population migration represents an infringement on the privacy of the tribe from a tribal perspective as opposed to from a researcher's perspective.

Because social work research is concerned with reflecting reality as accurately as possible, we must work creatively and strategically to encourage and enable a representative group of participants to safely participate. One method of encouraging participation is through the use of incentives.

Incentives for Participation

It is common and useful in research projects to provide small incentives for participants. For example, the researcher might give a small stipend or gift certificate to subjects to cover the costs of transportation to the research site or to compensate them for their time. Incentives, however, can be considered coercive when the value is such that people who would not ordinarily participate in a study feel that they must participate because they need the incentive. For example, from 1963 to 1971, a study involving testicular radiation and vasectomy was conducted in the Oregon prison system. Participants were paid $25 per session for up to five sessions. This incentive was offered at a time when prisoners generally earned 25 cents a day for their labor. In this case, the incentive may have "coerced" men to participate in the study when they otherwise would not have chosen to do so (Goliszek, 2003). Similarly in social work, a mother receiving TANF may feel that she "must" participate in a study of childhood sexual abuse experiences that offers a $500 incentive because the money would greatly benefit her children, even if she believes that engaging in this research would be traumatic for her. Social work researchers often conduct research with vulnerable and needy populations. Therefore, they should carefully consider the use of incentives when they design their projects. In Chapter 10 we discuss further the use of incentives to encourage participation.

Confidentiality and Anonymity

The promise of confidentiality that we so often make to a potential participant during the informed consent process is a promise not to reveal identifying information that the participant has provided. Fulfilling the promise of confidentiality can be especially problematic in some forms of qualitative research, in which (1) the intent is to obtain as much detailed information as possible, (2) everything about the participant has the potential to become data, and (3) the participant's words are used in the publication and presentation of the findings.

One research scenario in which confidentiality becomes highly problematic is the case study. The **case study** is a qualitative research strategy that seeks to examine a single unit of analysis, be it an event, a person, a family, a group, an organization, or a company, in order to generate an in-depth understanding of that unit. (We examine case studies in greater detail in Chapter 6.) Frequently, researchers engaged in case studies either cannot protect or do not desire confidentiality because of the level of detail that participants report. In such cases, the researcher must negotiate with the participants concerning which information they wish to reveal to other individuals and which information they wish to withhold.

Large quantitative studies can also put participants at risk of identification. This risk is especially prevalent in cases that involve a small number of participants who possess particular characteristics that might enable anyone reading the study to identify them. This is particularly true of participants whose demographic characteristics are rare within the sample. For example, in the Midwest, a 59-year-old male Pacific Islander may be the only individual in the sample who fits those demographic characteristics. Therefore, he may be relatively easy to identify. In such studies the researcher should not report results by categories that would permit identification.

The promise of **anonymity**—the agreement not to record a participant's name or other identifying information such as address or Social Security number—does not guarantee confidentiality. Although a promise of anonymity can make research participants more comfortable and more willing to participate, it does not guarantee that they cannot be identified by other revealing characteristics after the study is published. For example, a direct quotation from a participant in a research study may allow someone to identify the participant even if the name is not given. In one study, a social worker was quoted as saying, "Someone should just slap the management. They should check with the workers before changing policy." Although no name was given, many people at the agency knew who regularly used the expression "should just slap." Social work researchers must carefully consider issues of privacy and confidentiality when they are designing research projects.

THE ETHICS OF INTERNET RESEARCH

The proliferation of mobile devices coupled with advanced information and communication technologies (ICT) have made their use increasingly common in public service interventions. For example, applications have been functionally and routinely used to mobilize social justice efforts, to promote human well-being, and to support therapeutic interventions. Information and communication technologies (ICT) present new ethical challenges. Typically, ICT ethics have been concerned with respect for three things: the rights of privacy and intellectual property of IT users; copyrights and licensing agreements; and the integrity of data. Others who have contributed to the consequentialist approach (e.g., Bynum, 2006) have examined the impact of ICT upon human values like health, wealth, opportunity, freedom, democracy, knowledge, privacy, security, and self-fulfillment. Bynum (2006) called his approach one of *flourishing ethics*.

Reynolds and Picard (2005) suggest that new relational phenomenon potential with ICT challenges us to begin to develop a new ethical approach. They note that questions such as: "Could a user be emotionally manipulated by a program with the capability to recognize and convey affect?" and "Should an affective system try to change the emotional state of a user?" are now at the starting point when working with "computing that relates to, arises from, or deliberately influences emotion" (Picard, 1997, p. 3). This discussion implies that research on ICT applications should begin in the design phase and continue through to considerations related to the end user and application. Larger ethical considerations relate to potential challenges regarding data integrity, now that systems have been compromised across a variety of platforms, and also greater ability to disseminate findings broadly, which simultaneously increases opportunities for collaboration and in application raises the potential of misuse of participants' data.

CONCLUSION

The uniqueness of social work research is not in its research methods, theory, statistical analysis, or technology. Social work research can be distinguished from research in other disciplines by its purpose—the ends to which the research is conducted and its particular ethical structures. In brief, the mission of social work is the enhancement of human well-being with attention to the vulnerable, oppressed, and poor. Historically, these groups were the most likely to be the victims of ethical misconduct through research studies. They may also feel especially powerless to refuse requests to participate in research studies since they may feel that their access to needed resources and services is at stake. The social work researcher must be more than a technician. The social work researcher must be able to explain, promote, and use social work research in direct and policy practice. At the same time, social workers must have as their highest concern the protection of all those who participate in research and their ethical responsibilities to their clients. This requires a clear understanding of research ethics before engaging in the research methods described in the remainder of the text.

MAIN POINTS

- In working to achieve the mission of social work, researchers must pay attention to research and evaluation quality as well as clarity in reporting and interpretation. In addition, they must assist program personnel and advocates in using data to influence social policy.
- Research and research priorities are strongly influenced by funding, and funding is strongly influenced by politics. Research priorities can also be affected by the extent of knowledge in the field and the degree of advocacy for a particular issue.
- All social workers should be familiar with the ethical standards of the profession. The current version of the NASW Code of Ethics (2008) sets out 17 ethical standards relevant to evaluation and research. The NASW ethical guidelines and local IRBs are resources to aid in the conduct of ethical research.
- The principle of informed consent requires that potential research participants thoroughly understand the nature of their involvement in the research as well as the risks and potential benefits of the research. Moreover, participants must possess the legal and mental capacity to consent, and they must be given free choice as to whether to participate without fear of consequence.
- Privacy should be viewed from the perspective of the research participant and not from the perspective of the researcher. Protecting the identity of research participants goes beyond promises of anonymity and confidentiality in data collection and safe data storage. The researcher must be vigilant not to reveal a participant's identity through publication or presentation of information that is particularly revealing.

EXERCISES

1. Using the Riverton: A Community Conundrum case, describe how you might use the results of a community survey to work towards social justice. Consider the following:
   a. Who might serve as an audience for your findings?
   b. Who would you target as a change agent in the community?
2. Using the Riverton: A Community Conundrum case, list three perceived benefits and three perceived risks of conducting a community survey.
3. Consider The Sanchez Family: Systems, Strengths, and Stressors case. If you were to involve this family in research, what factors would you need to consider in order to protect their privacy?
4. Write a sample letter of consent that you could conceivably present to Mr. and Mrs. Sanchez to recruit them into a research study focused on parenting in

Hispanic families. Since getting consent from the Sanchez family members would require Spanish-language documents, outline the elements of an appropriate informed consent process particularly for the family.

5. Using the Carla Washburn: Loss, Aging, and Social Support case, discuss how you would apply each of the NASW Code of Ethics Ethical Guidelines for Research and Evaluation to a study aimed at exploring reactions of parents and guardians to the loss of an adult child through military service.

6. How would you ethically invite Ms. Washburn's participation in such a study? Consider for example, recruitment, incentives, privacy, and other matters discussed in this chapter. What might make Ms. Washburn reluctant to participate in research, and how would you address those concerns?

7. A staff member of RAINN is preparing to disseminate findings from an evaluation of their services and uncertain about the extent to which she must disclose that RAINN is only able to collect satisfaction data from those who complete a follow-up survey. She suspects that this is a relatively small group and not entirely representative of those RAINN serves. Compare and contrast the three approaches to ethics described in this chapter and then describe the ethical considerations that would arise from each approach in regard to the RAINN case and the worker's uncertainty.

8. What are some unique ethical consideration related to the RAINN case given that it is an Internet-based service? List and explain each consideration.

9. How has media coverage influenced your opinion of rape and incest? How might your personal opinions and biases influence the research questions you would ask with regard to RAINN?

10. If you were on an IRB panel considering a research proposal to study an environmental justice study to be conducted by the Brickville youth leadership development group (the group plans to assess community members' experiences with air pollution and litter, in particular), what questions might you have for the group? What would influence your assessment of whether this project needs full IRB review? What protections do you think would be important to put in place?

11. Imagine that you are putting together a RFP for an evaluation of Hudson City's disaster response system. What would you look for in researchers? What project elements would be important to you? What would researchers need to consider in order to make this inquiry valuable to those struggling in the aftermath of the disaster?

RESEARCH PROBLEMS AND RESEARCH QUESTIONS

Rowing harder doesn't help if the boat is headed in the wrong direction.
Kenichi Ohmae

At this point in your social work education, you may be more comfortable, or at least more familiar, with social work practice than with social work research. Social work practice, like research, is a systematic process. That is, social workers use a practice framework to guide their actions. Therefore, an effective strategy to become familiar with the steps in social work research is to relate them to your practice framework.

The first two chapters dealt with the need to base social work practice on knowledge and the ethics and the politics involved in generating knowledge. This chapter begins our journey into the "how to" of conducting social work research. As Enola Proctor, former editor of the premier journal *Social Work Research*, wrote, "The advancement of social work knowledge requires not only that we pose significant questions, but also that we answer them well" (2001, p. 3). This chapter provides you with the knowledge and skills you will need in order to pose relevant and researchable questions. The remaining chapters deal with the knowledge and skills you will need in order to answer research questions with confidence. By the end of this chapter you should be able to:

■ Explain the parallel between social work research and social work practice.
■ Explain how a working knowledge of the research process is important to all social workers.
■ List and briefly describe the first two steps in the social work research process: identifying the problem area and formulating a research question and hypotheses.
■ Describe the concept of operationalization and provide an example of its relevance to social work research.
■ Discuss how sensitivity to culture at each step in the research process will produce better information.
■ Apply criteria to critically evaluate a research problem and research question in a published research study.

UNDERSTANDING THE RESEARCH PROCESS

When you are conducting research in a social work context, the steps of the **research process** serve as the framework for your actions. Exhibit 3.1 presents the research process as a series of eight steps. It also illustrates how the steps in the research process parallel those in social work practice. Both social work practice and social work research use existing information to identify a problem, create a plan of action, seek valid and reliable measurement, collect data, and analyze and interpret the data to direct further action.

The research process consists of all the steps that must be considered in planning and carrying out research in a social work context. The word process implies that order is involved in conducting social work research. When social workers ignore that order or fail to make a connection between the steps in the research process, they waste a lot of time and resources producing information that is likely to be flawed and misleading. Worst of all, despite their good intentions, they will not benefit and may even harm the very people they aim to help—their clients, communities, programs, and organizations.

Good social work practice, at any level, begins with an assessment, defined as a thorough understanding of the problem area. For instance, a professional social work counselor or case manager begins with an assessment before she or he considers an intervention. Similarly, a social work manager writing a proposal for a new social program would be required to include an assessment of need and assets before specifying the overall purpose of the proposed program—its goal— and measurable statements of its intent, or objectives. The social worker engaged in policy practice would not lobby for new legislation without first becoming familiar with the problem that the proposed legislation

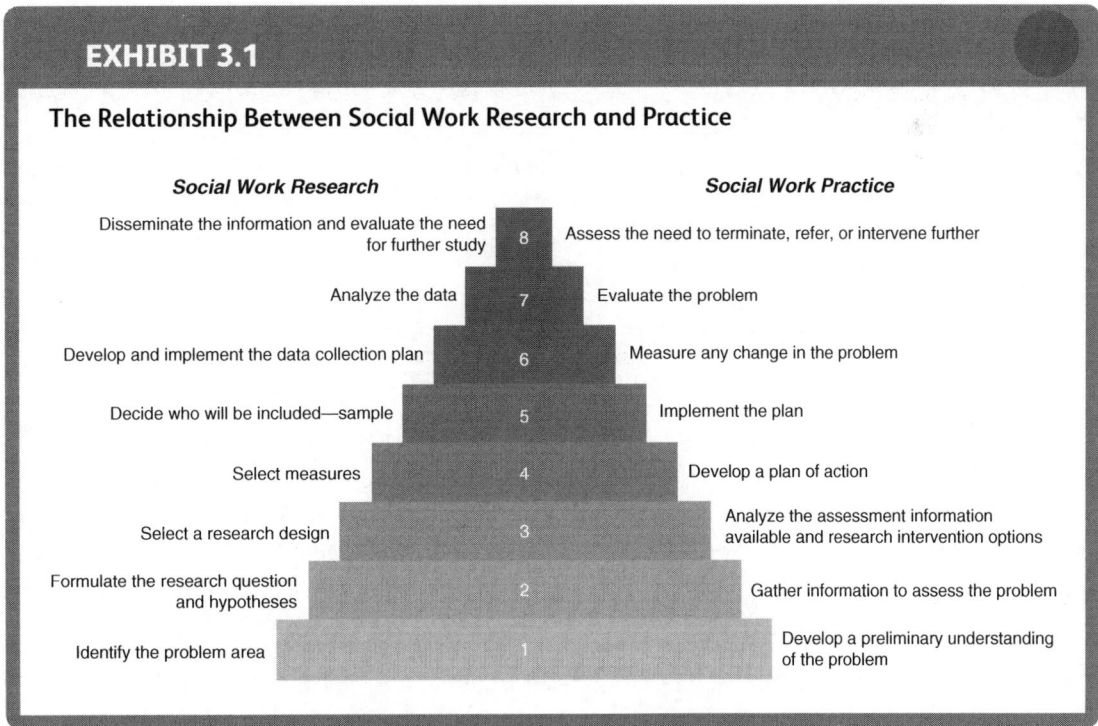

EXHIBIT 3.1

The Relationship Between Social Work Research and Practice

Social Work Research		Social Work Practice
Disseminate the information and evaluate the need for further study	8	Assess the need to terminate, refer, or intervene further
Analyze the data	7	Evaluate the problem
Develop and implement the data collection plan	6	Measure any change in the problem
Decide who will be included—sample	5	Implement the plan
Select measures	4	Develop a plan of action
Select a research design	3	Analyze the assessment information available and research intervention options
Formulate the research question and hypotheses	2	Gather information to assess the problem
Identify the problem area	1	Develop a preliminary understanding of the problem

is intended to alleviate. So too, social work research begins with identifying a problem. To say that something is "problematic" in a research context is to imply that something is unknown and we would be better off if we knew about it. In the absence of understanding the problem, effort and resources are wasted as implied in the opening quote of this chapter.

What if you want to be involved in human services and are not planning to be a social work researcher or an evaluator? Why should you spend time learning the research process? The answer is that, regardless of your role as a social worker, possessing a working knowledge of the research process will serve you well:

- Using the research process as a framework for evaluating existing information will help you become more critical in your thinking and better able to critique the effectiveness of your methods and those of other service providers.
- Knowledge of the research process is essential for the evaluation of social work practice, whether it involves work with a single client or an entire program of services.
- Social work administrators attempting to raise funds to support a new or existing program are more likely to succeed when they use the research process as a framework for deciding what information to include in their proposals.
- Policy makers, lobbyists, and advocates will appear more credible when they debate issues and create arguments using their knowledge of the research process.

Conducting research to produce useful information for social work requires careful planning, sound design, adequate resources, and a step-by-step process that begins with a definition of the problem.

IDENTIFYING THE RESEARCH PROBLEM

One of the most exciting aspects of social work is the breadth of populations and problem areas it addresses. This observation applies to social work research as well as to social work practice.

Research, the process of searching for an answer to the unknown, is a problem-driven enterprise. Problems become recognized in the public domain not because they exist but because they are identified and defined as problems. In other words, problems are socially constructed. For example, people sometimes claim that poverty was discovered in the 1960s, sexual abuse in the 1970s, and domestic violence in the 1980s. Reflecting on problems of the current decade—mass incarceration, opiate addiction, and racial profiling. In reality,

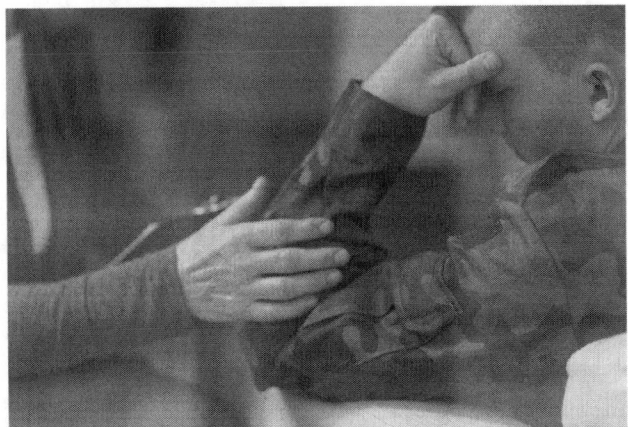

The Problem of Veteran Suicide

Veterans exhibit significantly higher suicide risk compared with the U.S. general population. However, deployment to Iraq or Afghanistan, by itself, was not associated with the excess suicide risk.
Credit: KatarzynaBialasiewicz/ThinkStock.

Kang, H. K., Bullman, T. A., Smolenski, D. J, Skopp, N. A., Gahm, G. A., & Reger, M. A. (2015). Suicide risk among 1.3 million veterans who were on active duty during the Iraq and Afghanistan wars. *Ann Epidemiol. 25*(2), 96–100. doi: 10.1016/j.annepidem.2014.11.020.

of course, all of these phenomena existed before these times. However, they did not receive sufficient attention to be defined as social problems.

Because social workers encounter social problems on a daily basis, they are in a unique position to bring their knowledge of these problems to the public's attention. In addition, they can help dispel popular myths and stereotypes by giving the affected populations a face and a voice through research. For instance, many social workers practicing in the area of homelessness have noticed that the clients of homeless shelters and soup kitchens are increasingly families with children.

The federal government has undertaken an enormous data collection effort to increase our understanding of the problem of homelessness in the United States. In 2001 Congress directed the U.S. Department of Housing and Urban Development (HUD) to collect data on the extent of homelessness at the local level (H.B. 106-988; Senate Report 106-410). As a result, jurisdictions that receive HUD funds are busily implementing management information systems to answer four questions: (1) How many individuals are homeless? (2) What are the characteristics of homeless individuals? (3) What services do homeless individuals need? (4) What services do homeless individuals receive? Some data collection efforts are statewide, and others are limited to cities and counties.

It is highly unlikely that a social worker will need to go looking for a problem that needs to be researched. Just the opposite, practicing social workers consistently encounter situations for which they need more information. For example, assume that your internship is in a middle school and a child who is being picked on by other children has been brought to your attention. Suddenly you are full of questions. Is this an isolated incident? If not, how long has it been occurring? How many other children are encountering the same problem? Are the teachers and administrators aware of the problem? If so, how have they responded? Is the problem limited to this school setting? What are the characteristics of the children being picked on and of the perpetrating children? What are the long-term consequences for the victims? What do the parents of the victims and the perpetrators know about the situation? How have they reacted? Are there any verified strategies for dealing with this problem? In your search for answers to these questions, you find that school bullying has received a lot of recent attention in the research literature. You also find that some of your initial questions have been answered, but that others require further research.

Although work-related opportunity is probably the most common way a social worker will identify problems for research, personal interest and experience can also play a role. Many social workers, for example, are personally committed to the social problems of developing countries, such as economic development in the face of transitional economies, child poverty, and the spread of HIV/AIDS.

Other social workers commit themselves to advancing knowledge in specific problem areas as a result of personal, and sometimes tragic, experiences. A social worker who has experienced the return of a deployed friend or family member and then loses him or her to suicide, for example, might feel a responsibility to expand the base of knowledge associated with PTSD and depression among veterans.

Exhibit 3.2 is a checklist for evaluating a research problem. Some of the items in the checklist are discussed in greater detail below.

EXHIBIT 3.2

Checklist for Evaluating a Research Problem

After identifying a problem area for study, evaluate it according to these five criteria:

1. The problem area is relevant to social work.
2. The need for research on the problem area is compelling.
3. The claim that the problem area warrants research is supported by credible sources of information.
4. Various sources of bias have been considered in identifying the research problem.
5. Potential participants in the study agree that research on the problem is needed and view it as potentially beneficial.

Defining the Real Problem

The problems that social workers encounter usually can be addressed in multiple ways. Critical to addressing a problem is figuring out what the real underlying problem is, and separating it from its more readily observable symptoms. A classic example of the failure to address the real problem is found in the area of posttraumatic stress disorder (PTSD). PTSD is found across populations of adults, for example veterans, child welfare-involved parents, and incarcerated individuals. Often the focus of research and treatment with these populations is on the symptoms of the disorder, i.e., the substance abuse, the unsanitary home, depression, and an apparent lack of motivation for change. Avoiding the tendency to rush to a solution, and taking the time to research and think critically about a problem, can help to identify the root cause as opposed to focusing on the symptoms. Acknowledging as well that many of the problems that we deal with are complex and have many layers also helps. Following the steps in the research process will help us identify the real problem. The following Case-in-Point illustrates what happens when the problem is misidentified. The research that is built on such a mistake can produce misleading results and waste time, resources, and the good will of the client system or the public at large. Thus a basic principle of social work research is that all of the steps in the research process should flow from an accurate identification of the problem.

CASE-IN-POINT: PREVENTION PROGRAM FAILS TO ACCURATELY IDENTIFY THE PROBLEM

A social worker was asked to consult with the administrator of a school-based substance abuse prevention program that targets children in 3rd through 8th grades. The program was designed around a standardized curriculum to discourage students in these grades from using alcohol, drugs, and tobacco. The administrator reported that for the second year in a row the evaluation of the program revealed no significant change in students' attitudes or behavior regarding these substances. What did this mean? Was the prevention program not working?

By examining the data and talking to groups of parents, the administrator determined that the vast majority of students in the program had not experimented with alcohol, drugs, or tobacco. They didn't need a substance abuse prevention program, or at least not one that focused on drugs and alcohol. Resiliency programs targeted at children at a young age that focus on school attachment, positive parent/child communication, etc. have been shown to be successful in preventing a number of risk behaviors that tend to surface later in childhood (Jenson & Fraser, 2016). On the basis of this feedback from the social worker, the administrator decided to use the scarce prevention funds to target the reduction of risk and increase resiliency rather than focus on substance use.

Making the Case to Study a Research Problem

Identifying a research problem can be quite easy. Unfortunately, there are more problems that merit research than there are resources for studying them. What factors, then, determine that one problem area warrants the time and resources associated with research more than another? To demonstrate the worth of a problem area for research, the social worker must be able to convincingly answer the question: Why is this important?

Possible answers to this question include the frequency with which the problem occurs, the extent of human suffering the problem produces, the costs of the problem to society, the lack of attention the problem has received in the past, and the belief that the problem can and should be addressed at the current time. Through an initial exploration of a problem area, social workers come to understand the magnitude, extent of suffering, and costs associated with a social problem, as well as the attention, or lack thereof, it has already received. Social workers seek answers to such questions as: How many people are affected, and in what ways? The information found in this initial exploration of the problem area will help social workers decide whether further research is warranted.

It is also likely that a social worker will be interested in more than one compelling problem area. In such cases, she or he must select one area based on some combination of personal interest and expressed agency or organizational need for the research.

Find Relevant Information Sources

There are several useful resources for conducting an initial exploration of a problem area. For instance, conducting a key word search on an electronic database of a library, reading agency case files, and browsing the annual program evaluation reports of agencies and organizations can give us a sense of the magnitude and nature of a problem area. Talking with social work colleagues and professors can also be helpful, particularly if they can suggest valuable sources of information.

The Internet will likely contain a great deal of information related to your problem area as well. A key word search may produce information from a wide variety of sources, including university-based projects, archives of government agencies, electronic journals, interest groups, magazines, and web pages from companies and individuals. Because the Internet contains so much information it will be important to sift through it and make a judgment as to what is relevant. An initial determination can be made as to whether it helps to answer questions on how many are affected, with what characteristics, how they are affected, for how long, and what causes the problem. However, not all information sources can be trusted. The following section helps you to evaluate the credibility of information sources.

Evaluate the Credibility of Information Sources

Although we should approach all information sources with a healthy amount of skepticism, information from the Internet is especially prone to error and bias because there are no controls on its publication. Consequently, we must carefully evaluate which Internet sources are credible and which are not using accepted principles of critical analysis.

One way to evaluate the credibility of a source is to use a framework such as the one presented in Quick Guide 2.

Striving for Cultural Proficiency

When social workers consider which research to undertake, they must take into account the cultural context in which the research will take place. There is a broad agreement within the social work literature on the need for social workers to be proficient in issues of culture. **Cultural competence** is the ability to perform effectively in multicultural settings based on an understanding of one's own and others' language, customs, values, and beliefs. **Cultural proficiency** is the culmination or endpoint on the continuum of cultural competence. It is characterized by knowledge, attitudes, and behavior that hold culture in high esteem (Cross et al., 1989).

Culturally proficient social workers seek to do more than provide unbiased services. Rather, they value the positive role that culture can play in their clients' health and well-being. Training for social work practitioners on cultural proficiency generally includes self-awareness, knowledge of different cultures, and intervention strategies that are tailored for specific cultures (Marsiglia & Kulis, 2015). When applied to social work research, cultural proficiency involves adding to the knowledge base of culturally competent practices by conducting original research, tailoring research approaches so that they are appropriate for the client's culture, and publishing and disseminating the results of research in ways that are accessible to varied cultural groups that may be interested in the research.

To achieve cultural proficiency in research—to produce knowledge that is respectful of culture and as error free as possible—social workers must be sensitive to culture during each step of the research process. Culturally proficient research begins with being sensitive to culture in identifying the research problem.

QUICK GUIDE 2 FRAMEWORK FOR EVALUATING THE CREDIBILITY OF INFORMATION SOURCES

Criterion	Explanation	Source 1	Source 2	Source 3
Authority	Is the source of the information identified by name? Is there a way to verify the legitimacy of the source, such as an address or telephone number? Does the source have a bias or reason to distort its information? What credentials does the source have to provide this information? Have experts subjected the information to a process of review?			
Currency	How recent are the facts and figures? Is there a date to indicate when the source was first published or last updated? Might things have changed considerably since this information was gathered?			
Fairness	Do the authors present the material in a balanced manner, or do they focus only on the positive or negative aspects?			
Intent	Is the motivation for providing the information clear? Is the intent informational, that is, to provide facts and figures? Is the intent advocacy, meaning that the source is sponsored by an organization attempting to influence public opinion? Is the intent advertising, meaning that the purpose of the source is to promote or sell something?			
Reliability	How did the authors derive the information? Do they cite their sources? Are the data consistent with other known sources? Did the authors follow accepted research procedures? Do they provide enough detail? Do they address the limitations of the information? Is the information well presented and free of grammatical, spelling, and typographical errors?			
	Total score			

DIRECTIONS:

List each source of existing information you have gathered by title or author in the top row. Next, for each of the five criteria, rate each source on a scale of 0–5. A score of 0 represents a failing grade, and a score of 5 represents excellence. When you have rated all five criteria, add up the total score for each source and record it in the bottom row. A total score close to 25 indicates a credible source; a low score suggests that the source should not be used.

Source: Courtesy of Janet Alexander and Marsha Ann Tate.

The guidelines that follow are a useful beginning in achieving culturally proficient research:

ACKNOWLEDGE PERSONAL BIASES

People are separated socially, economically, and educationally on the basis of ethnicity, race, gender, sexual orientation, and age. This separation frequently generates myths, stereotypes, attitudes, and assumptions regarding diverse groups and their cultures. Heightened self-awareness is necessary for the researcher to identify his or her personal biases.

ASSESS BIAS IN THE LITERATURE

Three kinds of bias can be found in the existing literature. First, certain cultural groups might not be represented in the literature because researchers simply have failed to study them. For example, researchers have paid a lot of attention to teenage mothers but very little to teenage fathers. Second, a study of a subset of people can overgeneralize the entire group. For example, researchers might make inferences about Hispanic immigrants in general based solely on a study of undocumented immigrants from Mexico. Finally, researchers can focus on the negative attributes associated with particular cultures at the expense of acknowledging positive features. Over time, this negative focus can lead to the development and reinforcement of destructive stereotypes, particularly the tendency to define differences as pathological. For example, a great deal of research on American Indians focuses on alcohol and drug use. In contrast, the concept of kinship care has been central to the American Indian culture for generations, but it has taken researchers decades to frame it as a positive practice that has conceptual relevance to the field of child welfare.

ASSESS BIAS IN AGENCIES AND ORGANIZATIONS

Bias in social service agencies can lead to the study of diverse populations in only limited contexts. For example, research may focus on poor African Americans but not on middle-class African Americans. Studying populations in limited contexts promotes stereotypes and masks within-group diversity. Bias within an agency can also lead to a narrow view of culturally diverse groups and the difficulties they face. For example, social service practitioners have tended to emphasize individual parenting deficits and to ignore external and institutional factors such as poverty, poor education and health care, and loss of culture that make parenting even more of a challenge for particular groups.

ACQUIRE PREREQUISITE KNOWLEDGE

Social workers need to invest time and effort in learning about the cultural groups of interest. At the very minimum, social work researchers should acquire knowledge of the cultural group's history, communication norms, language preferences, religion or spiritual beliefs, and attitudes toward gender and age.

DIFFERENTIATE "RESEARCH FOR" FROM "RESEARCH ON"

Research for can be conceptualized as an altruistic activity, pursued out of an unselfish concern for the welfare of others that promotes the expressed needs and perspectives of the group being studied. Research on, in contrast, can be perceived as an opportunistic activity, viewing the cultural group as merely a subject of study.

INVOLVE MEMBERS OF THE CULTURAL GROUP

Members of the identified group to be involved in the research should be consulted about decision making related to research. Research problems identified through involvement of participants may have a very different focus from research problems identified independent of such consultation. Researchers should be guided by the old saying "nothing about us without us."

Cultural proficiency in research is a developing domain, and it is imperative that social workers continue to advance this area.

REFINING THE RESEARCH QUESTION

After you identify the research problem, the next step in the research process is to formulate a research question. To make the research process more manageable, researchers often move from a general problem area to a narrower, specific research question, which is sometimes referred to as the funnel approach.

Formulating the General Research Question

One useful approach to formulating the general research question is to begin with a brainstorming session. Brainstorming involves writing down as many general research questions related to the problem area as you can think of, without being overly concerned about their wording. To expand your list of questions, engage your classmates and colleagues in brainstorming with you; after all, social work research is seldom a solitary activity. The rationale for beginning the process of formulating the research question by brainstorming is to avoid being limited to the ideas published in the literature.

Exhibit 3.3 is a checklist for evaluating a general research question. The items in the checklist are elaborated in the sections that follow. Use the checklist as a final evaluation after the general question has been formulated.

EXHIBIT 3.3

Checklist for Evaluating the General Research Question

- The question is logically related to the identification of the problem area.
- The question can be answered through research; it is not value laden.
- The question has not been answered. If it has been, what related questions might you ask?
- Answering the question will be useful for informing social work practice, developing social policy, or advancing theory.
- The question is sensitive to issues of culture.

Avoid Value-Laden Questions

Some of the questions produced in a brainstorming session are likely to involve values. Value-laden questions cannot be answered through research; their answers are purely a matter of personal opinion. Examples of value-laden questions are: Should transgender individuals be allowed to use the bathroom of their choice? Should abortion be legal? Is euthanasia morally acceptable? Is capital punishment moral? These questions cannot be answered by research.

Social workers may, however, be concerned with related questions, such as: What is the range of public opinion on transgender bathroom choice? How do women who have experienced an abortion view the procedure one year later? What are the psychological consequences of euthanasia for surviving family members? Does capital punishment deter violent crime? These questions differ from value-laden questions in that they can be answered through research.

Categorize Research Questions by Their Purpose

Once you have compiled a list of potential research questions, you can place each question into one of three categories of inquiry, depending on the purpose of the question. These are the three categories:

- *Exploratory research*: The purpose of **exploratory research** is to gain an initial understanding of the problem area. This type of research is especially important when we know very little about the problem.

■ *Descriptive research*: As the name suggests, the purpose of **descriptive research** is to describe. Descriptive research questions pertain to the characteristics of the problem and the characteristics of those affected by the problem. This involves questions such as: How many people are affected, and with what consequences? How does the problem differ by demographic and cultural characteristics?

■ *Explanatory research*: As you have probably deduced, the purpose of **explanatory research** is to explain how and why things happen. Explanatory research questions are designed to generate an in-depth understanding of the problem area. They often seek to establish cause-and-effect relationships that enable us to predict future events. We can use explanatory research to test such aspects of a problem as (a) the factors related to the presence or absence of the problem, (b) a common order or sequence in how the problem develops, and (c) the effectiveness of intervention strategies aimed at alleviating the problem.

The reason for classifying research questions according to purpose is to help identify which category of questioning is most appropriate for the problem area. We determine the most appropriate category of questioning by reviewing the literature to identify what we already know about the problem area and what we still need to learn.

To illustrate the question categorization process, we will refer to a current issue that has relevance to social work: same-sex marriage. In February 2004 San Francisco began issuing marriage licenses to same-sex couples (Murphy, 2004). In the ensuing month, more than 4,000 gay and lesbian couples from 46 states and eight countries were legally married in San Francisco. Then, in March, the California Supreme Court prohibited the city from issuing any more marriage licenses to same-sex couples. A flurry of legislative activity continued around the country as many state legislators worked to ban same-sex marriages through constitutional and statutory provisions. Then on June 26, 2015, the Supreme Court ruled in favor of same-sex marriage nationwide. The highest court in the U.S. ruled that states could not ban same-sex marriage.

The controversies surrounding same-sex marriage raise a number of potential research questions. We can classify these questions by their primary purpose: to explore, to describe, or to explain. Exhibit 3.4 provides examples of questions with the primary purpose of explore, describe, or explain.

Conduct a Literature Review

A significant step in formulating a research problem is to review the research that has already been conducted. A **literature review** is an account of what has

EXHIBIT 3.4

Purpose-Based Classification of Research Questions Relating to Same-Sex Marriage

Exploratory Questions:

1. How has marriage affected same-sex couples?
2. What significance does marriage have for the children of same-sex unions?
3. How has same-sex marriage legislation influenced the process of coming out whereby gays and lesbians publicly proclaim their sexual orientation?

Descriptive Questions:

1. What are the demographic characteristics of the gay and lesbian couples who have married versus those who have not?
2. How many same-sex unions are there in the United States, and what forms do they take?
3. What state-level spousal rights exist for the unmarried partners of same-sex unions?

Explanatory Questions:

1. What factors predict whether or not same-sex couples will choose legal marriage when it is available?
2. How does legal marriage impact the quality of same-sex relationships?
3. What types of interventions support healthy parental adjustment to a child's disclosure of homosexuality?

been published on a problem area by scholars and researchers. The purpose of the literature review in social work research is fourfold:

1. To gain an understanding of the knowledge and ideas that have been established in a problem area.
2. To identify the strengths and weaknesses of our existing knowledge.
3. To identify the controversies that exist in the literature.
4. To identify questions that require further research.

To achieve its purpose, the literature review may examine issues of theory, methodology, policy, and evaluation that relate to the effectiveness of a policy or intervention. The review can include information from a variety of disciplines other than social work, including health, psychology, sociology, medicine, law, political science, and women's studies, as long as the information is directly related to the problem area.

One way to begin the literature review is to conduct an electronic search of a library database for relevant books, journal articles, theses, dissertations, and conference proceedings. In addition, government documents may provide valuable statistical information on the problem, including the numbers and demographic characteristics of the people affected by it. Reference librarians can be particularly helpful in locating government documents and other unpublished sources of information such as evaluation reports.

An Internet search also might identify relevant printed resources, sometimes in the form of an annotated bibliography, meta-analysis, systematic review, or other online publications. Many journals now publish scholarly articles online before they appear in print, making the Internet the most current source of information.

Familiarity with the literature on the problem area will likely help you reword some of your original research questions and generate ideas for additional questions. When conducting the literature review, remember to perform the following activities:

- Look for information on the scope, severity, and relevance of the problem area.
- Assess the relationship between the theory related to the problem area and the available research.
- Note the problematic issues that the literature raises, and assess how these issues have been addressed in prior research.
- Identify areas of controversy related to the problem.
- Synthesize the literature review into a summary of what is and is not known.
- Identify questions that require further research.
- Make the literature search wide enough to ensure that you have included the relevant material yet narrow enough to exclude irrelevant material.
- Identify the leading researchers in the area of interest and be sure to include their research in your literature review. Leaders are usually those whose names appear again and again.
- Relate the study you propose to do to the previous literature.

Use Theory as a Guide

In its simplest of terms, theory is an explanation for why things are the way they are; it is an explanation of the relationships among phenomena. When we are developing research questions, theory can lead us to ask certain research questions or to word our questions in a specific way. When we are explicit about the theory or theories we use to help guide our study, we make clear our rationale for asking certain research questions.

Sometimes, if you are simply trying to determine if an intervention is helping a client or group of clients, there will be no explicit use of theory in your research. Not all research is guided by theory. The following Case-in-Point describes the use of theory as a basis for generating research questions.

CASE-IN-POINT: THREE THEORIES USED TO FORMULATE RESEARCH QUESTIONS ABOUT RELATIONSHIPS AND THE INTERNET

Megan Lindsay, a doctoral student in social work at Arizona State University, was interested in how the social relationships and developmental processes of young adults are influenced by their use of the Internet. By reviewing the literature, she discovered that little was known about this topic, even though young adults were reported to use the Internet at rates comparable to adolescents. Prior research had either excluded 18–24-year-olds, or had grouped them together with 10–18-year-olds. Megan drew from three theories to help advance her thinking in this area. First, the *theory of emerging adulthood*, formulated by Jeffrey Arnett (2000), claims that young adults aged 18–24 differ substantially from adolescents based on their living situations, societal roles, and the amount of responsibility expected of them. This is an expansion of developmental theories made popular by Erik Erikson and others. It proposes an entirely new stage that exists between adolescence and young adulthood. Emerging adulthood emphasizes identity exploration. The goal of emerging adulthood is the mastery of two qualities—independent decision-making ability and acceptance of greater responsibility (Arnett, 2000). Within this intensified period of identity exploration the focus is on three primary social experiences: love, worldviews, and employment. Taking this theory a step further, Megan considered that identity exploration in an emerging adult's life would be taking place in both offline and online spaces.

Select the Right Research Question for the Study

To determine whether the right research question is being asked, consider the results of the literature review:

- A literature review that fails to produce any reference to the problem area or very little information would indicate that exploratory research questions are the most appropriate avenue of inquiry. The purpose of exploratory research is to generate an initial understanding of the problem area and to identify relevant concepts.
- If the literature describes important concepts and variations of the problem but contains little information about the extent or costs of the problem or the people affected by it, descriptive research questions are warranted.

■ If exploratory and descriptive information is available, the most appropriate category of inquiry may be explanatory. Explanatory questions could involve replicating existing studies, clarifying controversies, evaluating intervention strategies, and advancing relevant theories.

After you have determined the most appropriate avenue of inquiry—exploratory, descriptive, or explanatory—you should review the list of potential research questions one by one to establish their relevance to social work. For each question ask the following:

■ Will the answer to this question inform social work practice?
■ Will the answer to this question influence social policy?
■ Will the answer to this question lead to a better understanding of the populations affected by the problem?

You should continue this process until you have identified the most useful general research question. As social workers we are far too busy—and our resources are far too limited—to pursue answers to research questions that are not going to make a valuable contribution.

Formulating a Researchable, Specific Research Question

General research questions need to be specified before they can be answered. The question needs to be put into a format that makes it researchable. The challenge is to make the question specific enough so that it can be answered but not so narrow that it loses its relevance. The following section describes the many tasks involved in this process.

Exhibit 3.5 is a checklist for evaluating a specific research question. The items in the checklist are elaborated on in the sections that follow. Use the checklist as a final evaluation after the specific question has been formulated.

Identify and Define Concepts

The first task in specifying the general research question is to identify the major concepts contained in the question. A **concept** is an abstract or a general idea, a symbol for some observable attribute or phenomenon. For example, if our general research question is: What is the recidivism rate of juvenile girls?, three concepts are readily identified: recidivism, juvenile, and girl. Some concepts leave less room for interpretation than others. For instance, the concept girl is the least ambiguous of the three concepts and may require no formal definition.

EXHIBIT 3.5

Checklist for Evaluating a Researchable, Specific Research Question

■ The major concepts contained in the research question have been defined in a way that will ensure a common understanding.
■ Choices made in the operationalization of major concepts have been well justified.
■ Answering the research question is feasible.
■ The research question clearly specifies a unit of analysis.
■ The research question specifies a time frame.
■ The research question is grounded in a specific geographic area.

The concepts of recidivism—whether delinquency is repeated— and juvenile, however, are subject to various interpretations.

Defining the major concepts contained in the research question is necessary so that (a) the social work researcher is clear about what she or he plans to study and (b) the study participants and eventual consumers of the research will define the concepts the same way the researcher does.

Concepts are usually defined with both a nominal definition and an operational definition. A **nominal definition** is one that describes a concept in ways similar to a dictionary definition. An **operational definition** defines concepts in ways that can be measured. To **operationalize** a concept means to define it in a measurable way. Operationalizing a concept provides conceptual clarity and removes all ambiguity about the meaning of the concept. Social workers can draw on prior research to help them identify the options for operationalizing a concept.

Using juvenile as an example, a nominal definition might be "a young person not fully grown or developed." This definition, however, makes it hard to know exactly who should be considered a juvenile. For instance, should we consider someone who is two years old a juvenile? What about a "late bloomer" who is 21 and has not yet reached full physical maturity? In order to avoid this ambiguity, we use operational definitions to specify exactly what should be included.

At times, operationalizing a concept is easy because an official definition already exists. Juvenile status, for example, will likely be determined by the state where the research is being conducted. The Arizona justice system, for instance, considers children as young as eight years to be juveniles. Thus, one possible operational definition of juvenile is "any child between the ages of eight and 17 years of age."

Many times, more than one official definition for a particular concept exists. In these cases, the researcher must select the most appropriate one. For example, recidivism is often operationalized according to a legal definition. In a study involving risk prediction, recidivism was defined as "any delinquent complaint, regardless of the final disposition, occurring within 365 days of the initial referral." Although using this definition of recidivism included more juveniles than were eventually judged to be delinquent, the definition represented the legal status that the Supreme Court was interested in predicting (Krysik & LeCroy, 2002). In contrast, other researchers have used a different definition of recidivism that includes re-arrest, adjudication, and incarceration.

More important than the operational definition we choose is the reasoning behind the choices we make. We must specify and provide reasons for the operational definitions we use. When it comes to social work research, our mantra is "justify, justify, justify!" The Case-in-Point below highlights the importance of specifying the definition of concepts.

CASE-IN-POINT: POVERTY: OUTDATED DEFINITION OF POVERTY LEADS TO MORE SPECIFIC ALTERNATIVES FOR RESEARCH

At times an official definition does such a poor job of representing a concept that we intentionally avoid using it. This can be true no matter how popular or embedded its use may be. As an example, consider the official definition of poverty used in the United States. This definition dates back to the 1960s when Mollie Orshansky, a worker in the Social Security Administration, developed what became known as the poverty threshold (Short, 2011). Orshansky created this measure by multiplying the cost of a minimum food basket by three, based on the assumption that the average family at that time spent one third of its income on food. Poverty thresholds are recalculated annually and vary according to the number of adults and children in a family and for some family types. Thus, the official definition of poverty is an economic measure based on a family's annual before-tax cash income and the cost of food. The poverty thresholds are used to determine eligibility for a host of federal, state, and local government programs as well as private-sector programs, including assistance with utility bills.

Since its development, the poverty threshold has been adjusted only for inflation. It has never been updated to account for changes in the consumption patterns of U.S. households. For example, expenditures for food accounted for about one-third of family income in the 1950s, but they now account for as little as one-seventh. Therefore, the current threshold might be unrealistically low and might not include many families whose incomes are too low for them to meet their expenses. Additionally, the official threshold ignores many costs associated with maintaining a job, such as child care and travel costs, as well as unavailable income such as child support payments that the wage earner must send to other households. It also disregards regional variations in the cost of living, especially the cost of housing, and it ignores differences in health insurance coverage and medical needs. From a different perspective, the official poverty measure has been criticized for excluding in-kind benefits such as food stamps and housing assistance when counting family income.

Due to the deficiencies in the official definition of poverty, some researchers have decided to use alternative standards. Recently, the Census Bureau has published a Supplemental Poverty Measure that will be released along with the official measure each year (Short, 2011). The supplemental measure takes into account the cost of food, clothing, shelter, and utilities; it adjusts for geographic differences in housing costs, and adjusts for the value of in-kind benefits as well as medical costs (Short, 2011).

Analyze the Feasibility of How the Concept is Defined

Many times the operationalization of a concept will be determined largely by what is feasible. The concept of recidivism, for instance, can be operationalized behaviorally as well as by legal status. To measure recidivism behaviorally, offenders self-report their criminal involvement.

Proponents of a behavioral definition argue that self-reports capture more variability in behaviors and yield higher occurrence rates than official crime records do (Herrenkohl et al., 2003). In contrast, official records are at least in part a measure of how vigilant officials are in catching offenders. They do not include people who committed subsequent offenses but were not caught. Despite these arguments, researchers commonly use legal definitions of recidivism because the data that are consistent with these definitions are readily available. Feasibility, then, is a primary consideration when we make choices about how to operationalize the major concepts contained in our research question.

Define the Unit of Analysis

The **unit of analysis** refers to the system level that will be studied. It is common for the unit of analysis in social work research to be people, including individuals, couples, and families. Sometimes the unit of analysis is made up of an aggregation of people like a household, tribe, community, city, county, state, school, school district, hospital, organization, or agency. In other cases, the units of analysis are **social artifacts**, the products of social beings and their behavior. Examples of social artifacts are suicide notes, stories and poems, drawings, newspapers, and agency case files. For instance, it is possible to study childhood trauma by examining children's drawings as the unit of analysis. Whatever the level, however, the unit of analysis should be explicitly stated in the research question.

One reason that researchers must clearly identify the unit of analysis is to avoid committing an **ecological fallacy**. This occurs when a researcher makes a statement related to one unit of analysis on the basis of data collected from a different unit of analysis. For example, we might find that cities with high percentages of Hispanics have higher rates of violent crime than cities with low percentages of Hispanics. In this case, the unit of analysis is cities, and we can draw conclusions about cities. On the basis of this information, we might be tempted to conclude that Hispanics commit violent crimes at higher rates than other ethnic and racial groups. This would be an ecological fallacy, because we did not make this statement on the basis of knowing the ethnic or racial characteristics of the individuals who committed the violent crimes. It is possible that in cities with large Hispanic populations, other racial or ethnic groups are committing the majority of the crimes. We cannot identify the actual characteristics of criminals by examining general data such as the crime rate per capita in relation to population demographics.

Anchor the Question in Time and Place

After you identify and define the concepts contained in the research question and decide upon a unit of analysis, you need to anchor the question in time and place. When the research question implies one observation at one point in time, the research is referred to as a **cross-sectional study**. For instance, a study of the impact of marital status on the poverty rates of elderly women in March of last year would be a cross-sectional study.

Cross-sectional studies exist in contrast to **longitudinal studies**, which examine some phenomenon at multiple points in time. There are three different types of longitudinal studies:

1. **Panel studies**: studies that follow the same individuals over time. A panel study of the economic well-being of elderly women would follow the same group of women as they age.
2. **Cohort studies**: studies that follow a group of individuals over time but are not concerned that they be the same individuals from one time to the next. A cohort study of the economic well-being of elderly women would make multiple observations but over time would observe different groups of women born during this period. One advantage of using cohort studies is that the researcher doesn't have to deal with the problem of participants leaving the study through the years since each group involves a different sample of people. The disadvantage is that the researcher cannot be certain that each cohort is actually similar.
3. **Trend studies**: studies that compare individuals with the same defining characteristics at different points in time. For example, it might compare the income composition of elderly women in the 2000s with that of elderly women in the 2010s.

At first glance, some research questions that are cross-sectional may appear to be longitudinal. Consider the question "What factors are predictive of recidivism within 12 months of the first juvenile offense?" The term "12 months" may lead to the erroneous conclusion that the study is longitudinal. The key to deciding whether a study is cross-sectional or longitudinal is to determine how many observations are involved. In this instance, one observation is required, occurring 12 months after the first offense. The research question, therefore, is cross-sectional.

The final consideration in specifying the research question is to anchor it in a geographic area. Is the research concerned with juvenile offenders in a particular county, with children in a particular school or school district, or with families living within the geographic boundaries of a particular community?

Many of the choices that we make in anchoring the question in time and place will be influenced by feasibility. Specifically, we must consider the time and expense involved in relation to the resources available for conducting the study. For example, we might want to conduct a national study of recidivism among juvenile offenders, but due to limited resources, we can study only a single state.

The Case-in-Point below provides a critique of the first two steps of the research process based on a research article titled "Physical activity for young children: A quantitative study of child care providers' knowledge, attitudes, and health promotion practices" (Lanigan, 2014). The article explores results from a pilot project designed to increase children's physical activity. Reading the critique should increase your familiarity with the steps in the research process discussed in this chapter.

CASE-IN-POINT: EXPLORATORY RESEARCH: PHYSICAL ACTIVITY AND YOUNG CHILDREN

The author—Lanigan (2014)—citing statistics related to the prevalence of young children in child care settings, raises the potential of child care staff to promote physical activity among young children as a strategy to reduce child obesity and support healthy development. This study is an examination of a pilot project aimed to improve child care staff attitudes with regard to their role in supporting increased physical activity practices. The general research question was "How do child care providers' role perceptions on children's physical activity relate to physical activity practices in child care settings?" Two hypotheses were postulated: (a) providers who view physical activity as part of their role are more likely to encourage children to be physically active, and (b) decreases in providers' perceptions of barriers to support physical activity will be associated with improved practices. Because child obesity is a serious and costly problem to individuals and society, the relevance of this question was easily established. The pilot program was guided by two theories: the Health Belief Model and the Transtheoretical Model. The theory guided the identification of concepts to measure in the research. For example, questions revolved around the concepts of perceived salience of the provider role, perceived leadership, and perceived barriers to physical activity. This study was guided by theory, had measures at two points in time (before and after the program), specified hypotheses, and identified concepts to be measured. What then makes it exploratory rather than explanatory? The study was considered exploratory because it was the first study to examine the relationship between providers' perceptions of their role in supporting physical activity and actual child care practices, and it studied a small sample drawn from one geographic area that did not represent the broader child care provider community. The researcher was not concerned with generalizing beyond the sample studied (description) or to demonstrating that the program was the reason for the change in physical activity (explanation). The results did suggest, however, positive program outcomes and feasibility of the measurement plan, which provides encouragement to move beyond exploration to description and explanation. An unexpected finding was that perceived barriers actually increased rather than decreased over the course of the intervention, which implies the need to better identify and address barriers over the course of the program and adjust the second hypothesis.

Developing Research Hypotheses

In addition to specifying the research questions, a researcher may also specify one or more **hypotheses**—tentative answers to a research question. Hypotheses are written as statements, not questions. For example, in a study of juvenile recidivism, a researcher may ask, "What factors influence whether a juvenile becomes an offender?" A related hypothesis is "The higher a juvenile's self-esteem, the less likely he or she will become an offender."

How do you decide whether your research study warrants a hypothesis? In general, when the theory pertaining to a problem area or prior research suggests with confidence what the answer to a research question should be, that is an indication that a hypothesis is appropriate. In contrast, where the state of knowledge on a problem area is not well developed and there is more speculation than research findings, a hypothesis is not justified. This is why a hypothesis sometimes is referred to as an "educated guess." For this reason, it would be uncommon to specify a hypothesis if the research question were exploratory or descriptive. Hypotheses are more likely to be developed in conjunction with explanatory research questions.

Exhibit 3.6 is a checklist for evaluating research hypotheses. Use the checklist as a final evaluation when a hypothesis is being specified.

> ## EXHIBIT 3.6
>
> ### Checklist for Evaluating a Research Hypothesis
>
> ■ The hypothesis can be tested through research and is capable of being refuted.
> ■ The hypothesis is in the form of a tentative answer to the research question and is not phrased as questions.
> ■ The hypothesis is specifically stated.
> ■ The hypothesis is in the form of a tentative answer to the research question and is not phrased as a question.
> ■ Statement of a directional hypothesis is justified on the basis of existing theory or research.

Variables and Constants

In order to discuss how to develop hypotheses, we must first understand two research terms:

■ **Variable:** a concept that can vary. For instance, the concept of recidivism is a variable because offenders can either commit another offense or not. The concept of sexual orientation can also be considered a variable, as individuals can identify themselves as heterosexual, gay, lesbian, bisexual, pansexual, and asexual.

■ **Constant:** a concept that does not vary. For instance, in a research study that is concerned only with females, gender would be a constant rather than a variable.

The research question should make clear which concepts are being considered as variables and which ones are being considered as constants.

All research is concerned with studying how concepts vary; that is, all research is concerned with studying variables. A hypothesis, then, is essentially a statement about the relationship between two or more variables. For example, a hypothesis related to juvenile offenders might be "The younger the girls are at the time of their first offense, the more likely they are to commit a subsequent delinquent offense." Note that this hypothesis is written as a statement, not a question. The variables implied in this hypothesis are age and recidivism. Gender, in this instance, is a constant, as only females are being considered.

Types of Hypotheses

There are important distinctions in the way hypotheses are stated. Two types of hypotheses indicate the existence of a relationship between variables.

■ **Null hypothesis:** a hypothesis that asserts that no relationship exists between two or more variables. The null hypothesis for the previous example would be "There is no relationship between age at first offense and recidivism for female delinquents." The null hypothesis suggests that any apparent relationship between two or more variables is simply due to chance and does not exist in a true sense.

■ **Research hypothesis**, or **alternative hypothesis**: the opposite of the null hypothesis. It proposes that a relationship exists between two or more variables.

The null hypothesis is the hypothesis that is tested in the subsequent analysis of the data. If the analysis fails to support the null hypothesis, in research terms we claim that the null hypothesis is refuted and support is provided for the research hypothesis.

Research hypotheses may also be specified in terms of the type of relationship that exists between variables:

■ **Directional (one-tailed) hypothesis:** specifies the nature of the relationship, either positive or negative. Our previous example hypothesized that age is negatively related to recidivism. That is, girls who are younger at the time of first offense are more likely to commit a subsequent offense than girls who are older at the time of first offense. Thus, as age decreases, recidivism increases.

■ **Nondirectional (two-tailed) hypothesis:** does not specify the proposed direction of a relationship. For example, "There is a relationship between age at first offense and recidivism." In this case, the researcher does not predict whether younger or older girls are more likely to experience recidivism.

A directional hypothesis should be specified if prior research or theory reasonably suggests a direction.

The more specifically a hypothesis is written, the more easily it can be tested and—when it is not valid—refuted. We explore hypotheses testing in Chapter 12.

The Case-in-Point below illustrates the first two steps of the research process by examining a research article titled "Current methods and attitudes of women toward contraception in Europe and America" (Johnson, Pion, & Jennings, 2013).

The purpose of providing this critique is to demonstrate the use of the evaluative criteria and research terminology introduced throughout this chapter with a research study that is descriptive in its purpose.

CASE-IN-POINT: DESCRIPTIVE RESEARCH: WOMEN AND CONTRACEPTION

The authors—Johnson, Pion, and Jennings (2013)—introduce their study by claiming that although the choice of contraceptive methods has expanded in recent years, women in the U.S. and Europe tend to rely primarily on the contraceptive pill, which was introduced in the 1960s. Further, they report that unplanned pregnancies have decreased among teens, however, remain high among adults. Limited information on women's awareness of alternative contraceptive methods, or their reasoning for selecting or changing methods, exists and thus provided a rationale for the study. If known, this information might help shape efforts to present women with additional birth control options with the desired result of fewer unintended pregnancies.

The general research question was "How do women's use and awareness of different forms of contraception compare across Europe and America?" The authors did not provide a rationale for the cross-national comparison design. The research question was, however, logically linked to the authors' conceptualization of the problem. The unit of analysis was individual women and the time period was at the time of the study. The geographic location spanned five countries: the United Kingdom, Germany, Italy, Spain, and the U.S.A.

The availability of the Internet enhanced the answerability of the research question. Only in Italy, data were collected through interviews due to the lack of Internet access. The criteria for study participation was based on gender (gender, i.e., female was treated as a constant rather than a variable in the study). Women were operationalized as those 25–45 years of age, who were not known to be infertile. The research question did not apply to all women, and therefore increased specificity in the question was important to how meaningful the findings would be. With regard to awareness, women were asked "When thinking about methods of birth control, what ONE method comes first to your mind?" And "What are ALL the other methods of birth control you have ever heard of?" These questions provided a measure of unprompted awareness. Women were also asked to respond to a list of contraceptive methods (i.e., prompted awareness) "From the list of birth control methods, please select the ones you have EVER HEARD OF or READ about." The lists were translated into the appropriate language of the women and only those birth control methods that were available were included on each country's list.

The purpose of the study was to describe behavior and awareness on a broad scale. This research article can be classified as descriptive in purpose as the intent was to describe. The information produced from the study can be used to inform efforts on family planning, a topic that is relevant to social work practice and policy.

Formulating Culturally Proficient Research Questions and Hypotheses

The seven guidelines presented below will assist you in achieving cultural proficiency in formulating the research question and hypotheses. These guidelines are not intended as a definitive list, but they are fundamental to becoming culturally proficient.

1. **Explore culturally specific meanings.** Always remember that concepts do not necessarily have equivalent meaning across all cultures. The concept of wealth, for instance, has a variety of meanings across culturally diverse populations. To one culture, wealth may mean money; to another culture, the presence of children; and to yet another, spirituality. For this reason, the researcher should always explore culturally specific meanings of concepts with the relevant group.

2. **Determine valued measures of success.** Measures of success and what is valued also differ across cultures. The concept of independence, for instance, is generally valued as a healthy developmental task for adolescents in North American families. To a traditional Hindi family, however, adolescent independence is not only irrelevant but also undesirable. What a social worker with a Western perspective might describe as an enmeshed and undifferentiated parent-child relationship may be considered healthy in the context of another culture.

3. **Anticipate potential consequences.** Consider how the collected data might be misused, and anticipate any harm, physical or psychological, that such misuse could inflict on the research participants or members of their cultural group. Research that relates race to intelligence is one of the most blatant examples of cultural destructiveness. As a general rule, the researcher should anticipate both the positive and negative potential consequences of conducting the research.

4. **Prevent exploitation.** The study regarding the Havasupai Indian tribe of Arizona cited in Chapter 2 is an example of research that was perceived as exploitative by the participants. Groups that already feel marginalized or stigmatized are at increased risk of feeling that they are being exploited through research. To avoid generating these feelings, as researchers we must show members of marginalized cultural groups how the benefits of the research will outweigh any efforts or sacrifices on their part. In addition, we should always define exploitation based on the participants' perspective, not ours.

5. **Consider issues of privacy.** All research is intrusive to some degree. As with exploitation, we should evaluate whether the research is overly intrusive from the perspective of the research participants and not our own. Using the same example, the question of whether the Havasupai originated from Asia was in direct opposition to the Havasupai's cultural beliefs of creation. Research should only be done and reported with the permission of the participants.

6. **Seek and use feedback.** Research participants should be directly involved throughout all phases of the research process. Ensuring that research

participants have input at the question/hypothesis formulation stage will help avoid feelings of surprise or exploitation on their part when the findings are reported. The review process should be continued until consensus on the research questions and hypotheses is reached.

7. **Use precise and sensitive language.** Culturally proficient researchers avoid using generic variable labels to indicate specific subgroups. For instance, a research question that refers to parents but studies only women, or a research study that refers to Hispanics but studies only Hispanics of Mexican origin, is neither precise nor sensitive with regard to language. Sometimes the myriad labels associated with cultural groups can be confusing. For instance, is the appropriate term Hispanic, Latino/Latina, or Chicano/Chicana? When in doubt, consult the research participants for their preference.

The Case-in-Point below illustrates the first two steps of the research process by examining a research article titled "Multidimensional treatment foster care (MTFC): Results from an independent replication" (Kyhle Westermark, Hansson, and Olsson, 2011). The purpose of providing this critique is to demonstrate the use of the evaluative criteria and research terminology introduced throughout this chapter with a research study that is explanatory.

CASE-IN-POINT: EXPLANATORY RESEARCH: MULTIDIMENSIONAL TREATMENT FOSTER CARE

In the article titled "Multidimensional treatment foster care (MTFC): Results from an independent replication," researchers from Sweden—Kyhle Westermark, Hansson, and Olsson (2011)—examined the outcomes of an experiment that compared 35 male and female adolescents with antisocial behavior. The youths were randomly assigned to receive MTFC or treatment as usual (TAU). The MTFC program is based on social learning and family systems theories. The rationale for targeting this group of adolescents was that they represented a sizable portion of youths and were the most difficult and expensive to treat. The Swedish researchers adopted the MTFC program based on a number published research studies conducted in the United States that provided support for the program. The Swedish study was the first experiment not conducted by the developers of the program, thus it was an independent examination. Neither the research question nor hypothesis was explicitly stated. The study followed the youths for 24 months and collected data at the beginning of the project, six, 12 and 24 months follow-up. The researchers found no significant differences in the adolescents' characteristics or behaviors prior to the experiment. Although both groups had reduced symptoms following treatment, MTFC produced a consistent and statistically significant reduction in problematic behaviors from entry to 24 months. The results of the experiment indicated positive treatment effects favoring MTFC over TAU. This study was explanatory because it attempted to explain or establish causality that the

program was the reason for the difference between groups. By setting up an experiment with participants assigned to each group at random, the authors created research conditions that could answer
the implicit research question and test the hypothesis, i.e., "MTFC produces better outcomes than TAU
in treating youth with antisocial behavior."

Finding Research Questions and Hypotheses in Published Research

One way to learn a new skill is to practice it. Practice in social work research is
not limited to conducting original research. In fact, practice should begin with
a critical review of the published research. Many social work journals publish
research-based articles. In addition, social workers publish research articles in
the journals of related disciplines.

When searching for research articles to critique, be aware that just because
an article is published in a journal does not mean that it is based on research.
Some journal articles are conceptual in nature; others describe a practice
approach or a specific practice skill; still others examine a statistical technique
and its application; yet others provide a summary of the research studies in one
problem area.

One way to identify a research-based article is to read the abstract, located
at the beginning of the article. The **abstract** is a brief statement of approximately
100 words that summarizes the objectives, methods, results, and conclusions of
the article. If the abstract mentions a research question or hypothesis, research
participants, a method of collecting or analyzing data, or findings, you can be
certain that the article is research based.

As you review research-based articles, you will quickly observe that the
authors follow a similar format.

1. The introductory or first section of the article consists of a discussion of
   the problem area addressed by the research study, including information
   on its relevance to social work.
2. A critical analysis of existing knowledge based on a review of existing
   research and theory. This analysis also considers which issues are con-
   tested and what is yet to be discerned.
3. The justification for the research study is customarily framed within the
   context of prior published work.
4. The research question is not always explicitly stated, but it may be implied
   or labeled as objectives of the research.
5. Hypotheses, if warranted, customarily follow the statement of the research
   question or study objectives.

These elements typically lead up to a discussion of the research methods, the findings, and a conclusion. You will learn more about these in the remaining chapters.

CONCLUSION

Good social work research, like good social work practice, has to be built on a strong foundation that begins with identification of the problem area. The information found in the initial exploration of the problem area will help social workers decide whether further research is warranted. To demonstrate the worth of a problem area for research, the social worker must be able to convincingly answer the question: Why is this important? It is likely that a social worker will be interested in more than one compelling problem area. In such cases, she or he must select one area based on some combination of personal interest and expressed agency or organizational need for the research.

As with social work practice, in research, the use and meaning of words is important. Asking the right question(s) and providing clear and measurable definitions of terms are essential to obtaining useful information. Careful consideration of cultural factors should be included when conceptualizing the research and defining variables. Specifying the research question makes the study of a problem area feasible and facilitates the research of others who wish to replicate or expand the study. Once the research problem has been identified, a research question has been specified, and maybe a hypothesis has been presented, it is time to move on to answering the research question.

The remaining steps in the research process must be logically consistent with the conceptualization of the research problem and the specification of the research question and hypotheses. The research design—the blueprint for how the research will be conducted—must allow us to answer our research question with confidence. How to choose an appropriate research design is the subject of Chapters 4, 6 and 7.

MAIN POINTS

- A working knowledge of the research process empowers social workers to be better practitioners, evaluators, administrators, advocates, and policy makers.
- Social work research and practice are complementary activities, such that through practice the social worker identifies problem areas that require research, and through research the social worker provides knowledge for practice.

■ Social workers are expected to base their practice on knowledge, and yet not all sources of existing information are equally valid. The research process can be used as a framework for critically evaluating existing information.

■ Culturally proficient research practices are necessary to dispel destructive myths and stereotypes and to avoid exploiting and harming those whom social workers aim to help through research. Cultural sensitivity should be considered at each step of the research process.

■ To demonstrate the worth of a problem area for research, the social worker must be able to credibly answer the question: Why is this important?

■ The research process begins with a broad conceptualization of the problem and narrows as a general research question is developed, followed by increasing specification as concepts are operationalized and the research is grounded in a time and a geographic area. Increasing specification makes the research problem researchable.

■ Research questions can be categorized into one of three types: exploratory, descriptive, or explanatory. Through a thorough literature review of the problem area, the social work researcher will determine what avenue of inquiry is most appropriate for the problem area.

■ There is no one correct way to do research. The social worker engaged in research must make many choices and must be able to justify those choices within the context of the research study.

EXERCISES

1. Using the Riverton case, how might you go about developing the research problem? Describe the role of theory and research in developing the research problem. Describe how the research process might unfold, beginning with what you might examine in the literature and identifying questions of importance to social work practitioners as well as to community members in Riverton.

2. From the information presented on the Riverton case, develop one research question that fits each level of knowledge: exploratory, descriptive, and explanatory. Describe how the questions differ. What would you attempt to answer with each question?

3. Consider the Sanchez Family case. Propose a culturally proficient research problem, research question, and hypothesis related to the Sanchez family. How would you incorporate dimensions of culture, gender, ethnicity, and power into your formulation of a research project here? How could research help to unravel myths and stereotypes that affect the Sanchez family?

4. Make a list of research problems that would be relevant to your personal life. How could advancing this knowledge contribute to improvements in

your quality of life? Now, make a list of research problems that would be relevant to the Carla Washburn case. What would you want to know in order to determine questions that would be valuable to Mrs. Washburn and the social workers engaged with her?

5. Outline a strategy that you would use for conducting a literature review related to the Brickville case. What factors would you consider in evaluating the credibility of the different sources of information? What might complicate your pursuit of valid data related to the Brickville context?

6. Conduct a search of articles related to the issues presented in Hudson City case. Describe the difference in what is produced from a keyword search on the Internet and a keyword search using a searchable database of peer-reviewed literature from the library. Describe any similarities and differences. When and where might you rely on these various sources of information?

7. If you were conducting research for RAINN, how might you involve practitioners in the design of the research question and study? How would you seek to present and share the research so that it is accessible and actionable for practitioners?

chapter
4

SINGLE SUBJECT RESEARCH

Develop a passion for learning. If you do, you will never cease to grow.
Anthony D'Angelo

Sometimes we are interested in answering research questions that are probabilistic. That is, research tells us which result is most likely to occur for groups of elements such as individuals or families. For example, group-level designs (see Chapter 7) allow us to evaluate whether one intervention, overall, is more effective than another.

When working with an individual, a group, or a family, however, social workers are interested in the results of a single case. This is especially true for social workers involved in clinical practice, and is also true for social workers involved in macro practice. It is not enough to know that "most" people or communities improve with a particular intervention. Rather, we need to know whether a specific situation is actually improving due to *this* intervention. To obtain this knowledge we need to engage in single subject research, the topic of this chapter.

There are two types of research that examine single cases: *single subject research* and *case study research*. People sometimes confuse these two different approaches:

■ **Single subject research (SSR)** focuses on a quantitative approach to documenting changes over time in a limited number of specific elements such as behavior or attitudes. SSR is often used to document the process and outcomes of change efforts in clinical practice or organizations. SSR answers the question, "Did change occur in this instance?" through the consideration of quantitative data.

■ **Case study research** (see chapter 6) is generally used to learn about a new phenomenon, to develop theories, to identify and understand important variables, and to provide specific examples of the phenomenon under study. The case study represents an in-depth, intensive, detailed qualitative study of an individual or particular unit of analysis such as a community. It may include quantitative data, but it focuses on more holistic processes. It answers the question, "What is the whole story here?"

Both types of research are based on scientific methods in that: (1) they are planned, (2) they are clearly delineated, (3) they require the collection and interpretation of data, and (4) they are open to scrutiny and replication. In addition, both methods contribute to evidence-based practice.

By the end of this chapter you should be able to:

■ Describe the difference between single subject research and case study research.
■ Describe the advantages and disadvantages of using SSR.

■ Clearly define and operationalize variables to be used in an SSR design in measurable terms.
■ List and describe the steps in carrying out SSR.
■ Describe and state the purpose of various SSR designs.
■ Use Excel to graph and analyze data collected in SSR.

THE VALUE OF SINGLE SUBJECT RESEARCH

Although research can help you decide which interventions are most likely to produce positive changes for clients, it will not tell you if an intervention will work for a specific client. For example, in trying to reduce alcohol-exposed pregnancies, are mail and online versions of a self-guided change intervention equally effective? Research suggests that they are, but the results are based on data collected from a group of people (Tenkku et al., 2011). As another example, does motivational interviewing have the potential to improve treatment outcomes in male domestic violence group therapy? Research suggests that it would not, although again the research is primarily based on group data (Zalmanowitz et al., 2013).

Group-level research has several limitations when it comes to applying the findings:

■ There may not be conclusive (or any) research evidence on the issue to be addressed.
■ The research evidence may show mixed or even contradictory results in several studies.
■ The research may not be generalizable to your specific client population. Studies with LGBT youth in foster care in an urban area may not generalize to rural LGBT foster youth, for example.
■ Even when studies find consistently effective outcomes, not *all* people in the studies show positive outcomes. Usually, at least some people show no change or may even get worse.

Social work values and our commitment to knowledge-based practice require us to evaluate the specific outcomes of our work with clients or participants. Single subject research (SSR), also known in the literature as *single system design*, *single case experimental design*, *within subject comparison*, and *n of 1 research*, provides us with systematic methods for answering the question: Does my intervention with this client system (individual, family, group, organization, or community) create change that is consistent with our agreed-upon intervention goals?

THE SINGLE SUBJECT RESEARCH MODEL

Single subject research is based on a research model that views social work as a problem-solving experiment. Repeated data collection provides information about the process of change over time. These data are especially useful because they monitor the outcomes of our interventions throughout the period when we are providing services or are engaged in an intervention. In addition, they do not require us to perform sophisticated statistical analysis in order to evaluate success.

SSR follows the logical steps of a scientific experiment.

1. Through assessment, areas for change, known as targets, are identified, and goals are established. The hypothesis is that intervention will change the targets in the desired direction.
2. Goals—the dependent variables in research—are operationalized. That is, they are defined in measurable terms. This process includes identifying the short-term objectives that must be accomplished in order to reach the long-term goals.
3. A specific type of single subject research design is selected.
4. A baseline phase is established in which the dependent variable is measured repeatedly before the intervention is introduced.
5. An intervention—the independent variable in research—is introduced.
6. After the intervention has been introduced, the dependent variable is measured over time on a regular basis. This step is known as the intervention phase.
7. The data are evaluated, usually using a graph, in terms of the desired goal(s).
8. Following the end of the intervention, data are collected in a follow-up phase to be sure that the individual/family/community, etc. maintains the change with or without continued assistance.

Variables for Single Subject Research

In social work research, as in any scientific research, we must clearly define and measure all of the relevant variables. Specifically in SSR, we must define the dependent variable (goals or targets of services) in a way that enables us to measure it. This process involves measuring the duration, frequency, or magnitude of the problem (see Exhibit 4.1).

Whenever possible, you should define your goals in terms of positive rather than negative behaviors. At the very least, your goals should include

EXHIBIT 4.1

Example of Operationalized Variables in Single Subject Research: Crying Behavior

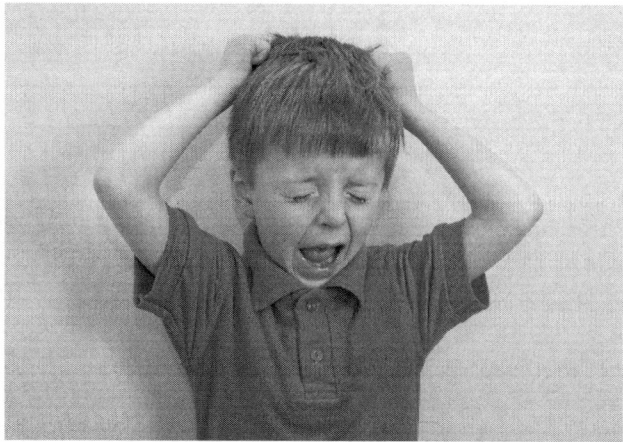

Operationalizing Crying Behavior

- Duration: "the number of minutes crying after being told 'No.'"
- Frequency: "the number of crying outbursts per day."
- Magnitude: "the intensity of the crying behavior."

Source: Thinkstock.com.

developing positive behaviors as substitutes for the negative behaviors that you wish to eliminate. A more positive approach to working with crying would be to define "compliance"—the number of times a child obeys a request the first time it is made—as a goal of the intervention. This definition is based on a measure of frequency.

When you are dealing with more complex behaviors, such as "depression," you can break them down into measurable objectives (subparts related to the goal) such as "number of negative self-statements," "time spent with friends and family," or "score on the Hudson Generalized Contentment Scale."

Whenever possible, you should assess the dependent variable using valid and reliable measures (see Chapter 9). Examples of these measures are behavior counts, self-reports of feelings or experiences, existing records such as attendance records and teachers' homework-completion charts, and standardized scales.

One strategy that can help you measure the dependent variable is triangulation, which involves using several different measures or sources to assess progress. For example, both compliance behavior and tantrums can be measured at home and at preschool, thus providing four indicators of a successful outcome. Fischer & Corcoran (2007) provide many measures useful for SSR.

Baseline Phase

A **baseline** is series of measurements taken before an intervention is introduced. During the baseline phase, researchers establish the pattern of behavior before the intervention. Ideally, during this phase, researchers take measurements until a stable pattern emerges. A minimum of five measurements is useful to establish a baseline. In general, the more baseline measurements that we take, the greater the certainty of the pattern.

As an example, a baseline may measure the number of times a child has a tantrum when told "no." The pattern of the baseline can fall into one of four categories:

- Ascending
- Descending
- Stable
- Unstable

See Exhibit 4.2 for examples of these patterns.

EXHIBIT 4.2

Example of Patterns of Behavior in Baseline Measurements

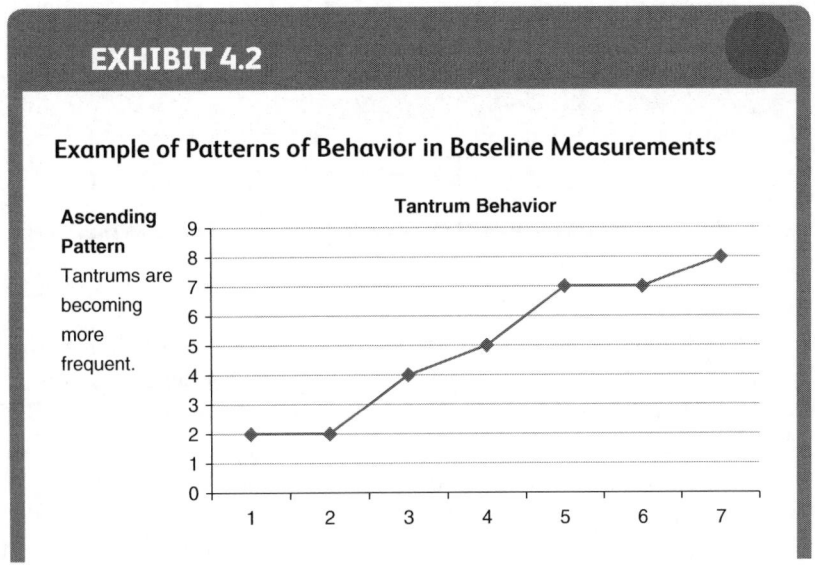

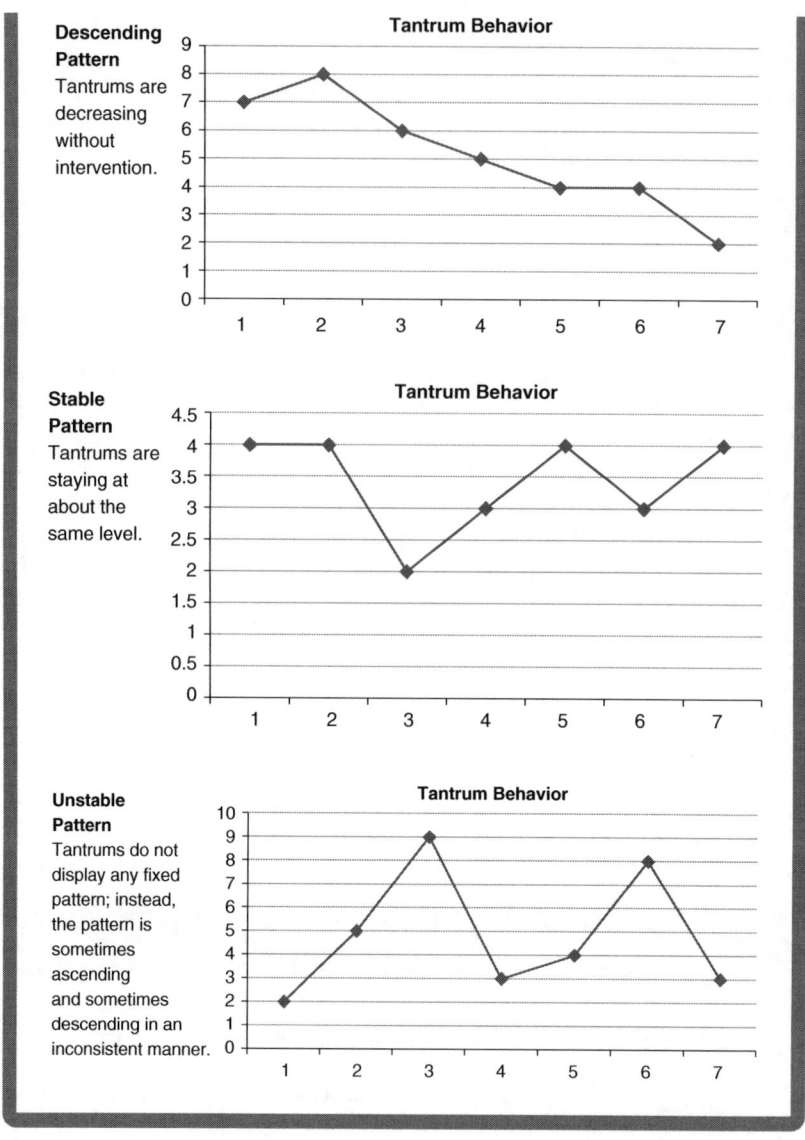

In the baseline phase, if the pattern in the data suggests a trend of dramatic or continuous improvement, intervention may not be warranted. Success in the intervention phase is defined as change relative to the baseline phase.

Social workers frequently establish a baseline during the assessment phase after they have identified the area or areas for change. This process may involve developing instructions to monitor behavior on a regular basis (for example, hourly or daily) or to complete assessment scales that have been validated for a series of measurements such as those included in the Fischer and Corcoran (2007) sourcebooks of measures. Measurement can be performed by the social worker, the receiver of services, a third party such as a teacher or family member, or any combination of these individuals. The decision about who will conduct the measurement is important. It is essential to devise a measurement plan that will not be overly burdensome and that can be carried out reliably.

The most commonly used method, except with children, is self-report. Self-report, however, can be subject to bias and reactivity, terms that you will learn more about in Chapter 9. For example, a youth reporting his or her own disruptive behavior in the classroom may minimize the extent to which this behavior takes place.

One way to minimize bias is through unobtrusive observation; observing a person in ways that he or she will not notice. For example, a teacher or parent aid may keep track of the youth's behavior during the day. Here again, triangulation of data can help to enhance the validity of our measurement.

In some cases, intervention must begin immediately, and there is no time to collect baseline data. In these cases, we can use a **retrospective baseline,** one based on past experience. Examples of retrospective baselines are descriptions of behavior that are based on personal memory, on notes from a diary or journal, or on formal records such as class attendance. As examples, a parent may be asked which days during the past week a child had a tantrum; or a teacher may provide attendance records for the past month. Clearly, we must carefully consider the validity and reliability of retrospective baseline data.

Intervention Phase

In SSR, data that are collected in the baseline phase continue to be collected in the intervention phase. The intervention, or independent variable, should be specified as clearly as possible. The intervention should clearly establish who will do what, when, and under what circumstances.

SSR is not associated with any particular theory, and it can be used with any intervention approach. Specification of the intervention, however, is easier in some instances than in others. For example, it may be easier to specify interventions that use behavior modification than those that use play therapy.

To the greatest extent possible, specification should include the following elements:

- The responsibilities of all parties
- The frequency of any task or activity

■ Expectations of behavior during intervention sessions as well as in the natural environment

■ Rules concerning how data are to be collected.

Follow-Up Phase

Interventions should also, whenever possible, include a follow-up phase. In the follow-up phase the client demonstrates that he or she can maintain the changes made without assistance from the social worker.

Exhibit 4.3 illustrates and summarizes the basic steps in single subject research. Note that the collection and evaluation of data is a key component in all phases.

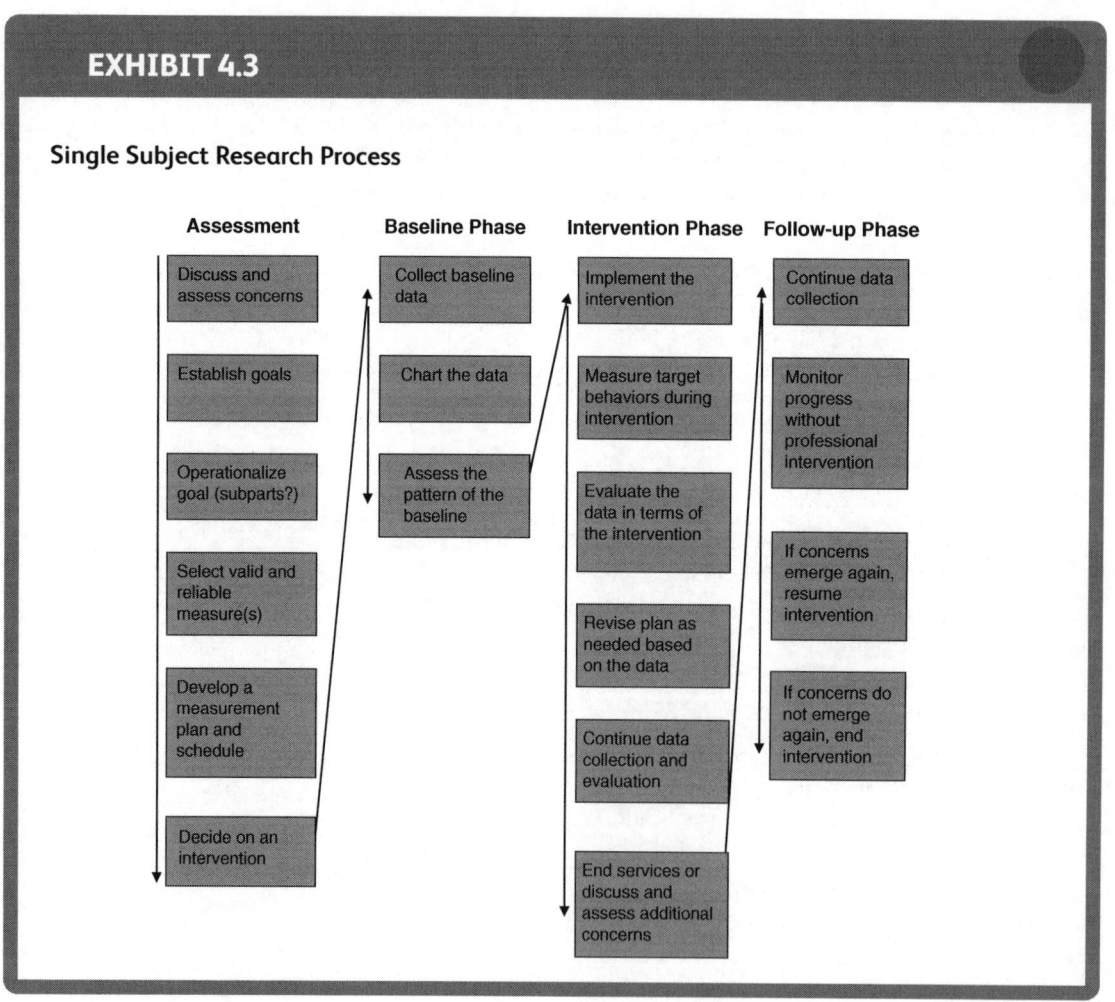

EXHIBIT 4.3

Single Subject Research Process

SINGLE SUBJECT RESEARCH DESIGNS

A variety of SSR designs have been used to evaluate practice in social work and other helping professions (Bloom, Fischer, & Orme, 2009). We will discuss the following designs in this section starting with the simplest and ending with the more complex: AB design, multiple baseline design, multiple component design, reversal design, and changing criterion design.

AB Design

An **AB design** measures the dependent variable during the baseline and intervention phases. By convention, the letter *A* is used to designate the baseline phase, *B* is used for the intervention phase. When these data are presented in a graph, a vertical line separates the baseline phase from the intervention phase.

An AB design measures the dependent variable during the baseline and intervention phases. Exhibit 4.4 shows a typical AB graph in which the dependent variable "tantrum behavior" is defined as the number of minutes the child

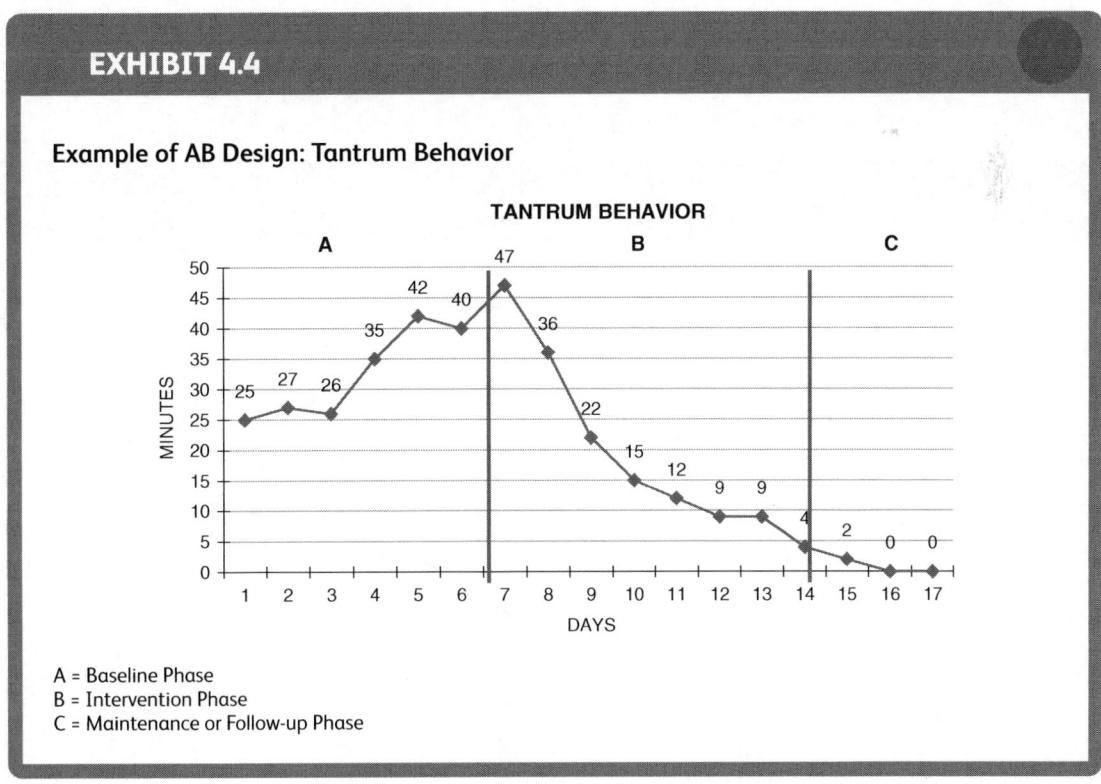

EXHIBIT 4.4

Example of AB Design: Tantrum Behavior

A = Baseline Phase
B = Intervention Phase
C = Maintenance or Follow-up Phase

spends pouting, begging, crying, or screaming after being told that it is bedtime. The line separating the baseline and intervention phases falls between Day #6 and Day #7. Note that the A phase or baseline is ascending, indicating that the behavior is getting worse. In contrast, the behavior appears to be improving, or descending, during the B or the intervention phase. These results suggest—but do not prove—that the intervention is succeeding since other factors may be responsible for the improvement.

In Exhibit 4.4, the letter *C* designates the maintenance or follow-up phase. This phase is introduced after Day 14. The data suggest that the client in this example is able to continue the progress independently of the intervention.

Multiple Baseline Design

A **multiple baseline design** is useful in illustrating whether the intervention does, in fact, account for the changes in the target behavior. Although the AB design shows whether change occurs with the introduction of the intervention, the change may be the result of other factors—such as, in the tantrum example, maturation, timing of the introduction of the treatment, or extraneous factors such as a change in baby sitters.

Exhibit 4.5 illustrates a multiple baseline design to track changes in compliance behavior with four different children using three different baseline

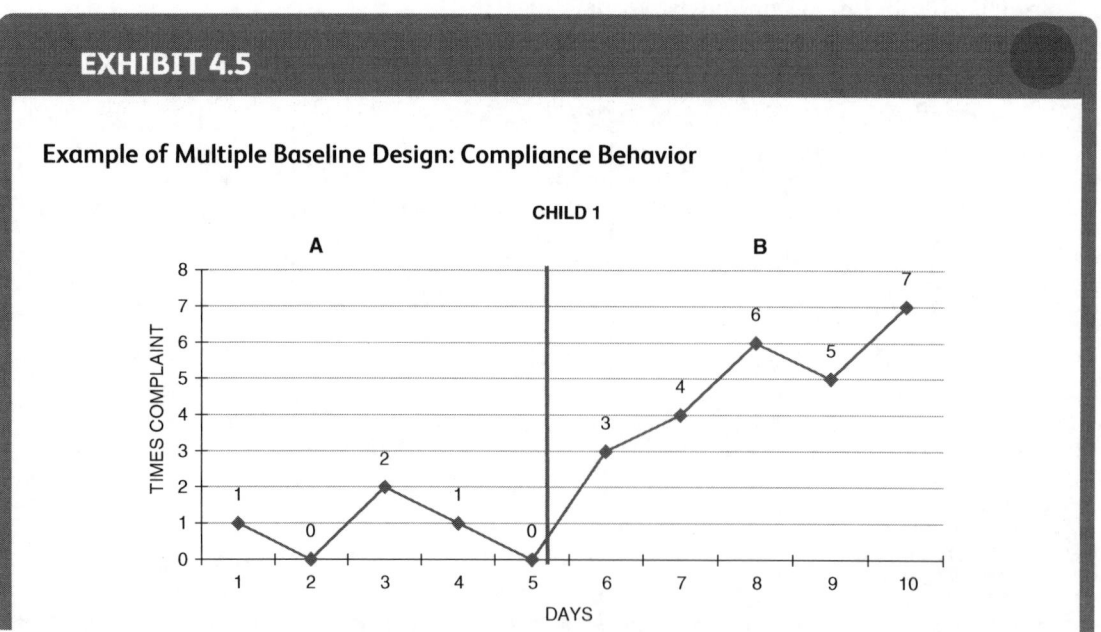

EXHIBIT 4.5

Example of Multiple Baseline Design: Compliance Behavior

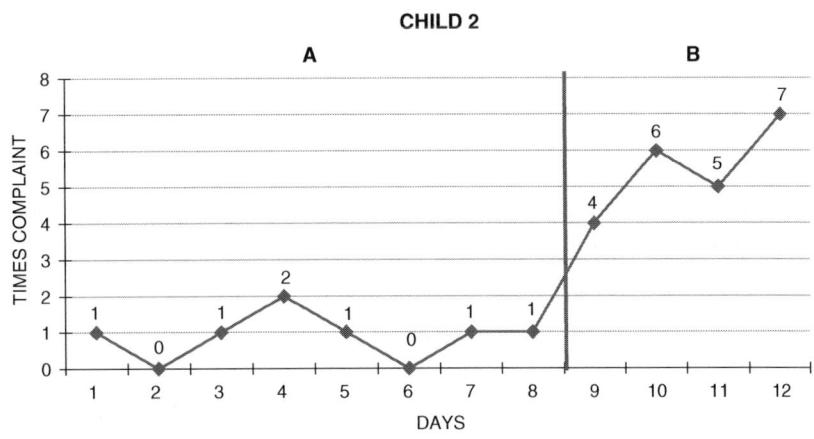

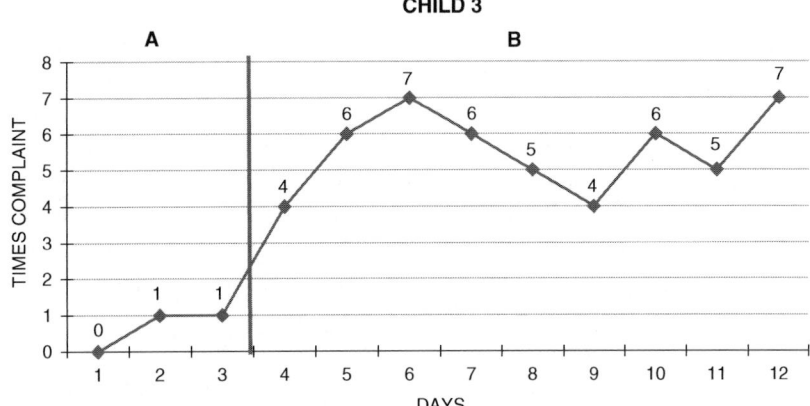

Multiple Baseline Suggestion Intervention Does Not Cause Change

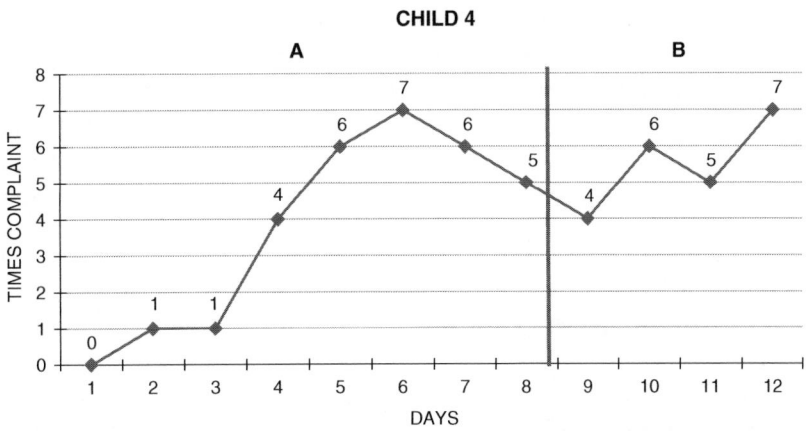

periods. In the first graph, the plotlines in the chart indicate that the intervention, which uses tokens to reward compliance, may be responsible for changes in behavior. The changes all occur following the intervention, even when the length of the intervention phase varies.

In the fourth graph in Exhibit 4.5, however, a different result is suggested. The data suggest that the passage of time rather than the intervention itself was actually responsible for the change of behavior since improvement was shown prior to initiation of the intervention.

Multiple Component Design

A **multiple component design,** sometimes known as the **ABC design,** involves the use of sequential interventions or changes in the amount or intensity of the same intervention. For example, in the case of an anxious six-year-old girl who was constantly biting her fingernails to the point of drawing blood, her parents recorded the number of times each week that they found her biting her fingernails. Meanwhile, the girl's social worker used play therapy for four weeks. Unfortunately, this intervention produced only limited results. The social worker and the parents then agreed to try a behavioral approach in which they made no comments when the nail biting occurred, but the girl was rewarded for each hour she went without biting her fingernails. Exhibit 4.6 graphs the results of both interventions. Clearly the girl's nail-biting behavior declined far more dramatically after the behavior therapy was introduced.

It should be noted, however, that a multiple component design does not specify which components were effective. In other words, we can conclude from Exhibit 4.6 only that play therapy followed by a behavioral approach was effective. We *cannot* determine whether continuing the play therapy or using the behavioral approach alone would have been as effective.

The different phases of a multiple component design can be defined in a key or legend. An alternative strategy in this case would have been to change the intensity rather than the mode of treatment. For example, the social worker could have increased the play therapy to three times per week. In that case, the *B* phase in Exhibit 4.6 would be weekly play therapy, and the *C* phase would be play therapy 3 times per week.

Reversal Design

Researchers use a **reversal design** to provide greater assurance that the intervention is responsible for the observed changes in behavior. In this method, as with the AB design, a baseline phase is followed by the intervention. In a reversal

EXHIBIT 4.6

Example of ABC Design: Nail Biting

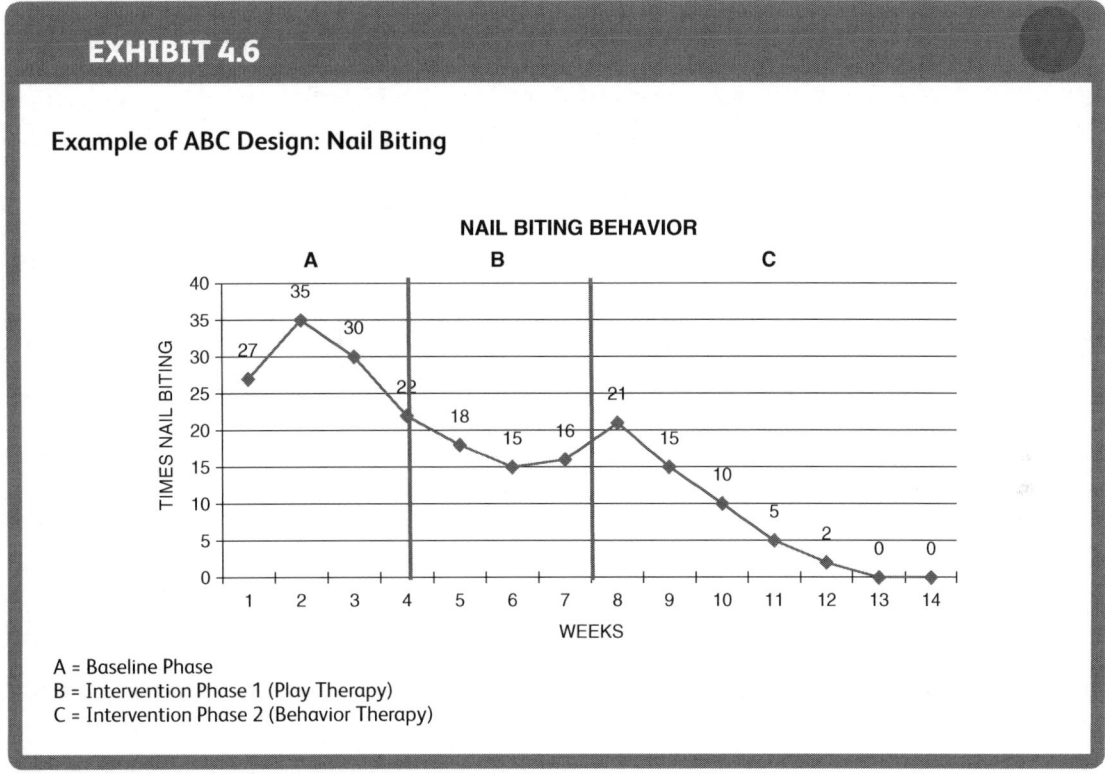

NAIL BITING BEHAVIOR

A = Baseline Phase
B = Intervention Phase 1 (Play Therapy)
C = Intervention Phase 2 (Behavior Therapy)

design, however, the intervention phase is then followed by a third phase in which the intervention is withdrawn. Next comes a fourth phase in which the intervention is reintroduced. This type of single subject research (ABAB) is common in drug studies.

Exhibit 4.7 illustrates a reversal design that is being used to test the usefulness of meditation for reducing the pain associated with migraine headaches. In the baseline phase, the subjective intensity of headache pain is charted on a 10-point scale for one week with higher scores representing higher intensity of pain. After 7 days, the intervention—meditation—is introduced. After the headache pain is successfully reduced for one week the meditation is stopped in the third phase and the headache pain is again monitored. In the fourth phase, the meditation is reintroduced and the headache pain is monitored.

Exhibit 4.7 illustrates a pattern in which the client reported a significant decrease in pain while using meditation and a major rebound after the meditation was stopped. These results strongly suggest that the meditation is a successful intervention for this client. In a reversal design, when the pattern of the behavior is increasing or decreasing after the intervention is withdrawn and

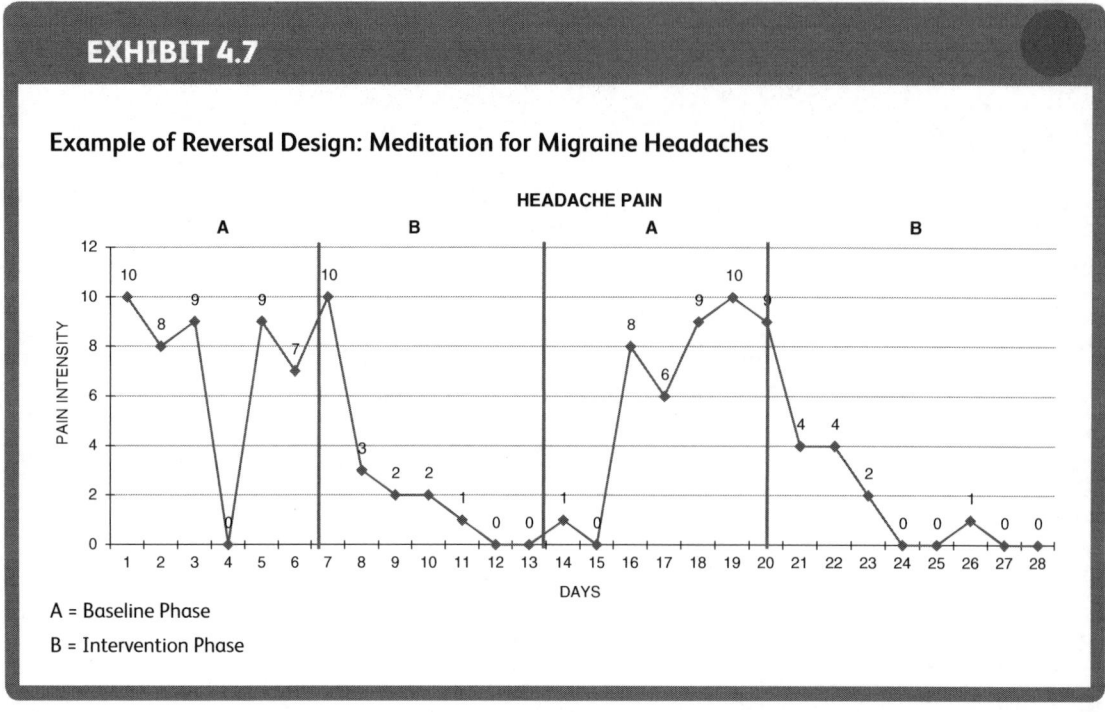

EXHIBIT 4.7

Example of Reversal Design: Meditation for Migraine Headaches

HEADACHE PAIN

A = Baseline Phase

B = Intervention Phase

reverts back to intervention levels once the intervention is reintroduced, it is likely that the intervention is the cause of the change. It should be noted, however, that a reversal design does not test the possibility that the meditation had a placebo effect, or that other chance circumstances were responsible for the pattern of improvement.

Reversal designs may not be appropriate for many social work interventions. First, withdrawing an intervention that was helpful just to test for reversal effects would be unethical. In addition, many interventions would not have reversal effects because attitude changes or new behaviors are expected to continue after the services are terminated. For example, a social worker would not expect parents who have learned better parenting skills through parent education classes to return to their former behavior after the classes have ended.

Changing Criterion Design

A **changing criterion design**, also referred to as a **changing intensity design**, is useful when the goal is to gradually reduce, or increase, a specific behavior. This approach is often used in monitoring interventions related to withdrawal from addictions to substances such as cigarettes or alcohol. Subphases in the

EXHIBIT 4.8

Example of Changing Criterion Design: Cigarette Smoking

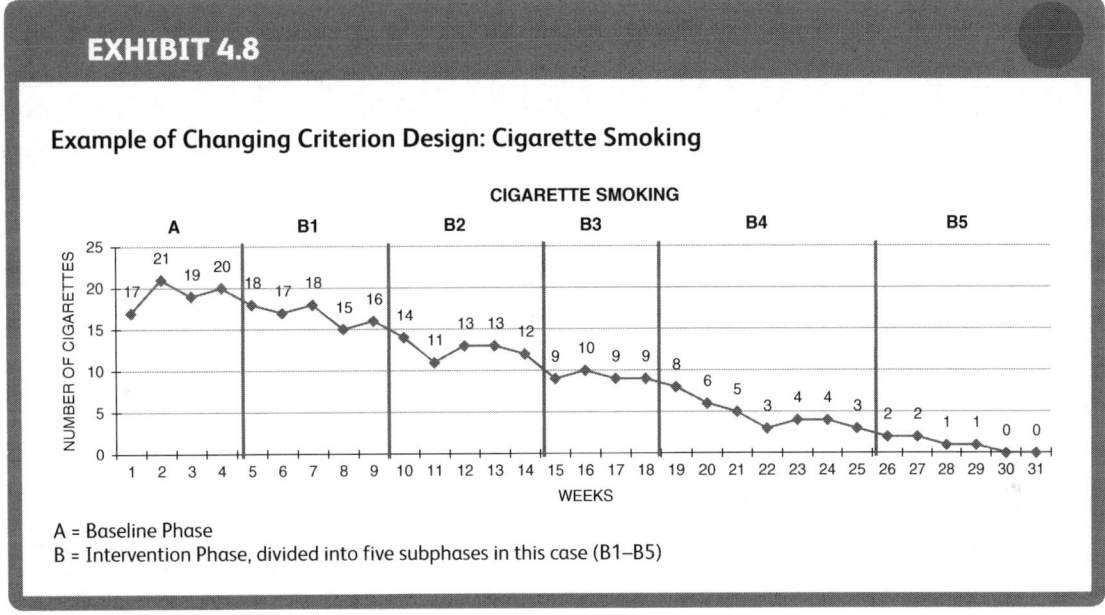

A = Baseline Phase
B = Intervention Phase, divided into five subphases in this case (B1–B5)

intervention phase can be numbered sequentially. Each subphase can last for a different period of time, depending on when the criterion for that subphase is reached.

Exhibit 4.8 shows the results of an intervention to reduce cigarette smoking. In this case, the client counts the number of cigarettes smoked each day on a paper attached to the cigarette pack. After the baseline phase (A), the client and social worker establish a goal of reducing the number of cigarettes smoked each day from an average of 16 to 13 (B1). When the client reaches the goal of 13, the goal is reduced in the next phase to 9 (B2). When the client reaches that goal, the goal is reduced to 4 cigarettes (B3), and so on until the client achieves the goal of not smoking at all (B5).

SUCCESS IN SINGLE SUBJECT RESEARCH

People may define the success of a social work intervention with a single subject in a number of different ways. Some people consider even the attempt to make positive changes as a success. Others may view any change in the desired direction a success, and still others might consider only the complete resolution of a problematic situation a success.

Clinical social workers are generally interested in **therapeutic success:** the situation for which a person seeks services is resolved, for example, abuse and neglect of a child has stopped; an adolescent is no longer missing school; a nursing home resident is participating in social events; a married couple is engaged in problem solving rather than in destructive communication. Therapeutic success is achieved when a client has reached the goal of the service. Whenever possible, clients should be involved in the evaluation of the success of the intervention. A client should indicate whether an intervention has attained the desired goal as well as demonstrate that he or she can perform their desired behavior independently.

Social work researchers may define other types of success, including experimental and statistical success:

■ **Experimental success:** the intervention has produced a clear improvement—that is, measures in the intervention phase are better than the average of the baseline phase—but the goal has not been completely reached. In the case of the child who throws tantrums, the child may have improved from having tantrums every night to having a tantrum only once or twice a week.
■ **Statistical success:** changes in the intervention phase are greater than would be expected by chance variation. For example, if a student missed 14 to 18 days of school per month (an average of 16 days) during the baseline phase but missed only nine days during the intervention phase, this difference would show statistical success because it indicates a great deal of change from a student's typical or average behavior. Missing nine days of school each month, however, cannot be considered therapeutic success.

The sections that follow outline methods for analyzing success from a researcher's perspective, as well as the way that clinicians measure the success of SSR. The benefits and drawbacks of using the results to inform clinical practice are addressed.

Analysis of Single Subject Research

In this section we consider various methods of evaluating the success of social work interventions through SSR. We can analyze SSR visually through a graph, statistically, or through a combination of these methods.

Graphing SSR Data

One method of determining the success of an intervention is to "eyeball" the data, that is, to look at the pattern of the data in the intervention phase in relation to the baseline phase. A common technique for representing the pattern is with a graph like those in Exhibits 4.4 through 4.8. In some cases, we can clearly see that goals have been reached and the intervention is successful (for example, in Exhibit 4.5, for compliance). In other cases, we can clearly see that the intervention has not been successful. We assume that an intervention has not been successful when (a) there appears to be no difference between the baseline phase and the intervention phase or (b) the intervention phase shows that the situation is getting worse rather than better.

Typically, researchers use a line graph to show changes over time. A graph of SSR should have a title, and each axis should be labeled. The horizontal (x) axis indicates units of time (days, weeks, or months). The vertical (y) axis indicates increments of the dependent variable (number of minutes, number of days' attendance, score on an anxiety scale, for example). As noted earlier, *A* denotes the baseline phase, and *B* indicates the intervention phase. Additional numbers (B1, B2, etc.) or letters (*C, D, E,* and so forth) denote changes in intensity of the intervention or additional interventions.

An alternative visual approach assumes that the trend of the baseline will continue over time if the intervention is not successful. It is called the **split-middle method** because the baseline is split in the middle (see Exhibit 4.9, for example). The mean of each half of the baseline is used as a point through which we plot

EXHIBIT 4.9

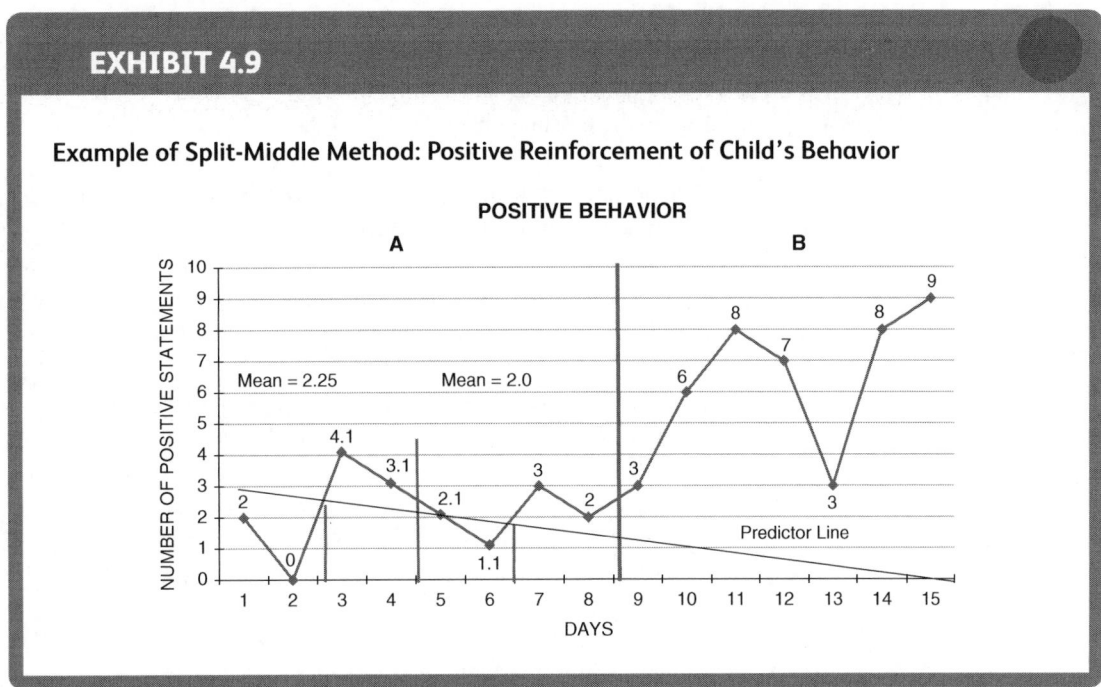

Example of Split-Middle Method: Positive Reinforcement of Child's Behavior

a predictor line. (If the baseline scores show extreme variation, we can plot the median rather than the mean.) We then extend the line connecting the plotted means or medians into the intervention phase. If most of the points in the intervention phase are above or below this line (depending on the direction of the goal), we consider the intervention to be successful.

For example, consider a situation in which a goal was to increase a mother's use of praise and positive reinforcement in changing her child's behavior. We can see in Exhibit 4.9 that the mean of the first half of the baseline is 2.25 and second half is 2.0. These points are plotted in the center of each half of the baseline, and a predictor line is drawn to indicate the trend of the data. Because all of the points in the intervention phase are above the predictor line, the intervention is considered a success.

Analyzing the Standard Deviation

Statistical analysis frequently draws on the concept of **standard deviation,** which is a measure of the amount by which a set of values differs from the mean. This concept is discussed at length in Chapter 12. As its name suggests, the **standard deviation method** assumes that the baseline represents a person's typical (or mean) behavior and that the behavior varies in a manner similar to a normal distribution:

- Approximately 68% of behavior will fall within one standard deviation of the mean of the baseline phase
- Approximately 95% of behavior will fall within two standard deviations of the mean of the baseline phase.

Based on this assumption, a social worker may assume that if the mean of the intervention phase is outside of one standard deviation of the baseline mean, the intervention is considered successful because it represents a shift away from previous "typical" behavior. Alternatively, a social worker may use more stringent criteria and choose a change of two standard deviations to represent success.

When we use this method, plotting the standard deviation lines on the SSR graph can help us represent the results visually. We can easily calculate the mean and standard deviation of the baseline phase and the mean of the intervention phase using a spreadsheet program such as Excel or statistical software such as SPSS. Quick Guide 3 is a tutorial on using Excel to create a graph plotting SSR results, as well as finding the mean and the standard deviation of the baseline phase; it is based on the circumstances described in the following Case-in-Point, which describes an intervention designed to improve a child's bedtime behavior. Other methods of SSR analysis involve the use of trend

analysis, t-tests of mean differences, chi-square analysis, and binomial probability, but they are beyond the scope of this chapter. Here we concentrate on
plotting standard deviation.

QUICK GUIDE 3 EXCEL TUTORIAL: GRAPHING THE RESULTS OF SINGLE SUBJECT RESEARCH

You are tracking the number of minutes of fussing behavior on a nightly basis:

Baseline Data:	25, 38, 27, 30, 25, 30, 20
Intervention Data:	30, 35, 25, 20, 15, 10, 15, 10, 10, 15, 8, 10, 8, 5, 5, 10, 5, 8, 5, 0, 5, 3, 5, 1, 0, 5, 0, 3, 0, 0,
Follow-up Data:	0, 0

Graphing with Excel

1. Open an Excel sheet and, in the first row, enter each data point listed above in order with Baseline data first. The data will be in cells A1 through AM1.
2. Highlight and select the data (click on the 1 in the first row, farthest left).
3. Click the Chart Wizard icon or icon associated with Recommended Charts under the Insert Tab; next select the **Line chart** (be sure the **Rows** option is selected); click **OK**.
4. Double click the **Chart Title** and type Bedtime Behavior and press enter.
5. Under the **File** tab, click on **Add Chart Element**, and then **Axis Titles**. Type in Days for the **Primary Horizontal Axis** and Minutes of Fussy Behavior for the **Primary Vertical Axis**.
6. Select: **Insert,** then the **shapes icon**, and then **line**. Place the cursor where you want to begin the line, then click the left button of the mouse, drag the mouse and then release where you want to end your line. You can move the line with the cursor and the drag and drop with the left mouse button.
7. Draw a vertical line at the end of the baseline just after the seventh data point on the X axis. Draw another vertical line at the end of day 21 to separate the B phase from the C phase. Draw a vertical line at day 35 to separate the C phase from the D (Follow-up) phase.
8. Use the **Textbox tool** under the **File** tab to add the letters A (for baseline), B (First Intervention phase), C (2nd Intervention phase) and D above each section.

Finding the mean and standard deviation of the baseline with Excel

1. Within the table that you constructed in part A, put the cursor in an empty cell e.g., A3.
2. Select the **Insert Function (fx)** button. Select *Average* to calculate the mean.
3. In the *Number 1* box type: **A1:G1** (that means, A1 through G1) to select the average of the first 7 days.
4. Move the cursor to another empty cell e.g., A4.
5. Select the **Insert Function (fx)** button. Highlight **STDEV,** which calculates the standard deviation.
6. In the *Number 1* box type: **A1:G1** (that means, A1 through G1).

7. In another empty cell, e.g. A5, subtract one standard deviation from the mean. In Excel you can do this by typing cell names or actual data, such as **+A3–A4** or **=27.86–5.64,** and striking the **Enter** key.
8. Use the Line tool to draw the mean and the one standard deviation and two standard deviation ranges on the graph. Note: using different colors for these lines will add visual clarity.

If you experience difficulty with any of these steps, conduct an Internet search on how to.... e.g., draw a line in Excel.

CASE-IN-POINT: USING STANDARD DEVIATION IN SSR GRAPH DEMONSTRATES SUCCESS IN IMPROVING BEDTIME BEHAVIOR

Mr. and Ms. C. sought assistance from a family service agency because they were "worn out" trying to get their son to sleep at night. Mr. and Ms. C. were caring and involved parents who spent a great deal of time interacting with their six-year-old son, Jon. Ms C. explained that things were fine during the day and evening, but they became chaotic and difficult at bedtime. When Jon was told that it was time to go to bed, he would cry and whine. He said he was afraid of ghosts and wanted to sleep in his parents' bed with them. If his parents put him in his own bed, he cried and shouted about monsters and ghosts, and he clung to whichever parent attempted to put him to bed. Further, he usually left his bed and slept with his parents before the night was over. The parents were inconsistent, alternately threatening, coaching, and usually giving in to get some sleep and "meet their son's needs."

The parents agreed that the goal was to have their son spend 15 minutes of quiet time with his parents, and then sleep through the night in his own bed. The goal (the dependent variable) was to decrease fussing and to have Jon sleep in his own bed. The social worker asked the parents not to change their behavior during the next week so they could establish a baseline. They were to keep a nightly journal noting the number of minutes Jon spent fussing before he went to sleep. (The baseline data in Quick Guide 3 are the numbers that Mr. And Ms. C. recorded to indicate the amount of fussing.) The parents noted that the week was typical of what they had been experiencing for the past year.

The intervention to which Mr. and Ms. C. agreed consisted of weekly parent training sessions focusing on the following strategies: implementing a consistent bedtime routine, setting limits, ignoring all talk of ghosts and monsters, and putting Jon back in his own bed when he left it. In addition, they were to praise Jon when he went to his own bed and reward him by reading him a story in the morning if he slept through the night in his own room. During the second week of the intervention, Jon's behavior began to show improvement, and it continued to improve throughout the intervention period.

After two weeks, the parents and the social worker agreed that additional support would be useful. Mr. and Ms. C. then began to attend a weekly support group in which parents shared experiences and engaged in mutual problem solving. Mr. And Ms. C. ended their parent training sessions after five weeks, but they continued to attend the parent support group for the next three months. Follow-up telephone calls one week and then one month after the end of their training sessions found that appropriate bedtime behavior continued.

EXHIBIT 4.10

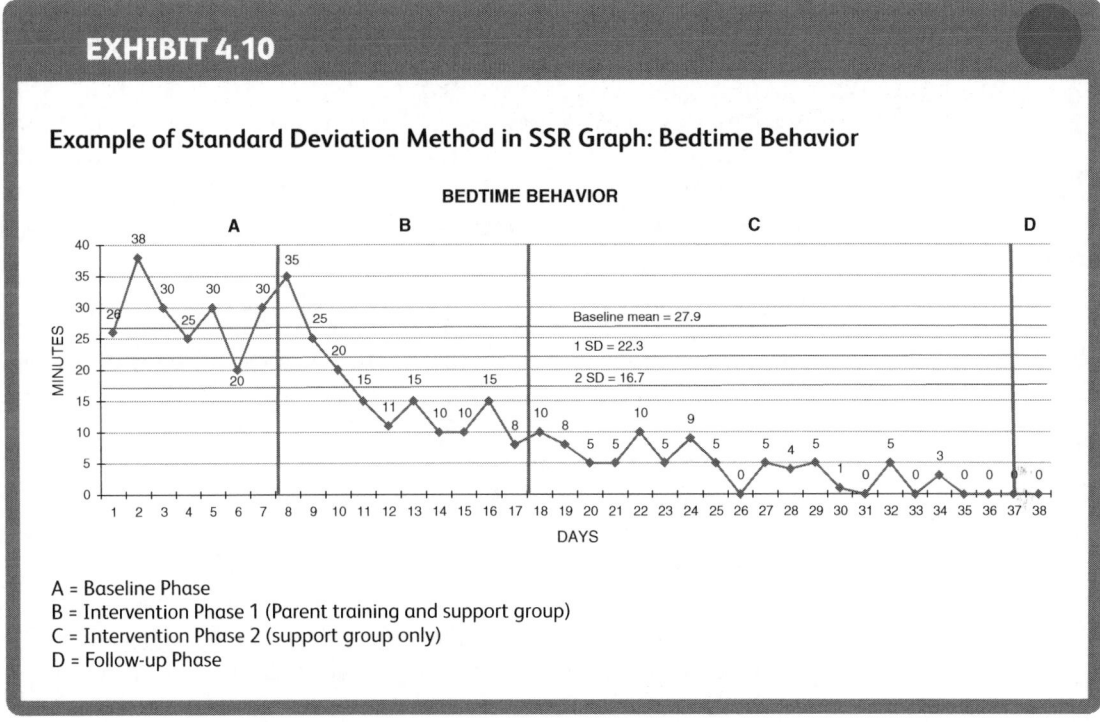

Example of Standard Deviation Method in SSR Graph: Bedtime Behavior

A = Baseline Phase
B = Intervention Phase 1 (Parent training and support group)
C = Intervention Phase 2 (support group only)
D = Follow-up Phase

Exhibit 4.10, an ABC design, shows the data for the baseline phase (A), the first intervention phase, which featured parent training sessions and, after two weeks, weekly support groups (B), the second intervention phase, consisting of the support group participation (C), and the follow-up phase (D).

When analyzing the graph in Exhibit 4.10, a social worker might discern a clear pattern of improvement suggesting that the goal had been reached. Further observation of the graph would provide more precise information:

- The baseline ranges between 20 and 38 with a mean of 27.9 (top line) and standard deviation of 5.6. The pattern is somewhat unstable with no clear direction.
- The middle line represents one standard deviation from the mean, and the bottom line represents two standard deviations. By the end of the first week of intervention, measurements already fall below two standard deviations from the baseline mean. These results would indicate experimental and statistical success, although the goal is not yet completely reached.
- By the end of the intervention phase, all measurements are well below two standard deviations from the baseline mean, and the goal of bedtime without fussing appears to have been reached.
- Follow-up at one week and then one month confirms that the behavior change has been maintained.

Benefits of Using Single Subject Research to Inform Practice

The purpose of single subject research is to inform practice by monitoring the effectiveness of social work interventions. The use of SSR should enhance the quality of services and help to build the social work knowledge base. It does so in several ways, which we discuss next.

Better Services

SSR promotes better services by documenting both the process and outcomes of services on an individualized basis.

- Social workers who monitor progress will know whether an intervention that works for most people is effective with a specific client.
- Social workers can change their approach when ongoing data collection indicates that it is not achieving the desired outcomes.
- By monitoring many cases, social workers will learn the typical process of change for an intervention. This information will help them to assess their progress during interventions and to educate clients about the process of change.
- SSR provides concrete evidence to consumers about the progress of interventions. For example, it provides important information about when to stop, change course, or refer elsewhere because the intervention is not working.
- SSR puts evaluation in the hands of the person most affected by the intervention: the client, who should verify whether an intervention has attained his or her desired goal, as well as demonstrate that he or she can perform this intervention independently if needed (Bloom, 2010).

Enhanced Relationships

SSR may promote a more collaborative relationship between social workers and their clients by opening up communication through a joint review of the data.

- SSR promotes discussions about the reasons that progress is or is not being achieved.
- Communication with others (such as a parent, teacher, or counselor) during the process of collecting data promotes better understanding of the problem during the baseline phase.
- Communication during the process further encourages everyone concerned to consider what factors other than the intervention may be impacting the problem.

View of the Larger Context

Social workers can use SSR to evaluate services in a larger context.

- Generalization to others with similar concerns is not possible from single cases. However, by using SSR with many cases, a social worker can accumulate information about the effectiveness of a particular type of intervention.
- Information can help answer questions about the usefulness of an intervention, the speed at which change can be expected to occur, and for whom and under what circumstances the intervention is successful.
- A social worker's cumulative SSR with a specific concern provides valuable feedback about practice. When such cases are collected and analyzed across all social workers in the agency, even greater generalization is possible. SSR can provide an inductive and empirical method for building evidence-based knowledge.

Promoting Critical Thinking

SSR uses an empirical, research-based orientation to services. For this reason, it may promote critical thinking about the efficacy of practice methods that have been based primarily on "practice wisdom" or authority. Thus, SSR both supports innovation and reinforces the use of interventions supported by research.

Efficiency

SSR is efficient in that it can be incorporated into practice with little additional time or expense.

- SSR avoids many of the costs and disruptions of group-level research as discussed in Chapter 7.
- There is no need for research consultants, random assignment, or the extensive collection, input, and analysis of data.
- Data collection in SSR can generally take place as part of the assessment and intervention processes.
- Data analysis is relatively simple and straightforward.

Drawbacks of Using Single Subject Research to Inform Practice

In spite of the potential of SSR to inform practice, there has been some criticism and resistance to its use in social work. These arguments are based on both pragmatic and methodological concerns. Any form of evaluation may be threatening because it can highlight ineffective practice. In addition, even simple evaluation methods require a social worker's time and commitment.

These are the major criticisms of SSR, along with rebuttals to those criticisms:

■ *SSR is impractical and takes away time that might otherwise be used for direct services.* The use of SSR, however, fits within an evidence-based practice approach, in which specifying goals, assessing systems, monitoring improvement, and documenting processes and outcomes are integral components of service delivery. The time needed for data collection is often minimal, and the use of computer software makes graphing and analyzing results a fast and simple task.

■ *SSR is appropriate only for behavioral interventions that focus on simple behavior change.* This is an erroneous belief. In practice, SSR is not tied to any particular theory or intervention approach. It can be used to monitor any kind of change, including changes in knowledge, attitude, relationships, and the environment.

■ *SSR does not have the internal validity needed to establish cause-and-effect relationships or the external validity needed to generalize to broader populations.* (See Chapter 9 for a discussion of validity.) Although these criticisms cannot be refuted, they also apply to the majority of research done on social work practice that relies on nonrandom samples, with small groups of participants, in limited settings. Nevertheless, SSR allows us to accumulate data that can lend empirical support to the use of specific practice methods.

■ *In SSR, many of the evaluation instruments used to measure more complex variables such as self-esteem, marital satisfaction, family environment, and community integration have not yet been shown to offer an accurate picture of change over time. For example, taking a self-esteem test on a weekly basis for several weeks may change a person's responses as he or she becomes either familiar or bored with the test. In addition, the test may not be sensitive to small changes that occur on a weekly basis.* When using SSR, indicators based on behavior rather than a written testing instrument may be more accurate measures of change. Behavioral indicators are often available for concerns brought to social workers, and some instruments have been validated for repeated administration. Much work, however, remains to be done in this area.

■ *SSR focuses on individual change rather than system change, which is a key focus of social work.* Although this criticism is valid, there is nothing inherent in SSR to prevent a focus on system change. Ultimately, it is people who seek services. For this reason, the results of services must be documented based on the well-being of those who seek them, whether the change effort is directed at people or at systems in the environment.

■ *There is no evidence that social workers that use SSR are more effective than those who do not evaluate their practice.* That is true. Little research has been done in this area, and further research to establish the benefits of SSR is needed.

CONCLUSION

Social workers need to assure the people they work with, themselves, and the public that their services are effective. Single subject research designs offer an efficient, cost-effective method for evaluating practice that is individualized and consistent with social work ethics and practice methods. SSR enhances practice in that it promotes specificity in assessment and accountability of results. SSR documents practice outcomes for individual social workers and can provide generalizable evidence of practice effectiveness when SSR data from many cases are combined and analyzed. Social workers need to know whether what they are doing works each time they use an intervention with an individual, family, group, or community.

MAIN POINTS

■ Social work values and ethics require that social workers use tested, effective methods to promote positive change. They also require that social workers document the outcomes of their services.

■ Although social work research is a good starting place for selecting an evidence-based intervention, we cannot know whether the intervention suggested by the research will be effective for a particular person, family, group, or community.

■ Single subject research provides systematic methods with which to monitor the process and outcomes of change efforts on an individualized basis.

■ Single subject research uses a clinical research model that follows the logical steps of good practice and research: formulating problems, setting and operationalizing goals; developing procedures to collect data; collecting baseline data; specifying and introducing the intervention(s) with ongoing data collection; analyzing the data; and making decisions based on the data.

■ A variety of single subject designs can be used depending on the goals to be reached and the degree to which the researcher needs to draw conclusions about the causal nature of the independent variable. These designs include: AB, multiple baseline, multiple component, reversal, and changing criterion designs.

■ Practitioners may define success differently from researchers. A practitioner may define success as reaching agreed-upon goals. A researcher may view success as reaching a significant level of change, even if the goals are not completely reached.

■ Social workers often use spreadsheet and statistical software programs to simplify the process of data recording, graphing, and data analysis.

■ Single subject research has advantages and disadvantages. Although it has been criticized as being inefficient, inadequate for many situations, and possibly ineffective, it is a practical, easy-to-use method to document the results of practice on an individualized basis. It promotes assessment and accountability, evidence-based decision making.

EXERCISES

1. Consider the Sanchez Family case, and list one research question that could be answered using single subject research. What type of SSR design would make it possible to answer the question you posed? Are there any cultural nuances that might affect how you formulated the question?

2. One of the challenges in culturally competent practice is the shortage of research testing evidence-based practices with particular racial and ethnic groups. What concerns might you have about how a specific evidence-based practice would "translate" to the Sanchez family's needs? How could you design a single subject research project that might provide some insights to inform this practice?

3. In single subject research, it is important to be able to operationalize the dependent variable—what you expect to see change. Considering the Riverton case, list four possible dependent variables you would track using SSR and provide an operational definition for each variable.

4. Use a spreadsheet program such as Excel to graph the design and results for single subject research on a new radio advertising campaign that was initiated in order to recruit online volunteers for RAINN. Be sure to include a baseline, intervention, and follow-up phase.

   a. Graph a baseline based on the number of people who had volunteered in each of the past six months using these data: month 1=12, month 2=15, month 3=22, month 4=14, month 5=24, month 6=15.

   b. Graph the number of volunteers during the six months of the radio campaign (the intervention): month 1=28, month 2=22, month 3=18, month 4=16, month 5=18, month 6=20.

   c. Enter vertical lines to represent the baseline and intervention phase.

   d. Find the mean and standard deviation of the baseline.

   e. Enter the one and two standard deviation lines on the graph.

   f. What do you conclude about the effectiveness of the intervention?

EXHIBIT 4.11

SSR Graphs for Analysis

Case A: Verbal Aggression

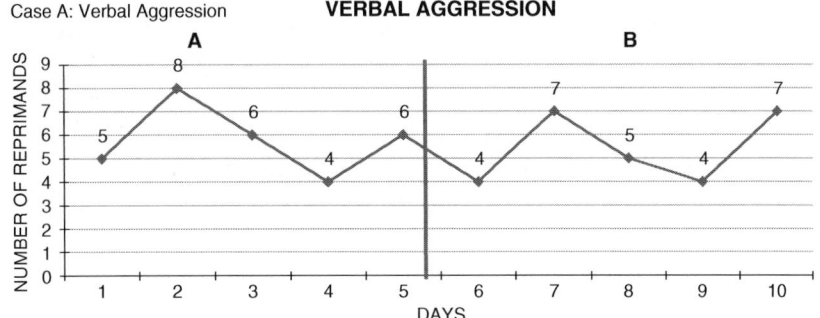

Case B: Truancy

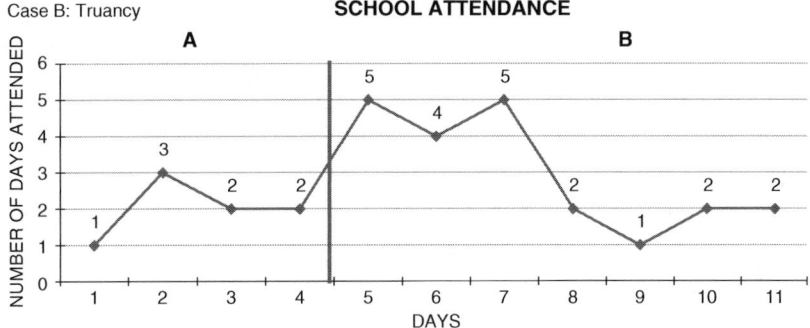

Case C: Anxiety

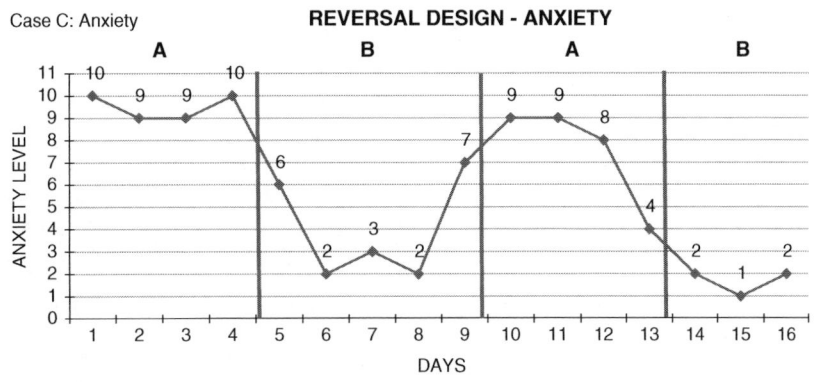

5. Visually examine the graphs in Exhibit 4.11. What can you conclude about the effectiveness of the intervention in each case?

6. A proposal is made at the agency serving Carla Washburn. The Director is proposing to make it an agency requirement to use SSR with all clients as part of both program evaluation and individual staff evaluation. How would you respond to this proposal? How could you include clients such as Mrs. Washburn in the process of formulating your response?

7. Imagine that you are putting together a plan to evaluate the Hudson City disaster response system using SSR. What questions would you answer pertaining to the disaster response system? How would you implement such a plan?

8. Select one of the interactive cases. Using the steps in the clinical research model as explained in the chapter, describe how you would: Formulate a problem, set and operationalize goals; develop procedures to collect data; collect baseline data; specify and introduce the intervention(s) with ongoing data collection; analyze the data; and make decisions based on the data. For example, perhaps you are a social worker at an agency in Brickville. You are concerned that many of your clients are not showing up for your appointments, and you believe that poor public transportation resources are part of the problem. What would you do in order to use the clinical research model to test the intervention you create to address this problem?

RESEARCH IN AGENCIES AND COMMUNITIES

If we help only one child, we consider ourselves a success!

P rogram advocates sometimes use the opening quote, or a version of it, when they are asked to discuss their goals and to show evidence of their success. The sentiments expressed in the quote, though likely well intended, represent dangerous thinking. More than ever before, we live in an age of evidence-based practice and accountability. Not only is social work's reputation as a profession dependent on providing scientific evidence that programs are successful and cost effective, but as social workers, our ability to live by our ethics and to secure funding for the programs we believe in is also at stake.

Social workers working in agencies and communities use their knowledge and skills in research in many ways:

■ Evaluating their own practice (see Chapter 4).
■ Engaging in research that describes community problems and needs in order to educate and design programs.
■ Evaluating practices and programs to find areas for improvement and to make decisions about funding based on demonstrated effectiveness and cost.
■ Involving consumers in the evaluation of programs.
■ Presenting evaluation findings at a community meeting, local or national conferences, or through publications online or in research journals (see Chapter 13).

In this book, we discuss the kinds of questions that can be answered by research, the methods and research designs we use to answer these questions, and the strengths and limitations of these methods and designs. Also in this book, we discuss research tools and methods that can be used by social workers to design and evaluate programs.

In addition to providing basic definitions related to program evaluation, and the functions and types of program evaluation, this chapter explains that program evaluation always occurs within a social and political context. The chapter concludes with a discussion of the politics of evaluation and strategies for maximizing the likelihood that program evaluation will be used to enhance social work services.

By the end of this chapter, you should be able to:

■ Define what is meant by program evaluation and list and explain the reasons that program evaluation is a necessary part of social work practice.
■ Define four different perspectives on need and describe strategies for the assessment of community needs.

- Describe a variety of strategies for the evaluation of programs and explain the methods and purpose of each one.
- Recognize and write specific and measurable objectives that can be used in program evaluation.
- Describe the use of a logic model in conceptualizing program evaluation.
- Explain the use of cost analysis and benefit/cost analysis in program evaluation.
- Explain the difference between participatory evaluation and other evaluation strategies.
- Describe the political and organizational issues associated with program evaluation and what can be done to minimize them.

This chapter deals with the application of research methods to answer some very practical questions about social work services. Is a social work program needed? If it is, does the social work program work? If it does work, is it cost effective? This chapter provides a basis for social workers to engage in the role of researcher using research-based methods to evaluate programs within their own agencies and communities. The research process and methods used for answering questions related to planning, evaluating, and improving social work programs are referred to as **program evaluation**.

To understand program evaluation, we must clearly define what we mean by *program* and *work*. A **program** is a set of activities designed to reach specific objectives. A program can be used to produce change at any system level. Some programs involve clinical change in individuals and families, whereas others attempt to change organizations or communities. For example, a program can focus on a specific objective such as improving communication among individuals. Conversely, it can encompass an entire agency's activities, such as a program to reduce targeted violence. Regardless of their scope, all social work programs are intended to improve the quality of life for people. If a program accomplishes this goal, we say it "works."

Finding out whether a program works is a complex process. We can think of a program as based on a theory of practice. Theory states that if we perform a specified set of activities, certain changes will take place. If these changes do not take place, then there is usually one of three explanations advanced:

- The program was not implemented with **fidelity**, that is, the program is not being delivered as intended. In order to determine whether this is the case, we must collect evidence about the ways the program functions.
- Our theory of practice was wrong. This is the case if we find that the program is operating as intended and yet the desired changes in people or systems are not occurring.
- A third possible explanation may be that our measures (Chapter 9) or data (Chapter 10) were inadequate to capture the change attributable to the program.

We use our knowledge and skills in research to help assess fidelity, and to avoid making erroneous conclusions based on poor measurement and flawed data. When measurement does not reflect what is intended, and data are flawed, valuable resources are wasted and there is a disservice to the potential recipients of the service as programs have been canceled on the basis of poor research methods.

Program evaluation is often divided into two major categories based on purpose:

■ **Formative evaluation** is research conducted for the purpose of informing program improvement efforts. For instance, examining immunization levels of program participants compared to overall immunization completion rate in the state may indicate that the program is doing well or, conversely, that the program should be doing better. Formative evaluation is directed at collecting information that can be used to target improvement efforts.

■ **Summative evaluation** is for the purpose of judging the overall effectiveness of a program and lends itself to decision making about the future of the program. Based on information from the summative evaluation, important decisions will be made regarding whether or not the program should continue to be funded as is, should be terminated, or should even expand.

TYPES OF PROGRAM EVALUATION

Whereas the formative-summative classification is based on purpose, there is also an evaluation typology based on focus. In this chapter, we discuss seven different types of program evaluation, each with a distinct focus: needs assessment, evaluability assessment, implementation evaluation, consumer satisfaction assessment, process evaluation, outcome evaluation, and cost evaluation.

These different types of program evaluations are related. For example, process evaluation provides information that the program is "doing things right," but not necessarily that it is "doing the right thing." Even when a program is implemented as designed, process evaluation does not provide evidence that it is producing the intended changes in the people or communities. This is the focus of outcome evaluation. Thus, understanding the questions that need to be answered, and then selecting the type of evaluation that best answers those questions is a first step in mastering program evaluation.

NEEDS ASSESSMENT

Many constituencies, including social workers, politicians, businesses, community leaders, interest groups, and others, may wish to develop new social programs that they believe are needed to better help community members. Given the reality of limited resources, the development of a program must first include evidence that the program is needed. **Needs assessment** is the application of research methods to determine the nature of the problem, whether the problem warrants a service, and whether services currently exist to address the problem. In addition, where a need exists, a needs assessment helps to identify the most effective program to meet that need.

Needs assessment can help social workers plan programs by identifying the extent of local problems or by documenting the existence of new concerns. It can also assist in establishing budgets by helping inform choices between funding new services or increasing support for existing services. Unless decisions are made based on systematic needs assessments, already limited resources can be wasted addressing lower-priority problems or even problems that do not exist.

Keep in mind that developing new programs and maintaining funding for existing programs are political processes. Funding depends on the outcome of conflicts among competing interests. Providing evidence that a program is needed can be essential to creating public awareness and convincing the community to establish and maintain social programs.

Needs assessments focus on questions such as:

- What are the major social problems in a community?
- What is the extent of unmet need in a community?
- Are enough people in need to justify a program?
- Do people know about an existing program? If so, how do they perceive it?
- If you develop services, will people use them?
- Where should services be located?
- What barriers prevent people from accessing existing services?
- How do stakeholders view the need for new services or the usefulness of existing services?

Types of Information for Needs Assessment

In order to assess need, we must identify the different perspectives that are being investigated. One widely used classification system identifies four perspectives on needs (Kettner, Moroney, & Martin, 2017):

- **Perceived Need:** what people say they need. Perceived need is generally assessed directly from the people involved through surveys, focus groups, and community forums. Always keep in mind that what people report they need or would utilize can differ dramatically from how they actually behave. For example, consider a study conducted shortly after September 11, 2001. The New York Department of Health and Mental Hygiene surveyed 414 people living in the area of the World Trade Center. They found that 28% of the sample received supportive counseling of some type after the destruction. Approximately 33% of the sample thought they would benefit from counseling. When projected to the 12,300 people residing in these neighborhoods, this result indicated that there were about 4,000 individuals who felt they would benefit from counseling (Community Health Works, 2001). This does not mean, of course, that all 4,000 people would participate in counseling services if they were actually offered it.

- **Expressed Need:** a need expressed in action. Consider the saying, for example, that people vote with their feet. Or consider a scenario in which 30 students come every week to an afterschool program that is designed for 15 pupils. This is an expression of the need for an expanded program. Documentation from waiting lists or other agency records can also be a source of expressed needs. Expressed needs often underestimate the actual need. For example, if students know the afterschool program is always crowded, many of them may not attend. Or, if a program does not exist, people may not have enough information to ask about its development. Also affecting expressed need is the cultural acceptance of help-seeking behavior. In some cultures, admitting a problem or reaching out for help may be a sign of weakness or a cause for shame.

- **Normative Need:** a perceived need defined by experts, not by the people themselves. A normative need reflects what the experts believe people generally need based on a set of data or criteria. According to the 2016 federal poverty guidelines for the 48 contiguous states and the District of Columbia, a family of four needs $24,300 per year on which to live (Federal Register, 2016). Accrediting organizations, guided by professional standards, are another source of normative need. They may mandate, for example, that a staff ratio of one social worker for each 15 nursing home residents is needed.

- **Relative Need:** what comparisons with similar populations indicate is a need. This approach is sometimes referred to as **rates under treatment**. For example, if most communities of approximately 50,000 residents have at least one group home for individuals with developmental disabilities, it may be reasonable to assume that my community of 50,000 needs a group home. Census data, information from other surveys, and rates of people under treatment in other communities can be used to show relative need and may be an inexpensive way to conduct a needs assessment. However, we must be careful to justify that the compared groups are truly equivalent in important ways.

Research Methods in Needs Assessment

Given the different perspectives on need, researchers use a variety of quantitative and qualitative methods to obtain information for needs assessments, including these five:

1. **Surveys.** Mailed questionnaires, telephone surveys, or face-to-face interviews can provide generalizable information about perceived needs. As discussed in Chapter 9, survey development involves recruiting participants and designing the questionnaire or interview.

2. **Focus Groups.** Also discussed in Chapter 9, focus groups are meetings of about five to 10 people that generally last from one to two hours. In needs assessment, participants discuss their perceived needs and/or expressed needs in some detail. Focus groups allow both the researcher and the participants to explore the relevant issues and to provide in-depth examples of experiences and opinions. Representation in the focus groups should be carefully considered and justified to avoid biasing the results. Focus groups may be repeated to look for similarities and differences in the results.

3. **Community Forums.** Inviting community members to discuss community needs is an important step in establishing commitment to new services. A community forum is especially useful when a program is thought to be controversial, because the individuals who agree to participate are likely to be those who feel strongly about the issue. Consider a scenario in which a school board in an inner-city neighborhood proposes a program in which truant youths will be arrested by police and held until their parents pick them up. A community forum may disclose that, although parents want their children to attend school every day, they view a policy of arresting their children as harassment of the minority community, and they strongly support other methods to improve school attendance.

4. **Key Informant Interviews.** Some members of the community may be known to have expertise about the needs and reactions of the community. Interviews with these key informants provide detailed, in-depth, qualitative information. They also can help researchers to discover the reasons that the community is not using existing services. Key informants may be professionals such as police, teachers, health specialists, and social workers who have direct experience with the populations to be addressed or the services to be developed. They may also be informal community leaders such as elders, religious leaders, business leaders, and activists. The rationale and justification for using particular key informants should be identified as part of the needs assessment.

5. **Analysis of Existing Records.** Census data, published reports, police and court records, agency case records, newspaper accounts, and even suggestion

boxes can provide information to help assess the need for a program. For example, an analysis of the zip codes of current users of agency services may reveal areas of the community that are not being reached by the program. Similarly, census data combined with published reports of similar communities may provide information to justify the need for new services. Similarly, census data may indicate a significant increase in the population of low-income senior citizens within the community, whereas published reports reveal that similar communities have food programs for this population. Together, these data suggest that such services are needed within this community.

The following Case-in-Point describes how a combination of quantitative and qualitative research was used to assess the need for an online sexual assault hotline.

CASE-IN-POINT: ASSESSING NEED FOR RAINN ONLINE SEXUAL ASSAULT SERVICES

Social work has traditionally been a face-to-face profession, but the proliferation of Internet-based services in other realms has led some social workers to investigate the online delivery of therapeutic services. However, in the past, many social workers believed that online services were either ineffective or inferior to face-to-face services (Finn, 2002). Others were concerned that the ethical requirements of practice cannot be met online. This controversy was a key part of the needs assessment for an online version of a sexual assault hotline established by RAINN (Rape, Abuse & Incest National Network).

RAINN's National Sexual Assault Hotline (1-800-656-HOPE) was established in 1994 and by 2016 had provided sexual assault services to over 2.2 million callers (RAINN, 2016). As early as 2005, RAINN staff began to report that callers to the telephone hotline were asking about the availability of online services.

The idea of establishing online services was appealing to the RAINN organization, but they needed more structured information before taking action. To evidence-based practitioners, healthy skepticism and "gut feelings" are useful, but ultimately, decisions to develop and use services must be based on available research evidence and professional ethics. The rationale for the development of the RAINN Online Services was based on: 1) the expressed need of users of the RAINN telephone hotline, 2) research evidence showing the increasing use of the Internet for health and human service information, and 3) research evidence showing the growth and effectiveness of online therapeutic services.

Researchers found that an estimated 80 % of Internet users, or about 93 million Americans, look online for health information and the percentage is higher for young adults (Pew Internet & American Life Project, 2013). Research also suggests that data quality is better when sensitive topics are discussed online rather than in-person (Lenhart, Madlin, & Hitlin, 2005).

The decision was made to offer services online. In order to evaluate its new service, RAINN developed:

■   A brief pop-up consumer satisfaction survey following each online session with space for consumers to write qualitative comments about their experience.

- A volunteer counselor's survey to be filled out following each session about the topics discussed, types of services provided, visitor demographics, difficulties in the session, and the volunteer's perceived helpfulness of the session.
- Focus group sessions with volunteer counselors to provide qualitative data about the operation of the program, training needs, and ideas for improving the program.
- An online supervisor survey of information about the quality of the volunteer's session and their own perceptions of the helpfulness of the session.
- Computer system data of the date, time, and length of each call, and the type of resource or referral that was given to the visitor.

Evidence of the need for online therapeutic services in sexual assault cases also came from experiences relayed by some of the consumers. For example, Sarah, age 19, lives with her mother in a small, conservative, rural community. Sara's father died when she was 16 years old. Sara's uncle occasionally visited on holidays. Three months before Sarah used the online services, while her mother was out of the house, her uncle told Sarah that he loved her and then threw her down on the couch and raped her. He later told her that she had seduced him, and to never mention what happened. Sarah was terrified, felt guilty, and didn't know what to do. Later she was relieved to have her period. At least she wasn't pregnant. But she became anxious and withdrawn. She wouldn't go out, except to church with her mother. She had trouble sleeping and was filled with shame and guilt. She was afraid to go to the police or tell anyone what had happened. She didn't want everyone in town knowing about what had happened. She sought help on the Internet. She read stories similar to her own. She soon came across a link to RAINN.org that promised confidential help and someone to talk with . . . and nobody in town had to know.

Another anecdotal example came from Alan, age 34. Alan is a successful young man, married with one child. He is employed as a manager at a grocery store where he has worked for the past five years. Although his life appears stable to others, he lives with great inner turmoil. When Alan was 13, he was gang-raped on his way home from school by three older boys. Out of a sense of deep shame, he had never told anyone, including his wife, about what happened. He reported having violent nightmares and horrific dreams of being humiliated and experienced high blood pressure, headaches, sleeplessness, and anxiety. He was prone to temper outbursts with his family followed by guilt and depression. He sometimes thought of suicide. One evening when he couldn't sleep he typed, "Help for Rape Victims" into a search engine. The first link he found was for RAINN.org.

EVALUABILITY ASSESSMENT

A determination of need may lead to the development of a new program or a critical examination of a program that already exists. To determine whether a program that exists, or one that is being designed, can be evaluated for effectiveness, researchers should first conduct an **evaluability assessment**. An evaluability assessment examines the clarity and consistency of the program's mission, goal, objectives, and data collection plan to measure the achievement of its stated objectives.

Foundations of Effective Program Structure

In order for a program to be evaluated, its objectives must be defined clearly enough for social workers to measure the extent to which it has reached its objectives. This process involves understanding the program in terms of administrative structure, resources, operationalization of objectives, activities to meet the objectives, assessment tools and methods, and the timeframe for achieving its objectives.

Program Objectives

The agency goal is not directly measurable and need not be fully accomplished for the organization or program to be successful. The articulation of specific, measurable, time-limited **objectives** is what matters. Two types of objectives are common in social service programs:

- **Process objectives** relate to the higher-order activities that the program must accomplish in order to achieve its goal, for example, recruit 50 families.
- **Outcome objectives** relate to changes produced by the program in people or in larger systems. A change in program recipients is often referred to as an **outcome**, whereas a change in the larger community or social system is called an **impact**.

To understand how these concepts apply to social work programs, let's use the example of a program such as DARE that provides drug and alcohol awareness and resistance education. These are some of the program objectives:

- Desired outcome: to increase the knowledge and influence the attitudes of students in the program.
- Intended impact: to decrease the number of arrests for drug-related problems by juveniles in the community.

These objectives focus on the accomplishments of the program.

Evaluators should clearly identify the program's objectives so that any evaluation can clearly and explicitly determine the extent to which the objectives are accomplished. To do this, the objectives should include the information listed in Exhibit 5.1—essentially, questions of what, who, how, and when.

The following are examples of clear and measurable objectives:

- At least 80% of parents will attend at least six sessions of the parent education classes during the next year. (Process objective)
- Staff will involve 20 high school seniors in developing two antismoking community awareness campaigns by the end of the year. (Process objective)

EXHIBIT 5.1

Checklist for Measurable Program Objectives

■ What specific, measurable changes will occur?
■ In whom or in what targets will change occur?
■ By what method will change be measured?
■ What is the time frame in which changes will occur?

■ The program will increase the number of female-owned businesses by 5% a year for the next three years. (Outcome objective)
■ All state mental hospital patients will be in community housing placements by June 2019. (Outcome objective)

In contrast, the following are examples of objectives that do *not* meet the criteria for clear and measurable objectives:

■ Increase the number of adoptions by 10%. (Among whom? By when?)
■ Staff will develop an appreciation of cultural diversity by the end of the training. ("Appreciate" is vague. How is it measured?)
■ Decrease the number of consumers who do not keep their appointment at the agency by 15%. (By when?)

Logic Model for Assessing Program Evaluability

When conducting an evaluability assessment it is useful to place the program goal, objectives, and measures in a more comprehensive format. For this reason, program evaluators frequently employ a **logic model** to chart the path from the social conditions that necessitate the program to the evaluation of the program benefits.

Exhibit 5.2 shows the types of information that are often included in a logic model. The focus of change in a logic model is on the benefits for the target population, not on the provision of services. Therefore, it is the desired benefits—that is, the desired outcomes and impact—that drive program development. The need for resources follows from the outcomes and impact. The resources are then used to implement program activities.

Formative evaluation involves selecting measures and research designs to provide information to assess the "Activities" section of the logic model. This process involves obtaining information about what, when, where, how often,

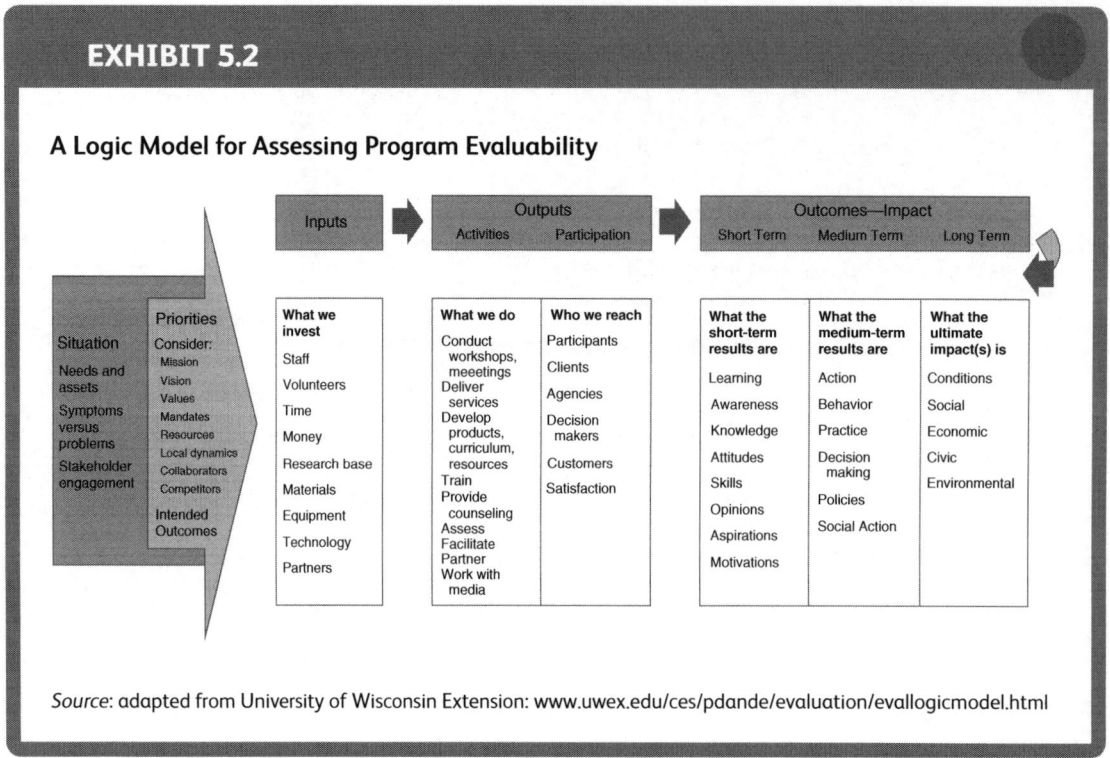

EXHIBIT 5.2

A Logic Model for Assessing Program Evaluability

Source: adapted from University of Wisconsin Extension: www.uwex.edu/ces/pdande/evaluation/evallogicmodel.html

by whom, and for whom services are delivered. Similarly, summative evaluation uses measures and research designs to provide information regarding the accomplishment of the "Outcome and Impact" sections of the logic model. The changes generated by the services may occur in many areas, including knowledge, skills, attitudes, values, behavior, status, and condition. In addition, they may include system changes in policies and procedures.

IMPLEMENTATION EVALUATION

After the need for a program has been established and the program has been designed and funded, it is ready to be implemented. Starting a new program involves a great deal of work. Staff must be hired and trained, consumers of services must be recruited, record-keeping procedures must be put into place, intervention processes must be developed, and interventions must be delivered. **Implementation evaluation** is a type of formative evaluation that focuses on the processes and activities that are established to implement the program. It helps workers develop the program by providing data in the early stages.

These data may include who uses the program, the types of services the program is to provide, the length of services for particular issues, the extent to which staff implement the program components, and the reaction of staff and consumers to the services.

Once a program has been implemented as designed, evaluators must continue to collect data about the program to be sure that it continues to function as intended. In addition, the program might have to be adjusted in response to changes in the environment. Therefore, evaluators need to collect program data to know what changes are taking place and to supply information for evidence-based decision making. There are two important methods to ensure that the program continues to meet the needs for which it was designed:

- **Quality Assurance** (sometimes known as the **model standards approach**). In quality assurance an accrediting body, outside consultant, or agency-based committee defines the standards for a quality program—for example, the staff-to-customer ratio, the types of records to be kept, and staff qualifications—as well as the procedures that are to be followed and charted on a regular basis. The entity that sets the standards reviews the evaluation. This approach often involves a regularly scheduled site visit in which the evaluators review a variety of data sources such as interviews, observation of the program, and agency records. Quality assurance generally focuses on agency policies, processes, and procedures. However, it may also evaluate the impact of services on consumers.
- **Program Monitoring**. Over time, an evaluator routinely collects and reviews data about the program. The data include the number of people seeking services, consumer demographic information, types of services requested, caseload ratios, dropout rates, and reasons for termination. Program monitoring thus provides ongoing data for program planning and management. The evaluator may also track the outcome of services for consumers, usually through ratings of perceived improvement by social workers. The widespread use of computers and database systems allows organizations to track and analyze such information.

The following Case-in-Point illustrates how a family services organization used implementation evaluation to help establish a computer-training program for foster children.

CONSUMER SATISFACTION ASSESSMENT

Quality assurance and program monitoring evaluate the functioning of the program from the organization's perspective. However, to evaluate a program

CASE-IN-POINT: IMPLEMENTATION EVALUATION IMPROVES TECHNOLOGY PROGRAM FOR FOSTER CHILDREN

Access to, and comfort with, information technology can be viewed as a form of privilege. Those who have it are advantaged in that they possess skills that are necessary to succeed in today's information society. More specifically, they have access to resources such as employment opportunities, college scholarships, internship opportunities, education and training, news, social commentary, social support, and entertainment that create both financial opportunity and involvement with the larger community.

One group who tends to lack access to technology and technology-related skills is foster children. This problem occurs for a number of reasons. First, foster children are more likely to be part of groups without access to technology—that is, low-income, minority, and single parent. Second, they frequently must overcome barriers such as residential instability, educational discontinuity, and emotional and behavioral problems associated with family disruption. Third, social workers perceive developing the children's technology skills as beyond the scope of their plans for developing independent living skills in foster youth.

Casey Family Services initiated a new program, Building Skills-Building Futures (BSBF), which provided computers and Internet connection to 32 foster families in order to bridge the digital divide. The program model was developed by a steering committee composed of agency administrators, information systems staff, the BSBF project director, foster care workers, foster parents, outside technology and education consultants, and a university-based evaluator. The model included the gift of a computer, printer, software, and Internet connection to each participating family; access to community training for foster family members in how to use the computer and Internet; and the integration of technology into ongoing foster care services through the development of an Information Technology Plan between foster family members and their social worker.

Three months into the program, the CFS evaluator conducted an implementation evaluation of BSBF. Among the questions included in the evaluation were the following: Did family members receive their computer and Internet connection? Were they able to set up and use the computer? To what extent were they actually using the computer? Did family members participate in community-based technology training opportunities? Did families develop an information technology plan? How satisfied were family members with the program thus far? The evaluator gathered information from telephone interviews with foster parents as well as from separate focus groups with foster parents, foster youth, and foster care workers.

Early experiences implementing the BSBF program resulted in changes to the original program model:

- ■ In one case, a new foster family who received the full complement of hardware and software left the program only three months later. The family refused to return the computer. As a result, the administration determined that, in the future, developing information technology plans with families would take place before hardware is installed in their homes. In addition, a family would receive hardware only after serving as a foster family for at least six months to insure that they are committed to the goals of the BSBF program.

- Several participants identified two additional workshops that would have been helpful to enhance computer security: introduction to virus protection software and Internet-filtering software. In response, BSBF provided filtering software to all participating families as well as training in monitoring Internet use by children.
- Fewer than 25 % of family members had made an information technology plan with their social worker. A major reason for this low percentage was that social workers did not believe they could "mandate" that parents and biological children develop a plan. In addition, social workers felt that they did not have the time to focus on technology when they needed to address other, more important issues. As a result, the program model was changed so that only foster children would develop an information technology plan, thus reducing the workload on social workers.
- Social workers' own skill deficits, whether real or perceived, presented another obstacle to integrating the model within ongoing services. Some social workers expressed doubts about their ability to help families develop technology skills due to their own limited knowledge in this area. As a result, the project director, who had extensive experience in information technology, took the lead in developing information technology plans with families. At the same time, she trained the accompanying social workers in the process of creating these plans.
- Finally, interviews with parents revealed that very few had either participated in community training themselves or involved their children in additional training, even though CFS would pay for the training. They claimed that time restrictions, child care needs, and other priorities prevented them from attending training sessions. As a result, the program began to explore other models of training, such as recruiting "computer buddy" volunteers who visit the child in the home and offering training at the agency in conjunction with other family appointments.

Although families expressed a high degree of satisfaction with the BSBF program, implementation evaluation found that the original program model required additional development in several areas: program eligibility, alternate training methods, responsibilities for developing information technology plans, training of social workers to help families develop their technology skills, and outcome goals to include only the foster children and not biological children.

Understanding the need for change early in the program contributed to the satisfaction of participants in the program and helped to overcome some of the initial resistance from social workers.

comprehensively, it is also important to assess the views of the consumers of the services. Research on consumer satisfaction seeks to provide consumers' assessment of the convenience, appropriateness, and outcomes of the services they receive.

Consumer satisfaction is a type of formative evaluation because it does not provide evidence of the actual impact of services on consumers' lives. Rather, it assumes that systems exist to produce specific outcomes and that, to achieve these outcomes, certain attitudes, processes, and services need to be in place.

Consider mental health services as an example. The desired outcomes of mental health services are to reduce symptom distress and help an individual to (a) function on his or her own, (b) improve his or her performance and productivity at work or school, (c) develop a system of natural supports, and (d) gain access to physical healthcare services. To achieve these outcomes, a mental health system must offer a wide range of service choices that are voluntary, easily accessible, culturally appropriate, focused on recovery, and designed to promote consumer inclusion (Kansas Foundation for Medical Care, 2010). Consumer satisfaction research may assess consumer's perceptions of all of these aspects of services. Again, however, it cannot assess how well the services are actually achieving these outcomes.

Often the answer to a question depends on whom we ask. For example, health providers may have a different perspective on the quality and outcomes of their services than the consumers of those services. For this reason, the consumer satisfaction movement has become more prominent in recent years, primarily in the areas of health and mental health. This movement is founded on the belief that the consumer "voice" is an important component in evaluating and improving a system. Consumer groups view themselves as partners in the health and mental health systems. They believe that they should be involved not only in evaluating services but also in developing the actual evaluation methods and tools. Social workers value the empowerment of people who are receiving services, and they can help to facilitate research on consumer satisfaction.

Obtaining the Information

Researchers can obtain consumer satisfaction information by a variety of methods, all of which have strengths and limitations. Some organizations are established specifically to assess consumer satisfaction. They generally conduct surveys based on a random sample of consumers who use the system. Other organizations survey consumers by mail or telephone at the time the consumers terminate services or as part of a quality-review process. More recently, organizations, especially those providing online services, have used the Internet to obtain consumer feedback. Focus groups are also useful when organizations are faced with specific issues about which they want consumer input. Exhibit 5.3 provides an example of consumer satisfaction questions developed by and for mental health consumers.

From a research perspective, information obtained from consumers is only as good as the methods and designs used to obtain it. Evaluators must employ a sampling method that ensures that they select a representative group. If evaluators give a survey only to consumers who complete services and not to consumers who drop out, satisfaction rates will be inflated. Similarly, if they provide surveys that are written only in English and that require a ninth-grade reading level, people who do not speak English and people with lower reading levels will not be represented. Reassuring consumers that their responses will remain anonymous will also help to reduce bias. Participants may worry that their answers will affect the quality of their services if their provider becomes aware of their responses. Collecting complete, valid, and reliable data is the topic of Chapter 10.

EXHIBIT 5.3

Sample Consumer Satisfaction Survey Questions

Consumer Satisfaction Evaluation Questions

1. I know whom to call to ask questions about my HealthChoices plan.
2. I was given the necessary information on how to access other services that I needed.
3. I have a choice in selecting or changing my service provider.
4. I know whom to call if I have a complaint or grievance about my services.
5. I am satisfied with the scheduling of my appointments.
6. Lack of reliable transportation has prevented me from keeping my appointments.
7. My service provider spends sufficient time with me.
8. Program staff respects the role of my ethnic, cultural, and religious background in my recovery/ treatment.
9. I trust my service provider.
10. I feel that I am an equal partner on the treatment team.
11. I was informed of the advantages and disadvantages associated with my therapy or treatment.
12. My treatment promotes recovery.
13. I feel that my service provider and I work together as a team.
14. My service provider focuses on my strengths.

1 = Strongly disagree 2 = Disagree 3 = Neither agree or disagree 4 = Agree 5 = Strongly agree NA = Not applicable

Outcome Evaluation Questions

15. I can deal with daily problems.
16. I'm able to control my life.
17. I'm able to deal with crisis.
18. I like how I feel about myself.
19. I feel optimistic about the future.
20. I enjoy my leisure time.
21. I'm building a social support network.
22. I handle school or work.
23. I can deal with people and situations that used to be a problem.
24. The specific issues or problems that led me to seek services are . . .

1 = Much worse 2 = Worse 3 = About the same 4 = Better 5 = Much better NA = Not Applicable

Source: Finn, 2004, Consumer Satisfaction Consultation Report. Consumer Satisfaction Services, Harrisburg, PA

Evaluators should also consider the consumer's ability to complete a survey. In mental health services, for example, low energy and lack of concentration can make answering a survey difficult. Thus, surveys should be kept short and simple. When necessary, interviewers should assist consumers, for example, by reading the questions to them or writing their responses for them. Finally, the survey results should be made available to consumers, along with an explanation of how the information will be used to improve services.

Understanding the Limitations

Although consumer satisfaction surveys are an important component of formative evaluation, they have certain limitations. We need to understand these limitations when we are interpreting the results. To begin with, as we have discussed, satisfaction is not equivalent to actual changes or outcomes, although we often assume that that they are highly associated. Satisfaction may be related to expectations as much as to actual performance. Assume, for example, that a well-designed survey with a high return rate was given to a sample of mental health consumers in two counties. The results indicated that consumer satisfaction in County A is much higher than in County B. How should we interpret these results? Here are three different but viable conclusions.

- Services are, in fact, better in County A, accounting for higher consumer satisfaction.
- Services are not better in County A, but the culture of county A is one in which people are more likely to say "nice" things.
- Services are not better in County A, but people's expectations of services are lower. Thus, people give high ratings even to mediocre services because the services met or exceeded their low expectations.

You should always interpret satisfaction surveys with caution. Whenever possible, use several measures when you evaluate the quality of services. The following Case-in-Point is another example of how consumer satisfaction can be assessed and analyzed, this time using information technology.

CASE-IN-POINT: POP-UP SURVEY RATES CUSTOMER SATISFACTION WITH RAINN ONLINE SEXUAL ASSAULT HOTLINE

Following an online chat session, those who visit the online sexual assault hotline established by RAINN are asked to evaluate the services they have received. A pop-up survey appears on the screen that asks 5 questions and provides space for comments. Questions are scored on a 5-point scale: 1=Strongly

Disagree, 2=Disagree, 3=Neither Agree or Disagree, 4=Agree, and 5=Strongly Agree. Higher scores indicate stronger agreement and greater satisfaction.

These are the questions:

1. I will use the services recommended by RAINN during my session.
2. I am satisfied with the trained specialist's (counselor's) knowledge and skills.
3. I would recommend the Online Hotline to someone else.
4. The Online Hotline was easy to use.
5. Overall, I am satisfied with this service.
6. Please write any comments you wish to leave about your session.

During one six-month period, the RAINN online hotline received 2,050 completed consumer satisfaction surveys, a 30% response rate. Exhibit 5.4 shows the results.

EXHIBIT 5.4

Results of RAINN Consumer Satisfaction Online Survey

Answer to Question	Mean Rating	Percentage Rating 4 or 5	Percentage Rating 1 or 2
1. I will use recommended services	4.06	76.9	10.4
2. I am satisfied with volunteer's knowledge and skills	4.27	79.6	14.3
3. I would recommend hotline to someone else	4.37	79.6	12.2
4. Hotline was easy to use	4.87	97.8	2.1
5. Overall, I am satisfied	4.31	79.6	10.2

Rating Key:

1 = Strongly Disagree
2 = Disagree
3 = Neither Agree nor Disagree
4 = Agree
5 = Strongly Agree

From these data, a researcher might consider the following:

■ Overall, the program appears successful with a mean of over 4.0 in each category and more than three-fourths of consumers satisfied with all aspects of the service.
■ With a response rate of only 30%, the sample may be biased. How can we increase the response rate?

- More than one in ten consumers are dissatisfied according to the ratings for questions 1, 2, 3, and 5. What factors are associated with low satisfaction? In an anonymous hotline, how can we get information about *why* some consumers are not satisfied?
- The hotline technology (question 4) does not appear to be problematic for users.

The quantitative data cannot answer these questions:

- Are there demographic differences (e.g., age, race, sex) in satisfaction? (No demographic data were collected in order to promote a sense of privacy and confidentiality.)
- What is the impact of RAINN services on consumers? For example, do they actually use the services recommended by RAINN? Do they have a reduction in symptoms such as flashbacks, anxiety, and depression?
- Who fills out the survey? For example, do satisfied consumers fill out the survey whereas dissatisfied consumers ignore the survey?
- Why are some consumers dissatisfied?

Information from the analysis of consumer satisfaction data is reviewed regularly in efforts to improve the program.

PROCESS EVALUATION

Process evaluation is an assessment of the activities performed by the organization and the quality with which the organization delivers these activities. For example, an agency that provides mental health services might collect information about the number of people served, the size of the workers' caseloads, the time between intake and ongoing services, the number of contacts before services are terminated, and the number of people who drop out of services before the goals of the program are reached. Process evaluation helps ensure that both the theoretical model upon which the program is built and the steps that are necessary to carry out the program are implemented as intended.

Because process and outcome evaluations are interrelated, researchers use both methods to test the program's theory of intervention. Unless researchers know whether the program is being delivered as intended, they cannot draw conclusions about the program's ability to achieve its goals.

OUTCOME EVALUATION

After researchers have completed process evaluation, they use **outcome evaluation** to seek evidence that the program has made positive changes in the target population. To accomplish outcome evaluation, researchers must first identify the types of changes that are being sought (a political decision), how these changes would best be measured (a research methods decision), and whether the changes are worth making (a political decision).

In the past, human service agencies could obtain funding and legitimacy for their programs by reporting process evaluation findings such as the number of clients served or the number of units of service delivered. More recently, funding decisions are being made on the basis of the outcome of the program for people and the impact of the program on the larger community. The Government Performance and Results Act of 1993 specifically sought to hold federal agencies accountable for achieving results by setting program goals, measuring program performance against those goals, and reporting publicly on the program's results (Office of Management and Budget, 1993). The emphasis on outcomes has also been adopted by nonprofit organizations and private foundations in making their funding decisions. As a result, evaluation now must include both process and outcome evaluation.

In undertaking an outcome evaluation, the question "Does the program work?" is far too simplistic. A more useful question has multiple components, based on a combination of process, outcome, and cost assessments (see Exhibit 5.5). The components of the larger question include the following:

EXHIBIT 5.5

Components of Process and Outcome Evaluations

Does the Program Work?

Process components	**What services** were provided?
	To whom were the services provided?
Outcome components	**What changes** did the program produce?
	For whom were the changes produced?
	Under what circumstances were the changes produced?
	For how long did the changes last?
	How did the changes compare with changes due to other services or programs?
Cost component	**At what cost** were the changes produced?

- **What Services?** Services may include therapy, support, education, training, access to concrete resources, recreational experiences, changes in environment, or other activities used by social workers to create change. Regardless of the type of intervention, the services must be described, and the evaluation must assess whether the program is being carried out as planned.

- **Provided to Whom?** The targets of the program must be specified. In addition, it is useful to know to whom the program is actually being delivered. For example, a program aimed at adult education is restricted to people over 50 years of age. In this case the demographic characteristics of the program recipients—including age, race, sex, income level, and education—as well as other characteristics that are believed to be relevant to the program outcome (such as severity of difficulty at intake) should be tracked. These data are essential to ensure that the target audience is being reached. Moreover, they enable researchers to generalize the results to the population actually being served.

- **Producing What Changes?** The objectives of the program must be stated in terms of outcomes in the target system and, when possible, the program's impact on the larger community. The extent to which change can be attributed to the influence of the program will depend on the research design (see Chapter 7).

- **For Whom?** Just as demographic and other relevant characteristics can influence who attends a program, they can also affect which people benefit from the program. It is useful to collect and analyze demographic and other information that suggests who has benefited in order to examine the reasons for differences in success and to appropriately generalize the results.

- **Under What Circumstances?** After identifying the individuals or groups who have benefited from the service, the next step is to specify how the program is to be delivered. For example, is the program delivered by professionals or by volunteers? If by professionals, what is their academic degree or theoretical orientation? Is the program delivered in six weeks or in 10 weeks? Is it voluntary or court-mandated? Although the range of circumstances seems infinite, the analysis should focus on those variables that are considered to be important.

- **For How Long?** This question refers to the length of documented changes. Is the program measuring change only at the conclusion of the program? Is change maintained? If so, for how long? Are there follow-up data? This information is useful in determining both the success of the program and appropriate generalizations.

- **Compared to What?** This question focuses on the ability of the research design to establish a cause-and-effect relationship between the program and the outcomes (Chapter 7). Some evaluations do not use comparison or control groups. They are interested only in changes at the end of the program. Therefore, they assume—and not always correctly—that changes are a result of program interventions. Other evaluations are interested in the relative effectiveness of the program compared to a different intervention or to no intervention at all. When programs use random assignment and control groups with reliable and valid measures, they are better able to establish both the effectiveness of the program and the link between the program and its outcomes.

■ **At What Cost?** Human services rely on funding to deliver their programs. Service providers seek to deliver the best services in the most cost-efficient manner. Program evaluation can assist providers in this process, which is described in greater detail in the section on cost evaluation.

Program evaluation can focus on one or any combination of these questions, depending on the needs of the organization, the resources available, and the feasibility of conducting the evaluation.

CASE-IN-POINT: PROGRAM EVALUATION SEEKS TO DETERMINE WHETHER DARE WORKS

Perhaps you are familiar with the program Drug Abuse Resistance Education (DARE). DARE began in Los Angeles in 1983 and has since been adopted in school districts in all 50 states. The DARE program is generally a 17-week curriculum ranging from 45 minutes to 1 hour once a week. It is administered by uniformed police officers that attend classes in fourth through eighth grades to provide information about alcohol, tobacco, and other drugs and to teach strategies for students to resist the use of these drugs. The primary purpose of the program is to prevent substance abuse among youth.

A number of positive outcomes have been attributed to DARE. These outcomes, however, are related specifically to the attitudes and opinions of students, teachers, and parents, rather than to their actual behaviors. For example, an evaluation of DARE in South Carolina with 341 fifth graders in 1989–90 found that after three months the program had improved participants' scores on attitudes toward avoiding substance use, assertiveness, positive peer association, avoiding association with drug using peers, and avoiding alcohol use (Harmon, 1993).

In contrast, however, several studies, especially longitudinal studies of long-term impact, found that DARE had no effect on actual drug or alcohol *use* when equivalent comparison groups or control groups were used. For example, a five-year study of 2,071 students in Kentucky found no significant differences between intervention and comparison schools with respect to cigarette, alcohol, or marijuana use at post-program intervals of either one year or five years (Clayton, Cattarello, & Johnstone, 1996). Similarly, a 10-year follow-up study of 1,000 students in a Midwestern area compared students who had attended DARE at age 10 with students who had not. The study found few differences between the two groups in terms of either actual drug use or attitudes toward drugs. Significantly, in the follow-up, in no case did the DARE group have a more successful outcome than the comparison group (Lynam et al., 1999).

In another study in New Mexico, positive perceptions of a DARE antidrug program among 6th grade and 9th grade students were highly related to attitudes towards the police. In contrast, among high school seniors, perceptions of the DARE program were most closely associated with patterns of drug use. The conclusion was that programs offered in the 5th or 6th grade would help to build a more positive attitude toward police among students; with older students the program should focus on people who are already using illegal substances (LaFree, Birkbeck, & Wilson, 1995).

These results raise a fundamental question: How and why did a program that has been shown to be ineffective or, at best, no more effective than standard education become so popular and widely used? One explanation is that few would argue with the goal of teaching children to refrain from drug use (Lynam et al., 1999). These "feel-good" programs are ones that everyone can support; therefore, few people consider it necessary to critically evaluate their effectiveness.

A second possible explanation is that programs such as DARE *appear* to work. In fact, most children who go through DARE do *not* abuse drugs or become delinquent. What many people fail to realize, however, is that the same conclusion applies to most children who *don't* attend a DARE program.

A final explanation is the tendency of policymakers, practitioners, and the public in general to embrace short-term programs to solve complex social problems. Some experts believe that the public is looking for a *panacea*, a "cure" that is simple, available, effective, and inexpensive. In the case of DARE, the public wants to believe that a little education at an early age by a person in authority will solve the nation's substance abuse problem. Therefore, they avoid examining the outcomes too carefully, lest they discover that their "solution" isn't really solving the problem.

Overall, the results of program evaluations focusing on the effectiveness of DARE are mixed and contradictory. Attitudes change in the short run, but behavior does not change in the long term. A 2004 meta-analysis of the research on DARE concluded that the program was ineffective (West & O'Neal, 2004). These evaluations highlight the importance of asking the broader question: What services, to whom, are effective, for whom, under what circumstance, for how long, compared to what, at what cost? Now, owing to years of research, the new DARE has integrated evidence-based substance abuse prevention strategies into its curricula (Nordrum, 2014).

COST EVALUATION

Funding for human service programs is limited, and organizations compete for these scarce funds. Therefore, service providers must be able to offer evidence that their services are cost-effective in order to make optimal use of funds and to maintain support from funders and the public. A variety of questions are related to cost evaluation: Is this program the most efficient way of delivering the service? What are the benefits and costs of the services? Are the benefits worth the cost? Although financial considerations are not the only reason for making decisions about funding for programs, they are becoming increasingly important.

Three types of cost evaluation are typically conducted:

1. Cost analysis: the costs of delivering the program
2. Cost-effectiveness analysis: the comparative costs of delivering different programs or different levels of the same program
3. Cost/benefit analysis: the cost in relation to quantifiable benefits.

We examine the second and third types of cost evaluation here.

Cost-Effectiveness Analysis

Cost-effectiveness analysis (CEA) estimates the net costs and effects of an intervention compared with some alternative. It assesses the costs of the program per successful outcome.

CEA assesses program outcomes in natural, or nonmonetary, units. For instance, if the program were aimed at preventing premature births, one non-monetary outcome would be the rate of premature births.

A CEA might also compare the costs of two alternative methods of producing the same outcome. This is a form of CEA called **cost minimization analysis**. It is concerned with such questions as, "Is individual or group counseling more cost-effective?" "Is a 12-week program as cost-effective as a 16-week program?"

To compute a cost-effectiveness ratio, you divide the total cost of the program by the success rate. Exhibit 5.6 compares the cost-effectiveness of two

---

EXHIBIT 5.6

Example of Cost-Effectiveness Analysis: Two Men's Domestic Violence Treatment Models

Program A		Program B	
Number of participants:	60	Number of participants:	50
Cost per participant:	$1,000	Cost per participant:	$1,500
Total cost:	$60,000	Total cost:	$75,000
Success rate:	40%	Success rate:	70%
Number of successes:	$60 \times 0.40 = 24$	Number of successes:	$50 \times 0.70 = 35$
Cost-effectiveness:	$60,000/24	Cost-effectiveness:	$75,000/35
	$2,500		**$2,142.85**
	per success		**per success**

programs that use different models to provide treatment groups for men who engage in domestic violence. As you can see, although Program B treats fewer men at a greater total cost, it has greater effectiveness, so its actual cost per successful outcome is lower.

Cost/Benefit Analysis

In contrast to CEA, **cost/benefit analysis (CBA)** expresses all costs and benefits in monetary units. All of the researcher's assumptions and sources must be clearly specified and available for scrutiny in the presentation of the cost/benefit analysis.

For instance, the health care cost of a premature birth is $49,000 (March of Dimes, 2009). This total takes into account all costs over and above the normal birth expenditure of $4,551 for a healthy, full-term baby. To arrive at a cost/benefit analysis of a program to prevent premature births, the researcher would multiply the number of premature births prevented by the health care cost of $44,449 for the total dollars saved by the program. She or he would then subtract this total from the cost of operating the program to arrive at a final cost savings. A benefit/cost ratio can then be computed. If the overall benefit is $44,449 per birth and the cost of the program is $15,000 per birth, the benefit/cost ratio is 44,449/15,000 = 2.96. A ratio greater than 1.0 indicates more benefit than cost. Cost/benefit analysis is increasingly used in decision making regarding the funding of social programs.

THE POLITICAL CONTEXT OF PROGRAM EVALUATION

Program evaluation involves more than methodological decisions. Political decisions focus on the relative value of the goals to be accomplished and the allocation of resources to reach those goals. Politics are also concerned with who makes decisions about how the evaluation will be conducted and how the results of the evaluation will be used. Program evaluation is costly in terms of time and money, and it can lead to political difficulties if the results are not as the organization had wished.

Nevertheless, most organizations routinely evaluate their programs and make the results known to various concerned parties. Clearly, these organizations perceive some value in this process. In this section we will discuss how an organization can benefit politically from an effective program evaluation. We will then explore the political concerns regarding the evaluation process that are common among social workers and administrators.

Participatory Action Research and Evaluation

The question of whom to involve in planning and implementing a program is both philosophical and political. In many cases, professional program evaluators have carried out the evaluation methods described in this chapter without involving the people who are being evaluated, whether those people are agency staff, clients, or other community members. This lack of involvement has sometimes engendered resentment and resistance from the targets of the evaluation and from agency staff who may be needed to assist in data collection. These negative feelings may be due to the belief that the evaluation does not focus on the right outcomes, the evaluation is disruptive and wastes time, and the information from the evaluation will not be shared or will not be of use to the people being evaluated.

Some evaluations include participants in the entire evaluation process. **Participatory action research (PAR)**, sometimes known as **empowerment evaluation**, is the use of research and evaluation concepts, methods, and findings to promote program improvement and self-determination while making conscious efforts to include the subjects of the research or evaluation in the process of research design and selection of outcome criteria. It is based on principles that view research as a means of empowering people and creating social change by creating a partnership between researchers and the people they are studying.

Participatory evaluation is designed to help people help themselves and improve their programs using a form of self-evaluation and reflection. It differs from more traditional evaluation in that the program participants, including administrators, service providers, and people receiving services, serve as a group to conduct their own evaluation. The participants are involved in, and make decisions about, all phases of the evaluation. An evaluator's function in this model is to provide a consultative, facilitative, or coaching role while members of the evaluation team determine for themselves the best way to evaluate the program.

Empowerment evaluation typically involves the group in a number of steps or phases:

1. The group defines and refines the mission of the program. Thus, the final mission statement is produced by a democratic group process rather than imposed by the administration or the history of the organization. For this reason it creates a shared vision and direction.
2. "Taking stock," involves prioritizing and evaluating the organization's current activities and practices. The group generates a list of key activities that are crucial to the functioning of the program. For example, in a parent education program, key activities might include recruiting parents at local

schools, offering parent education classes, providing volunteer telephone support for parents, and maintaining a 24-hour crisis line. The group prioritizes the list of activities by identifying the ones that are most important to evaluate. The evaluator's role is to facilitate this process rather than to predetermine the focus of evaluation. Group members then rate how well the organization is functioning on each activity. These ratings are used to promote a dialogue about the functioning of program activities.

3. The group makes plans for future improvements in the program based on the previous phase of assessment. The group decides on goals and objectives and then selects strategies for achieving them. In addition, it identifies and collects evidence that the program is achieving these objectives.

Participatory evaluation has been used in a variety of social work intervention settings including tribal reservations, inner-city schools, battered women's shelters, adolescent pregnancy prevention programs, and substance abuse prevention programs (The Data Center, 2011).

Benefits of Program Evaluation

Why do organizations evaluate programs? An effective evaluation can benefit the organization in at least five key areas:

■ *Supporting Professional Ethics.* The NASW *Code of Ethics* (5.02) has established standards that govern evaluation and research. These standards define an ethical social worker as one who works in the best interests of his or her clients. This work includes expanding the knowledge base, evaluating the implementation and effectiveness of programs, and using research to improve services.

■ *Influencing Social Policy and Practice.* Hard data from program evaluations document the effectiveness of programs and can influence the development of policy and practice. For example, data from the evaluation of mental hospitals indicated that these facilities were ineffective in treating mental illness. Thus these studies played a large role in establishing deinstitutionalization policies (President's Commission on Mental Health, 1978). In addition, evidence that community-based alternatives were more effective and cost-efficient led to the adoption of community mental health services nationwide. The Program of Assertive Community Treatment (PACT) in Madison, Wisconsin, demonstrated that an intensive approach to the treatment of people with serious mental illnesses using a multidisciplinary team including case managers, a psychiatrist, nurses, social workers, and vocational specialists could provide a "hospital without walls." In addition, well-designed studies demonstrated that assertive community treatment and similar models of intensive case management substantially reduced the use of inpatient services, promoted continuity of outpatient care, reduced time in jail, improved family relationships, and increased residential stability for people with serious mental illnesses (Lehman, 1998; Stein & Test, 1980).

■ *Securing Funding.* We live in a time when evidence-based practice and accountability are rapidly increasing. Social work organizations must fund their services, whether from federal and state programs, nonprofit umbrella organizations, private foundations, or any combination thereof. Good intentions and a history of service are no longer sufficient to guarantee funding. Funders want to see evidence that the services they are financing are effective and efficient, and this evidence must be based on well-designed evaluations. New services are unlikely to be funded without an evaluation plan, and ongoing services will need evaluation data so funders can decide whether to increase or even continue funding.

■ *Improving Program Decision Making.* Social work organizations must constantly make decisions about programs. Decisions might include a response to the following types of questions: Should a program be continued? Would 12 sessions be as effective as 16 sessions for an educational program? Should we hire people with a four-year degree or only MSWs? Do we need additional outreach to minority consumers of agency services? If we begin an after-school program, will community members participate? Should the community initiate a policy of arresting truant youth? Although tradition and politics generally play some role in agency decision making, program evaluation data can and should be used to promote rational decision making about programs. For this process to be conducted properly, the data must be accurate, relevant, available, and correctly interpreted and used. Unlike many research studies, program evaluation can provide continuous information to the organization about the quality and effectiveness of its services in order to promote continuous program improvement.

■ *Promoting Efficient Services.* Social work agencies are obligated to use the most effective and efficient services available to them. To meet this obligation, an organization must document the cost of providing services, provide evidence that it is operating in a cost-effective manner, and document the benefits of its programs. Organizations that meet these goals are more likely to provide effective services, receive and maintain funding, and maintain the goodwill of the general public.

Concerns Related to Program Evaluation

In spite of the many benefits of evaluating programs, some social workers are reluctant to engage in program evaluation for a variety of reasons, including the following:

■ *Evaluation Uses Valuable Time and Resources.* Social workers who oppose program evaluation argue that they do not have time to devote to evaluation because their caseloads are already too great or their waiting lists too long. Collecting data and writing reports take time and resources away from direct services. In addition, workers worry that evaluation will divert already limited funds from providing direct services.

■ *Evaluation Will Harm Clients.* Another major concern of social workers is that evaluation will harm their clients, in several ways. To begin with, some workers worry that clients will perceive filling out evaluation forms and participating in other non-service-based activities as an imposition and a distraction from the actual intervention. In this way, data collection will disrupt the worker-client relationship. A related concern is that the needs of the evaluation will take priority over the needs of the people who are seeking services. For example, a research design may call for random assignment, whereas agency workers would rather assign individual clients to the intervention they think will work best for each client. Finally, some workers express concern about violating client privacy, security, and confidentiality of records when an outsider such as a consultant or a university-based entity is conducting the evaluation.

■ *Evaluation Will Harm Social Workers and the Organization.* In addition to harming clients, evaluation has the potential to embarrass or negatively affect workers, supervisors, and administrators if negative results are made public. In addition, it can have serious political consequences. For example, evaluation data may show that one worker or unit is much more successful with cases than another. If administrators use this information in a heavy-handed way to blame, threaten, or harass the less-successful worker or unit, social workers will soon distrust the evaluation process. The administration also may feel threatened by evaluation, especially one imposed from the outside. Evaluation information can highlight poor agency performance and thus threaten the agency's funding as well as its reputation in the community.

■ *Evaluation Results Cannot Be Trusted.* Political pressures and vested interests may influence who is hired to do the evaluation, what types of data are reported and not reported, which methods are used to obtain data, and how the data are interpreted. In some cases, the administration may report the program evaluation data in ways that put a positive "spin" on the results. At other times, when an administrator wishes to end a program, she or he may interpret data from an outside evaluator in such a way as to justify termination.

All of these concerns are legitimate and should be addressed before an evaluation project is initiated.

Finally, the results of the evaluation should always be used to improve services and not to embarrass or intimidate agency workers. For example, administrators might look for reasons why a worker is unsuccessful. Is the worker's caseload too high? Does the worker need additional training and support? Is this a chance event outside of the worker's usual performance? Is the worker experiencing burnout? Similarly, outside evaluators such as accrediting or funding agencies must use evaluation information constructively with organizations just as with individual workers or units. In general, social workers will support efforts that they perceive as leading to an improvement in agency services, and they will undermine evaluation efforts that appear irrelevant or punitive.

Evaluators should be aware of the political context in which evaluation occurs when they plan evaluation studies. Similarly, social workers should critically examine the political context of the study when they consider the results and conclusions. The following Case-in-Point offers an example of how the political environment can be acknowledged in planning for evaluation.

CASE-IN-POINT: PROGRAM EVALUATOR ADDRESSES POLITICAL CONCERNS IN LARGE-SCALE STUDY OF SEXUAL ABSTINENCE PROGRAM

The Arizona Abstinence Only Education Program was a broadly implemented school initiative. Over a five-year period (1998–2003), the program served approximately 123,000 children in grades 4 through 12, most of them adolescents, in 12 of 15 Arizona counties. At the height of its implementation, the program reached as many as 175 middle and high schools, 42 detention and residential facilities, and 32 community and after-school settings. The program also implemented an extensive media campaign with statewide coverage through radio, television, and non-broadcast forms of advertising such as posters and signs on bus benches.

The 17 program contractors responsible for implementing the program used 14 different curricula with varying emphases. For example, some contractors emphasized the health benefits of abstinence, including the avoidance of sexually transmitted diseases. Others stressed refusal skills and communication, and some provided ancillary services such as youth groups and parent meetings.

The Arizona Abstinence Only Education Program presented many challenges to evaluation. This is how the external evaluator dealt with three of the challenges:

- *Aggregating diverse data.* The program was marked by diversity in target population, program delivery setting, curricula, and supplemental activities. The state believed that creating diverse programs was necessary to respond to the unique needs of local populations and settings. Although diversity was critical to the program's effectiveness, evaluating a diverse program as an aggregate is problematic. Unless the evaluation findings are overly positive or negative, they are likely to appear average when some sites do very well, some are in the middle, and others perform poorly. The evaluator for the program dealt with the diversity issue by designing the program evaluation to describe the operations of each contractor. The analysis was conducted and reported separately for different subgroups, including three age groups and four different settings (parochial versus public schools, detention and residential youths, after-school settings, and public schools). The media campaign was evaluated separately using a statewide telephone survey.
- *Detecting primary prevention results.* It is undoubtedly more difficult to measure the prevention of behavior than its occurrence. In the case of the Arizona program, how does an evaluator measure whether children and youths are abstaining from sexual behavior? And how is it possible to tell whether or not the abstinence program played a role? In addition to asking preteens and teens about their attitudes and intentions regarding abstinence, the evaluator also asked teens whether they had engaged in a continuum of sexual risk behaviors ranging from kissing to intercourse. Perhaps the most innovative strategy used to assess the preventive impact of the program was to match names and birth dates of participants with birth certificate data from the state Department of Vital Statistics. This strategy enabled the evaluator to calculate the number of live birth rates for female program participants and then compare these data with the rates for nonparticipants of the same age.
- *Dealing with sensitivities.* Sex is a sensitive topic for parents and their children. Parents are also sensitive about research in the schools and the use of school time for nonacademic endeavors. In the early days of the program, participant recruitment was a problem because many students were not returning their signed parental consent forms. Once this problem was identified, the school administration changed the parental permission form from active consent to passive consent. Instead of asking parents to sign the permission form to allow their child to participate in the program, the administration required that parents who do *not* want their children to partici-pate to sign the permission form. Switching to the passive consent process increased enrollment numbers. As Chapter 2 explains, passive consent is controversial, but proponents contend that once researchers have made such good-faith efforts as mailings, school meetings, sending forms home with children, and calling parents directly, passive consent is an acceptable method.

Overall these measures were successful in reducing political fallout and allowing the evaluation to be completed with integrity.

CONCLUSION

Social work practice exists in a political context that is strongly influenced by a marketplace mentality. The desire to be of help is not enough to ensure that programs will develop and continue. Programs that do not evaluate their services or that focus only on the number of units of service provided will not convince stakeholders that these services should be continued, no matter how efficiently they are managed. For both ethical and pragmatic reasons, it is essential that social workers present evidence of the effectiveness and benefits of their services. Systematic and research-based evaluation of social programs provides evidence that programs are needed, are operating as intended, and are producing the expected beneficial results.

Program evaluation is directly linked to social work practice by helping to focus services on outcomes for participants, improving practice through ongoing feedback about program processes, and providing evidence that workers are improving the quality of people's lives in the most cost-efficient manner.

Once the program evaluation or other research projects are designed and implemented and the data are collected and analyzed, the evaluator needs to write a report describing the process, results, and conclusions of the study. What should go in a research report and how to present the report to the intended audience is the focus of Chapter 13.

MAIN POINTS

■ A program is a set of activities designed to reach specific objectives. Program evaluation is the use of research methods to answer questions related to planning, evaluating, and improving social work programs. It seeks to answer the broad question: "What services, to whom, are effective, under what circumstances, for whom, compared to what, for how long, at what cost and benefit?"

■ Types of program evaluation include needs assessment, evaluability assessment, implementation evaluation, consumer satisfaction assessment, process evaluation, outcome evaluation, and cost evaluation. All of these types of evaluations use scientifically based research methods.

■ Program evaluation requires that the program goals are consistent with the organizational mission in which the program is housed and that clear goals and specific, measurable objectives are identified.

■ A logic model is a program planning and evaluation tool that charts the linkage between social conditions, specification of goals and objectives, program activities, and program outcomes.

■ Program evaluation always occurs in a political and organization context that can help to facilitate or undermine the evaluation. In reviewing or developing a program evaluation, social workers must consider who is doing the program evaluation, the reasons that an evaluation is being conducted, who stands to gain or lose from the evaluation, the ways the information is used, and who is included in development and ongoing program evaluation efforts.

■ Benefits of conducting program evaluation include compliance with ethical responsibility to use the most effective methods and to provide proof that services are effective; providing information for ongoing program improvement and promoting policy and social change; and improving the opportunities for funding of needed programs. Possible negative effects of program evaluation occur when the evaluation disrupts direct services or reduces resources for services; when management uses information from the program evaluation to threaten workers; and when evaluation results threaten the program's funding or reputation.

EXERCISES

1. Considering the Riverton case, you would like to know if the substance abuse prevention program is changing attitudes and behavior among Riverton community youth.

    a. How will you operationalize substance abuse "attitudes" and "behaviors"? What alternatives exist for how you operationalize these concepts, and how would different decisions influence your evaluation?

    b. What measures would you use in formative/implementation evaluation to be sure the program is being delivered as intended?

    c. What outcome measures would you propose in your evaluation to assess the impact of the program on youth in the program?

    d. What longer-term measures might be used to assess the benefits and costs of the program?

    e. How might you examine participants' satisfaction with their experiences in the program? How might consumer satisfaction be an important measure in this case? How might it not be as valid as other measures?

    f. There are different approaches to addressing youth substance abuse, and these programs have been subjected to various types and degrees of program evaluation. Use the Internet or other sources to find information about the *Scared Straight* program. What outcomes measures were used to evaluate that program? From your findings, would you recommend that your community adopt the *Scared Straight* program? Why or why not?

2. RAINN provides a hotline and online services to individuals who are victims of rape, sexual abuse, and incest. This service delivery model shapes the organizational context in which program evaluation occurs. As you consider how you might approach an evaluation of RAINN's work, think about your beliefs about delivering crisis and other social work services online. Do you believe people would use them instead of face-to-face services? Do you believe they are as effective as in-person services? On what

do you base your beliefs? On what should you base your beliefs? How might you design a research project that takes these views into account, reducing the likelihood that they influence your findings?

3. Use a search engine to locate The California Evidence-Based Clearing-house for Child Welfare on the Internet. Familiarize yourself with what the Clearinghouse does.

   a. Search for programs that you feel might assist any members of the Sanchez family. What makes it appealing to you as a practitioner?

   b. What is the evidence for or against that program? What is the program's overall rating, and how would that encourage or discourage you to use the program?

   c. What alternatives might you explore, and how does evidence about this other project inform your thinking about its applicability?

4. Using the Carla Washburn case, search the peer-reviewed social work literature to find evaluations of programs aimed at helping the elderly with grief and loss.

   a. What type of evaluations do you find?

   b. What are the outcome objectives that are specified in some of the programs?

   c. What activities are engaged in to achieve two of the outcome objectives?

   d. How are the outcome objectives measured? How do the research designs employed compare, and how should these considerations inform your thinking about the findings presented?

5. You wish to create an evaluation for the Hudson City Disaster Response System. Specifically, you are interested in both the outcomes produced and the costs to implement the intervention.

   a. What costs are involved in the program?

   b. What benefits might you expect?

   c. Translate some of the non-monetary benefits into monetary terms. How would you put a value on these other outcomes, and what makes this a difficult exercise?

   d. In a time of disaster, implementation may be compromised. What would you want to look at in an evaluation of the process of implementation of the Hudson City Disaster Response, in order to be sure that you are correctly assessing the outcomes of the plan?

6. Considering the Brickville Youth Leadership Development Group, you attend a community meeting where someone suggests that a program be started in which the police arrest students who are truant and bring them to juvenile hall until their parents come and get them.

   a. What would research-based evidence suggest about the likely outcomes of such a program?

   b. What type of evaluation might you suggest that the community engage in to determine how to address truancy in the community?

7. You are a social worker working in a program that provides housing subsidies to low-income families. There are many people on the waiting list, as the program is perennially under-funded. You see that families who receive the housing support are thriving, and you want more families to get this valuable support. How might you use research to document the effects of this program?

   a. How could you use the existence of the waiting list to strengthen your research design and increase confidence in your findings?

   b. How would you use the NASW Code of Ethics to convince a reluctant supervisor that it is worth the resources, to invest in program evaluation here?

QUALITATIVE RESEARCH

with Dr. Robin Bonifas

Grownups like numbers. When you tell them about a new friend, they never ask questions about what really matters. They never ask: "What does his voice sound like? What games does he like best? Does he collect butterflies?" They ask: "How old is he? How many brothers does he have? How much does he weigh? How much money does his father make?" Only then do they think they know him.
ANTOINE DE SAINT-EXUPÉRY, *THE LITTLE PRINCE*, 1943/2000, P. 10

This chapter introduces students to the qualitative research paradigm. As stated in Chapter 1, qualitative methods stem from the interpretive or narrative tradition and seek to understand the deeper meanings of human experience. Such meanings are best captured with words and images rather than with numbers and counting things as in quantitative research. One could say that the grownups in the quote above are more interested in the outcomes of quantitative research, whereas the narrator is more interested in the outcomes of qualitative research—the knowledge that enables him to better understand the essence of the new friend. This chapter will also present how qualitative and quantitative approaches may be combined to shed light on both of these areas of interest.

Qualitative research methods are highly applicable to social work due to our interest in the nuances of peoples' lives and what it is like to experience certain phenomena, such as living in poverty, leaving an abusive relationship, or coping with multiple sclerosis. Consider the nature of homelessness among gay and lesbian youth as an example of the type of knowledge generated by qualitative research compared to that of quantitative research. Through quantitative research methods, we might learn that there is an association between homelessness and parental rejection of the youths' sexual orientation. This is important and valuable information. Through qualitative research methods, we might learn what this rejection feels like and the range of emotions gay and lesbian youth experience related to their family of origin and life on the street. This too is important and valuable information, but of a completely different nature. Rich descriptions of the lived experience of homeless gay and lesbian youth can help us understand these individuals on a deeper level, generate greater empathy for the challenges they face, and inform the development of micro and macro social work interventions that are appropriately tailored to fit their unique needs, values, and beliefs. Exhibit 6.1 provides another comparison of the results of quantitative and qualitative methods, this time exploring coping in the context of chronic illness. Notice how the participant's comments featured in the qualitative approach section are quoted verbatim and include grammatical errors.

By the end of this chapter, you should be able to

■ Describe the differences between qualitative and quantitative research.
■ Discuss the strengths and limitations of qualitative research and for what types of research questions such methods are appropriate.

EXHIBIT 6.1

Example of Results Generated from Quantitative and Qualitative Research: Chronic Illness in Elderly

Quantitative	Qualitative
What is your level of agreement with the following statement? It is difficult to cope with chronic illness. 1.1 Strongly agree 1.2 Agree 1.3 Neither agree/disagree 1.4 Disagree 1.5 Strongly disagree <u>Results</u>: 85 % of the sample age 80 and over strongly agree that it is difficult to cope with chronic illness.	*"I wish there was some way I could tell you what I feels like. I wouldn't want you or nobody else to be in this bad shape. But how else could you know? I don't feels like myself, but I don't know what happened to me. Like on this beautiful day, this warm day. I don't even belong here on this day. . . . I feels like my life is over, but it won't stop. What I mean to say is my life as I see it is over. You see I can't walk, and I can't hardly see a thing. I can't hardly even get up. I'm just trapped here in a body that ain't even mine."*

Source: Quote from Burnette, 1994, p. 16.

- Distinguish among several types of qualitative research methods.
- Articulate how qualitative research can augment quantitative research and vice versa.
- Describe methods of collecting data in qualitative research.
- Articulate basic techniques for analyzing qualitative data.
- Describe what is meant by rigor in qualitative research and provide suggestions for maximizing the rigor of qualitative studies.

USES FOR QUALITATIVE METHODS

Some social work students are initially attracted to qualitative research because qualitative methods seem easier than quantitative methods, after all there are no numbers so that means no statistics, right? This is not a good rationale for the use of qualitative methods! As we present in the qualitative data analysis section, qualitative methods are not any easier than quantitative methods, and in many ways can be even more challenging due to the voluminous data generated.

What then is a good rationale for employing qualitative methods? When are such methods indicated in research? The answer is simple: When the research question requires it. If, for example, the research question involves comparing outcomes for two different groups—perhaps clients who receive an intervention featuring solution-focused therapy and clients who receive an intervention featuring motivational interviewing—quantitative methods are warranted. If, however, the research question centers on participants' perceptions, impressions, or experiences of involvement in one of those groups, qualitative methods are called for. The following questions are qualitative in nature: *What is it like to experience solution-focused therapy? How do social workers describe the development of a therapeutic alliance when using motivational interviewing?* Morse and Richards (2002) detail five reasons for using qualitative methods:

1. When very little is known about a topic and initial exploration is needed to even begin to know what to study.
2. When understanding is sought regarding a complex situation that is constantly changing.
3. When there is interest in studying participants' reactions to a natural setting or process (as opposed to a laboratory setting) to determine their experience of it, the meaning they ascribe to it, or their interpretation of it.
4. When the goal is to develop new explanatory theory that is grounded in reality or the lived experience.
5. When the research aim is to cultivate a deep understanding of certain human phenomenon.

STRENGTHS OF QUALITATIVE RESEARCH

One of the hallmarks of qualitative research is the rich understanding such methods generate. Burnette's (1994) narrative in Exhibit 6.1 is an example of the depth of knowledge that can stem from this paradigm. Simply incorporating the respondent's grammatical errors provides an additional level of insight into who this person is. A second rich description produced by qualitative methods follows, this time a reaction to the aging process:

> *I have always known her to be strong and to see her allowing herself to become weak, it frightens me . . . just seeing her become sicker, seeing her become forgetful, and seeing that she is really getting older, it frightens the hell out of me.*
> Sheehan & Donorfio, 1999, p. 168.

This quote illustrates both the fear and the sadness that the speaker feels witnessing her mother growing increasingly frail over time. Note that the depth of these emotions could not be captured through quantitative methods, and that the richness provides insight into the aging process far beyond what could be conveyed with numbers reporting the extent of chronic illness or level of physical dependence among this population, or even for this person.

Qualitative methods are also highly flexible in that the data collection is ongoing and occurs simultaneously with data analysis, which allows the research plan to be altered as needed. Initial data analysis may reveal an aspect of a phenomenon that the researcher had not previously considered. Subsequent data collection efforts could then be targeted to shed additional light on that area. As new insights arise, the focus of data collection can change accordingly.

LIMITATIONS OF QUALITATIVE RESEARCH

As rich a method as qualitative research can be, it does come with some criticism. The two main criticisms include its subjectivity and its limited generalizability.

Subjectivity

The results of qualitative research are frequently based on the researcher's interpretation or judgment. Interpretations are by nature highly personal and are influenced by the researcher's own values and individual biases. These criticisms are considered subjectivity and are telling in an era of evidence-based practice.

Given these characteristics, qualitative research findings are not replicable in the same way as quantitative findings. Consider, for example, two qualitative researchers, one with more optimistic tendencies and the other with more pessimistic views, each studying the same phenomenon and even interviewing the same people. It is possible that they may arrive at different conclusions because the interpretive process would be impacted by their dissimilar world views.

It is important to point out that a primary emphasis in designing rigorous qualitative studies is taking steps to minimize researcher bias. Additional detail is provided later in this chapter on how to enhance rigor in qualitative research.

Limited Generalizability

Qualitative research findings typically do not generalize to populations beyond the study sample. This is due in part because of the subjectivity of results, but also because they are so specific to the sample. In the quote presented in Exhibit 6.1, we cannot assume that *all* persons with chronic illness feel the same way as that particular respondent, nor can we surmise that all caregiving daughters witnessing their mothers growing older experience the same emotions as the interviewee in the example. What these findings help us understand on a deeper level is what these experiences *can* be like.

As noted previously in this chapter, qualitative research questions differ from quantitative research questions. Qualitative methods diverge from quantitative methods in other important ways as well. One of the fundamental differences between the two approaches relates to the research purpose. As discussed in greater detail in the next chapter, one of the primary aims of quantitative research is **generalizability**, or being able to apply what is learned from a representative sample to the understanding of a larger population with similar characteristics.

Generalizability is not, however, the aim in qualitative research. The goal in qualitative research is to develop a rich understanding of some aspect of human experience. Consider the qualitative research abstract below.

> *Using grounded theory methodology, this research identified the major themes or meaning systems that caregiving daughters and their aging mothers apply to their caregiving. In depth interviews with 11 mother-daughter pairs explore attitudes toward filial responsibility and actual caregiving experiences.*
> Sheehan & Donorfio, 1999, p. 161

Everything is data

Source: Brigitte Wodicka/ThinkStock

After reading this excerpt, students new to qualitative research typically react negatively, with comments such as "That study is no good; the sample size is too small!" Because qualitative and quantitative research have dissimilar aims, the meaning of sufficient sample size is also different. In qualitative research, because understanding rather than generalizability is the aim, data collection typically continues until no new information emerges. This is termed **saturation** and it occurs with relatively small sample sizes of 30, 20, or even 10 participants. The 11 mother-daughter pairs interviewed above is a perfectly acceptable sample size for qualitative research.

Lest students get overly excited thinking "Wow! That's easy! Eleven interviews and my project is done instead of processing 300 close-ended surveys; this qualitative research is where it's at!"—those eleven in-depth interviews likely generated text for analysis equal in size to several copies of this textbook! The voluminous amount of data can at times seem overwhelming. This brings us to another difference between qualitative and quantitative methods: the nature of the data.

QUALITATIVE DATA COLLECTION

There are many types of qualitative data, which vary depending on the data collection method used. In qualitative social work research there are three primary methods for collecting data: interviews, observation, and review of existing records.

Individual Interviews

An interview in qualitative research is different from an interview in quantitative research. First, the questions used in qualitative interviews do not ask participants to select from a number of predefined responses, as is often the case in quantitative research. Typical questions in qualitative research revolve around how people experience being part of a cultural group or subculture, how they describe or comprehend an experience or an event, and the discovery of regularities and patterns in people's experiences. Attention is given not only to the words the respondent provides in response to interview questions, but also to his or her nonverbal behaviors, including body positioning, facial affect, and emotional tone.

The structured interview protocols characteristic of quantitative approaches and discussed in Chapter 10 are rarely used in qualitative research, rather open or unstructured interviews, semi-structured interviews, standardized open-ended interviews, and informal conversations are employed.

Open or **unstructured interviews** are free-flowing in nature and do not seek to guide the respondents' answers after the initial question has been posed.

Semi-structured interviews are guided by a list of topics and subtopics or broad questions that an interviewer should cover in the interview, but allow the interviewer to modify the sequencing and wording of questions to fit each particular interview situation.

Standardized open-ended interviews consist of pre-developed questions that are worded exactly how they are to be asked in the interview; specific probes are included and may be asked if needed at key points during the interview. Exhibit 6.2 provides an example of a standardized open-ended interview.

Informal conversations are spontaneous interactions between an interviewer and a respondent that occur naturally in an unplanned way during a field observation.

With respondents' permission, qualitative interviews are typically audio-recorded to ensure the data are captured verbatim and can be referred to again and again such that the researcher need not rely on memory. Another benefit of audio-recording is that it allows the interviewer to keep his or her full attention focused on the respondent rather than scribbling notes. Verbatim recording also helps address interviewer bias. Relying on handwritten or word processed notes alone tends to contribute to data inaccuracies in that the interviewer tends to remember interview components that appeal to him or her in some way. Verbatim recordings are usually later transcribed into verbatim text for subsequent analysis, a topic discussed later in this chapter.

EXHIBIT 6.2

Example Standardized Open-Ended Interview Schedule— Research Topic: University Reaction to a Mass Shooting Incident

1. What has been your role in the incident?
2. What has happened since the event that you have been involved in?
3. What has been the effect on the university community of this incident?
4. What larger ramifications, if any, exist from the incident?
5. To whom should we talk to find out more about campus reaction to the incident?

Focus Group Interviews

A special kind of interview popular in qualitative research is the **focus group**. This group interview method typically involves a skilled moderator who interviews about five to 10 people in an environment that is conducive to sharing information. Focus groups are often easier to facilitate than other in-person methods of data collection because they are limited in time and in the number of questions that the interviewer can ask. Researchers generally repeat focus groups with different groupings so that they can identify trends and patterns in the responses.

Although the moderator has a great deal of flexibility in asking follow-up questions and providing clarification and prompts in the focus group, the actual interview questions are carefully predetermined. The majority of the questions are open-ended. The questions are arranged in a logical sequence that contributes to the flow of the discussion by beginning with the more general and proceeding to the specific. Due to the limited amount of time, the number of participants, and the open-ended nature of the questions, the number of predetermined questions is usually restricted to about seven to 12. The number

---

EXHIBIT 6.3

Example of Focus Group Questions

Introduction

Where is everyone from?
How long have you been in Greencourt?

1. What brought you to Greencourt?
2. What is life like for a person who is homeless in Greencourt? (Can you compare it to homeless life in other places?)
3. What are the major challenges you face on a day-to-day basis? What is keeping you homeless?
4. Where do you go to get help with the challenges you face?
5. Do you have any needs that are not being met? (Prioritize your three top needs.)
6. Do you think anyone should be doing something to address these needs? If yes, who (what organization or agency)?
7. What advice would you have for any agencies, organizations, or other groups trying to address the unmet needs of homeless individuals/families in Greencourt? What would a service have to look like in order for you to use it?

of questions will also depend on the time allotted for the group. The interview questions can deal with feelings, attitudes, experiences, and knowledge, but given the public nature of the discussion, the focus group is usually not appropriate for research related to sensitive topics. Exhibit 6.3 is a sample of focus group questions that were used as part of a community needs assessment. The focus group was conducted with single adults who were homeless.

The most important consideration in deciding whether a focus group is the best data collection method for the research is the type of research question being considered. Whereas in-depth interviews, observations, and surveys can be used to answer exploratory, descriptive, and explanatory research questions, focus groups generally are limited to answering exploratory questions. Exhibit 6.4

EXHIBIT 6.4

Guidelines For Using A Focus Group

Respondent characteristics	• Suitable for hard-to-reach populations, from school age onward. • Difficult if participant mobility is a problem and with disabilities that limit successful group participation. • Possible to encourage participation through incentives.
Survey questions and presentation	• Limited number of open-ended, carefully sequenced questions; few closed-ended questions to provide information on demographics and context. • Not suitable for sensitive information considered too personal to share in a group context. • Length will depend on the target group, but the interview generally lasts from one to two hours. • Best suited to exploratory research questions.
Resource requirements	• Comfortable space. • Recording method (field notes, audio recording, flip charts, observation) may require transcript preparation. • Incentives (monetary or otherwise).
Skill requirements	• Skilled facilitator with interviewing and group skills. • Organizational skills to invite participants and arrange space. • Attention to appearance and attending behavior.
Examples of target groups	• Resident subgroups of a community, consumers of a service, employees, members of a professional group, volunteers.

summarizes the conditions for selecting the focus group interview as a method of data collection.

Observation

The advantage of observational research as a means of data collection is summarized in the saying "actions speak louder than words." Observation eliminates the need to rely on participants' self-reports of their behavior and intentions. Observational research also avoids the problems of people providing socially desirable answers and having trouble with recall, which can be present in interview data collection.

Types of Observation

There are two main forms of observational research: pure and participant.

In **pure observation**, the observer remains apart from the group, event, or person being observed. For this reason, pure observation is especially appropriate for use with nonverbal populations like infants. It is also useful for studying behavior across contexts, for example, in the classroom and in the schoolyard. Pure observation also tends to be highly structured in the sense that the researcher begins with a limited number of defined behaviors to be observed within a specified time and location. The researcher can observe behaviors in terms of three characteristics:

1. Their frequency, defined as how often they occur
2. Their duration, meaning how long they last
3. Their magnitude, or intensity

As an example, consider crying as the target behavior. This behavior could be measured by the number of times the individual cried during a defined period, the duration in minutes of each crying spell, or the intensity of the crying.

In **participant observation**, the observer becomes actively involved in the research setting. The degree of participation varies with the context of the research. A researcher may live in a housing project for people with mental illness to gain insight into their daily routines. Alternatively, a person may "hang out" on the street corner talking with men who are homeless to better understand their lives. Participant observation makes use of interviews. The researcher uses interviews in participant observation to clarify and interpret data rather than simply to record the information. Moreover, the interview will vary across participants depending on the topics the participants wish to discuss. Nevertheless, the primary purpose of the interview in observational research is to collect data.

Limits of Observation

Observational research has certain limitations, two of them significant.

- **Reactivity**. What the researcher observes in a specified segment of time is not always an accurate representation of what is typical. In fact, as we explain in Chapter 5, studies have shown that participants sometimes adjust their behavior simply because they know that they are being observed. This problem of reactivity can interfere with accurate measurement. To illustrate by example, a popular measure used in research on parenting programs requires the observer to record within a one-hour home visit the number of times a parent makes eye contact and verbalizes to his or her infant. The problem is that when parents are aware that their parenting behavior is being observed, they may be more attentive than usual to their child.
- **Observer inference**. This refers to the meaning that the observer attributes to what he or she observes. The way an observer explains or understands a behavior, feeling, or attitude may be different from the way that the person being observed experiences it or would report it.

Field Journals

Observations are usually recorded in a field journal. In observation, handwritten or word processed notes are appropriate. Similar to social work documentation in general, the goal is to write journal entries that are both comprehensive and concise. Such journal entries include the researcher's empirical or objective observations and his or her interpretations of those observations. In other words, the researcher documents what he or she sees happening and what he or she thinks is the meaning or reason behind that happening. Using the example of observing crying behavior, a researcher might make the following notation in the field journal:

> _Observation:_ _Infant B noted to be crying loudly for five minutes with bright red face, clenched fists, tightly closed eyes. Sitting on mat in corner of play room with no one else around other than infant H sleeping on back 12 feet away. Room quiet other than Infant B's wailing; cries even more loudly when caregiver G approaches; then abruptly stops, opens eyes, looks up, and lifts arms upward with open palms._

> _Interpretation:_ _Infant B possibly crying due to feelings of isolation as seems excited at sound of Caregiver G's approach and then reaching out for attention while simultaneously stopping crying behavior._

Such field notes are made as soon after an observation as possible to minimize the researcher's potential memory lapses.

Review of Existing Records

Paper and electronic documents, databases, and other nondocument artifacts of human behavior are included in the category of existing records. Research using nondocument sources of existing records such as the analysis of trash are rare in social work. Existing documents are valuable sources of information for social work researchers. We could, for instance, use existing records to answer the question: What are the similarities and differences in how home health social workers describe terminally ill clients relative to non-terminally ill clients in psychosocial assessments?

SAMPLING IN QUALITATIVE RESEARCH

Sampling, the topic of Chapter 8, refers to the activity of selecting entities from which the data will be gathered. As the goal of qualitative research is comprehensive understanding, sampling choices are made with the goal of yielding rich knowledge regarding the phenomenon of interest. For this reason, **purposive sampling,** the intentional selection of **elements** to be included in the sample, is the sampling method of choice. Qualitative researchers may choose the elements they believe are good sources of information, possess varied perspectives or common experiences, or are extreme or deviant. Focus group participants, for example, are selected for the type of perspective the researcher is seeking. Depending on the issue, the researcher might select the participant for his or her age, gender, position, occupation, interests, common experience, or area of residence.

Purposive sampling is sometimes referred to as *expert sampling* because the researchers choose individuals for their special knowledge and not necessarily for their formal training or education. The key to purposive or expert sampling is that selection is intentional and is consistent with the goal of the research. The researcher may be guided in sample selection by his or her judgment or the advice of others.

Choosing a Purposive Sampling Method

There are many sampling techniques useful in qualitative research, which vary depending on the purpose of the study. Consider the 16 potential methods depicted in Exhibit 6.5. Here, however, we will focus on three of the most common types of purposive sampling methods used in qualitative research: snowball, deviant cases, and quota.

EXHIBIT 6.5

Sixteen Purposive Sampling Methods

Type of Purposive Sampling	Description	Rationale
Combination or mixed	Selects sample by multiple methods	Offers triangulation and flexibility, meets multiple interests and needs
Confirming and disconfirming cases	Seeks exceptions, looking for variation	Elaborates on initial analysis
Convenience	Selects participants based on availability	Saves time, money, and effort, but at the expense of completeness and credibility
Criterion	Selects all cases that meet some criterion	Is useful for quality assurance
Critical case	Selects case most germane to research problem	Permits logical generalization and maximum application of information to other cases
Deviant or extreme case	Selects highly unusual manifestation of the phenomenon of interest	Permits understanding of range
Homogeneous	Selects participants who are alike in key characteristic	Focuses, reduces, simplifies, and facilitates group interviewing
Intensity	Selects information-rich cases that manifest the phenomenon intensely but not extremely	Aids in understanding coping mechanisms
Maximum variation	Selects participants who represent as many different characteristics as possible	Documents diverse variations and identifies important common patterns
Opportunistic	Selects participants by following new leads, taking advantage of the unexpected	Provides new insights
Politically important cases	Selects cases on the basis of their visibility to entities with political power	Attracts desired attention or avoids attracting undesired attention

Type of Purposive Sampling	Description	Rationale
Quota	Selects cases from purposeful sample that represent certain subgroups of interest	Illustrates subgroups and facilitates comparisons
Random purposeful	Selects participants at random from purposeful sample that is too large	Adds credibility to sample
Snowball or chain	Selects cases of interest from people who know cases that are information-rich	Useful when gaining access is difficult
Theory-based	Finds examples of a theoretical construct	Elaborates on and examines theoretical construct
Typical case	Selects participants or cases that represent the most common characteristics under study	Highlights what is normal or average

Source: Adapted from Miles and Huberman (1994)

Snowball Sampling

In **snowball sampling**, the researcher asks the initial participants to identify other potential participants until data saturation is achieved. The number of participants builds as each person identifies multiple new potential recruits, thus the term snowball. The researcher can deliberately ask participants to identify potential participants who have divergent ideas or perspectives. In this manner, the researcher can diversify the range of attitudes, behaviors, and other elements represented in the sample. Snowball sampling is useful for locating hard-to-access populations, such as sex workers, persons who are homeless, users of intravenous drugs, or members of gangs. This sampling method is based on the idea that people often know others in situations similar to their own. Snowball samples are limited in generalizability because a common thread unites all participants, and this thread, no matter how extensive, may be unlike others not connected to this group. Note that question 5 in Exhibit 6.2 is designed to generate a snowball sample.

Deviant Cases

Focusing on cases that do not fit the usual pattern and represent the extremes of a phenomenon of interest is referred to as **deviant cases** sampling. Often understanding what is going on at the margins can inform our understanding of the phenomenon as a whole. For example, if your research interest centers on the lived experience of youth in foster care and you surmise that the number of foster care placements influences the nature of the experience, you might want to interview youth who have moved around a lot as well as youth who have moved around very little. Similarly, if you want to learn more about students' impressions of the role teaching style plays in the learning experience, it would be useful to access the perspectives of learners who are performing well and learners who are having greater difficulty.

Quota Sampling

Quota sampling applies to populations that have distinct categories of membership or participation. In this case, qualitative researchers often want to ensure that all subgroups of a larger population are studied. In its least structured form, quota sampling strives to include the voices of all subgroups regardless of the actual size of the subgroup. In its most structured form, quota sampling seeks to represent all subgroups in proportion to their prevalence in the population; quotas for each subgroup are set according to their estimated representation in the population. As an example of these two extremes, consider a study aiming to understand social work students' reaction to online learning.

A less structured quota sample would seek input from bachelor's and master's level students, from female and male students, from older and younger students, from students of color and students not of color, from students focusing on micro practice and those focusing on macro practice. In contrast, a more structured approach would seek input from members of each of these specific subgroups in proportion to the subgroup's size relative to the population. In other words, if 60% of the social work students are MSW students and 40% are BSW students, then 60% of the sample would also be MSW students and 40% would be BSWs. Exhibit 6.6 reviews the process of conducting a structured quota sample.

Accessing Participants

Sampling in qualitative research is not always as easy as just locating some interesting participants and inviting them to participate in your study. Often we must first gain access to potential participants through what is known as a **gatekeeper**—that is, the individuals or groups who are essential in providing access to the research participants. The process of accessing the target participants is called **gaining entry**. The basic considerations in recruitment at this level are much the same regardless of whether the research is qualitative or quantitative.

EXHIBIT 6.6

How To Draw A Quota Sample

1. Identify key variables, and establish discrete categories or subgroups.
2. Determine the representation of each subgroup in the population based on prior knowledge.
3. Establish the desired sample size.
4. Calculate the quotas by multiplying the desired sample size by the proportion of each subgroup.
5. Sample using convenience or snowball sampling until you fill the quotas.

For instance, new parents are invited to participate in the Healthy Families Arizona program in the hospital at the time of birth. Efforts to recruit program participants for research, however, must begin with the Department of Economic Security, which funds the program. From there, researchers must clear their recruitment efforts with the program administrators and ultimately with the hospital administrators who offer the program to the parents.

To succeed in the process of gaining entry the researcher should understand who the gatekeepers are and should strategize as to the best way to approach them, and what messages to communicate to them. The researcher must then anticipate and respond to any barriers to participation.

Strategizing about recruitment at the gatekeeper level involves many of the same considerations that are involved at the participant level. Gatekeepers have to be convinced that the research will produce more benefit than harm, that the participants' rights will not be violated, and that the research will be sensitive to the participants' needs and preferences. The gatekeepers must also be assured that the researcher has adequate skills and resources to carry out the research as described.

In addition to these considerations, gaining entry is a process of building trust. It can be a quick process, or it can take considerable effort over a period of time, depending on the research context. Whatever the specific circumstances, the researcher must nurture those relationships over the life of the research project. This approach will ensure that the relationship will not end once the gatekeepers give their approval to proceed.

COMMON QUALITATIVE METHODS

There are several different qualitative research methods. Four that are especially relevant to social work research are the case study, ethnography, grounded theory, and phenomenology. Each of these methods is discussed below and is reviewed briefly in Exhibit 6.7. Although biography is also a common qualitative method, the four methods highlighted in this section were chosen due to their utility for social work research.

Case Study

A case study is the rich, detailed, and in-depth description and analysis of a single unit or small number of units. The unit may be at any system level: individual, family, group, organization, community, or even the larger social system. Case studies focus on discovering key system elements, such as history, motivation, and worldview, as well as on deriving patterns and processes that explain how the system functions. Case studies appear in the form of narratives of events and descriptions of personalities and situations.

EXHIBIT 6.7

Four Common Qualitative Methods in Social Work Research

Case study: Develops understanding of a phenomenon through in-depth analysis of one or a few single case examples. The case can be an individual, group, organization, or event. The focus is on understanding a single case rather than the entire group of cases.

Ethnography: Focuses on understanding an entire culture or subculture through extensive participant observation. The ethnographer becomes immersed in the culture as an active participant and records extensive field notes. Development of explanatory theory as well as description of processes are the goals of the research.

Grounded theory: Begins with raising broad questions and ends with construction of theoretical concepts and their relationships, clearly linked to the data. Theory development is based on intensive observation and is an iterative process in which the researcher repeatedly observes and then refines the theory.

Phenomenology: Focuses on people's subjective experiences and interpretations of the world. The goal of the researcher is to describe the world from the point of view of the person(s) being studied.

In social work research, case studies often center on individuals or families who seek social work services and document the background, history, environmental context, and reasons for seeking services. Case studies help social workers develop empathy by encouraging them to see the world from the perspective of the person or people being studied. A case study also documents the process of the intervention, using detailed notes and recordings to keep a record of services and to hypothesize the reasons why interventions are, or are not, effective. The goal is to understand the person in his or her environment in order to increase understanding of human behavior and to help develop effective interventions.

Social work researchers can also use case studies for exploratory research when they know little about a phenomenon. A researcher might, for example, use a case study to understand the experiences of *throw-away* teens—homeless teenagers who have been forced to leave home by parents or caregivers. The researcher's goal would be to obtain an in-depth understanding of the motivations, lifestyle, and consequences of being a throw-away teen and the culture in which this phenomenon exists. The researcher would study one teen, or a few teens, in this situation and attempt to understand his or her worldview, needs, motivations, and social niche. This effort might involve in-depth interviews with the teen; the teen's family, friends, and acquaintances; neighbors; school and medical personnel; and the police. In addition, the researcher would carefully document relevant treatment strategies and issues, including engagement strategies, background, assessment, and successes and failures. From this cumulative data, the researcher might develop and test a theory of throw-away teens.

In this context it would be possible to use a case study for explanatory research as well, with the goal to establish cause-and-effect processes and to explain the reasons why things happen the way they do. Social workers could use this material to increase their understanding of and empathy for these teens, to inform intervention efforts, and to provide information that might be useful in prevention campaigns.

Case studies can additionally be utilized to understand larger systems such as organizations and communities. The qualitative methods that researchers use to study larger systems include those presented in this chapter: participant observation, in-depth interviews, informal conversations, and examination of existing documents such as letters and records. The goal of such methods would be to obtain the subjective experiences of individuals in the system and to understand their social construction of the world. Researchers might also collect quantitative data as part of an overall description.

A case study that focuses on a larger system is presented in the following Case-in-Point. It provides insights into the social and cultural dynamics of an inner-city urban neighborhood. As with individual case studies, researchers who are focusing on larger systems generate data through case notes and record-ings. They then analyze the data to develop or test theories, insights, patterns, themes, and processes.

CASE-IN-POINT: CASE STUDY OF INNER-CITY NEIGHBORHOOD ILLUMINATES THE CODE OF THE STREET

Elijah Anderson, in his 1999 book *Code of the Street*, focused on understanding the impact of poverty and lack of opportunity on the everyday life of an urban inner-city neighborhood in Philadelphia. He explained street behavior and why it differs from mainstream culture.

Anderson, a university professor living in Philadelphia, became a "regular" in the neighborhood, spending a great deal of time as a participant observer. Using a combination of purposive, snowball, and convenience sampling, he conducted intensive interviews with a wide range of community members, including "old heads" (elders), families, pregnant teens, students, drug dealers, and store owners. From his interviews and observations, he provided rich detail to support his explanations of the reasons for interpersonal violence, teen pregnancy, crime, drug use, and other social problems of the inner city.

Anderson divided families in the inner city into two broad categories. The first category, "decent" families, adhere to mainstream values. In contrast, "street-oriented" families do not identify with the broader society. Anderson focused on the daily pressures that shape the choices and goals of both types of families.

Regardless of a family's values, everyone must learn the "code of the street." Anderson explains that the code is based on "respect," that is, being treated with the deference one expects based on his or her status in the community. This unwritten set of rules is based largely on an individual's ability to command respect through physical violence or the threat of violence. In addition, every individual must understand when and how to defer to others. The code is a powerful and pervasive form of etiquette that dictates the ways in which people learn to negotiate public spaces. The code of the street is functional. Its purpose is to establish status and reduce violence.

Through narrative examples from interviews and descriptions of daily life, Anderson explains the code as a response to poverty, racial prejudice, alienation, and lack of opportunity. These forces create an economy based on illegal activities and a subculture at odds with mainstream culture. Both stable and street families must learn to negotiate this subculture. He concludes that the causes and solutions to social problems in the inner city are social and economic, not personal.

Code of the Street illustrates many strengths of a case study. It provides detailed accounts of people's motivation, behavior, activities, and responses to their environment in a way that makes them real for the reader. It examines and explains behavior that outsiders may not understand. It uses a flexible research design that could be altered by the needs of the study. The author's choice of who is interviewed about what topics emerges as he begins to understand the community. Finally, the study is based on actual experiences and firsthand accounts, and it is not time-limited. In general, it provides a comprehensive, holistic view of community processes and events.

This study also illustrates the limitations of the case study method. How do we know that this neighborhood is like other inner-city neighborhoods? How much did the author himself, a middle-aged

African American professor, influence the material that he gathered? The author provided money to one respondent as part of their relationship. Might this act have influenced what the respondent told him? How representative are the people Anderson selected for his interviews? Did people respond to Anderson as a professor and a professional person, thus limiting and shaping what they said? Would another researcher of a different age, race, and gender reach similar conclusions?

Ethnography

Ethnography aims to understand an entire culture, subculture, or social group through extensive participant observation. Ethnographers are interested in the patterns of daily living among group members. As such, the researcher immerses him or herself in the culture as an active participant and takes extensive field notes with the goal to develop explanatory theory and descriptions of processes implicit within the culture.

This method stems from cultural anthropology and indeed, the traditional depiction of the anthropologist "becoming one" with an isolated tribal group is an example of classical ethnography. Ethnography is not reserved for the study of culture in the narrowly defined sense of race and ethnicity, but can be utilized to study culture from a broader perspective as well. Culture is defined as the "beliefs, behaviors, norms, attitudes, social arrangements, and forms of expression that form desirable patterns in the lives of members of a community or organization" (LeCompte & Schensul, 1999, p. 21).

Using this broad definition, ethnographic methods can be applied to the study of institutions and groups of people who share similar characteristics. One researcher, for example, studied the culture of nursing assistants working in skilled nursing facilities (Foner, 1995). Other potential cultures include persons who use intravenous drugs, persons awaiting a kidney transplant, parents who home school their children, or even social work students studying research methods.

Data collection using ethnographic methods employs participant observation, in-person interviews, and the collection of materials that help describe the culture. This method requires attention to several issues inherent in fieldwork. For example, gatekeepers are needed to enable the researcher to gain access to the group of interest. In addition, **key informants** are necessary to both provide information relevant to the group's culture and direct the researcher to other individuals likely to provide useful information.

Ethnographers are also highly sensitive to reciprocity and reactivity. **Reciprocity** refers to an interest in giving something back to the group in exchange for the information and insights the group shares. **Reactivity** refers to avoiding change or impact to the group by the researcher's presence during the study. Indeed, while immersing him or herself in a culture of interest, an ethnographic researcher aims to hold two contradictory perspectives at the same time.

1. **Emic** perspective: The researcher tries to adopt the beliefs, attitudes, and points of view shared by the members of the culture being studied.
2. **Etic** perspective: The researcher tries to maintain the objectivity of an outsider and ask questions about the culture that would not occur to members of that culture.

As an example of the emic perspective, Lewinson (2010) examined the coping strategies of individuals living in extended stay hotels while living in one of the hotel rooms herself. She explained how struggling to store favorite food items in her room's tiny refrigerator led her to include questions about food storage in her interview guide: *"While at the hotel, I came to understand how the small freezer in the kitchenette limited my ability to purchase the type of ice cream I wanted because of space considerations. As I listened to other residents' descriptions of the kitchenette space, I was able to identify with comments about limitations in storing frozen foods, and I listened for the commonality of this limitation across each interview"* (p. 183).

Participatory action research (PAR) stems from the ethnographic tradition in that the researcher is deeply engaged in a cultural group of interest. PAR differs from ethnography because rather than studying group members, PAR researchers *partner with* group members to study topics of interest to the group. PAR used in program evaluation is discussed in greater detail in Chapter 5.

Grounded Theory

Grounded theory refers to both a qualitative research tradition and a qualitative data analysis method. As a research tradition, it seeks to generate theory that is "grounded" in data or arises from the data itself rather than being generated a priori based on the researcher's knowledge and experience before data collection has occurred. Theory in this context simply refers to the potential relationships among concepts and sets of concepts within the data that can explain or predict phenomena of interest (Strauss & Corbin, 1998).

Grounded theory is based on symbolic interactionism, or the idea that reality is socially constructed and stems from the relationships and interactions that occur between people; its aim is to uncover this underlying social reality. Given that human interactions are dynamic and, therefore, constantly changing, grounded theory is particularly relevant for studying processes and events that are expected to change over time.

Data gathering methods used in grounded theory include both observation and unstructured interviews or narrative reports. A highlight of the grounded theory approach is the use of **constant comparison** (Strauss & Corbin, 1998):

1. The researcher identifies codes of meaning within the data and combines these codes to form categories.
2. The researcher continually compares subsequent data with those categories to **saturate** the categories, or describe them completely in terms of their **properties** and **dimensions**. Properties are the characteristics of a category or what gives it meaning; dimensions are the range of properties within a category, its extremes and variability

Saturating the categories often means employing a "zigzag" pattern of returning to the field to gather more data to fill out a category's properties and dimensions, analyzing the new data, developing additional insights into the category and returning to the field to learn more (Creswell, 1998). Grounded theory is especially illustrative of simultaneous data collection and analysis typical of qualitative research.

Phenomenology

Phenomenology aims to capture the essence or meaning of the lived experience, or the individual's perception of his or her being in the world. In terms of phenomenology, human behavior is considered in relation to things, people, events, and situations.

In applying phenomenology to a research question, researchers first **bracket** their preconceived notions of a particular phenomenon by documenting their assumptions, knowledge, and expectations about it. The idea is to suspend all judgments about what is "real" because, in the phenomenological tradition, reality can only be understood in the context of the meaning assigned to it by an individual. As with grounded theory above, reality is a socially constructed phenomenon, but phenomenology takes this one step further and asserts reality is not only socially constructed, but personally constructed as well. Indeed, the meaning individuals ascribe to an event or experience is deeply influenced by their own point of view.

Perhaps this complex idea can best be understood through the classic "monster entering the classroom" example: imagine being in one of your social work classrooms with an interesting lecture in progress when all of a sudden a big hairy monster enters the classroom. How might you and your fellow students react? Well, some students might scream, some students might laugh, others might be annoyed, and still others might not even notice. Which one of these reactions constitutes the "real" lived experience of the monster entering the classroom? The answer is, of course, all of them! It depends on each student's individual perception of the meaning underlying the event. Students whose prior experience with monsters labels them as scary creatures, say those who watched a lot of horror films as children, might be more inclined to scream, while those who associated monsters with being rather funny, perhaps from viewing many Looney Tunes or Disney videos, might be more inclined to laugh. Uncovering these underlying meanings or "realities" would be the focus of phenomenological inquiry.

Data are collected for phenomenological research through in-depth interviews of persons who have experienced the phenomenon of interest. Interviews center on the everyday lived experience of such individuals. Example topics of inquiry might be the experience of living with cancer, of being a parent of a child with autism, or the experience of visiting the welfare office.

Combined Research Approaches

Another powerful research approach is the mixed-methods study, introduced previously in Chapter 1. Mixed-methods studies combine both qualitative and quantitative elements and allow for the limitations of one method to be offset by the benefits of the other. A project may, for example, begin with a qualitative component that explores the lived experience of a given phenomenon. The project may then culminate with a quantitative component that identifies the distribution of that phenomenon and measures various aspects of its characteristics, with the goal of further describing the phenomenon. Alternatively, a research study may initially comprise a quantitative component that generates unexpected or puzzling findings, which are then explored more in-depth via a qualitative approach (Morse & Richards, 2002). Creswell, Plano-Clark, Gutmann, and Hanson (2003), drawing on the work of Steckler, McLeRoy, Goodman, Bird, and McCormick (1992), present four models of how qualitative and quantitative approaches can be combined depending on the aim of the research: (1) qualitative methods are used to develop quantitative measures and instruments; (2) qualitative methods are used to embellish a primarily quantitative study; (3) qualitative methods are used to help explain quantitative findings; and (4) qualitative and quantitative methods are used equally and in parallel (p. 167). For example, Gao (2015) used a qualitative approach consistent with model 1 to identify definitions of elder mistreatment among older Chinese Americans, which were then used to guide quantitative data collection instruments.

In social work research, case studies and quantitative research often complement each other. Researchers use case studies to develop theories and share new methods while using quantitative methods to test hypotheses derived from these theories and to test generalizations. Quantitative methods often show the extent of a problem in numerical terms, while qualitative methods show the true human impact in an emotionally powerful way. Researchers often use this combination of quantitative and qualitative data in writing grant proposals for the funding of human service needs.

The following Case-in-Point illustrates how two social work researchers used both methods to study a political development in Ohio that had consequences for social policy. An additional example of a mixed-methods approach to program evaluation is featured in Chapter 5.

CASE-IN-POINT: EXAMPLE MIXED-METHODS APPROACH

Through case study research, Janenne Allen and Richard Boettcher (Allen & Boettcher, 2000) described two attempts to pass a tax levy that would be used to fund the majority of mental health and alcohol and drug treatment services in Franklin County, Ohio. The first attempt to pass the tax failed. The second attempt saw the tax pass by an overwhelming margin. The research question addressed by this case study could be characterized as "How can social workers promote a successful tax campaign to ensure the funding of mental health services?"

Allen was a participant in the second campaign. She describes herself as "an informal, behind-the-scenes liaison among the providers, the Board, and the political professionals." This role enabled her to outline in a comprehensive manner multiple perspectives on why the first attempt failed and to describe in detail the processes put into place for the second campaign. Allen and Boettcher's article offers two especially useful pieces of learning for social workers confronted with a similar problem:

- The authors explain both campaigns in reference to theories of community practice. For instance, they discuss theories on coalition building, conflict management, and influence in relation to the campaign. Thus, the reader knows not only what was done, but why.
- The authors present detailed data on fund-raising and expenditures for the second, successful campaign. This material makes the political process more transparent. In addition, it allows social workers and other activists to replicate or adapt the authors' strategies to a different setting.

This study is an example of the power of combining qualitative and quantitative data. The qualitative data used in the case study include observations, the researchers' perceptions, and the findings of a focus group. In addition to the specific information about income and expenditures, the quantitative data presented in the case study include the findings from polls that were used to shape the message to the voting public. For instance, Allen and Boettcher write:

> It was clear from the previous election and from polling that 40 % of the voters were solidly against the levy, no matter what messages they heard during the campaign. Another 40 % were solidly for the levy at the outset. The persuadable 20 % tended to be Republican and politically Independent women. . . . It was essential to victory that most of the campaign efforts and dollars be pitched to this 20 %.
> (p. 33)

Case study research, as this example illustrates, is a form of qualitative research in that it is holistic. However, this fact does not preclude the use of quantitative data. Without the combination of qualitative and quantitative data, the researchers would not have been as successful in describing the efforts to pass the tax levy.

DATA ANALYSIS AND RESULTS REPORTING IN QUALITATIVE RESEARCH

There are many types of qualitative research, each with a different purpose and focus of inquiry. However, similarities exist across the qualitative traditions regarding how the data are prepared and analyzed. Perhaps the most basic feature common to qualitative data is that they tend to be in the form of words. The words can appear in various formats, including written documents such as letters, spoken and recorded words from interviews, and observational notes written by the researcher.

Qualitative data are also quite lengthy. One 60-minute interview can generate as much as 20 pages of text, making the qualitative researcher feel a little like the man shown on p. 156. Here is an eloquent description of that tendency:

> The data generated by qualitative methods are quite voluminous. I have found no way of preparing students for the sheer massive volumes of information with which they find themselves confronted when data collection has ended. Sitting down to make sense out of the pages of interviews and whole files of field notes can be overwhelming.
> (Patton, 1980, p. 297)

This section describes how to handle such enormous amounts of data by first preparing the data for analysis, conducting the analysis itself, and reporting the findings.

Preparing the Data

Qualitative data have to be processed before they can be analyzed. If the data are from an interview or handwritten notes, it is useful to transcribe or transfer them into a word processing program. Transcription takes time, so the researcher should plan for a ratio of approximately 1:3: one hour of recording will require about three hours of transcription. Transcription is a budget item that the social work researcher should not overlook. Transcription can also involve equipment and software costs or perhaps the expense of hiring someone to do the transcription.

Even if the researcher who collected the data employs others to assist with the transcription, he or she must spend time reviewing and editing the transcript for errors. For example, in a recent qualitative study, a participant referred to Arizona's Medicaid program, the Arizona Health Care Cost Containment System, which is commonly known as AHCCCS and pronounced "access." The person transcribing the interview wrote, "I didn't know if I was approached because I had access." The transcription was not consistent with what the participant intended, which was, "I didn't know if I was approached because I had AHCCCS." Checking for errors as the data is being prepared for analysis is important in qualitative research.

The transcript of an in-depth interview or participant observation may include what was said, what was observed, and the researcher's thoughts and reflections. These three different types of information must be kept distinct from one another. The researcher can use labeling for this purpose. Additionally, if there was more than one person being observed, it may be necessary to know who said or did what. Assigning each person a brief identifier can make this task manageable. The researcher can use a simple system like A, B, C or something more descriptive such as Mum, Dad, and Grandma. In most cases, confidentiality concerns are the same in qualitative research as in quantitative research.

A key issue that arises when researchers prepare to analyze data is whether or not to use qualitative analysis software. Many computer-assisted qualitative data analysis software (CAQDAS) programs are available, and all have strengths and limitations and can perform different functions. Some CAQDAS can be used with graphics, audio, and video sources in addition to text. Two main questions researchers will need to answer are: Should I use a CAQDAS program, and what program would best suit my needs?

Most CAQDAS programs have online tutorials that allow exploration of the software's functionality. For information about programs, researchers can consult published reviews in books, articles, and online commentaries for help in choosing the program that will best meet their needs and budget.

Keep in mind that CAQDAS programs aid in analysis, but they cannot *perform* analysis. The researcher must provide the guidance, while the computer makes the process less manual. In addition, these programs cost money and require time to learn. The researcher must decide whether the investment in time and money, as well as the potential benefits, are justified given the scope of the research and whether the researcher will have additional use for the software in the future.

Analyzing the Data

The analysis of qualitative data is very different from the analysis of quantitative data. In quantitative research, when all necessary data have been collected from the selected sample, the researcher proceeds with numerical data analysis (Chapters 11 and 12) to reach the end point of reporting the findings. In qualitative data analysis, however, data collection and data analysis occur simultaneously. To state this another way, in quantitative research, data analysis and reporting are the final stage of the research process, but in qualitative research, data analysis is an iterative process. This process consists of data collection, concurrent data analysis, and purposive collection of additional data. For example, Westerfelt (2004) conducted a study of how faithfully a group of men infected with HIV adhered to their treatment schedules. Westerfelt describes the iterative process of data collection and analysis:

> *I attempted to offset any bias on my part (that is, hearing only what was most important to me) by including another note taker and conducting three focus groups, modifying the interview guide after each group for inclusion of the new areas of inquiry that emerged.*
> (p. 233)

Qualitative analysis also differs from quantitative analysis in its treatment of **outliers**. Whereas outliers are problematic—and sometimes excluded—when quantitative data is analyzed, when conducting qualitative research, researchers often specifically look for outliers to make the research inclusive and holistic as opposed to reductionist.

Not only are there different methods of qualitative research, there are also many different approaches to analyzing qualitative data. The researcher's task is to take a large amount of raw data, usually in the form of text, and condense it into something that is manageable without sacrificing meaning. There is no one right way to analyze qualitative data. The lack of a clear procedure for analyzing qualitative data does not imply, however, that this process is haphazard, unsystematic, or purely subjective. In fact, good qualitative analysis does follow a systematic process and there are guidelines for enhancing analytic rigor and the validity of the subsequent findings. Whatever process is utilized, this should be made clear when the results of the study are reported.

Our goal in this section is to present an overview of some of the major steps that are common in qualitative data. The process we present includes four steps: (1) organizing the data into concepts, (2) developing the story, (3) maximizing rigor by validating conclusions, and (4) reporting the findings. To illustrate the process, we present examples from two published studies. The first is Alex Westerfelt's (2004) study of men who are HIV positive. The second is a study by Susan Saltzburg (2004) of the responses of parents upon first learning that their adolescent child is gay or lesbian.

Organizing the Data into Concepts

By the time the researcher has prepared the data for analysis by transcribing interviews and compiling observations and field notes, his or her first task is to read through the entire collection of data. This is an important part of the analysis, and it can lead to different perspectives from those the researcher adopted when he or she considered the data piece by piece. As the researcher progresses through the data, he or she will note that some data have nothing to do with the research question and other data are not particularly relevant. This is the beginning of process known as **data reduction**.

During data collection and preliminary analysis, the researcher made theoretical notes that included his or her thoughts about what the data meant, potential themes and concepts that seemed to emerge from the data, and additional questions. Now that the researcher has had a chance to consider the full text, including these notes, he or she can begin to identify concepts in the data, fitting them into categories. These concepts may or may not be consistent with those developed earlier. Nevertheless, the initial thoughts provide a good starting place. This process is described as follows by Westerfelt (2004):

> I undertook a general thematic analysis, repeatedly reviewing both sets of notes [his and those of a graduate student assistant] to categorize recurring topics. These topics were further modified, adding others and grouping related categories together.
>
> (p. 233)

Once the researcher has selected the relevant categories, he or she begins coding the data. **Coding** is a method of categorizing qualitative data to make it manageable for analysis. Note that not all methods of qualitative data analysis involve coding, but many do. There are two potential types of coding:

1. **Theoretical coding**, also called hypothesis-driven coding, is used when the researcher has an underlying theory in mind regarding the themes present in the data. For example, based on an in-depth literature review or previous research, an investigator studying job satisfaction among social workers might surmise that key categories associated with this construct are quality of client contact, recognition and appreciation of effort, and coworker relationships. Knowing this, the researcher might then analyze the data attending specifically to how the data relates to those categories.

2. **Open coding** does not assume an underlying theory ahead of time. In open coding, categories are allowed to emerge from the data itself. For example, Bonifas (2015) used research participants' own phrase "knowing your residents" as a code to assign meaning to nursing home social workers' descriptions of the importance of being familiar with residents' personal histories and preferences in developing effective psychosocial interventions. This is considered an open code because it stems from the data itself rather than any existing knowledge. As you may surmise, open coding stems from the grounded theory tradition.

In coding, the researcher marks portions of the text, notes included, with labels to indicate data that fit with the identified categories. This involves going through the data line-by-line and circling, underlining, or highlighting key words or sentences that stand out as meaningful or interesting relative to identified categories. Next to the indicated words or sentences, the researcher then writes brief comments that provide insight into the importance of those elements.

Researchers should keep a running log of their in-depth thoughts, concerns, questions, and ideas about certain concepts that stand out during the coding process; this is known as **memoing**. Coding and memoing can be accomplished manually or with the assistance of CAQDAS as discussed previously. In terms of the characteristics of codes, both first-level codes and related subcodes are typically utilized. For instance, in qualitative observations of the parent-toddler relationship, first-level codes might include attachment,

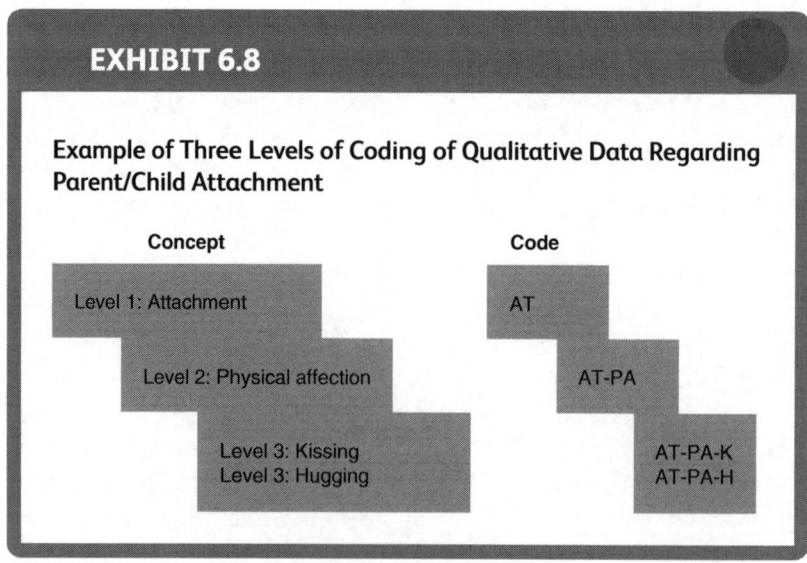

EXHIBIT 6.8

Example of Three Levels of Coding of Qualitative Data Regarding Parent/Child Attachment

Concept	Code
Level 1: Attachment	AT
Level 2: Physical affection	AT-PA
Level 3: Kissing Level 3: Hugging	AT-PA-K AT-PA-H

discipline, play, and education. Subcodes within the category of attachment might include observations of physical affection such as kissing, hugging, and touching. The researcher records the codes and their meanings on a master list that organizes them by the different levels. Exhibit 6.8 illustrates three levels of coding for the category of parent-child attachment that could be used to mark text.

Coding is an iterative process. The researcher works through the text and refines the coding system, adding new categories and codes as required. The researcher must be aware of the different perspectives in the data and include them in the coding. Specifically, the etic perspective is that of the researcher, whereas the emic perspective offers the insight of the participant. It is important that the emic perspective be considered in the analysis, along with that of the researcher.

When the researcher has completed coding, she or he can reduce the data by extracting coded segments and organizing them by code. The researcher typically accomplishes this task through indexing the codes as to their location in the data so that the appropriate text can physically be brought together, compared, and summarized. Using a qualitative analysis software program makes the extraction of text an easier task. The researcher can also use the copy and paste functions of a word processing program. Finally, the researcher can extract segments manually by literally cutting the text apart and organizing it by code.

Qualitative research is generally an inductive process, meaning that the researcher identifies categories and codes while collecting and analyzing data. Coding allows the researcher to move from raw data to the generation of concepts and theories. This approach is different from a deductive process that begins with a theory or framework and examines the data for the major concepts that are consistent with that theory or framework.

Developing the Story

The researcher engaged in the process of coding the data must constantly question how the emerging patterns or themes in the data relate to the initial research question. She or he will look for deviations from the themes in the data, areas of disagreement, and contrast. When the researcher finds contrasting data, she or he will search to identify the factors that can help explain the deviations. At times this may mean returning to the field for additional data collection.

A helpful tool in moving from data coding to the development of conclusions is to organize the categories, themes, and patterns into **data displays**. These can take many forms, but their basic purpose is to help the researcher describe and explain visually how the concepts in the data are linked. The data display further reduces the amount of text, making the task of drawing conclusions more manageable. A data display can take the form of a role-ordered matrix with defined rows and columns, like the one in Exhibit 6.9, or it may map the relationships among concepts, as depicted in the concept map in Exhibit 6.10. Alternatively, the chronology of a process, the steps involved in decision making, or a typology might also be presented. Data displays are limited only by the creativity of the researcher.

As with analyzing qualitative data in general, designing a data display is an iterative process. The researcher moves back and forth between the display and the data, revising and testing to see if the display fits for all of the data. When the researcher finds contrasting data, he or she must revise the display. As in

EXHIBIT 6.9

Role-Oriented Data Display to Illustrate Perception of the Implementation of a New Foster Care Training Curriculum

Role		Anticipated Impact of Change	Perceived Role in Change	Perceived Preparedness for Change	Perceptions of External Support for Change	+ OR − Perception of Change
Administrator	Olivia					
	David					
	Kelly					
Case manager	Cowden					
	Terry					
	Alonso					
	Karina					
Foster care training personnel	AVC					
	Shalom					
	Pasqua					
	Delaney					
Foster parent	Mum J.					
	Dad C.					
	Mum I.					
	Mum T.					

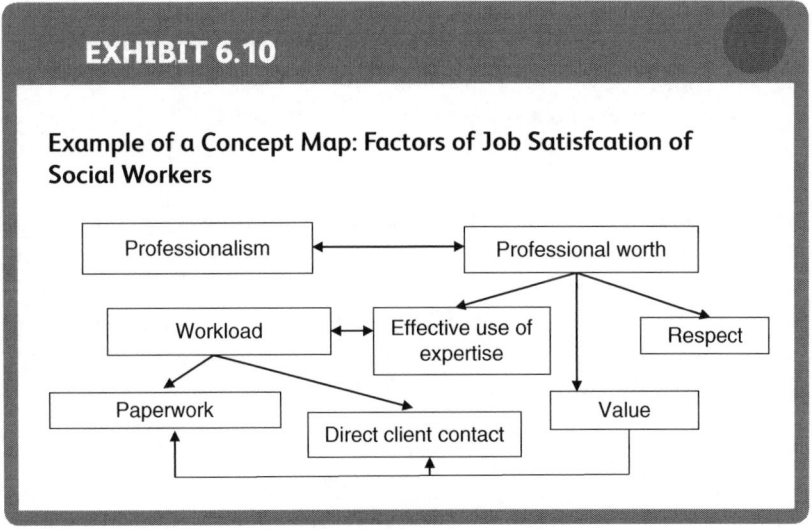

EXHIBIT 6.10

Example of a Concept Map: Factors of Job Satisfcation of Social Workers

quantitative analysis, the researcher must note the decision rules governing the design of the display for later reference and reporting.

As the reviewer refines the data displays, he or she inevitably observes patterns and themes, exceptions, and consistencies. Based on these observations, the researcher begins to draw conclusions that he or she must explain in writing. Conclusions do more than summarize the data. Rather, they can involve rich descriptions with interpretations, theories, and questions and hypotheses for further research. At the same time, however, the researcher must be careful to avoid generalizing beyond the data. He or she should always check any conclusions against the original full-text data. If the conclusions do not fit with a subsequent reading of the data, they will need to be revised. Once the conclusions fit with the data, yet another layer of validation will occur. Susan Saltzburg (2004) effectively describes this process:

> *The steps for analysis include transcribing texts, discerning themes, reflecting on variations of meaning, translating to social work language, moving back and forth between the individual protocols (that is, interviews) to ensure that a structure emerging in one was not overlooked in another, and finally synthesizing the themes into the phenomenological summary.*
> (p. 112)

Maximizing Rigor by Validating the Conclusions

The process of validating conclusions involves judging whether the conclusions that have emerged from the analysis are credible, defensible, and able to withstand alternative explanations. Researchers use numerous methods to validate the conclusions of qualitative data analysis. Here we discuss six of these methods: (1) triangulation, (2) respondent validation, (3) an explicit account of the data collection and analysis methods, (4) reflexivity, (5) attention to negative cases, and (6) the audit trail.

1. **Triangulation** is the process of making comparisons among the results from different methods of data collection or different sources. For example, the researcher could compare the results obtained from observations to those obtained from interviews. Similarly, she or he could compare the results from a group of homeless individuals to the accounts of staff members at the homeless shelters.

2. **Respondent validation**, or **member checking**, as it is often referred to, involves reviewing the results of the data analysis with the participants of the research. For example, Lewinson (2010) in her qualitative study of coping strategies used by individuals residing in extended-stay hotels describes "intermittently checked preliminary and emergent interpretations with participants at the hotel to confirm [her] understanding of the information collected" (p. 184). In respondent validation, the participants' reactions may be included in the report of the findings. This strategy is common in participatory action research, discussed in Chapter 5.

3. **Explicit accounting of the methods for data collection and analysis** allows other researchers to validate the claims of the study. If the researcher coded the data, he or she must explain how the early coding was refined. Were some of the transcripts coded by an independent researcher and compared for reliability? How did the researcher create the data displays? How did the researcher structure additional data collection efforts based on the findings from the preliminary analysis? These are only some of the questions the results section of the research report should answer. The following excerpt from Bonifas, Simons, Biel, and Kramer (2014) illustrates how the researchers describe their analysis procedure.

    > *Coding began with the principal investigator, who established the preliminary codebook. Then two additional research team members examined the coded data, revised the codes, and added new codes based on separate reviews. All three team members reviewed coding results a final time and made conjoint modifications to achieve consensus. . .Codes were grouped into subthemes and overarching themes based on content similarities and differences.* (p. 1325)

4. **Reflexivity** refers to the researcher's own reflections on how she or he might have directly impacted the research process, including the

conclusions. Here, the researcher must take into account such factors as her or his age, gender, ethnicity, economic background, and profession as well as any relevant personal experiences. Reflexivity should be ongoing throughout the qualitative research process and should be addressed in the research report.

5. **Attention to negative cases** involves the provision of evidence that the researcher explored data that seemed to contradict her or his conclusions, sought cases that differed from the norm, and considered rival explanations for the findings.

6. **Auditing** is a procedure in which an independent third party reviews the evidence of data collection in qualitative research. For instance, in relation to in-depth interviews, the audit trail could include the interview guides, audiotapes or videotapes, transcripts, list of participants, and the researcher's notes regarding the data collection procedures. Although auditing occurs after the study is completed, it must be planned in advance. Moreover, even if the audit does not occur, the researcher should keep the evidence available in the event that questions arise concerning the credibility of the study.

Reporting the Findings

Whereas the style of writing required for reporting quantitative analysis is highly technical, qualitative analysis can be presented in a more literary style. In fact, the researcher often uses the first person ("I"). Nevertheless, qualitative research sometimes reports statistical information as well, especially to describe the sample. Zayas, Wisniewski, and Kennedy (2013), for example, report, "Overall, men and women were approximately equally represented, mean age was 76.2, 38 had an 8th grade education or less, 33 had annual household income of \$15,000 or less, and all had healthcare insurance coverage, primarily Medicare, Medicaid, or both" (p. 1791). The descriptions of the methods of analysis and the results are not as distinct in the qualitative research report as they are in the quantitative research report. In the qualitative report, the researcher will want to clearly explain her or his esoteric approach to the analysis. She or he also will likely present the data display or a revised version of it.

One of the most distinguishing features of the qualitative research report is that the author intersperses quotes both to illustrate and to support the conclusions and to reflect the voices of the participants. In the Saltzburg example, the author discovered five common themes in her analysis. She used the themes as headings in writing her manuscript, and she provided quotes to illustrate each one. Although she includes verbatim quotes, Saltzburg is careful to protect the identity of the participants by labeling each with a title and a letter such as

"Mother M" or "Mother J." An effective use of presenting quotes is found in the following excerpt from Saltzburg (2004), under the heading "Emotional Detachment."

> *I can't stop the thoughts I have about homosexuality. This is what I've learned and what I believe. And now these apply to my child. It's awful to have these thoughts about one of your children. And I think that is what the depression and drinking was about. I felt so torn by all the awful thoughts I had about the child I loved. And I shut down from her and felt so empty." (Mother M)*
> (p. 113)

In drawing a conclusion, the researcher should note for what proportion of the sample the conclusion applied. For example, Saltzburg reports, "Whereas all of the parents spoke about feeling stunned by the finality of their adolescent's disclosure, five alluded to a level of semiconscious awareness that they believed existed as far back as childhood" (p. 112). At the same time, however, the researcher must be careful not to turn the qualitative report into a quantitative study by reporting the frequency of occurrence for each coded segment of participant data.

The way in which the report is written will depend to a great extent on the qualitative method. Case studies, for example, are intended to provide a holistic view of a subgroup, organization, or other single entity. Ethnography describes the culture of a group. Grounded theory aims at explaining a phenomenon. Phenomenology strives to capture the meaning of an event or experience. Whatever the qualitative method, the most important evaluative question for judging the qualitative report will be: Did the findings fulfill the intended purpose of the research?

Qualitative Content Analysis is a common approach used to analyze text in social work research, especially text associated with interviews and focus groups, although the method can also be applied to analysis of existing records. The process of qualitative content analysis incorporates the four steps described above, with emphasis on classifying textual data by assigning codes to related elements to identify underlying themes or patterns (Hsieh & Shannon, 2005). Qualitative content analysis may be *inductive*, whereby codes arise from the data itself, or *deductive*, whereby codes are assigned based on pre-existing knowledge derived from prior research or theory (Elo & Kyngäs, 2008). Inductive content analysis is used when little is known about a phenomenon, or when what is known is not well-integrated, whereas deductive content analysis is used when the research aim is theory-testing based on existing knowledge.

Inductive content analysis proceeds using the following steps: (1) open coding the text; (2) grouping codes into subcategories based on similarity and

EXHIBIT 6.11

Example of Themes, Categories, and Codes

Assessment Approaches	Intervention Approaches	Collaborative Strategies
Gathering information	**Determining appropriate interventions**	**Consultation to determine triggers**
1. Careful investigation	1. Ad hoc communication following incidents	1. Ad hoc individual interviews with other discipline
2. Ad hoc individual interviews	2. Planned team meetings	2. Planned team meetings
3. Witness statements	3. Incorporating strengths-based framework	3. Active review of other disciplines' documentation
4. Planned team discussion	4. Incorporating person-centered framework	**Intervention planning**
Knowledge of causal factors to rule out	5. Differential approaches for dementia versus non-dementia	1. Sharing knowledge about residents' needs and preferences with other disciplines
1. Physical factors	**Preventive approaches**	2. Planned team-based discussions to develop plan of care collaboratively with other disciplines
2. Psychological factors	1. Preadmission screening	**Collaborative intervention delivery**
3. Environmental factors	2. Setting the tone	1. Care coordination with other discipline
4. Past triggers	3. Thoughtful roommate assignments	2. Synchronous or asynchronous intervention by each discipline
Determining psychosocial impact	4. "Know your residents"	3. Collaboratively evaluating intervention effectiveness
1. Follow-up visits	**Psychosocial interventions**	**Capitalizing on professional strengths**
2. Staff perception	1. Room changes	1. Social worker's role
3. Observation	2. Behavioral contracts	2. Nurse's role
4. Monitor changes	3. Procedures for extreme situations	3. Reciprocal roles
	4. Liaison with families	**Barriers to collaboration**
	5. Supportive counseling to minimize psychosocial harm	1. Social workers inconsistently notified of RRA incidents
	6. Negotiating roommate difficulties	2. CNAs not positioned to share knowledge of residents' needs or effective approaches
	7. Facilitating support groups	
	8. Monitoring adjustment to change	

Source: Bonifas, Simons, Biel, and Kramer (2014), unpublished table informing results discussion in Bonifas, R. P. (2015). Resident-to-resident aggression in nursing homes: Social worker involvement and collaboration with nursing colleagues. *Health and Social Work.* DOI: 10.1093/hsw/hlv040

dissimilarity, and (3) abstracting subcategories into higher-level main categories (Elo & Kyngäs, 2008). Deductive content analysis, on the other hand, begins with creating a categorization matrix based on existing knowledge or theory and then coding proceeds based on the pre-identified categories (Elo & Kyngäs, 2008). New categories may be added if themes emerge that do not fit existing theory. In this way, results of deductive content analysis can help expand or modify existing theories to fit knew understandings of phenomena. The goal of both approaches is to systematically determine the meaning of textual data generated from participant interviews, focus groups, or other qualitative data collection methods.

Results of qualitative content analysis are often presented in terms of the number of identified themes, subthemes, and associated codes followed by a rich description of the nature of each theme with key participant quotes to illustrate key concepts. Exhibit 6.11 provides an example of a display depicting the codes, categories, and themes generated by qualitative content analysis in a qualitative study of collaboration between social workers and nurses in addressing aggression between nursing home residents (Bonifas, 2015).

CONCLUSION

This chapter has focused on qualitative research, a collection of approaches that support the in-depth exploration of human experiences at a level that is not accessible through quantitative approaches. Attention has focused on the unique characteristics of the qualitative tradition, specifically its aim to generate rich descriptions of human phenomena rather than findings that are generalizable to larger populations. This overarching goal necessitates smaller sample sizes, purposive sampling techniques, data collection methods that center on interviews and observation, and the analysis of text and other non-numerical data. Several qualitative approaches relevant to social work have been reviewed, including the mixed-methods study that combines qualitative and quantitative traditions and maximizes the strengths of each approach. Exhibit 6.12 presents a summary of the qualitative data collection techniques discussed in this chapter, in relation to the qualitative methods with which they are most commonly paired.

The iterative nature of qualitative data analysis has also been presented, along with key steps in deriving meaning from qualitative data in ways that generate rigorous and trustworthy results. The next chapter shifts attention from the narratives that are of interest in qualitative research to the numbers that are of interest in quantitative research, specifically focusing on group research designs.

MAIN POINTS

■ Qualitative research is based on the interpretive or narrative tradition and seeks to understand the deeper meanings of human experience.

■ Qualitative research is indicated when the research question calls for description of the lived experience or individuals' impressions, reactions, and perceptions of phenomena of interest.

■ Primary methods for gathering qualitative data include interviews, observation, and review of existing records; data are captured via tape recording for later transcription and field notes.

■ The aim of qualitative research is rich understanding rather than generalizability, therefore sample sizes are appropriately small and generated via purposive sampling strategies.

■ Qualitative methods include case study, ethnography, grounded theory, phenomenology, and the mixed-method approach, which combines elements of both qualitative and quantitative traditions.

■ Qualitative data analysis is an iterative process and typically involves the analysis of text.

■ Qualitative data analysis includes three steps: organizing the data into concepts, developing the story, and maximizing rigor by validating conclusions.

■ Qualitative content analysis is a common method for analyzing text data in social work research.

EXERCISES

1. Using the Riverton case, describe how you might gain entry in order to begin interviewing residents from your neighborhoods' homeless shelters to determine their perspective on neighborhood concerns. Consider the following:
   a. Who might serve as a gatekeeper?
   b. Who might serve as a key informant?
   c. What type of participant incentive would be appropriate for the homeless shelter residents?
2. Using the Riverton case, list five questions you would use to conduct a focus group with residents of the homeless shelters in your neighborhood. What process would you use to arrive at this list? Then list five questions you would use to conduct a focus group with neighborhood residents who are not homeless.
3. Consider a case study based on the Sanchez family case. What information would likely be included in such a case study?

EXHIBIT 6.12

Techniques of Qualitative Data Collection

Technique	Characteristics	Used Commonly In
Unstructured, interactive interviews	Relatively few prepared questions; may be only one or more grand tour questions. Researcher listens to and learns from participant. Unplanned, unanticipated questions may be used; also probes for clarification	Ethnography, grounded theory, case study
Informal conversations	Researcher assumes a more active role than in interactive interviews	Phenomenology, ethnography, grounded theory
Semi-structured interviews	Open-ended questions are developed in advance, along with prepared probes. Unplanned, unanticipated probes may also be used	Ethnography, grounded theory
Group interviews/ focus groups	Tape-recorded or videotaped; Six to eight open-ended questions asked. Facilitator stimulates dialogue among participants	All methods
Observations	Field notes may be recorded as notes (and later expanded) or into a dictaphone and later transcribed. Participants or nonparticipant observation (dependent on the extent to which the researcher participates) may be used	Ethnography, grounded theory
Video tapes	May be retained whole for replaying and reviewing or summarized or transcribed (optionally with illustration retained)	Ethnography
Photographs	May be used to illustrate and facilitate recall	Many methods, especially ethnography
Maps	May be stored and referenced	All methods where understanding a site is important
Documents	May be collected during project and used to give background or detail	All methods
Diaries, letters	May be retained and studied in detail or summarized	Many methods
Indirect methods of representing	Researcher finds ways of simulating or representing the phenomenon studied	All methods

Source: Adapted from Morse & Richards, 2002, pp. 91–92.

     a.   Describe how such a case study could guide social work practice with other families similar to the Sanchez family. What research questions could a case study be designed to examine?

     b.   Describe how such a case study could guide policy development related to social service delivery for clients seeking services similar to the Sanchez family.

     c.   Would a case study be the best qualitative research design for these purposes?

4.   Using the transcription of the video depicting Emilia Sanchez's interview with the social worker, practice inductive qualitative content analysis by open coding to identify the range of challenges she experiences.

5.   Using the Carla Washburn case, describe how a study aimed at exploring reactions to the loss of an adult child might look different from each of the following qualitative traditions:

     a.   Case study

     b.   Grounded theory

     c.   Phenomenology

     d.   Ethnography

     e.   Mixed methods

6.   How would cultural competence inform your selection of a qualitative research method with the Carla Washburn case? How might time, money, and other resource constraints affect your selection of a method?

7.   Using the Carla Washburn case, develop a semi-structured interview guide listing questions and probes to explore her feelings of both physical and emotional pain. How could you draw on the theoretical understanding of mind-body connections, as well as other research literature, to help you formulate your questions? What parameters (length of interview, level of comprehension required, cultural competence) should inform your development of the interview guide?

8.   Conduct a literature review on using Photovoice as a technique for eliciting qualitative data using pictures to illustrate and facilitate recall. Design a qualitative research study for the Brickville youth leadership development group using Photovoice. Include how you would prepare the youth for data collection and how you would seek to maximize rigor during the analysis phase, by confirming data with other sources.

9.   If you were to analyze the content of the RAINN online hotline, what qualitative method would you suggest and why? Would you propose a sampling method, why or why not? If you would propose a sample, what method of sampling would you use and why?

chapter
7

GROUP RESEARCH DESIGN

A research design should be selected for its ability to answer the research question and test the research hypothesis.

This chapter could have alternatively been titled "Now that I have a research question, what do I do with it?" Social work research is about asking good research questions and answering them with confidence. The choice of a research design, which serves as the blueprint for answering the research question, should always be guided by what the research question requires.

There is an important distinction to be made in research designs. Basically, there are two classes of research design:

1. **Group research designs** are appropriate for answering research questions that deal with groups of elements, such as people, organizations, and agencies.
2. **Case-level research designs** are appropriate for answering research questions about a single element: one person, one family, one organization, one community, and so on. Case-level research designs include single subject research designs and case studies. We have already examined single subject research in Chapter 4 and case studies in Chapter 6.

This chapter is about group research designs. It addresses such topics as how to select a group research design based on the research question, how many groups to study, how groups are formed, the number and timing of measurements, and the exposure of groups to an experimental condition, also known as the **independent variable**.

Experimental conditions in social work are the interventions used to produce positive changes. There are many possible experimental conditions. Interventions such as cognitive behavioral therapy, a change in the eligibility criteria for the Free and Reduced Price Lunch Program, and the implementation in a middle school of a curriculum aimed at preventing bullying are examples of experimental conditions.

Mastering the material in this chapter and the two following chapters on sampling and measurement is critical to planning, conducting, and critiquing research. Although mistakes in the analysis of data at the end of a research study can be corrected, errors in specifying the study's research design, how many subjects to study, or the data to be collected are costly. Moreover, once they are made, they cannot be undone. Decisions related to the choice of group research design, sampling, and measurement will impact how the evidence generated by the research study will be accepted and, ultimately, whether the results will be used to affect practice.

By the end of this chapter you should be able to:

■ Describe the difference between group research design and case-level research design.
■ Suggest an appropriate group research design based on what the research question requires.
■ Understand group research design notation as the building blocks of research design.
■ Describe the strengths and weaknesses of the different types of group research designs.
■ Explain what is meant by internal validity and how threats to internal validity vary with the choice of group research design.
■ Explain what is meant by external validity and how threats to external validity vary with the choice of group research design.

A PURPOSE-DRIVEN APPROACH TO SELECTING A GROUP RESEARCH DESIGN

Different group research designs are appropriate for generating different kinds of information or knowledge. Chapter 3 presented three different types of knowledge: exploratory, descriptive, and explanatory. Before selecting a group research design, you need to decide where on the knowledge continuum the research question fits. You must then purposively select a research design capable of producing that type of knowledge. The research question should drive the research methodology, not the reverse.

QUICK GUIDE 4 CHOICE OF RESEARCH DESIGN BASED ON THE RESEARCH QUESTION

If your answer is yes . . .	. . . Choose this
• Does the research question pertain to an area of research that is new or that has not been investigated in depth? • Is the research question designed to help us acquire a preliminary understanding of a phenomenon? • Is the intent of the research question to determine what variables and concepts are important in relation to a certain phenomenon? • Is the purpose of the research to discover what the research questions should be or to derive working hypotheses and theories? • Is the intent of the research to study some phenomenon as it is, without trying to alter it?	Exploratory design

If your answer is yes . . .	. . . Choose this
• How prevalent is a certain condition in a set geographic area? • What is the relationship between two or more variables? • What demographic characteristics are associated with the condition? • How much change has occurred in knowledge, skills, behaviors, or attitudes after the administration of an independent variable? • What is the trajectory of a developmental process such as dying, a behavior disorder, or a stage of maturation? • Has some minimum standard of outcome been achieved at a specified point in time?	Descriptive design
• What is the etiology of a problem—that is, the chain of events that caused it? • How effective is a program in making specified changes? • Which approaches are the most effective means to produce specified changes? • How will altering an intervention (independent variable) change the outcome (dependent variable) of the intervention?	Explanatory design

Exploratory Research Questions

To determine whether a particular research question is exploratory, we can ask several questions, as shown in Quick Guide 4. If the answer to any of these questions is yes, a group research design capable of producing exploratory knowledge is required.

The following are examples of exploratory research questions:

■ How does culture influence medical outcomes among people with HIV?
■ What contact do incarcerated parents have with their children?
■ How does adolescent disclosure of a gay or lesbian sexual orientation affect the parent-child relationship?

These questions are exploratory because they have been subject to very little investigation until this point. The important variables and concepts related to the cultural influences on medical treatment for HIV, incarcerated parents' contact with their children, and the parental experience of learning that an adolescent child is gay or lesbian have yet to be identified.

Exploratory research questions often call for an **inductive,** or indirect, approach to research. Instead of starting with conclusions and then trying to support them, researchers collect and analyze observations and then reach tentative conclusions based on those observations.

Descriptive Research Questions

All research is descriptive to some extent. A descriptive research question, however, is concerned with describing some phenomenon in a holistic way. See Quick Guide 4 for examples.

If the research question calls for description, a research design capable of producing descriptive knowledge is required. The following are examples of descriptive research questions:

■ What is the return rate of parental consent forms when a specified set of procedures is used to obtain active parental consent for child participation in research?
■ How does the prevalence of material hardship (food, housing, and medical care) in the United States differ among ethnic/racial subgroups?
■ What factors in adolescence are associated with the presence of serious violent behavior at age 18?

It may be difficult to differentiate a descriptive research question from an exploratory one. For instance, what makes the previous question on youth violence descriptive rather than exploratory? The answer is based on the amount of theory and research that already exists in the area. In the study of serious violent behavior in adolescence, a great deal of research has already been conducted, theories have been postulated, and important variables have been identified. The research therefore is seeking mostly to describe the incidence of factors associated with those theories and variables. If there were not so much prior research, the question would indeed be exploratory.

Explanatory Research Questions

Explanatory research questions are difficult to answer, and yet they are crucial in terms of accountability and furthering our social work knowledge base. Explanatory research questions focus on understanding the relationship between variables, especially on cause-and-effect relationships. For some examples, see Quick Guide 4.

The following rule can help you determine whether a research question is explanatory or descriptive: If the question addresses effectiveness, it is explanatory. For example: Did the training on the identification of sex trafficking victims in the child welfare system lead to an increase in identified victims? If the question asks to describe the outcomes observed in a social program or demonstration project, it is descriptive. For example: What was the change in the rate of sex trafficking victims identified before and after the training on the identification of sex trafficking victims? If the research question is related to cause and effect, a group research design capable of producing explanatory knowledge is required. The following are examples of explanatory research questions:

- Does home visitation by child-welfare workers prevent child abuse and neglect for children born to at-risk parents?
- How do parents' characteristics influence their methods of disciplining young children?
- How effective are paraprofessional home visitors compared with nurse home visitors in preventing child abuse and neglect?

Explanatory research questions are answered through **deductive reasoning**, or a direct approach, which involves first developing hypotheses and then collecting observations. The hypotheses are then either accepted as probable or rejected on the basis of the evidence produced by the observations. Note that hypotheses are never proven one way or the other. Rather, the cumulative evidence leads to their support or rejection. (See Chapter 12 for an explanation of hypothesis testing.)

NOTATION AND TERMINOLOGY OF GROUP RESEARCH DESIGNS

Before addressing the issue of how to select a group research design, some basic notation and terminology is needed. The basic notation of group research design involves three symbols: the letters O, X, and R. These symbols can be thought of as building blocks that researchers put together in different ways to enable them to address research questions. Although there are some common group research designs, there is no limit to the number of ways that we can put the building blocks together to answer research questions. In the following sections, we will describe what the symbols mean and how they are used.

Observation (O)

The first symbol, O, denotes an observation or measurement of the **dependent variable**—the condition or behavior of interest, or the one that is to be changed by our interventions. Examples of dependent variables include substance abuse, sexual behavior, employment outcomes including income, and child abuse.

All group research designs involve at least one O. If there is more than one O, numeric subscripts (for example, $O_1 O_2 O_3$) are used to identify the sequence of the observations. The subscript 1 represents the first observation, 2 the second observation, and so on. When there is only one observation, there is no need to use a subscript after the O.

We read research design notation the same way that we read the text in a book, from left to right. The activities represented by the notation to the left precede the activities represented by the notation to the right.

In addition, we can use a key or a legend, similar to that found on a map, to describe the subscripts. For example, if our interest is in prenatal care during pregnancy, the key might explain that O_1 is the number of prenatal visits completed at the end of the first trimester, O_2 at the end of the second trimester, and O_3 in the third trimester until birth. The purpose of repeated observations is to examine variation in the dependent variable over time.

When we are considering a group research design, it is important to justify the timing and number of observations. One key factor in determining the number of observations is feasibility: "How many observations are possible given the type and amount of resources available?" Research budgets are usually limited, and each observation point requires additional resources for collecting, entering, and processing data, as well as incentives to participants when appropriate.

Multiple observations over an extended period are especially difficult to implement with transient and unstable populations. Examples of such populations are graduating high school students, individuals who are homeless, victims of domestic violence, frail elders, and people afflicted with chronic diseases such as AIDS. Another factor in determining the number of observations is participant burden. There is a concern for how much researchers should ask of participants and the amount of time it consumes.

The Intervention, or Experimental Condition (X)

The second symbol used in group research design notation, X, denotes the introduction of an experimental condition, also known as the independent variable. Although all group research designs have an O, not all have an X. The absence of X denotes the absence of an experimental condition or an independent variable. This is the case when we want to observe a phenomenon as it naturally exists or evolves. For example, we might want to understand the meaning of social support in a rural community or the prevalence of breast cancer screening on an Indian reservation.

Numeric subscripts placed after an X (X_1 X_2 X_3) are used to denote variations when more than one independent variable is being studied. For example, X_1 might be a targeted direct-mail marketing campaign designed to motivate low-income women to access breast cancer screening. X_2 might represent a general advertising campaign for breast cancer screening that uses public service announcements broadcast over local radio stations. When there is only one experimental condition, there is no need to use a subscript after the X.

The number of groups of participants in the research design will depend upon the number of experimental conditions we want to observe. For example, we may want to study the difference between X present (the intervention) compared to X absent, or more of X compared to less of X. Each variation of the experimental condition requires a separate group of participants. The number of groups then will be equal to the number of variations. Similar to the Os, the Xs can also be described in a key or a legend.

Note that each group involved in the research study is given its own line in research design notation. If there are three groups, there should be three corresponding lines of notation. Two events that occur simultaneously are represented by notation placed vertically one above the other.

In the following example of group research design notation, for instance, two different groups, a treatment group and a wait list group, are given an anxiety scale at pretest (O_1) at approximately the same time. The first group is given an intervention (X), cognitive behavioral therapy, while the second group is still on the wait list. At the end of the intervention program, both groups are given the anxiety scale again (O_2).

O_1 X O_2 (treatment group)
O_1 O_2 (wait list group)

Random Assignment (R)

The third symbol, R, when placed in front of a row of group research design notation, denotes **random assignment** to groups. Random assignment is assignment by chance, not based on already existing groups, self-selection, or some defined characteristic. Random assignment can be accomplished in many ways:

- Assign every other person who applies for services to one group or another.
- Flip a coin for each participant. Heads go in one group, and tails go in another.
- Assign a computer-generated random number to each participant. Put odd numbers in one group and even numbers in another group.
- Put all participants' names in a hat and draw them out one at a time. The first person is assigned to the first group, the second person to the second group, and so on.

When groups are randomly assigned, as illustrated in the research design below, the group with the experimental condition (or independent variable) is called the **experimental group**, and the group without the experimental condition is called the **control group**. For example, in the study of anxiety described earlier, if the members of the intervention group and the wait list group are randomly assigned, the notation below can describe the study.

R O_1 X O_2 (experimental group)
R O_1 O_2 (control group)

The purpose of random assignment is to create **pretreatment equivalency**, also referred to as **between-group equivalency**. The assumption is that groups that have been randomly assigned should be similar to each other in terms of the distribution of major variables that might impact the dependent variable. The rationale for using random assignment is that if the groups are equivalent before the introduction of the independent variable, any differences between the groups at posttest can be attributed to the independent variable.

The assumption of pretreatment equivalency can be tested statistically by examining the equivalence of the groups on any variables believed to be important in terms of the dependent variable. When the observation involves individuals, the most common variables include age, gender orientation, education, race/ethnicity, income, and family size. What variables are important in any particular context typically are identified through a review of the literature. For example, we know that both education and gender orientation are important in the study of life time earnings. The beauty of random assignment, however, is that you can assume that all variables will be equivalent between groups, including variables that you cannot measure and those you would never even think about measuring.

When you are conducting group research, you need to distinguish between random assignment and random sampling. **Random sampling** is a means of selecting elements from a population so that each and every element has an equal chance of being selected. The intent of random sampling is to ensure that the subjects involved in the research represent the population from which they were drawn. Random assignment, in contrast, seeks to create between-group equivalence and is not concerned with the group's similarity to the population. For example, 50 people attend a program for parent education and are each assigned to one of two conditions: one is a 12-week course and the other is a six-week course. If these 50 parents are randomly sorted into the six- or 12-week course, that is random assignment. It does not tell us whether these parents, as a group, represent the population of parents in the community, the state, or the United States. Random sampling involves selecting the 50 parents at random from the total population before assigning them to a group. We discuss random sampling in Chapter 8.

Assignment that is Not Random

Generally speaking, if the notation does not include an R for random assignment, we can safely assume that the procedure was not random. Significantly, when the assignment procedure is not random, we cannot assume between-group equivalency. In such cases, the groups are said to be nonequivalent. In the absence of random assignment, the group that is not subject to the independent variable is called a **comparison group** rather than a control group:

O_1 X O_2 (experimental group)
O_1 O_2 (comparison group)

Although we cannot assume pretreatment equivalency in the absence of a control group, we can examine the similarity between the comparison and experimental groups by using statistics. (We examine statistics in detail in Chapter 12.) A statistical analysis of the characteristics of two or more groups can gauge just how similar the groups are on observed variables that are believed to impact the dependent variable. In the study of child neglect, for example, the literature identifies family size and composition as important factors. In the absence of random assignment to groups, the social work researcher would want to know how equivalent the experimental and comparison groups were on family size and composition before administering the independent variable, such as assignment to a home visitor mentor. The social worker would also want to know how similar the groups were regarding other important variables related to child neglect, such as history of previous abuse, parent's stress level, parent's history of abuse, extent of social support, and substance abuse by a family member.

The use of comparison groups is common in social work research. In many cases, either random assignment is not practical or there are too many objections to its use. For example, some agency administrators may prefer to assign clients based on which intervention or which social worker they believe will be most beneficial to the client rather than on a random basis. When random assignment is not a viable option, researchers frequently recruit participants from *preexisting groups*. Not only are preexisting groups plentiful, but they tend to be captive audiences. Classic examples are the students in a classroom and the consumers of a service. We discuss the use of preexisting groups in the next chapter.

Terminology and Notation Describing Group Research Designs

Researchers often need to communicate about group research designs in words as well as notation. To do so, they use descriptive terminology. Different sources will sometimes use slightly different terminology to describe the same design. As long as the descriptions are clear, the terminology used is generally acceptable.

Cross-Sectional Research

The terminology used to describe the Os, or observations, depends in part on whether an experimental condition is present and the number of observations in the design. If there is only one observation, the group research design may be referred to as a **cross-sectional research design**.

Pretests and Posttests

If there are two observations and the first observation, O_1, occurs before the independent variable is administered, the first observation is called a **pretest**. Exhibit 7.1 presents some useful guidelines concerning when and when not to use a pretest.

If a second observation, O_2, follows the independent variable, it is called a **posttest**. Group research designs including pretests and posttests are sometimes referred to as **before-and-after research designs**.

The interval between the pretest and posttest will usually depend upon the length of time it takes to administer the independent variable. For example, most programs designed to stop teenagers from engaging in sexual activity range from two to eight weeks in duration. In a research design to evaluate change in teenagers' intentions to abstain from sexual activity, the pretest would be administered just before the start of the curriculum, and the posttest would be administered at the conclusion of the curriculum.

Sometimes two pretests are administered before the independent variable is introduced. In these cases, the second pretest is referred to as a **delayed pretest**. We use delayed pretests when we want to assess the *normal* amount of change that occurs between two measurements before the introduction of an independent variable. The use of delayed pretests, although not common, is typically found in research when there is no opportunity to observe the changes that occur in a control or comparison group or when the population is maturing relatively quickly.

For example, in a study of teenage abstinence from sexual behavior, the researchers used a delayed pretest to assess changes in attitudes toward sexual abstinence that were occurring as part of the maturation process. The first pretest was administered eight weeks before the delayed pretest, which was essentially the same questionnaire. Eight weeks later, the independent variable, in this case an abstinence-based curriculum, was introduced. Significantly, changes were found to be taking place in the absence of the independent variable.

EXHIBIT 7.1

When and When Not to Use a Pretest

When to Use a Pretest

■ When the assignment to groups is nonrandom and between-group posttest results will be compared, use the pretest to evaluate whether the scores of the assigned groups were comparable before the independent variable was introduced.

■ When researchers need to know how much change has occurred in the dependent variable over time, that is, from pretest to posttest.

■ When the assumptions that have been made in planning an intervention need to be checked. For instance, is it true that parents identified as being at risk for child abuse and neglect have little knowledge of time-out techniques before their involvement in a program to promote parenting skills?

■ When recruiting the target population for a program is difficult. For example, voluntary screening programs for breast cancer that are designed specifically for low-income women from ethnic minority communities often attract minority women from higher income and education levels. Pretests can be used to select potential participants into the program or into the analysis according to some preset eligibility criteria.

When Not to Use a Pretest

■ When it is important to cut costs or save time.

■ When the act of taking the pretest would demoralize research participants. This might occur if the participants were to perceive the test as overly difficult or the subject matter as overly intrusive for a first meeting.

■ When taking the pretest would alter the way participants respond to the posttest, irrespective of the independent variable. For example, a pretest to measure knowledge of human sexuality may spark curiosity that leads to additional discussions or readings on sexuality before the posttest.

Sources: Adapted from Fitz-Gibbon & Morris, 1987; Abbott, Barber, Taylor, & Pendel, 1999

Follow-Up Observations

When two observations follow an intervention, the second one is referred to as a **follow-up observation**. These are required to determine whether observed differences between the pretest and the posttest are maintained over time. Follow-up observations help answer questions related to the durability of outcomes.

In the study on teenage abstinence, for example, a six-month, post-program follow-up observation assessed whether changes in attitudes toward sexual behavior were consistent with or stronger than posttest levels or whether they had regressed to pretest levels or below. Using group research design terminology, the abstinence example would be described as a one-group pretest-posttest research design with a delayed pretest and six-month follow-up. Using group research design notation, it would be represented as $O_1 O_2 X O_3 O_4$.

Many research studies do not include follow-up observations. In some instances, there are not enough resources to pursue follow-up data collection. In other cases, follow-up observations simply are not necessary. For example, the group research design $O_1 X O_2$ is commonly referred to as a pretest-posttest research design. In contrast, some designs employ three or more observations before and/or after the introduction of an independent variable. These designs are referred to as **time series** or **longitudinal** research designs.

Number of Groups Involved

Another part of the descriptive label given to group research designs relates to the number of groups that are involved. Group research designs employing only one group are commonly referred to as one-group research designs. For example, the design $O_1 X O_2$ is commonly known as a one-group, pretest-posttest research design. There is only one group, a pretest (O_1) followed by the introduction of an independent variable (X), and then a posttest (O_2).

With the addition of another group to the one-group, pretest-posttest research design, it becomes a two-group, pretest-posttest research design. Research designs with more than two groups are commonly referred to as **multigroup research designs**.

Prospective and Retrospective Studies

A final distinction in describing group research designs has to do with the timing of measurement. In a **prospective research study**, the researcher collects the pretest data and then observes the dependent variable as the independent variable is administered. In contrast, in a **retrospective research study**, the researcher does not observe the dependent variable until after the independent variable has been applied. In other words, the prospective research study looks ahead in time, whereas the retrospective study looks back.

The advantage of the prospective study is that the researcher can exert greater control over the research design, including sampling and measurement. The advantage of a retrospective study is that it probably costs less and requires less time. Whether research is prospective or retrospective is often a matter of feasibility.

At times the examination of a single phenomenon can involve both retrospective and prospective research. In the study of a home visitation program designed to prevent child abuse and neglect, for example, researchers conducted a retrospective study to identify the factors that predicted substantiated child abuse and neglect in the participant population. The researchers examined the records of more than 8,000 families involved in the Healthy Families Arizona program since its inception in October 1991. They then used the results to ensure that the program was addressing the major risk factors identified in the study, such as premature birth and high levels of parental stress. The retrospective research was one step in helping the program prepare for a prospective, experimental study of child abuse and neglect prevention. The prospective study involved random assignment of at-risk parents to a treatment group and a control group, and follow-up observations over the course of two years (LeCroy & Krysik, 2011).

Retrospective research can also be a means of examining old data under a new lens. For example, researchers have used retrospective studies to provide more accurate counts of suicide, domestic violence, and shaken baby syndrome, which are often overlooked or improperly classified. Retrospective research in these areas is often conducted by reexamining medical records as well as coroners' and crime reports.

TYPES OF GROUP RESEARCH DESIGNS

Once we are clear about the type of research question to be answered, it is time to select a group research design. Group research designs have been classified into a threefold system that includes pre-experimental, quasi-experimental, and experimental designs (Campbell & Stanley, 1963).

Differentiating experimental designs from the other two classes of research design is easy. Most sources, however, fail to present criteria on how to differentiate pre-experimental from quasi-experimental designs. The exception is William Trochim (2006), and the decision tree for classifying research designs presented in Exhibit 7.2 is based on his work.

As you can see in Exhibit 7.2, if the research design involves random assignment to two or more groups, it is an **experimental design**. In **random assignment**, all elements—whether they are individuals, families, communities, organizations, and so on—have an equal chance of being assigned to each group. If there is no random assignment to groups but there is more than one group, or more than one round of measurement, the research design is **quasi-experimental**. If the research design involves only one group or one round of observation and there is no random assignment to groups, it is considered **pre-experimental**.

The usefulness of classifying research questions and group research designs is in matching the type of knowledge sought with the class of group research design that is able to produce that type of knowledge:

■ If the research question calls for *exploratory* knowledge, a *pre-experimental* group research design is likely sufficient.

■ If the research question calls for *descriptive* knowledge, a *pre-experimental* research design can answer it. However, other questions that inquire about change over time or a comparison of outcomes achieved according to different independent variables will require a *quasi-experimental* research design.

■ If the research question calls for *explanatory* knowledge, an *experimental* group research design is required to answer the research question with confidence.

Although it is possible to answer exploratory and descriptive research questions with an experimental research design, it would be a great misuse of resources, comparable to using a sledgehammer to pound a tack. Similarly, you could not expect to answer an explanatory research question with a pre-experimental research design. There will be times, however, when the research question is explanatory and an experimental design is not feasible. Similarly, there will be times when the only option is a pre-experimental design.

EXHIBIT 7.2

Simple Decision Tree for the Classification of Group Research Designs

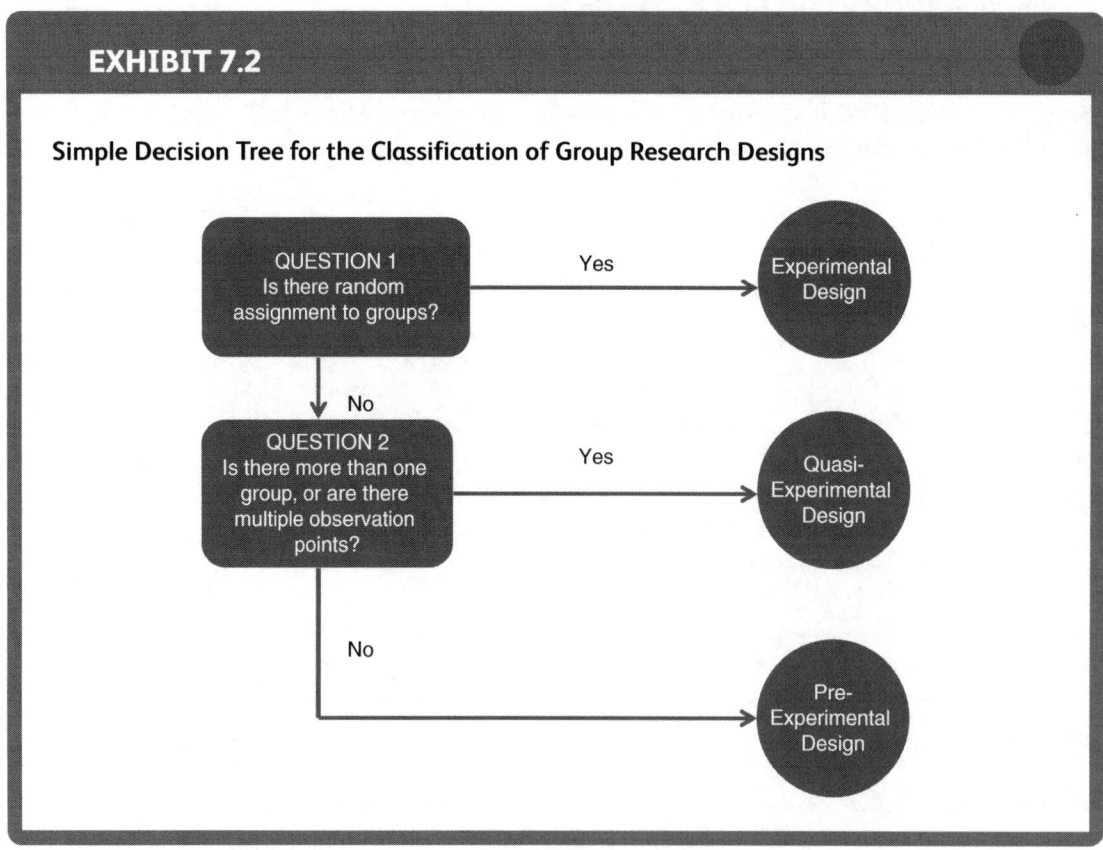

In these instances, it is helpful to be aware of the limitations of the group research design used to answer the research question and to be explicit about them when presenting the research findings. Descriptive and exploratory research designs can produce findings that suggest causation. In such cases, if it is warranted, the hypotheses that are generated can then be tested with experimental designs. The Case-in-Point that follows shows that all three classes of group research designs have value in social work research.

CASE-IN-POINT: VARIETY OF RESEARCH DESIGNS CONTRIBUTE TO UNDERSTANDING THE ROLE OF HOME VISITATION IN PREVENTING CHILD ABUSE AND NEGLECT

Communities across the United States have become increasingly invested in preventing child abuse and neglect and enriching early childhood experiences. Significantly, more than 500 of the programs developed to prevent child abuse and neglect in the past three decades involve home visitation by paraprofessionals or professionals trained to teach and support new parents identified as at risk for child abuse and neglect. Given the substantial investment in home visitation programs, it is not surprising that there is a great need for research in this area. All three classes of group research designs have been used for these studies by social work researchers:

- *Exploratory studies* using pre-experimental designs have provided insight into the experiences of new parents considered at risk for child abuse and neglect. They have also helped us to understand the nature of the relationship between the home visitor and the parent and they have examined the problem of parents terminating home visitation services earlier than expected.
- *Descriptive studies* in home visitation using quasi-experimental designs are used largely to evaluate program outcomes and to identify risk and protective factors associated with child abuse and neglect. Quasi-experimental research designs are implemented to describe changes in parents' stress levels over time, to document improvements in the home environment that are conducive to healthy child development, and to determine whether prevention targets involving substantiated incidents of child abuse and neglect are met.
- *Explanatory studies* using experimental research in home visitation, although rare, are highly valued by program personnel, child advocates, and state government officials responsible for funding decisions. These studies provide evidence as to whether home visitation works to prevent child abuse and neglect and to improve child development outcomes in both the short and the long term.

Whereas pre-experimental and quasi-experimental research studies lead to improvements in program theory and practice, experimental studies play a vital role in deciding the future of home visitation. Several new online, searchable, databases provide easy access to social workers who are searching for research literature on an area such as home visitation. One such site is the California Evidence-Based Clearinghouse for Child Welfare (www.cebc4cw.org). Social workers must always be careful to examine the studies presented and search for new studies that may not be represented on the database.

Pre-Experimental Research Designs

The simplest of all group research designs are those classified as pre-experimental. As we discussed earlier, a pre-experimental research design involves only one group or one round of observation, and participants are not assigned to groups through random assignment. Pre-experimental research designs tend to be less expensive and time consuming than experimental and quasi-experimental research designs because they do not involve multiple groups or multiple waves of measurement. We discuss two pre-experimental designs: the one-shot case study and the one-group, posttest-only.

One-Shot Case Study

The simplest of all pre-experimental group research designs is the **one-shot case study**, also known as the **cross-sectional study**. The one-shot case study is appropriate for answering exploratory and descriptive research questions related to what exists at a certain point in time. It can be used to answer questions about the level of knowledge or about functioning, attitude, behavior, or environmental circumstances at one point in time. It does not involve the introduction of an independent variable. An example of a research question that can be answered with a one-shot case study is: What do this year's incoming BSW students know about group research design?

The one-shot case study can be used with research approaches that use only qualitative methods, only quantitative methods, or a combination of the two. When using group research design notation, the one-shot case study is illustrated simply as O.

One-Group, Posttest-Only

If the one-shot case study is implemented after the independent variable is administered, it becomes a **one-group, posttest-only research design**. This design can answer questions related to whether some minimum standard of achievement has been met. An example is the question: What do graduating BSW students know about group research design? In this case, the BSW program is the independent variable.

The function of the one-group, posttest-only research design is to explore. It cannot produce knowledge about change because there is only one observation. Neither can it measure the impact of the independent variable, e.g., the social work program, because there is no means for comparison. This design only describes the dependent variable following the introduction of the independent variable. This design could not, for instance, answer the question of whether social work students increased their knowledge of research design while engaged in the BSW program. Nor could it determine whether students' knowledge of group research design at graduation was a result of participating in the program. The one-group posttest-only research design is illustrated as X O.

Quasi-Experimental Group Research Designs

Quasi-experimental group research designs are similar to pre-experimental designs except in that they involve additional observation points or additional groups selected without random assignment. Quasi-experimental research designs are useful for answering research questions related to changes that occur over time. They are often employed when experimental research designs are not feasible. These designs are also employed in cases in which there are strong objections to implementing an experiment. In this section we discuss six quasi-experimental research designs.

One-Group, Pretest-Posttest

The simplest of all quasi-experimental designs, the **one-group, pretest-posttest research design**, measures the dependent variable both before and after the independent variable is introduced. Thus, it is useful for measuring change over the course of an intervention. For example, unlike the pre-experimental designs discussed earlier, the one-group, pretest-posttest design could answer the research question "How much did BSW students' knowledge of group research design change over the course of their social work education program?"

A major limitation to this design is that the observed change cannot be attributed to the independent variable because possible alternative explanations have not been ruled out. We discuss the most common of these alternative explanations later in this chapter in the section "Threats to Internal Validity." A second limitation of this particular design is that it cannot answer whether changes in the dependent variable are maintained over time. The one-group, pretest-posttest design is represented as $O_1 \, X \, O_2$.

Posttest-Only with Comparison Group

In the **posttest-only with comparison group research design**, a group receiving the independent variable and a comparison group are observed at posttest. An example of a question this research design might answer is "What are the differences in attitudes toward sexual abstinence among eighth graders who receive the 'ABC' abstinence curriculum and eighth graders who do not receive any school-based instruction in abstinence?"

Because the posttest-only with comparison group research design compares a group that has received the independent variable with one that has not, researchers sometimes interpret the findings as a measure of the impact of the independent variable. In fact, this design cannot answer questions on impact because it does not rule out competing explanations for the between-group differences. For example, let's assume that students in the abstinence program exhibited more positive attitudes toward sexual abstinence post-test than students in the other group. Can we automatically attribute this difference to participation in the program? The answer is that we cannot, because other factors might have shaped the students' attitudes. It is possible, for instance, that the 8th graders in the group showing more positive attitudes were younger, were more likely to have previously attended a parochial school, or had greater overall extra curricula participation than the eighth graders in the other group. The posttest-only, comparison group research design is illustrated as follows:

X O
O

Pretest-Posttest with Comparison Group

Unlike the posttest-only comparison group research design, the **pretest-posttest with comparison group research design** compares two groups at pretest as well as at posttest. Because the groups are not assigned randomly, we cannot assume that they are equivalent at pretest on important factors that may influence the dependent variable. However, although we cannot assume pretreatment equivalency, we can test it to some degree by using the pretest. As with the posttest-only design, even if the study finds a greater amount of change in the experimental group, the design does not allow for any statement on impact or causality.

Regardless of its limitations, the pretest-posttest comparison group design is useful for identifying changes from pretest to posttest and speculating about the impact of the independent variable. This design is illustrated as follows:

O_1 X O_2
O_1 O_2

Multigroup, Posttest-Only

The **multigroup, posttest-only research design** can be used to determine whether a certain standard has been achieved. In this design, several groups are observed, each group exposed to different levels of the independent variable or to different independent variables. For instance, this design can be used to compare the outcomes among groups of students subjected to three different sex education curricula. This design also might suggest the best approach for achieving a particular outcome. In turn, this process could lead to the development of hypotheses and further testing employing a more rigorous experimental research design.

The multigroup, posttest-only research design cannot tell us anything about within-group change because it does not include a pretest. The multi-group, posttest-only research design is illustrated as follows:

$$X_1 O_1$$
$$X_2 O_1$$
$$X_3 O_1$$

Simple Time Series

A **simple time series research design** relies on a series of observations with a single group. It can be either interrupted or non-interrupted:

- *Interrupted time series design* involves making at least three observations before the independent variable is administered followed by at least three observations after it is administered. There is, however, no maximum number of observations that may occur either before or after the intervention. The simple interrupted time series design is illustrated as $O_1 O_2 O_3 X O_4 O_5 O_6$.

- *The non-interrupted time series design* is similar except that no independent variable is introduced. It is used to assess the actual changes of a variable without outside intervention. It is based only on a series of measurements and is appropriate for descriptive research when the interest involves the trajectory of a problem or state, for instance, living with HIV/AIDS. The non-interrupted time series design is illustrated as $O_1 O_2 O_3 O_4 O_5 O_6$.

Time Series with Comparison Group

Adding groups to a simple time series design with alternative interventions, or adding a comparison group, changes the simple time series design into a **time series with comparison group research design** or a **multiple group time series research design** if there are more than two groups. This design is used to lend greater support to the hypothesis that the independent variable is responsible for the changes that are occurring. For example, student attitudes about drug use may be measured in the three years before a Drug Awareness Resistance Education (DARE) program and three years following the program.

A comparison group that does not have the DARE program is also measured. This design is illustrated as follows:

$$O_1 \; O_2 \; O_3 \; X \; O_4 \; O_5 \; O_6$$
$$O_1 \; O_2 \; O_3 \quad O_4 \; O_5 \; O_6$$

Time series designs can be difficult to manage because participants frequently drop out before the study is completed. The tendency of participants to withdraw prematurely from a research study is known as **attrition**. Attrition occurs for many reasons, including illness, death, refusal to continue participation, and the inability to contact participants who have relocated. When attrition rates become excessive, researchers are unable to fulfill the goal of the study. The longer the study the greater attrition generally is.

Although researchers agree that attrition can be a serious problem, they have not achieved consensus on what constitutes too much attrition. Most researchers aim for a retention rate of 70% to 80%. However, in some studies an attrition rate of even 20% is unacceptable. An example is a research study that involves two or more groups in which the resulting between-group differences in outcome are small. In such cases, it is impossible to know which way the missing 20% would have tipped the scale. Conversely, if the research involves only one group, and there is not a great deal of within-group variation, a 20% attrition rate might not be viewed as problematic.

Researchers often assume that those who dropped out would have looked worse on whatever outcome is being considered. For example, a study of satisfaction with mental health services would assume that those who dropped out had lower satisfaction, which could explain their decision to drop out of services as well as the study. Maintaining low rates of attrition requires time and resources. We consider specific strategies to address attrition through sampling in Chapter 8 and through data collection in Chapter 10.

Experimental Research Designs

If the research design includes random assignment to two or more groups, it is a true experimental research design. Experiments are extremely powerful research tools for producing explanatory or causal knowledge. The true experiment is marked by five common characteristics (Campbell & Stanley, 1963):

■ There is a temporal order in which the presumed cause (the independent variable, or X) occurs before the presumed effect. If one variable is presumed to be the cause of a second variable, then logically it must be present before the second variable is observed.

- The independent variable (X) is manipulated. For example, the researcher might examine X present versus X absent, smaller versus larger amounts of X, or variations of X.
- The relationship between the independent variable and the dependent variable must be established. This is accomplished primarily through a combination of theory and prior pre-experimental and quasi-experimental research.
- There is random assignment to at least two groups, including an experimental group and a control group.
- Rival hypotheses, defined as alternative explanations apart from the independent variable that might account for the outcome, can be ruled out by the experiment (an example of a rival hypothesis is that the difference in the observed outcome is attributed to differences between the two groups prior to exposure to the independent variable). Ruling out rival hypotheses is achieved primarily through the use of random assignment.

True experiments have merit because they enable researchers to make valid conclusions about cause-and-effect relationships and they offer the highest internal validity of all research designs. Despite these benefits, however, when researchers suggest conducting an experiment, they often encounter resistance from social work practitioners and program administrators. Exhibit 7.3 presents some common objections to conducting experiments and potential responses to address each objection.

The following sections review three experimental designs: the classic experiment; the posttest-only, control group experiment; and the Solomon four-group design. We also discuss the technique known as matching, which can be used with both experimental and quasi-experimental designs to reduce sampling error.

The Classic Experiment

In the **classic experiment**, also known as **pretest-posttest with control group**, equivalent groups are formed through random assignment. The group called the experimental group is subject to the independent variable, whereas the control group is not. The changes that are expected to occur as a result of the independent variable are measured in both groups. Simply put, if the experimental group changes in the expected way but the control group does not change, experiences change of a lower magnitude, or changes in the opposite direction, then the independent variable was the likely cause of the difference. Using group research design notation, the classic experiment is represented as follows:

$$R\ O_1\ X\ O_2$$
$$R\ O_1\ \ \ O_2$$

EXHIBIT 7.3

Objections (and Responses) to Experimental Research Designs

Objection	Response to Objection
It is unethical to deny potentially beneficial services to otherwise eligible members of the population who will be included in the control group.	Often the control group receives the services that are typically offered by the agency. They do not go without services. Or a wait-list control group, created because a limited number of people who can be served at any one time, is used.
People are not to be experimented upon.	It is unethical to subject people to an intervention on the basis of faith more than fact. It is unethical to spend scarce dollars for social services on programs when there is no evidence that they actually work. Experimentation is the best way to demonstrate the effectiveness of an intervention. Experiments are also valuable because their results can help build needed support and cooperation for policy initiatives.
Assignment for treatment should be based on need and not randomization.	Random assignment does not violate social work ethics. Research can be done so that all who need services receive them. Research can help provide information about which clients might benefit most from a particular new service.
Steps taken to protect ethical standards, such as informed consent, may keep some potential participants away and thus may actually make the findings less relevant.	This is true. Informed consent, however, is essential in protecting the rights of human subjects and takes priority over other concerns.
Experiments do not generalize to real-life situations. Because people are not "randomly assigned" in real life, the likelihood that there will be differences between those who volunteer for a random experiment and those who volunteer for the actual program may be great, especially if recruitment mechanisms differ.	Experiments are one step in establishing the effectiveness of interventions and social programs. Additional evidence is needed to assess the transfer of the results to the "real world."

Objection	Response to Objection
The quality and effectiveness of a program implemented in a tightly controlled experiment will be different when the program is implemented on a broad scale.	Experiments should be conducted on tightly managed pilot programs as well as social programs that are broadly implemented so that the results will be applicable beyond the research context. Theory-building requires replication of the experimental research findings—that is, demonstrating consistent results across comparable studies.
Experiments may overlook subtle but valuable program effects—for example, behavior change but not changes in self-esteem.	Use of theory and discussions with program staff should identify the relevant outcomes to be measured in experiments.
Experiments may impose on program operations. Program operators (e.g., social workers) who struggle with the loss of control may not cooperate, declining to assist with evaluation tasks, limiting access to participants, or sabotaging records.	Program staff should be made aware of the benefits of the research, receive an orientation to the project, be given a chance to express their concerns, and be given the results of the study. Concerns about experimental design should be addressed early, and researchers should notify stakeholders about the practical and political aims of the project, how the mission of the program will be advanced, and how the experiment can add a rational dimension to policy making and funding decisions. In addition, researchers must design experiments to cause minimal program disruption—which may require assigning individuals other than program staff to recruit participants and collect data.

Posttest-Only with Control Group

As we saw in Exhibit 7.1, there are situations in which the use of a pretest is either not feasible or inappropriate. In these situations, an experimental research design that fills the requirement of an experiment without using a pretest is the **posttest-only with control group research design**. Rather than employ a pretest, this design assumes that random assignment negated any significant initial differences between the experimental and control groups before subjecting the experimental group to the independent variable. In other words, the groups are assumed to be equivalent. In group research design notation, the posttest-only, control group research design is represented as follows:

$$R\ X\ O_1$$
$$R\ \ \ \ O_1$$

Solomon Four-Group

The **Solomon four-group research design** combines the classic experiment and the posttest-only, control group design. This design is particularly useful when the act of taking the pretest might influence the posttest. This is the notation for a Solomon four-group research design:

1. $R \ O_1 \ X_1 \ O_2$
2. $R \ O_1 \quad O_2$
3. $R \quad X_1 \ O_1$
4. $R \quad O_1$

Comparing the second group ($R \ O_1 \ O_2$) with the fourth group (RO_1) allows the researcher to estimate the amount of change, if any, that is attributable to taking the pretest—a phenomenon known as a **testing effect**.

For example, in a study of attitudes about HIV/AIDS, the independent variable is an education program. Four groups are used, and members are assigned randomly to all four conditions. The first group (1) is given a pretest about their attitudes, the educational program, and then a posttest. The second group (2) is given the pretest and posttest, but not the educational program. The third group (3) is given the educational program and the posttest. The fourth group (4) is given only the posttest. If group (1) posttest scores differ from the third group's (3) scores, the pretest can be assumed to account for the difference since both got the educational program. If groups' (1) and (3) scores are similar but higher than groups' (2) and (4), the independent variable is assumed to have accounted for the difference.

LIMITATIONS OF GROUP RESEARCH DESIGNS

All group research designs have limitations that social work researchers should acknowledge. We have already discussed one major limitation—namely, that each specific group research design can answer some types of research questions but not others. For example, consumers of research, and even some researchers themselves, frequently want to generalize and to infer causation from even the simplest research designs. Other limitations relate to the way that a research study is managed, such as taking preemptive steps to minimize attrition, and additional considerations in measurement and data collection that are discussed in Chapters 9 and 10.

Fortunately, researchers can predict common problems such as attrition and poor quality control in the management of a research study. Consequently, they can take steps to prevent these problems or at least to diminish their impact.

The following Case-in-Point is an example of what can happen when an experiment is conducted before a program is properly implemented.

CASE-IN-POINT: A GOOD EXPERIMENT GOES BAD WHEN THE HEALTHY START PROGRAM BEING STUDIED HAS NOT BEEN PROPERLY IMPLEMENTED

Experiments tend to be lengthy and expensive to implement. For these reasons alone it is doubtful that researchers would undertake an experiment unless they felt that there was a reasonable chance of rejecting the null hypothesis, that is, rejecting the conclusion that there is no difference between the experimental and control groups at posttest. As a study reported by Anne Duggan and her colleagues (2004a; 2004b) illustrates, strong research designs cannot compensate for weak or poorly implemented treatments.

The Hawaii Healthy Start Program, a home visitation program designed to prevent child abuse and neglect, undertook an experimental research study of its services in the mid-1990s. Eligible families were randomly assigned to intervention and control groups and were interviewed annually for three years with an impressive follow-up rate of 88%. In the final analysis, the researchers found that the program had no significant impact on any risk factor for child abuse, on child abuse and the use of nonviolent discipline, or on the use of community services by at-risk mothers to address specified risks for child abuse and neglect.

The researchers provided several reasons for the fact that the program did not appear to be effective in any way. To begin with, they discovered that only 50% of all referred families received the recommended number of home visits according to schedule. The program also experienced a high attrition rate. Although it was designed for a three-year period, 10% of families had dropped out at three months, and 50% at one year. In addition, the program paid scant attention to the factors known to increase the risk for child abuse and neglect, particularly substance abuse, mental health, and domestic violence. The major reason for this shortcoming was that the home visitors lacked the training, skills, and supervision to address family risks for child abuse and neglect, to motivate families to change, and to link families with professional services. There was a lack of formal referral arrangements with professional services in the community to address risks and promote healthy family functioning.

The lesson learned from this evaluation is not that home visitation is ineffective but, rather, that no program should engage in experimental research until it has implemented a well-planned model of change or has developed a program based on prior research and theory. Research should have been conducted to determine whether the program was meeting the needs of the target population. Program implementation should have been monitored on an ongoing basis using pre-experimental and quasi-experimental research methods before an experimental study was conducted. The information obtained through research on the program should have been used in a continuous quality improvement process.

In addition, the program theory, which helps clarify how the program differs from the status quo, or what is regularly available in the absence of the program, should have identified the factors that the program must address in order to prevent child abuse and neglect. The training and hiring of home visitors should have been guided by the knowledge and skills necessary to address the identified risk factors.

Program theory, attention to implementation, and attention to quality are essential if, as Duggan and her colleagues have demonstrated, there is to be a fair test of the intervention through experimental studies. Owing in large part to the studies published by Duggan and her colleagues since 2004, the program is currently rated on the California Evidence Based Clearinghouse as "Evidence Fails to Demonstrate Effect" for child abuse and neglect (see http://www.cebc4cw.org/program/healthy-families-america-home-visiting-for-prevention-of-child-abuse-and-neglect/detailed).

Threats to Internal Validity

Internal validity is the amount of confidence we have that changes in the dependent variable are the result of the independent variable and not some other factor. Factors that jeopardize that confidence are known as *threats to internal validity*. Perfect internal validity in a research study is rarely assumed to exist. The design features of a research study, however, can enhance the likelihood of an acceptable level of internal validity (Campbell & Stanley, 1963).

Nine of the most common threats to internal validity are described here:

- **History effects** are important when the observed effect in a research study is influenced by an event that takes place between the pretest and the posttest. For instance, recent mass shootings targeted at law enforcement could influence the outcomes of a study that measures anxiety among the spouses of law enforcement officers. When the event that influences the outcome occurs in one group and not the other, we call it a threat of **intra-session history**.

- **Maturation** is a threat that occurs when an observed effect is due to the respondent's growing older, wiser, stronger, and more experienced between the pretest and posttest. Certain groups such as infants and children are more prone to maturation effects in the short term.

- **Testing effects,** as mentioned earlier, involve the danger that observed effects are due not to the independent variable but to the fact that performance on a test is influenced by taking a pretest. Testing effects may be due to the number of times particular responses are measured and the chance that familiarity with the test enhances the participant's performance. In some cases, what we are measuring may be the ability of participants to remember the answers they perceive as correct.

- **Instrumentation** refers to unintended changes in the way the dependent variable is measured over time. Instrumentation can arise from problems with the measuring instrument, the observer, and so on. For example, an observer may get bored or change his or her rating style during an experiment.

- **Statistical regression** can occur whenever a group is chosen because they are extreme. In such cases, the tendency is for both very high scores and very low scores to move toward the mean for the population regardless of the treatment being offered. For example, the most anxious members of a group are likely to be somewhat less anxious at the next measurement.

- **Selection bias** exists when the groups are not comparable before the study. In such cases, the change observed in the dependent variable could be due to pretreatment differences between the groups rather than to the independent variable.

- **Experimental mortality** is the danger that an observed effect is due to the specific types of persons who dropped out of a particular group. For example, mortality can be a threat to the internal validity of a study that involves the GPA of high school students if those who drop out of high school are included at pretest but not included at posttest.

- **Treatment contamination** can occur when the participants in one group learn about the treatment being offered to the members of another group, or when program personnel provide some compensatory benefits to those who form the control group. In some cases, treatment contamination is serious enough to cancel an experiment. In other cases, treatment contamination occurs naturally, for example, when youth in the experimental group discuss on the playground what they learned in an HIV/AIDS education program with youth not in the program but in the control group.

- **Resentful demoralization** is a reaction to being part of the control group. Sometimes membership in the control group is believed to be a negative state, causing resentment, anger, and demoralization that can inflate the difference among the two or more groups. For example, youth may see going to a climbing wall activity as a privilege and those not selected to participate may be resentful, thus affecting their scores on a measure of commitment to the school.

Researchers generally assume that random assignment to treatment and control groups can negate the first six of the above threats. In contrast, the final three cannot be avoided by randomization. Rather, careful planning and preparation can often reduce their impact. Experimental design is often referred to as the "gold standard" of research, or "the Cadillac of research designs." Experiments, however, are expensive, difficult to manage, and, at times, impossible to implement. Assessing beforehand the conditions under which an experiment is likely to succeed or fail can help to avoid wasting valuable resources, as this example illustrates.

Threats to External Validity

A study with a high degree of internal validity allows us to make causal inferences about the program or intervention with regard to the sample and the setting that was studied. The question then becomes: What about other settings and the larger population? These are matters of **external validity**—the degree that the research findings can be generalized to other cases not studied as well as to the population in general.

The basic issue behind external validity is whether an experiment is so simple, contrived, or in some other way different from the everyday world that what we learn from it does not apply to our everyday world. To maximize external validity, the study group must be representative of the larger target population so that the results can be generalized. We discuss strategies to achieve this objective in Chapter 8 on sampling. **Replication**, the process of duplicating the study involving differences in time, location, and target population also contributes toward confidence in the results. For now, we consider three major threats to external validity:

- **Reactivity** occurs when the situation being studied produces different results than would otherwise be found. Put simply, when people become aware that they are being observed or studied, they behave differently than they would under normal circumstances. Reactivity is also known as the **Hawthorne effect**. This term is derived from an experiment conducted in the 1920s to determine what factors would improve worker productivity in the Hawthorne factory of the Western Electric company in Cicero, Illinois. The study found that workers became more productive simply because they were aware that they were receiving more attention than they were accustomed to.

- **Researcher bias** occurs when researchers see what they want to see. In such cases, researchers interpret findings toward the positive for the experimental condition and toward the negative for the control and comparison groups. This is especially true when subjective judgments such as level of "empathy" or "creativity" are made. Researchers may be unaware of their tendency toward bias. In order to avoid researcher bias, it is best to use a **double-blind** study, that is, one in which neither the researcher nor the participant knows to which group a participant is assigned.

- **Multiple treatment interference** occurs when the effects of two or more treatments cannot be separated. This problem is common in social work because research takes place in real life rather than in a laboratory. Researchers have no control over what other resources people can access voluntarily or to whom they will speak. For example, in the research on the abstinence-only program in middle schools, it was difficult to find children who had not been subject to multiple forms of sex education in the schools before entering the program.

CONCLUSION

The right research design is the research design that will do the best job of answering the research question while dealing with the contextual complexities of the environment. Instead of limiting themselves to a restricted number of preset group research designs, social work researchers should focus on design features such as the number of groups and observations, timing, and variations in the independent variable in order to construct the optimal design for the research context at hand. Identifying the potential for common problems like resistance to experimentation and participant attrition is key to the successful implementation of any research study.

Experimental studies that examine research questions related to impact require additional attention so that the research results in a fair test of the independent variable and does not fail because of measurement problems (Chapter 9) or implementation problems (Chapter 10). The next three chapters continue the discussion of the planning process that must occur before a research study can be successfully implemented.

MAIN POINTS

- When selecting a research design, you want to match the level of knowledge implied by the research question with the class of research design that is capable of producing that level of knowledge.
- Mastering the concepts represented by the three symbols of group research design notation—O, X, and R—puts the beginning social work researcher in a position to understand, communicate about, and select group research designs.
- All three classes of research designs—pre-experimental, quasi-experimental, and experimental—have value in the creation of knowledge for social work.
- Experiments are essential for testing causal processes.
- Research designs that do not include a pretest do not allow for an assessment of within-group change.
- Participant attrition threatens the success of any research study.
- Six of the nine threats to internal validity can be dealt with through random assignment.

■ Before engaging in experimental research, the social work researcher should assess and deal with any contextual complexities that could derail the study. Particular attention should be focused on conditions that might lead to treatment contamination, resentful demoralization, and attrition.

EXERCISES

1. Using the Riverton case, develop three research questions. Demonstrate your skills at developing exploratory, descriptive, and explanatory research questions. For each research question:
   a. Identify an appropriate group research design that would allow you to answer the question.
   b. Provide a rationale for your selection of each research design.
   c. Outline the strengths and limitations of each research design for answering the question.
2. Describe a research design that could allow you to conclude that the substance abuse treatment program you operate in Riverton is the *cause* of a decrease in admissions to the hospital Emergency Room for alcohol- and drug-related illness and injury.
3. Formulate a group research design that would involve a comparison between two groups that receive services from RAINN. Describe the research design using group research design terminology and in research design notation.
4. Explain the differences between a pre-experimental, quasi-experimental, and experimental research design. Consider a possible program that you might offer to individuals experiencing loss similar to Carla Washburn and how you might evaluate some aspect of that program. Discuss the advantages and disadvantages of each design for this situation. What type of design might you begin with and why? What factors might influence your selection of a design? How could you attempt to compensate for the perceived limitations of the chosen design?
5. If you were to randomly assign the survivors of the Hudson City disaster to an intervention and a control group, what might be some of the associated ethical concerns? How might you respond? What would be the practical constraints to random assignment in this context?
6. Consider the Sanchez family case. When we deal with individuals in research studies, it is impossible to say that two groups are ever equal. When we randomly assign individuals to groups, we say that the two groups are equivalent. What does equivalence mean in the context of random assignment to groups? Use characteristics of the Sanchez family as examples. For instance, think about variables that might make it difficult

to compare the Sanchez family to another family that appears fairly similar to them, in terms of immigration status, country of origin, date of migration, or other variables.

7. It can be particularly difficult to assess the effects of a policy, since contextual complexities can interfere. Describe how treatment contamination, resentful demoralization, and attrition could affect research attempting to investigate how immigration policies affect mixed-status families such as the Sanchez family.

8. Search your library database for a peer-reviewed research article on environmental justice efforts by youth groups similar to that in the Brickville case. Considering the article, answer the following questions:

    a. What is the research question?
    b. Are any hypotheses tested?
    c. What type of research design is used to answer the research question or test the hypotheses?
    d. Is the research design appropriate? Why or why not?

chapter
8

SAMPLING

Selecting a sample is often a balance between what you want to accomplish and the resources available.

Researchers have found that among seniors age 65 and older in the United States, 51 percent report that they exercise three or more days per week (Mendes & McGeeney, 2012). Those seniors who reportedly exercise frequently are much more likely than those who do not to claim that they are in excellent or very good health—51% compared to 34%. How many of the more than 38 million (U.S. Census Bureau, 2012) adults over 65 years of age living in the United States do you think the research staff at the Gallup Organization contacted in order to make this assertion? It might surprise you to know that the number was as few as 150,984, which is less than one half of one percent.

So far, we have addressed the questions of how to select a research problem and how to formulate a research question and hypothesis (Chapter 3). Chapter 7 dealt with the topic of selecting a group research design to answer the research question and test the hypotheses. This chapter focuses on the issue of where we get the data—that which is collected usually in the form of numbers or words—that will allow us to answer our research question or test our hypothesis.

To accumulate our data, we need a **sampling plan** that outlines where the data will come from and justifies the choices we make along the way. Important choices in the formulation of a sampling plan include what to study and whether to collect data from the whole population or to limit data collection to a sample. A **population** is the totality of persons, events, organizational units, and so on that the research problem is focused on. A **sample**, in contrast, is a subset of the population. As one example, if a researcher conducted a study of students at your school, the population would consist of the entire student body. Any subset of that population—for example, 100 students picked at random—would represent a sample.

In instances when sampling is the preferred approach, researchers must decide how to select the elements they wish to study. In sampling, the term **element** refers to each member or entity in the population. Another question that the sampling plan must address is "How big should the sample be?" Finally, the plan must indicate whether the sampling method will permit inferences. By making an **inference**, the social work researcher is claiming that what holds for the sample is likely true for the population from which the sample was drawn. In the example just cited, the researcher would assume that the results of the study of 100 students could be generalized to the entire student population.

Exhibit 8.1 outlines the steps that the researcher will address in the formulation of a sampling plan. This chapter prepares you as a beginning social work researcher to engage in sampling and to critique the most commonly used sampling methods.

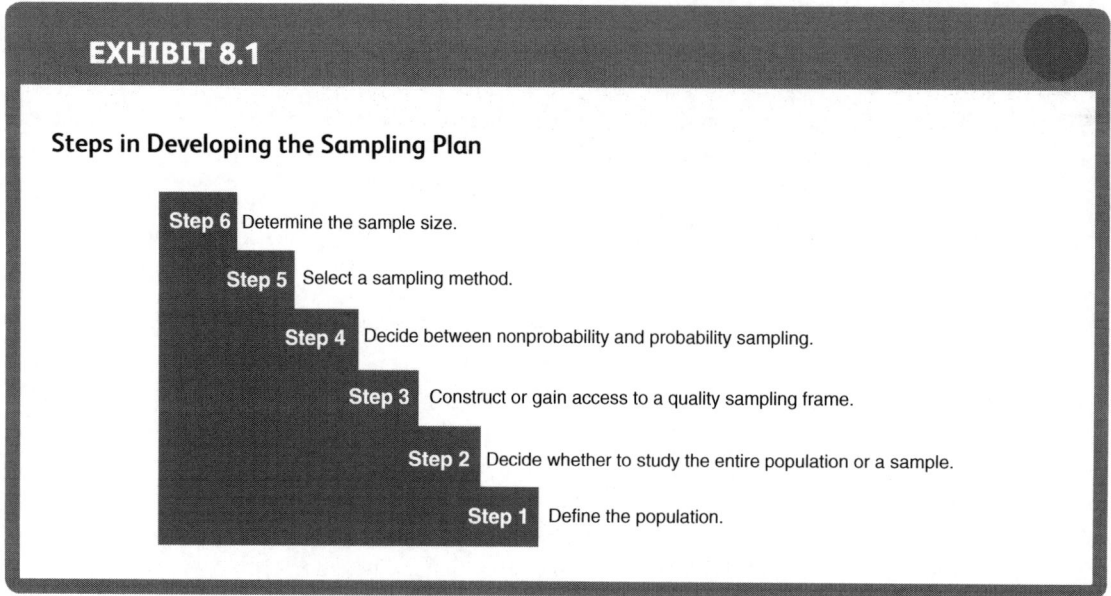

EXHIBIT 8.1

Steps in Developing the Sampling Plan

Step 6 Determine the sample size.

Step 5 Select a sampling method.

Step 4 Decide between nonprobability and probability sampling.

Step 3 Construct or gain access to a quality sampling frame.

Step 2 Decide whether to study the entire population or a sample.

Step 1 Define the population.

By the end of this chapter, you should be able to:

■ Describe the difference between a sample and population.
■ Explain the rationale for choosing to study either an entire population or a sample.
■ Identify the two main approaches to sampling, and explain their key differences.
■ List and discuss four types of probability sampling.
■ Discuss the concept of sampling error, and identify strategies to minimize it.

DEFINING THE POPULATION

The first step in developing a sampling plan is to develop clarity on the population that you wish to study. This task may sound straightforward and even simplistic. In reality, deciding on the population can sometimes be tricky. Social work research sometimes focuses on individuals and at other times on aggregates of people such as families, couples, and entire communities.

Let's assume that we are conducting a study in which the population elements are families. Although the category of "families" is very familiar, it nevertheless raises several basic questions. To begin with, within a given household, whom should we include in our definition of "family"? For example, do we

define "family" simply as parents and dependent children? What about adult children and extended family members who live in the household? Going further, if we are studying adults, at what age do we begin to place older children who are living at home into this category? Does an individual become an adult at 18, 19, or 21 years of age?

Researchers can use dimensions such as place, time, demographic characteristics, behavior, membership, attitudes, and beliefs to help define the population. The goal in specifically defining the population is to help the researcher achieve greater clarity about the focus of the research so that decisions are well thought out and there is greater precision in reporting the research procedures and findings.

For example, suppose our population consisted of elderly Chinese people. Would we restrict our study to American-born Chinese people, or would we also include elderly immigrants from China? What about immigrants from Taiwan and Hong Kong? A researcher must decide the boundaries of the population that is the focus of the study, and define it so that others will be clear about exactly who is included and who is not.

There will be times in research when the population elements are not exactly the same as the **sampling units**, the entities from which the data are gathered. For instance, a social work researcher may be interested in a population whose elements are preschool children, but the sampling units may be the parents of the preschool children because they are the ones who will respond to the researcher's request for information. The first step in developing a sampling plan, then, is to specifically define the population in terms of the elements and the sampling units.

The Sampling Frame

Once the researcher is clear about the population and has made the decision to sample, his or her next step is to obtain access to a **sampling frame**—a list of all the elements in a population from which the sample is selected. Together, the totality of population elements on the sampling frame is referred to as the **sampling universe**. The closer the sampling frame approximates the actual population, the less error that is introduced into the research study. The researcher's goal, then, is to gain access to a sampling frame that is comprehensive and free from error. For example, when the population is all schoolchildren in a district, the sampling frame may be a list of students obtained from the registrar's office in each school.

Suppose that, in the list of students, some are missing because they are new to the district and the list is not yet updated. It might seem obvious, but it must be made clear in a case like this that the lack of inclusiveness is due only or primarily to error in the collection of data. In contrast, **sampling bias** is defined as a problem with the selection of elements that produces systematic error in the research study. If all students with low test scores were left off the sampling frame, the study could be criticized for sampling bias. A sample that is drawn from a biased sampling frame cannot accurately represent the population.

At times, gaining access to a sampling frame is easy because it already exists, for example, a list of all juveniles in a detention facility. In other instances, you will have to develop the sampling frame, for example, a list of parents with adopted children in a specific school district. In either case, make certain to assess its quality very carefully. Is the sampling frame current? Is it inclusive of all the elements in the population? Is the information free of error and bias? If possible, crosscheck the sampling frame with other available sources. Sometimes you might have to add to or improve on an existing sampling frame. Don't worry if the elements on the sampling frame do not appear to be in any particular order—they don't need to be.

Social work researchers must be careful to include all of the elements on the sampling frame in the sampling process. If they exclude any part of the sampling frame, the elements no longer have an equal or a known chance of being selected. In such cases, the sample will not represent the population. For example, let's say that a researcher has a sampling frame of 150 individuals. Of these individuals, 100 provide contact information, and 50 do not. If the researcher selects only from the 100 who provide contact information, the sample will likely be biased. In other words, there will be a systematic difference between the sample and the population. The reason for this difference is that those individuals with contact information are probably different in some important ways (personality or motivation) from those individuals without contact information.

Sources of Error

How well we can generalize from a sample to the population depends on both sampling and nonsampling error. Error introduced by the sampling process can be of two types: sampling error and nonsampling error. We discuss strategies to reduce sampling error later in this chapter.

Nonsampling error is not related to the actual sampling procedure and includes inadequate sampling frames, high levels of attrition or nonresponse, and measurement and data entry errors. We examine strategies to reduce nonsampling error, including assessing the quality of the sampling frame before sampling and implementing a plan to maximize retention, in Chapter 10. Finally, we address strategies to reduce measurement and data entry errors and attrition in Chapters 9 and 10.

SELECTING A SAMPLING APPROACH

The next step in developing the sampling plan is to decide which of the two main sampling approaches to use:

- **Probability sampling** is a procedure in which every element in the sampling universe has a known chance (probability) of being selected. Note that all probability sampling approaches involve random sampling. Recall from Chapter 7 that the process of random sampling is the best way to ensure that there is no systematic bias in the way elements are selected. Similar to flipping a coin or rolling the dice, chance alone determines which elements will make it into the random sample and which will not. There is no purposive inclusion or exclusion of any element. If the researcher randomly selects enough elements, the sample should be representative of the population. The major advantage of probability sampling is that it permits **generalization**, the process of applying the findings from the sample to the population from which the sample was drawn.
- **Nonprobability sampling**, in contrast, is a procedure in which all of the elements in the population have an unknown and usually different chance of being included in the sample. Thus, nonprobability sampling does not support the claim that the sample is representative and therefore does not permit generalization, only speculation. The other side of the coin is that nonprobability sampling is simpler to manage and less expensive than probability sampling. In addition, it is better suited to answer some types of research questions.

The decision regarding what sampling approach to use will depend to a large extent on the goals of the research. Nonprobability sampling is most commonly used in exploratory research, in which the goals of the research are more concerned with discovery than with generalization. Recall from Chapter 3 that exploratory research tends to be qualitative because its purpose is to understand and give meaning rather than to quantify and generalize. For this reason, nonprobability sampling methods are often associated with qualitative research. In addition, nonprobability sampling methods are appropriate for situations in which it is either unfeasible or impossible to draw a probability sample. Such situations tend to develop when populations are difficult to access or when greater resources are required than are available. Nonprobability sampling is particularly appropriate if the study is a trial run for a larger study.

In contrast, research studies focused on descriptive and explanatory goals are better served by probability sampling because probability samples permit the researcher to generalize to the population. Also, because each element has a known probability of being selected, the researcher can estimate how well the findings for the sample will apply to the population. Because descriptive and explanatory studies are often quantitative in nature, probability sampling is most commonly associated with quantitative research. The following research example illustrates what happens when there is a mismatch between the sampling approach and the type of knowledge called for in the research question.

CASE-IN-POINT: STUDY OF FEMALE SEXUALITY FLOUNDERS ON SAMPLING BIAS

Shere Hite is known for her pioneering research on female sexuality in the 1970s. Her research has always commanded a lot of attention, and her study on the sexual practices and opinions of American women was no exception. Her 1989 report on the study contributed substantially to water cooler and locker-room conversations. It reported that 84 % of American women were not emotionally satisfied with their relationships and 70 % of women married five years or longer were engaging in extramarital affairs. How did she come up with these rather astounding findings?

Hite conducted her research by distributing more than 100,000 questionnaires to women across the United States over a seven-year period. Many of her questionnaires were distributed through organizations, including churches, political and women's rights groups, and counseling centers. Other women received questionnaires by responding to Hite's calls for volunteer respondents. In the final analysis, approximately 4,500 completed questionnaires were returned, a response rate of 4.5 %. Hite claimed that the 4,500 women included in her sample were representative of women in the United States based on demographic characteristics such as age and ethnicity.

Despite these assertions, several critics claim that Hite's research represents an extreme case of sampling bias. In Hite's study, what segment of the female population do you think would have been most likely to respond to her 127-item, essay answer, questionnaire? Would some women be more likely than others to respond? What characteristics might make a difference in responses? Unfortunately, because Hite selected a nonprobability sampling method, no one will ever be able to answer these questions accurately.

The point here is not that Hite's research has no value. In fact, her pioneering work on female sexuality has opened the dialogue on many topics that formerly were considered taboo, including cultural barriers to expressions of female sexuality. The problem is that the sampling method that Hite chose did not allow her to adequately answer her descriptive research question on the sexual behaviors and opinions of American women. Because Hite's objective was to generalize from her study to the female population, she should have selected a probability sample. Had her sample been selected randomly, 4,500 responses would have been more than sufficient.

Probability Sampling Approaches

This section presents five common methods of probability sampling. They include three single-stage methods—simple random sampling, systematic random sampling, stratified random sampling—and one multistage method, known as cluster sampling. Each method has advantages and limitations. Here we describe the types of situations in which each is used.

Advanced Skill Development 8.1 presents simple instructions for drawing these types of probability samples. All of them begin with a well-defined population and a quality sampling frame.

ADVANCED SKILL DEVELOPMENT 8.1

How to Draw Five Types of Probability Samples

Simple Random Sample:

1. Decide on the sample size.
2. Number consecutively all of the elements on the sampling frame.
3. Consult a table of random numbers. Decide in advance whether you will read down the columns or across the rows of the table. Then select a random or arbitrary starting point.
4. Select the numbered elements from the sampling frame that correspond to the numbers chosen from the random numbers table. Ignore redundant or out-of-range numbers.
5. Stop when you have selected enough elements to meet the desired sample size.

Systematic Random Sample:

1. Decide on the sample size.
2. Compute the sampling interval as follows:

   Sampling interval = N (population)/n (desired sample size)

3. If the computed sampling interval is not a whole number, alternate between using the first whole number immediately less than and greater than the computed interval. For example, if the sampling interval is 5.5, alternate between selecting elements at intervals of 5 and 6.
4. Select a random start within the first sampling interval. If the sampling interval is 5.5, the random start would be a number ranging from 1 to 6.
5. From the random start, select each element according to the sampling interval.
6. Stop when you reach the end of the sampling frame. You will have achieved the desired sample size by selecting according to the sampling interval.

Stratified Random Sample (Proportionate):

1. Stratify the sampling frame into relevant, mutually exclusive categories.
2. Decide on the sample size.

3. Sample each stratum as described under simple random or systematic random sampling.
4. Stop when you achieve the desired sample size.

Disproportionate Stratified Random Sample:

1. Stratify the sampling frame into relevant, mutually exclusive categories. Categories are mutually exclusive when each element belongs to one and only one category.
2. Decide on the sample size.
3. Divide the sample size by the number of strata to come up with the number of elements to be sampled from each category.
4. Sample each stratum as needed to represent that stratum. Oversampling of some strata may be necessary.
5. Stop when you achieve the desired sample size.

Cluster Sample:

1. Develop a sampling frame of broad clusters of elements within the population; stratify the clusters if justified.
2. Randomly select the clusters to be included in the sample.
3. After you have completed the broadest level of cluster sampling, develop a sampling frame for the next level of clusters—and so on, until the individual sampling element can be feasibly approached.
4. Randomly sample the chosen clusters using simple, systematic, or stratified random sampling.

Simple Random Sampling

In **simple random sampling,** the researcher selects elements from the entire sampling frame one at a time at random, so that each element has a known and equal chance of being selected. For example, if the sampling frame contains 50 elements, each element has a 1/50, or 2%, chance of being selected. The process is described in Advanced Skill Development 8.1.

The procedure used to select the simple random sample will likely depend on the size of the sampling frame and the researcher's comfort with using computer software. If the sampling frame is relatively small, a manual process is manageable. Any random method can be used. For instance, the researcher can write the sampling units on pieces of paper, put them in a container and shake them, and then pull them out at random until she or he reaches the desired sample size.

If the sampling frame is large, manual methods can be tedious. The researcher would instead want to use a computer program to number each element and generate a list of random numbers that matches the size of the desired sample. For example, if the desired sample size is 50 and the sampling frame contains 75 elements, the researcher would generate a list of 50 random numbers ranging from one to 75. The final step would be to match the list of 50 random numbers with the elements on the sampling frame.

A more common method of simple random sampling involves the use of a random numbers table, as described in Exhibit 8.2. A table of random numbers can be found through an Internet search using the term "table of random numbers."

Simple random sampling works best with a population that is relatively **homogeneous**, that is, in which there is not a great deal of variation on variables of interest to the study. For example, a study of attitudes in a Mormon community in Colorado City might safely use simple random sampling, whereas the same study would require a different sampling method in the more diverse areas of Los Angeles. If there is a great deal of variation on key variables in the population, a stratified random sampling method, as discussed later in this chapter, may produce a sample with less error—in other words, one that is more representative of the population.

EXHIBIT 8.2

Use of the Random Numbers Table

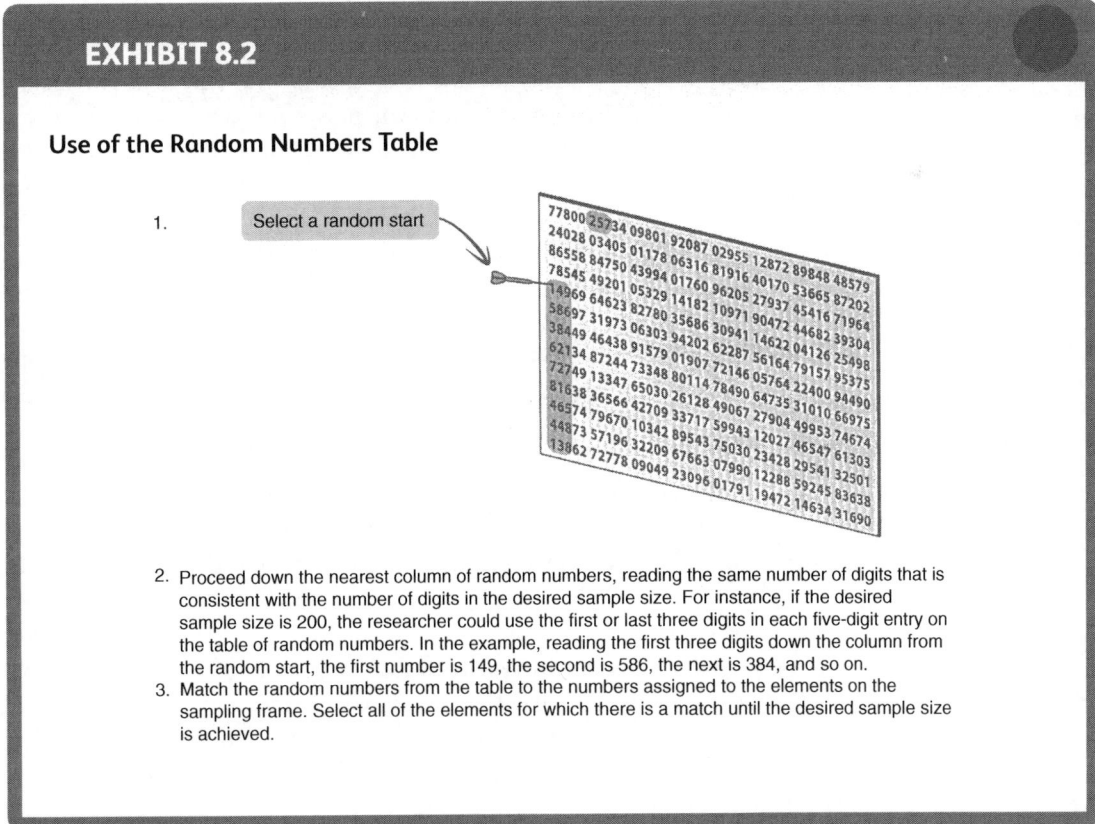

1. Select a random start

2. Proceed down the nearest column of random numbers, reading the same number of digits that is consistent with the number of digits in the desired sample size. For instance, if the desired sample size is 200, the researcher could use the first or last three digits in each five-digit entry on the table of random numbers. In the example, reading the first three digits down the column from the random start, the first number is 149, the second is 586, the next is 384, and so on.

3. Match the random numbers from the table to the numbers assigned to the elements on the sampling frame. Select all of the elements for which there is a match until the desired sample size is achieved.

Systematic Random Sampling

In **systematic random sampling,** the researcher computes a sampling interval based on the number needed for the sample. For example, if a researcher has a list of 300 names and plans to sample 50, she or he would select every sixth name (300/50 = 6). The researcher then selects the first element using a random start within the sampling interval of 1 through 6. Finally, beginning with the random start, the researcher selects every sixth element until she or he reaches the end of the sampling frame. The process of systematic random sampling is described in Advanced Skill Development 8.1. As with simple random sampling, the elements in systematic random sampling have a known and equal chance of being selected.

Systematic random sampling has several major advantages over simple random sampling:

■ The researcher does not have to number all of the elements on the sampling frame, a tedious task if the sampling universe is large.
■ The researcher does not need to match randomly chosen numbers with the numbers assigned to the sampling units.
■ The researcher does not need a sampling frame if the elements are organized in a way that permits the researcher to select elements at a regular interval—for instance, in a manual filing system or a computer directory of electronic file names when the filing system is representative of the population.

When researchers use systematic random sampling, certain quality control issues arise, even when a sampling frame is not used. For example, it is not unusual for filing systems, both paper and electronic, to have missing files that generally go undetected until an audit is conducted. Thus, researchers must take care to ensure that the entire sampling universe is available for selection.

When using systematic random sampling, researchers must also be alert to the possibility of order bias. **Order bias** occurs when the ordering in the sampling frame corresponds with the random start and the sampling interval in such a way as to underrepresent or overrepresent particular subgroups in the population. Consider, for example, a large child welfare agency and a sampling frame that is ordered by operational unit. Each unit is listed with the unit supervisor first, followed by five caseworkers. In this instance, drawing a systematic random sample could either overrepresent or underrepresent the caseworkers and the unit supervisors. If the researcher chose an interval of 6, for example, he or she would end up selecting only the supervisors.

Stratified Random Sampling

Researchers should adopt the method of stratified random sampling when they have reason to believe that the outcome of interest varies among the different subgroups in the population, and those subgroups run the risk of being overlooked or underrepresented in simple or systematic random sampling. For example, when researchers from the Gallup Organization examine health habits among seniors, they know that the results may vary by those who use landline phones and those who use cell phones. For this reason, they make certain their samples include representatives from both subgroups. Using this method can reduce error by helping to ensure that the sample is more representative of the population than it might have been with simple or systematic random sampling.

The process of stratified random sampling is spelled out in Advanced Skill Development 8.1. To draw a sample, the researcher first divides the sampling frame into two or more strata to be sampled independently. The strata are categories of variables determined to be important on the basis of prior knowledge. For example, in a study of literacy in childhood, the parents' primary language is an important variable. The researcher in this case may decide to create three strata: children whose parents speak only English, children whose parents speak only one non-English language such as monolingual Spanish speakers, and children with parents who are bilingual. Sometimes the researcher may stratify the sample on more than one variable. For example, the study may further stratify the groups by language, such as Spanish and Korean if these are the primary languages of the participants. The more variables, however, the greater the number of strata, and the larger the sample size needed to ensure that each category or stratum is adequately represented.

The task of creating the strata makes stratified random sampling considerably more complex than simple random or systematic random sampling. Thus, researchers who use stratified random sampling should limit the number of strata to only the most relevant categories. As with any research decision, researchers must be prepared to justify their choice of strata. They must also ensure that categories are mutually exclusive, which means that each element can belong to one and only one stratum.

Disproportionate Stratified Random Sampling

Stratified random samples can be of two types:

- In **proportionate sampling**, the proportion of each stratum in the sample corresponds to its respective proportion in the population. That is the method described above as stratified random sampling.

■   In **disproportionate sampling**, the size of the stratum is not the same as the proportion it constitutes in the population.

Disproportionate sampling is used when the numbers of elements with certain characteristics are so few in the population that they need to be over-sampled in order to be examined adequately as a subgroup and to be compared to other subgroups. **Oversampled** implies that the elements are sampled in greater proportion than their proportion represents in the population. For example, in a study of students' needs with a sample of 100 students, if only eight speak English as a second language, all eight might be included in order to better understand their needs.

When a researcher uses disproportionate stratified sampling, the probability of each element in each stratum being selected is no longer equal. Just the opposite, the elements in some strata have a greater chance of being selected than the elements in other strata because the strata vary in size. In such cases, if the researcher wants to make inferences from the sample back to the population, the sample data must be weighted to account for the influence of the oversampled elements. **Weighting** involves adjusting the values of the data to reflect the differences in the number of population units that each case represents.

For example, if we chose to study homelessness and our population of interest was U.S. military veterans, we know that gender would be an important variable. The National Coalition for Homeless Veterans (2010)[Q1] reports that 92% of sheltered homeless veterans are men and 8% are women. If we wanted to study the incidence of lifetime homelessness among the veteran population in Washington, DC, we would want to ensure that female veterans were represented in sufficient numbers in our sample. In other words, we would need to use stratified random sampling, disproportionate to size, to ensure an adequate sample of female veterans.

The pie charts in Exhibit 8.3 illustrate the difference between proportionate and disproportionate sampling. Imagine that we have a population of 40,617 veterans, as shown in Exhibit 8.3a, and we know that approximately 91% are men and 9% are women. Given a target sample size of 220, if we were to use proportionate sampling, we would sample 200 men (91% of our total sample size) and 20 women (9% of our sample size), as shown in Exhibit 8.3b. We calculate the proportion of men by multiplying the total sample size (220) by their percentage within the population (91%) represented as a decimal (91/100 = .91). In this instance: 220 x .91 = 200. For women, the sample proportion was calculated by the equation 220 x .09 = 20.

When we look at Exhibit 8.3, we must ask if our randomly chosen subgroup of 20 women would be representative of the entire population of 3,552 female veterans. This is a small sample. We would introduce

EXHIBIT 8.3

Proportionate and Disproportionate Stratified Samples

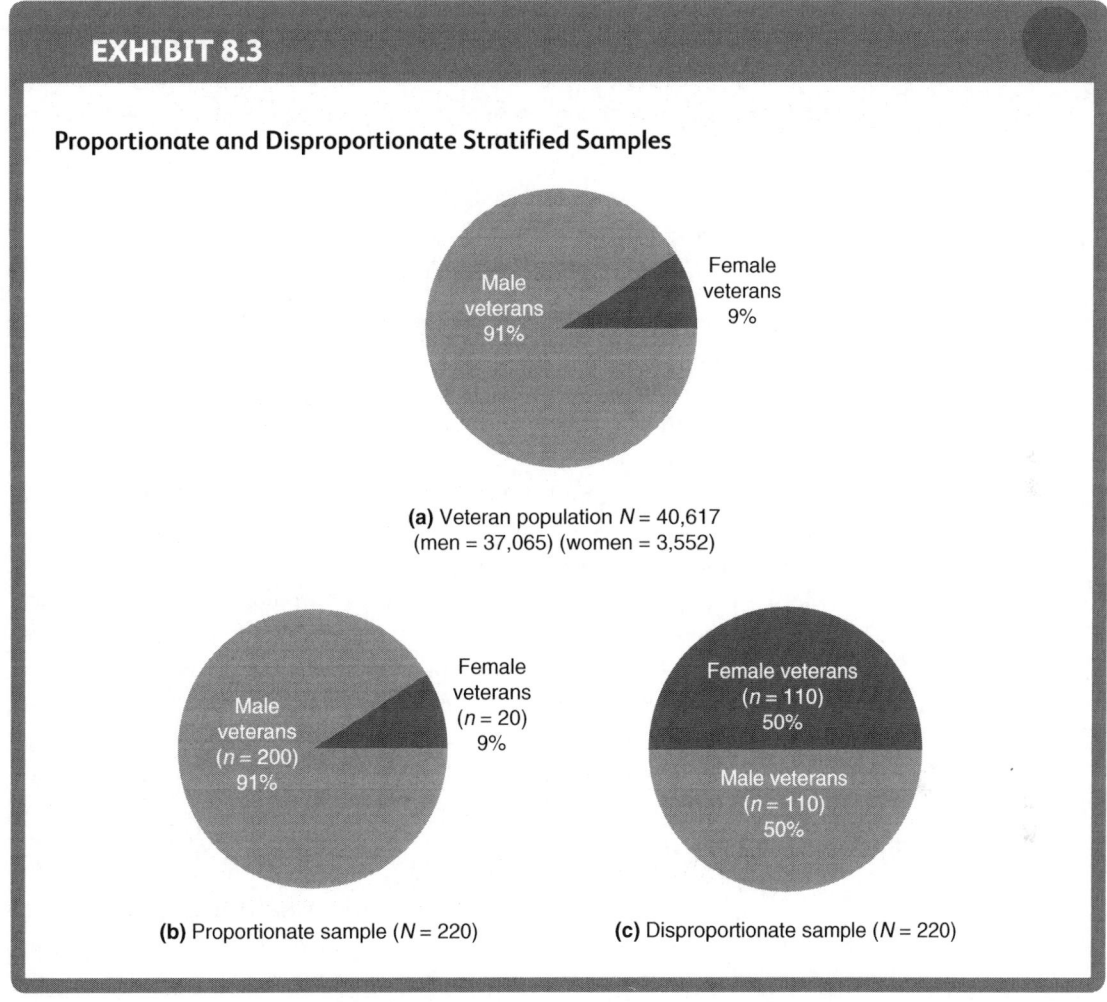

(a) Veteran population $N = 40,617$
(men = 37,065) (women = 3,552)

(b) Proportionate sample ($N = 220$)

(c) Disproportionate sample ($N = 220$)

significant error if we made inferences to the entire population based on a sample of 20 women.

Perhaps more important, we could not make any valid comparisons between male and female veterans if we had 200 men and 20 women. One strategy to deal with this shortcoming is to use a disproportionate sampling technique, as shown in Exhibit 8.3c. In this case, 50% of our sample would be female veterans, and 50% would be male veterans. Given our total sample size of 220, this would yield equal samples of 110 women and 110 men. If we randomly selected a sample consisting of 110 individuals in each subgroup, we could now examine male and female veterans separately and make between-group comparisons.

If, however, we then wanted to estimate the average income for the population of veterans from our disproportionate sample, we would need to weight the data for each case to take into account the overrepresentation of women—who typically have lower incomes than men—and the underrepresentation of men in the sample.

Cluster Sampling

Some populations cannot easily be represented on a sampling frame because they are so large or dispersed. One way to deal with this problem is through **cluster sampling**, the selection of elements from aggregates (groups) of elements. As an example, let's use individual students as a sampling unit. Obviously, the national student population is immense. How can we randomly sample such a population?

One approach is **multistage cluster sampling,** a method of repeating random samples until we reach a manageable cluster of sampling units. Exhibit 8.4 continues the student example. In this case, the first clusters are counties. If we were to end our sampling at this level, we would have performed a basic cluster sampling. However, because we want to sample individual students, we need to repeat the random sampling at increasingly targeted levels until we reach our sample population. That is, after we sample counties, we would then sample school districts, then individual schools within districts, and then classrooms within schools until we finally get to the students within the classrooms. Note that the more stages of random sampling, the greater the chances for sampling error, because error is introduced at each stage. The process of cluster sampling is described in Exhibit 8.4.

Cluster sampling can easily be combined with stratification. Within the level of school district, for instance, it may be important to stratify by size. Similarly, at the school level, it may be important to stratify by type: for example, public, charter, and parochial. At the school district level, sampling proportionate to size would likely be the best option to ensure that the sample reflects the distribution of school districts in the population. In contrast, at the school level, disproportionate sampling would likely be the method of choice because there are usually fewer parochial and charter schools than public schools.

Cluster sampling can make a large research project manageable, and it can be useful when a population sampling frame is not initially available. It can also help the researcher to manage research that covers a large geographic area. However, the researcher must be concerned with representativeness at each stage of cluster sampling and stratify if appropriate. The Homeless Street Count, described in the following Case-in-Point, illustrates the creative use of cluster sampling with a population that is relatively small in number, underserved, and stigmatized.

EXHIBIT 8.4

Multistage Cluster Sampling

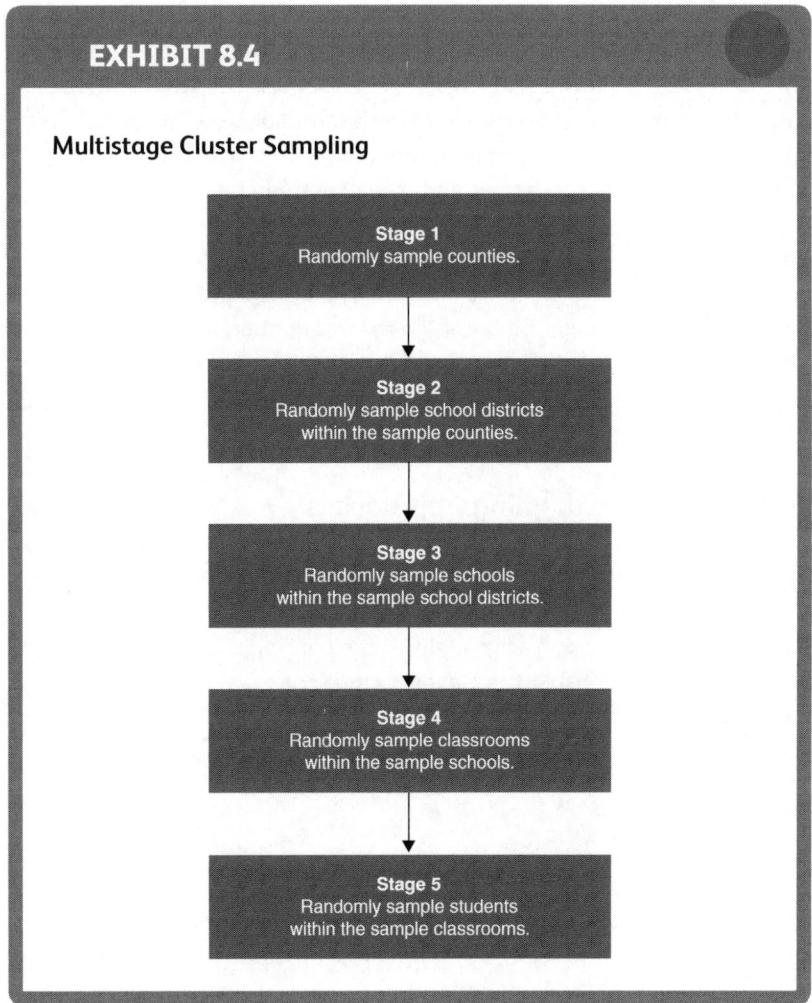

Stage 1
Randomly sample counties.

Stage 2
Randomly sample school districts
within the sample counties.

Stage 3
Randomly sample schools
within the sample school districts.

Stage 4
Randomly sample classrooms
within the sample schools.

Stage 5
Randomly sample students
within the sample classrooms.

CASE-IN-POINT: CLUSTER SAMPLING AND THE ANNUAL HOMELESS STREET COUNT

Each year all across the United States in one particular week, communities select one day to engage in an annual count of the homeless population. To guide the Count, the Department of Housing and Urban Development (HUD) has provided the following definition of homelessness: adults, children, and unaccompanied youth sleeping in places not meant for human habitation. Examples of settings that fit HUD's definition are streets, parks, alleys, dumpsters, abandoned buildings, campgrounds, vehicles, and stairwells. Note that this definition does not include individuals who move from home to home sleeping on couches. The existence and clarity of the definition, however, make the Count possible.

Some jurisdictions participating in the Count use sampling in combination with straight count-ing. Researchers in the city of Phoenix, Arizona, for example, stratify geographic areas of the city into grids of low-density and high-density numbers of homeless individuals. The stratification is based on information obtained from previous Counts. Homeless individuals in all high-density areas are counted, whereas only the homeless individuals in randomly selected low-density areas are counted. Sampling the low-density areas saves time and resources, thereby making the task manageable.

From the sample data, researchers compute the average number of homeless individuals in the low-density areas and then assign this number to the low-density areas that were not included in the sample. In other words, they estimate the population based on the information they obtain from the sample.

Nonprobability Sampling Approaches

As we discussed in Chapter 6, nonprobability samples do not use random sampling and therefore do not permit generalization. The decision to use a nonprobability sampling approach should be intentional, as should the choice of the particular nonprobability sampling method. The nonprobability sampling method that you select should be the method that best matches the goal of your research.

Convenience Sampling

This section describes one common type of nonprobability sampling: convenience sampling. Three additional types of nonprobability sampling, purposive, snowball, and quota, were presented in Chapter 6 in the context of qualitative research. As with probability sampling, the sampling units in nonprobability sampling do not have to be human, with the one exception being snowball sampling; snowball sampling depends on recommendations provided by human informants.

As its name suggests, **convenience sampling** selects the most available elements to constitute the sample. Convenience may be based on geographic closeness, ease of access, or other opportunity, such as presence at a conference. The use of convenience sampling is common in social work research because it is relatively quick and inexpensive. The caution with convenience sampling is not to generalize to the broader population because there is no justification to claim that the sample is representative of the larger group. Unfortunately, there is a tendency among some researchers to make this leap, as was illustrated in the first Case-in-Point above regarding the Hite study of female sexuality.

DECIDING ON THE CORRECT SAMPLE SIZE

One of the major questions a researcher must address in planning a study is "How big should my sample be?" There is no simple answer to this question. In the beginning of the chapter, we discussed a survey of people 65 and older living in the U.S. that was based on 150,984 adults. Can you imagine how long the survey would have taken and how expensive it would have been if researchers at the Gallup Organization had tried to contact every senior adult in the United States to elicit her or his opinion on exercise and health? The difficulty and cost involved in surveying the entire senior population probably explain why the U.S. Census, which seeks information from every American adult, is conducted only once every 10 years.

Conversely, in instances when the size of the population is relatively small, the researcher may want to study the entire population rather than a sample. This is the situation in many agencies and organizations that employ social workers. One guideline used as a practical matter is to restrict random sampling to populations with more than 100 elements. However, even when a population contains 100 or fewer elements, the researcher might have only enough resources to collect data on a smaller sample. Given this scenario, a small, carefully crafted research study based on a sample is better than no research study at all.

Another key factor that affects the decision on sample size is whether the researcher has chosen to use a probability or a nonprobability sampling approach. In nonprobability sampling, sample size is based on conceptual rather than statistical considerations, as discussed in Chapter 6. As a general rule in nonprobability sampling, the researcher selects elements until no new insights or observations are revealed. Convenience sampling often involves a small group of participants such as the students in a classroom. In such cases, the entire group should be included if resources permit. In purposive sampling, the sample size will be determined by the variation in experience, knowledge, and attitudes the researcher considers important to represent. For quota sampling, the desired sample size will be based at least in part on the number of categories that the researcher has predetermined to be important.

As with all research, sample size is a balance between what is desired and what is feasible. An increase in sample size in nonprobability sampling will not allow the researcher to claim that the findings are any more representative of the broader population than she or he could claim with a small sample. Nonprobability sampling does not involve random sampling; therefore, a nonrandom selection process is likely to introduce bias. The Case-in-Point above regarding the sexuality study illustrates the fallacy that increasing the size of a nonprobability sample will generate more accurate results. It will not.

Probability samples are typically larger than those found in nonprobability sampling. In probability sampling, an increase in sample size actually does permit the researcher to claim greater representation of the larger population. For probability sampling approaches, sample size will be determined by a combination of the following factors, each of which is described below:

- desired precision
- degree of variation in the population on key variables
- number of variables and the plan for the analysis
- estimated nonresponse or attrition rate

Determine the Desired Precision

The question of how big a sample should be is determined to a large extent by the amount of sampling error the researcher is willing to accept. **Sampling error** is the degree of difference between the sample and the population from which it was drawn. In determining an acceptable degree of sampling error, the researcher must select a confidence level and a confidence interval:

- **Confidence level:** tells us how sure we can be that the results from our sample represent the population. The confidence level is selected by the researcher. By convention, most researchers in the social sciences use a confidence level of 95% as their standard. A confidence level of 95% means that if the same study were conducted 100 times with random samples drawn from the same population, it would represent the true population value 95 times. Of course, this definition implies that five times out of 100, the sample would not represent the true population value. In other fields such as the medical sciences, in which decisions literally can relate to life or death, and the physical sciences, in which decisions can be a matter of public safety, a confidence level of 99% or higher might be chosen because the consequence of being wrong five times out of 100 is considered much too high.
- **Confidence interval:** indicates how far the sample's results can stray from the true value in the entire population. This is the plus-or-minus **margin of error** (usually expressed in percentage points) that we see mentioned in public opinion polls. The margin of error of a sample depends on the number of elements included in the sample. Margin of error, or the confidence interval, is calculated by dividing 1 by the square root of the number of elements in the sample. Thus, if the sample size is 50, we divide 1 by 7.1 (the square root of 50). This equation produces a margin of error of plus-or-minus ($\pm$) 14%. To illustrate what this means, if we conducted a survey to which 40% of those interviewed answered that they routinely used spanking as a means of disciplining their toddlers, we could be 95%

confident that the true population figure would fall $\pm$ 14 of 40, somewhere between 26% and 54%. Conversely, there is a 5% chance that the true population figure would not fall between 26% and 54%; it could be higher or lower.

A range of plus-or-minus 14 percentage points is very large and does not tell us anything with an adequate degree of precision. A sample of 100 individuals, in contrast, would provide a narrower margin of error, plus-or-minus 10 percentage points. A sample of 200 would reduce the margin of error to plus-or-minus 7 percentage points. If our goal were a margin of error of plus-or-minus 3 percentage points, we would need a sample size of 1,000.

The margin of error considered acceptable depends on how accurate we require the research to be. For example, since a close election may be decided by 1% of the vote, a very small margin of error is needed by political pollsters. On the other hand, if we need to know whether or not people are generally in favor of an after-school arts program, a larger margin of error (such as 10–15%) would suffice.

Although the size of the sample influences the margin of error, the size of the population does not. That is, it does not matter if we are interested in 200 million adults in the United States or in 10 million adults from Los Angeles County. In both cases, a randomly drawn sample of 1,000 is sufficient if we are willing to accept a margin of error of plus-or-minus three percentage points. This explains why the Gallup Organization often relies on sample sizes of approximately 1,000 people to represent large populations. The law of diminishing returns states that at a certain point, more does not mean better. In sampling, once we pass a particular point, what is gained in accuracy is not usually justified by the cost. Researchers must keep in mind, however, that if they want to make statements about population subgroups, they need to consider the size of the subgroup in the sample when calculating the margin of error.

The ability of a probability sample to represent the population from which it was drawn depends, however, on more than sample size. As discussed next, it also depends on other factors related to the population and the research design.

Manage Variation in the Population

Recall that when population elements are similar to a large extent on key variables, we say that they are homogeneous. In contrast, populations with greater within-group diversity are **heterogeneous**. Generally speaking, the more heterogeneous the population, the larger the sample size needed to accurately reflect the population. For a population with little variation on key variables, a relatively small sample usually is sufficient.

Fortunately, tables like the one in Advanced Skill Development 8.2 are available to help us determine a base sample size—the smallest sample size that will adequately represent the population—while taking into account the degree of variability in the population. If we do not know the variation in key variables, we should use the first column under the heading "Variability" because it assumes the greatest amount of variation, a 50/50 split. The column on the

ADVANCED SKILL DEVELOPMENT 8.2

Base Sample Sizes with a ±5% Margin of Error, Determined from Population Size and Variability

	Variability				
Population Size	50%	40%	30%	20%	10%
100	81	79	63	50	37
125	96	93	72	56	40
150	110	107	80	60	42
175	122	119	87	64	44
200	134	130	93	67	45
225	144	140	98	70	46
250	154	149	102	72	47
275	163	158	106	74	48
300	172	165	109	76	49
325	180	173	113	77	50
350	187	180	115	79	50
375	194	186	118	80	51
400	201	192	120	81	51
600	240	228	134	87	53
800	267	252	142	90	54
1,000	286	269	147	92	55
2,000	333	311	158	96	57

This table assumes a 95% confidence level.
The base sample size should be increased to take attrition into consideration.

Source: J. Watson, 2001. How to determine a sample size: Tipsheet 60, University Park, PA: Penn State Cooperative Extension. Available at www.extension.psu.edu/evaluation/pdf/TS60.pdf.

far right with the heading "10%" assumes that the distribution on the variable of interest is 90%/10%. Social work researchers would define such a population as homogeneous.

In some instances, researchers must undertake a pilot study to understand the degree of variability before they make an informed judgment on sample size. One method of reducing variation in the population is to focus on a more homogeneous group of elements, that is, to define the population more narrowly; for example, they could sample only a specific income bracket rather than the full range of incomes.

Consider the Number of Variables to be Analyzed

Another factor that influences sample size is the number of variables that researchers will consider in the analysis. The literature review the researcher conducts to help formulate the research problem and question is vital to identifying important variables for the study. The sampling plan must then take into account anticipated statistical analyses.

When researchers break down the data into categories that consist of multiple variables, what initially appeared to be a substantial sample size may no longer be large enough. Take the Healthy Families America program discussed in other chapters as an example. When researchers examined parental stress across four categories of age and five categories of ethnicity, they ended up with 20 cells (see Exhibit 8.5). Each cell must contain data about the number of people who fall into each age-ethnicity cell, such as Hispanic parents ages 26–32.

EXHIBIT 8.5

Example of Income by Ethnicity

AGE IN YEARS	AFRICAN AMERICAN	HISPANIC	NATIVE AMERICAN	WHITE/ CAUCASIAN	ASIAN, PACIFIC ISLANDER
<19					
19–25					
26–32					
33+					

When the data are cross-classified this way, the sample size must be sufficient to support the analysis. If the base sample size was determined from a table such as the one in Advanced Skill Development 8.2, the researcher would want to use the general rule of a minimum of 10 elements per cross-classified variable included in the analysis.

However, if the variables are not numeric, the researcher must also consider the number of categories in each variable. For example, if the analysis will include the variables age (classified into two categories, young or old), race (classified as African American, Hispanic, White, and Other), and gender (Male or Female), a 16-cell table is required. That number is calculated by multiplying the number of categories for each variable—in this case 2 x 4 x 2 = 16 cells. In this instance, the rule of 10 elements per variable would not be sufficient.

When the sample size is small, the number of elements in each cell can become quite sparse. A **sparse table** is one in which 30% of the cells have five or fewer elements. The use of sparse tables will invalidate many statistical tests. It would be better to use the rule for sparse tables; that is, no more than 30% of the cells should contain five or fewer elements. If the base sample size does not support the number of variables to be examined, or if several of the variables have multiple categories, the researcher will want to increase the base sample size.

Account for Attrition

It would be highly unlikely not to observe at least some level of attrition in a research sample. If the research involves observation at one point in time, we are concerned with **nonrespondents**, those who do not respond for whatever reason: refusal, language problems, illness, or lack of availability. If the study involves more than one round of measurement or observation, the researcher must be concerned with **attrition**, elements that are lost from one observation to the next.

To avoid an additional round of sampling, we can estimate the expected level of attrition before the study begins and then compensate for it when we determine the initial sample size. To estimate attrition, we might look at the dropout rates in similar studies. In studies of home visitation programs to prevent child abuse and neglect, it is common to sample an extra 20% in addition to the desired sample size to account for attrition. If the desired sample size was 220 and the estimated attrition rate was 20%, we would calculate the number of additional sampling units needed by multiplying the total sample size by the percentage of expected attrition represented as a decimal: $220 \times .20 = 44$. Thus, the total sample size needed to account for attrition would be 264 (220 + 44). Chapter 10 provides strategies for managing attrition once the study is implemented.

CONCLUSION

The power of random sampling is evident in national opinion poll surveys that allow researchers to generalize findings to the nation based on the responses of 1,000 people. Social workers are often concerned with large numbers of people as well, for example, when studying attitudes about social policies, the adjustment of people with mental illness in the community, or the stability of placements for foster children.

This chapter has presented the development of a sampling plan as a process requiring six steps. Together these steps can be used as a guide in developing a sampling plan, as well as to evaluate the sampling procedures used in other studies.

The ability to generalize from a sample to a population is not as dependent on sample size as it is on the sampling approach. Researchers should keep in mind the limitations of different sampling approaches and exercise caution not to generalize beyond what the sampling approach will support. Reduction of error is a goal in research, and prior knowledge of the research topic and the population can be used to tailor the sampling plan to minimize the potential for sampling error.

Once a sample has been selected, the researcher is ready to measure variables in the sample and engage in data collection. The following two chapters present additional strategies for minimizing error associated with measurement (Chapter 9) and data collection (Chapter 10). Unless appropriate sampling is used, even the best measuring instruments and the most sophisticated data analyses will yield inaccurate results.

MAIN POINTS

- A sample is a subset of the population.
- Key to good sample selection is the development of a sampling plan that addresses how the population will be defined, the justification for sampling or including the entire population, the quality of the sampling frame, the sampling approach, the sampling method, and the sample size.
- Probability sampling is a procedure in which every element in the sampling universe has a known probability of selection. If enough elements are randomly selected, the sample should be representative of the population. The major advantage of probability sampling is that it permits generalization.
- Nonprobability sampling is a procedure in which all of the elements in the population have an unknown and usually different probability of being included in the sample. Thus, nonprobability sampling does not support the claim that the sample is representative of the population and therefore does not permit generalization.

■ Sample size must be estimated in the design phase of the research. There are guidelines on how many subjects to sample based on population size. However, these guidelines can be improved upon through the consideration of desired precision, the number of variables considered in the analysis, the degree of variability within the population, and estimates of attrition or nonresponse.

■ The amount of difference between the findings based on a random sample and the true value in the population, if it were known, is sampling error.

EXERCISES

1. Access the sampling frame and a table of random numbers that can be located through an Internet search. Select a simple random sample of 20 youths in the Riverton case. Then answer these questions:
   a. How did you choose your random start?
   b. Which 20 random numbers did you select?
   c. Which 20 names did you select?
   d. What factors might influence how well this sample represents the population? What could you do in order to assess the representativeness of the sample?

3. Using the same materials as in the previous exercise, consult the sampling frame and select a systematic random sample of 20 youths. Then answer these questions:
   a. What was the sampling interval you calculated?
   b. How did you select a random start within the first interval?
   c. Which names did you select?
   d. How well do you believe the sample represents the population? How do you think that this sample would compare to the random sample from Question 1?

3. Using the sampling frame as in the previous two exercises, select a stratified random sample of 20 youths. Then answer these questions:
   a. Which categories will you choose to stratify the sample?
   b. If you use proportionate sampling, what percentage of the sample will you select from each stratum?
   c. If you use disproportionate sampling, how many elements will you sample from each stratum?
   d. How did the sample composition vary in proportionate sampling, compared to disproportionate sampling?
   e. How does your sample compare to the simple random and systematic random samples you selected for exercises 1 and 2?

4. Consider the Sanchez family case. Create a hypothetical sampling plan for a community needs assessment of similar families. Would you use probability sampling methods, nonprobability, or a combination of the two? Justify your decisions. What cultural considerations would enter into your sampling plan? What would you need to know about the population in order to determine the representativeness of your sample? How might it be difficult to assess the necessary sample size given uncertainty about the true size of the Latino immigrant population in the United States?

5. Use the RAINN interactive case. Access the data from Phase 4 in the interactive case. What would you describe as the sampling plan for the visitor dataset? Is the sample a probability or nonprobability sample? Given the reported response rate and the sampling method used, what are the implications for the findings related to these data? What recommendations would you make to RAINN to improve the quality of the data they collect?

6. Consider the Hudson City case. You want to understand how the residents of Hudson City are coping after the disaster. Devise a sampling plan and justify your choices. How might the community context, in the aftermath of the disaster, influence your choice of sampling approaches?

7. Suppose you have been hired as a consultant to develop a sampling plan for a survey of attitudes in Brickville toward environmental protections related to air quality in the city. The leaders would like a high degree of accuracy in the survey (plus or minus three percentage points). What does it mean when it is reported that the survey is accurate within plus or minus three or five percentage points? What pieces of information would you need in order to determine the recommended sample size? How might differences among groups within Brickville affect your proposed sampling plan? What might make it harder to get an accurate sample in some subgroups than in others?

chapter
9

MEASUREMENT

One foot is short. One inch is long.

Qu Yuan, Chinese poet and patriot (340 BC–278 BC)

Measurement in everyday life is commonly associated with the tools of our time. Activity and sleep trackers worn similar to wristwatches measure concepts such as pulse, calories burned, steps taken, total sleep time, and the number of times woken during sleep. How well we measure these concepts depends to a large extent on the tools we use. An atomic wall clock provides a much more accurate measure of time than eyeballing the position of the sun. Similarly, new advances in nanotechnology—technology at the level of the atom—are changing the ways in which doctors diagnose and treat cancer. Doctors can now detect cancer at its earliest stages, pinpoint its exact location within the body, and direct anticancer drugs to the affected cells.

These examples involving time and medicine illustrate the fact that measurement involves choice. To a large extent, the choices we make in measurement depend on the available technology, the skill level of the people who administer the measure, access to resources such as time and money, the need for precision, and the social context. The same is true of measurement tools used in social work research. Despite the emphasis on the mechanics of measurement in this chapter, the one thing that is certain is that measurement is not a pristine science.

Measurement is so important in social work research that it is the focus of two chapters in this book. This chapter is concerned with the concept of measurement and the questions we must ask in order to make critical choices in selecting and evaluating measures. Chapter 10 then focuses on the process of measurement, which begins after we have selected the appropriate measures and are preparing to implement them.

By the end of this chapter, you should be able to:

- Describe the concept of measurement.
- List the pros and cons of different measurement options.
- Know how to construct your own questions for use as measures in social work research.
- Know where to search for existing measurement instruments.
- Discuss the issues of measurement reliability and validity and their relationship.
- Explain the four levels of measurement.

MEASUREMENT IN SOCIAL WORK RESEARCH

The most fundamental thing to understand about measurement is that there is no one right way to measure each of the many concepts that are the subject of social work research. Take, for example, the concept of poverty. We often hear statements referring to the percentages of certain subgroups within the population who are living in poverty. Poverty statistics are bandied about as if there were an absolute division between people who are poor and people who are not poor. According to the official poverty measure in the United States, known as the poverty threshold, a four-person household with two dependent children earning $24,036 in 2015 was considered poor, while a household of the same size and structure earning $24,040—$4 more—was not poor (U.S. Department of Health and Human Services, 2016). What this example illustrates is that all measures, even well-established and accepted measures, have benefits and limitations.

Measurement can be defined as the process of assigning numbers or other symbols to characteristics or attributes of a concept according to specified rules. Thus measurement is the representation of a concept, not the actual condition itself. Measurement is reductionist in the sense that it filters the information that will be considered. For example, the poverty threshold is based solely on income and family type and does not consider other things, such as health care costs and geographic differences in the cost of housing. Measurement is also a social construction in the sense that it requires a decision about what to include and what to exclude.

Social workers must be diligent in critiquing the fit between concepts and their representation through measures. The choices we make regarding measurement have important implications. Measurement is a vital component of our communication both within and outside the social work profession. It also forms the basis of our conclusions in social work research. Finally, we use measures such as the poverty threshold to target individuals for research and to determine whether or not they are eligible for important programs and benefits.

The Role of Concepts in Measurement

When we think of measurement, we often envision the process of measuring or the tool used to conduct the measure. Before the tool or the process, however, we need to think about the concepts underlying the measurement. In social work research, we are interested in measuring concepts, which are called variables. In the context of measurement, a **variable** is simply something with no fixed numerical value; that is, its value can change or vary. For instance, if we were interested in the way parents discipline their preschool children, parental discipline would be the variable.

Various options or categories within the concept of parental discipline include spanking, yelling, pushing, explaining, and imposing a time-out. The options within a variable, in this instance the different forms of discipline, are referred to as **attributes**. Variable attributes such as spanking, yelling, pushing, explaining, and imposing a time-out would be the focus of measurement. In other words, we are concerned with measuring the attributes of variables.

Careful definitions are important when measuring the attributes of variables. As discussed in Chapter 3, the type of definition we would find in a dictionary is referred to as a *nominal definition*. The concept of disability, for instance, might be defined in a dictionary as a lack of physical or mental ability. However, in order to consider a concept for inclusion in a research study, we have to go beyond a nominal definition to define it in a way that enables us to measure it. We call this type of definition an **operational definition.** The process of creating an operational definition involves defining a concept in detail so that it is highly likely to mean the same thing to one person as it does to another.

In social work research, we can often adopt or build on operational definitions that have already been developed. Take the concept of childhood disability, for example. The U.S. Social Security Administration has defined childhood disability as "a physical or mental condition(s) that very seriously limits his or her activities and the condition(s) must have lasted, or be expected to last, at least 1 year or result in death" (U.S. Social Security Administration, 2016, p. 6). We could add to this operational definition by defining in greater detail the concepts of "child" and "mental condition." For example, we could define a child as an individual less than 18 years of age. We could adopt the definition for mental condition from the Americans with Disabilities Act: "any mental or psychological disorder such as mental retardation, organic brain syndrome, emotional or mental illness and specific learning disabilities" (Americans with Disabilities Act, 2010). The greater the detail in the operational definition, the less room for ambiguity in interpreting the results of a research study.

The Context of Measurement

Measurement is greatly affected by the cultural and social contexts as well as the prevailing political climate in which it is constructed and applied. Take for example the concept of elder abuse. Although there are some specific indicators that would seem to indicate elder abuse, it is not as simple as it seems. For example, two indicators would include the personal use of an elderly person's financial resources, and repeated and unexplained bruises. Both of these indicators correspond with typical changes in older adulthood. Some elderly adults, for instance, mismanage their money as their short-term memory declines with age. As a result, adult children and caretakers often assume responsibility for the elder's financial responsibilities. As for the bruising, elderly individuals tend to bruise more easily than younger adults. They may not be able to accurately explain the origin of their bruises due to memory loss, deteriorating mental status, and communication problems. Thus, bruising may indicate issues with declining balance rather than abuse.

Culture also complicates operationalization of elder abuse. Some cultures would define the placement of an elder in a skilled nursing home facility as a form of abuse, whereas other cultures would interpret it as a sign of caring. The problem with operationalizing elder abuse, as with many concepts, is that it involves subjective judgments and culture-bound definitions. No one operational definition is right for all research contexts.

The issue of cultural context can be sensitive. In the past, measurement has at times been used to oppress population subgroups. Classic examples of this practice are found in studies of biological determinism that rank people of different races and genders on measures of intelligence. Many of these studies concluded that women and minority groups were less intelligent than white males. Critics have denounced these works in part due to the studies' inadequate measurement techniques (Gould, 1981).

Talking about measurement without referring to the research context in which measurement occurs can be misleading. Measurement will also vary depending on whether the researcher chooses a quantitative or qualitative approach to answering the research question. The researcher's decision regarding the appropriate approach is based in part on the types of information that the researcher needs in order to answer the research question.

Measurement in Qualitative and Quantitative Research

The type of measurement used in social work research is related to the research approach being employed in the study. As discussed in Chapter 1, quantitative and qualitative research are different approaches, with different assumptions and methods. Quantitative and qualitative research also approach measurement differently:

- Quantitative research focuses on a limited number of predefined variables that generate primarily numeric data; qualitative research is holistic in its approach, and the data tend to be rich narrative descriptions.
- The main sources of data for quantitative research are structured observations, experiments, and survey research; qualitative research relies on unstructured observation and in-depth interviews, as discussed in Chapter 6.

Interviews are used in both types of research, but they are designed, conducted, and analyzed quite differently. Qualitative research makes use of unstructured interviews, although the interviewer may be guided by a list of topics and subtopics or broad questions. In addition, the questions used in qualitative research do not ask participants to select from a number of predefined responses, as is often the case in quantitative research. Typical questions in qualitative research revolve around how people experience being part of a cultural group or subculture, how they describe or comprehend an experience or an event, and the discovery of regularities and patterns in people's experiences.

Quantitative and qualitative approaches to measurement both have advantages and limitations. As a result, some researchers combine aspects of qualitative measurement in quantitative research. Consider a study of home visitation by social workers to prevent child abuse and neglect. Because it is difficult to find a quantitative measure that captures the nature and quality of the parent-child relationship, the researcher may choose to use qualitative methods such as observations of parent-child interaction and in-depth interviews with the parents. An early feminist researcher, for instance, observed female sweatshop workers and their male employers, conducted in-depth interviews, and incorporated statistical data from existing records in her book *Prisoners of Poverty: Women Wage-Workers, Their Trades, and Their Lives* (Campbell, 1883/1970).

SOURCES OF MEASURABLE DATA

Regardless of the particular approach the researcher chooses, at the most basic level there are only three ways to measure concepts: ask questions, make observations, and consult existing records. The first two options involve the collection of **primary data**, or new data compiled by the researcher. The third option involves the use of **secondary data**, defined as data that were previously collected for a purpose other than the research at hand. In conducting a study, the researcher selects the approach to measurement that will provide the kind of data that will answer the research question.

This section describes three common tools used to collect data in social work research: surveys, standardized instruments, which both yield primary data, and existing records, which is the source of secondary data. Observational research is discussed in Chapter 6.

Survey Research

Survey research, which relies on questioning, is a popular method of gathering data in social work research. A **survey** is a systematic way of collecting data from a number of respondents. The survey can be used to determine what respondents know, believe, feel, and how they say they behave. Some surveys ask respondents to describe what they have done or how they felt in the past, whereas others ask respondents to speculate about their future intentions.

Every research study that uses a survey as a data-collection method can be included under the umbrella of survey research. In contrast, efforts to sell, collect donations, or to educate or persuade under the guise of a survey are not true forms of survey research, although they may be falsely identified as such. What differentiates selling and educating from survey research is that the sole purpose of survey research is to collect data.

The measurement tool used to collect data in survey research, the survey instrument, is identified differently depending on the means of survey administration:

- A survey that is mailed to potential respondents or that is given in person is called a **self-administered questionnaire**.
- When interviewers ask survey questions in face-to-face or telephone interviews with respondents, the measurement tool is called an **interview schedule**.
- Another way of administering an interview schedule is through the use of **computer-assisted telephone interviewing (CATI)**, in which the computer asks the questions and records the responses. Surveys administered via the Internet are also popular.

Chapter 10 discusses Internet surveys and presents guidelines on how to choose among the different forms of survey research.

Structured and Semi-Structured Surveys

The degree of standardization in a survey instrument is reflected by the degree of structure in the questions. Survey research can be characterized on a continuum between structured and semi-structured:

- In a **structured survey**, the interviewer asks the questions as they are written with the aim of standardizing the administration process as much as possible. The questions included in a structured survey are primarily **closed-ended questions**—they require the respondent to choose from a limited number of predefined responses. Closed-ended questions are useful because they produce uniform responses. Even probing questions such as "Can you please explain what you mean by that?" are scripted in a structured survey.
- In a **semi-structured survey**, the interviewer is free to clarify the questions and follow up on participants' responses. Unlike structured surveys,

semi-structured surveys make use of **open-ended questions**, which ask respondents to respond in their own words rather than to select from a number of predefined responses. Open-ended questions are useful when the researcher cannot anticipate all of the answer categories and does not want to limit the responses. A researcher would seldom administer a semi-structured survey by any means other than an interview because of the length of time and writing required in answering the open-ended questions.

Exhibit 9.1 presents examples of closed, partially closed, and open-ended questions.

EXHIBIT 9.1

Types of Survey Questions

Closed-ended Question

1. What have you been doing in the past four weeks to find employment?
    a.   Checked with public employment agency
    b.   Checked with private employment agency
    c.   Checked with employer directly
    d.   Checked with friends or relatives
    e.   Placed or answered ad
    f.   Read want ads

Partially Closed-ended Question

1. What have you been doing in the past four weeks to find employment?
    a.   Checked with public employment agency
    b.   Checked with private employment agency
    c.   Checked with employer directly
    d.   Checked with friends or relatives
    e.   Placed or answered ad
    f.   Read want ads
    g.   Something else, please specify_____

Open-ended Question

1. What have you been doing in the past four weeks to find employment?

Limitations of Survey Research

A major drawback of survey research is that individuals are not always honest about what they have done, nor do they always follow through with what they say they intend to do. Researchers refer to the pressure to respond in a certain way regardless of whether the response is true as **social desirability**. Polls on voting behavior, for instance, customarily show the same skewed pattern, with more people reporting that they vote than actually do.

Another problem associated with survey research is recall. Simply stated, people's memories are not always accurate or reliable. This problem is especially acute for questions that either ask for a great deal of specificity or span a broad time period. How many adults, for instance, could accurately report how many newspapers they have read in the past six months? In contrast, most adults probably could accurately recall how many newspapers they have read in the past week.

Standardized Instruments

For many concepts we are interested in measuring, a measurement instrument has already been developed. We call these existing measures **standardized instruments**. Standardized instruments are published and are readily available for use in social work research. Exhibit 9.2 presents an example of a standardized instrument, the first page of The Healthy Families Parenting Inventory.

EXHIBIT 9.2

Sample Standardized Instrument: Healthy Families Parenting Inventory

Healthy Families Parenting Inventory©

Directions: Please choose ONE answer that best fits for you and color in the circle. ↓	Rarely or never	A little of the time	Some of the time	Good part of the time	Always or most of the time
	①	②	③	④	⑤
1. I feel supported by others.	①	②	③	④	⑤
2. I feel that others care about me.	①	②	③	④	⑤
3. I discuss my feelings with someone.	①	②	③	④	⑤

Directions: Please choose ONE answer that best fits for you and color in the circle. ↓	Rarely or never	A little of the time	Some of the time	Good part of the time	Always or most of the time
	①	②	③	④	⑤
4. If I have trouble, I feel there is always someone I can turn to for help.	①	②	③	④	⑤
5. I have family or friends who I can turn to for help.	①	②	③	④	⑤
6. I learn new ways of doing things from solving problems.	①	②	③	④	⑤
7. I deal with setbacks without getting discouraged.	①	②	③	④	⑤
8. When I have a problem, I take steps to solve it.	①	②	③	④	⑤
9. When I am faced with a problem, I can think of several solutions.	①	②	③	④	⑤
10. I am good at dealing with unexpected problems.	①	②	③	④	⑤
11. I remain calm when new problems come up.	①	②	③	④	⑤
12. I feel sad.	①	②	③	④	⑤
13. I feel positive about myself.	①	②	③	④	⑤
14. The future looks positive for me.	①	②	③	④	⑤
15. I feel unhappy about everything.	①	②	③	④	⑤
16. I feel hopeless about the future.	①	②	③	④	⑤
17. There isn't much happiness in my life.	①	②	③	④	⑤
	Rarely or never	A little of the time	Some of the time	Good part of the time	Always or most of the time
	①	②	③	④	⑤

Standardized instruments differ from questionnaires in that they can be used across a number of projects, whereas questionnaires are often used only for one particular research project. In addition, unlike questionnaires, standardized instruments tend to focus on either one concept or a number of related and narrowly defined concepts. For example, the Center for Epidemiologic Studies Depression Scale measures a single condition, namely, depression. In contrast, the Mental Health Inventory is multidimensional and includes separate subscales on depression, anxiety, positive affect, and feelings of belonging. Questionnaires, in contrast, are usually designed to collect data on a number of areas.

Standardized instruments can be either self-administered or administered via an interview. These types of standardized instruments are referred to as self-report, because the participant provides the answers. In contrast, other standardized instruments are completed by parents, teachers, or even the researcher while observing the subjects of the research.

Norms and Cutting Scores

Standardized instruments are also more likely than questionnaires to have developed **norms**, meaning that they often contain information about how different groups score on the instrument. The usefulness of the norms depend on how accurately the normed population represents the target population. For example, norms are often developed based on college or university populations. These norms might not apply to non-college populations of a different age or social class. Similarly, norms developed only on men may not apply to women. Researchers also must consider when the norms were established, as they may be outdated.

Some standardized instruments also have **cutting scores**, which measure the difference between two levels of a condition or performance. For example, a cutting score on a depression scale may indicate the level at which clinical depression is likely to occur. Researchers can develop cutting scores by calculating the difference in scores between a normative group and a group that is experiencing the problem. The development of norms and cutting scores is a major advantage of standardized instruments.

Overall, as you can see in Exhibit 9.3, standardized instruments have many advantages relative to their limitations. When these instruments are available and are suitable to the research purpose, researchers should use them rather than develop new measures.

How Researchers Use Standardized Instruments

Standardized instruments measure a particular concept by combining several items. In this context, the term **item** refers to a single indicator of a variable.

EXHIBIT 9.3

Advantages and Limitations of Standardized Instruments

Advantages

- Standardized instruments are readily available and easy to access.
- The development work has already been done.
- They have established reliability and validity estimates.
- Norms may be available for comparison.
- Most are easy to complete and score.
- In many instances, they are available free of charge.
- They may be available in different languages.
- They specify age range and reading level.
- Time required for administration has been determined.

Limitations

- The norms may not apply to the target population.
- The language may be difficult.
- The tone might not fit with the philosophy of the program, for example, deficit-based versus strength-based.
- The target population may not understand the translation.
- The scoring procedure may be overly complex.
- The instrument may not be affordable.
- Special qualifications or training might be required for use.
- The instrument may be too long or time-consuming to administer.

Standardized instruments use multiple items to avoid the biases inherent in using a single item to measure a concept. Earlier in this chapter, for example, we saw that the measurement of elder abuse takes into account multiple items such as bruising, financial responsibility, and cultural expressions of caring, because using only one of these items may not accurately measure the concept.

As with other forms of quantitative measurement, standardized instruments are reductionist. That is, although a standardized instrument can include multiple items, the researcher tabulates those items to achieve a single score. The way that the researcher tabulates the total score depends on whether the standardized instrument is an index or a scale:

- An **index** is constructed either by adding the scores assigned to specific responses or by adding the scores and dividing by the total number of responses to calculate an average score. For example, an index of depression would have items such as "Feels blue," "Has suicidal thoughts," and "Unable to sleep." Each item would be counted as yes or no and given equal weight. The total number of items would indicate the level of depression.

■ A **scale** differs from an index in that it takes advantage of any intensity structure that might exist among the individual items—for instance, by weighting the responses to the individual items differently. In a scale, each item might be scored on a one-to-5 scale, from "Never" to "Almost Always." In addition, some items might be weighted. "Suicidal Thoughts" might be weighted as being three times as important in a depression scale as "Feels Blue."

How Researchers Access Standardized Instruments and Questionnaires

Fortunately for today's social work researcher, the Internet has made the process of locating standardized instruments much easier than in the past. Researchers can locate many standardized instruments simply by typing keywords into an Internet search engine. In addition, most university libraries have a measurement section, and reference librarians can help researchers locate standardized measures. There are also published questionnaires that can be adopted or adapted for use in survey research. Examples are The American Drug & Alcohol Survey and The American Tobacco Survey. In some instances, scoring and report preparation services are advertised with the sale of questionnaires and standardized instruments.

Despite the availability of standardized instruments, using such a measure can involve more than just locating it and photocopying or retyping it. Some standardized instruments are copyrighted, and users must pay a licensing fee to use them. Others are available free of charge when they are used for research but not when they are used for clinical practice or program evaluation.

In some instances, the developers of standardized instruments specify minimum qualifications for the persons who will be administering the instrument. For instance, some instruments require "a 4-year degree in Psychology, Counseling, or a related field, including coursework in the administration of psychological tests." Typically, the qualifications are posted along with the information on purchasing the instrument.

For some measures, it is difficult to find information on qualifications, the permission process, and cost. In these cases, the researcher must search the literature and possibly even contact the developer.

Many instrument developers or publishers will mail or fax sample instruments upon request to a researcher who is considering adopting an instrument for research or evaluation. In some cases, publishers post copies of instruments on their web sites. Other instruments must be purchased up front, with a money-back guarantee. The social work researcher must be very clear about the costs of purchasing standardized instruments and questionnaires as well as the applicable refund policies, should they prove to be inappropriate.

Existing Records

Paper and electronic documents, databases, and other nondocument artifacts of human behavior are included in the category of **existing records,** or secondary data. Research using nondocument sources of existing records such as the analysis of trash are rare in social work. However, existing documents are valuable sources of information for social work researchers. We could, for instance, use existing records to answer our question about the prevalence of donations to the tsunami relief efforts in the immediate aftermath of the 2011 Tohoku Tsunami that struck Japan. One way of conducting this task would be to examine charitable donations reported on 2011 tax returns.

Using existing records as a data source for social work research has many advantages. For example, using secondary data can:

- Help the researcher avoid the time and expenses involved in collecting primary data.
- Reduce the data-collection burden on respondents.
- Facilitate research that requires access to large samples of the population (through large organizations such as the U.S. Census Bureau).

Existing sources of data also have limitations. Perhaps the most serious limitation is that the researcher has to work with whatever data are available, even if they do not include important variables for the study. A further problem is that the data might not be standardized. Consider, for example, a researcher conducting cross-national policy research that involves census data. One problem he or she will encounter is that some countries, such as the United States, collect information on marital status, whereas other countries, such as France, do not. In addition, the number and types of categories used to record marital status vary from country to country. This lack of standardization can cause the researcher to exclude entire countries as well as certain key variables from the analysis. Despite these limitations, existing records are a significant source of data for social work research, and they should not be overlooked.

PRINCIPLES OF MEASUREMENT DESIGN

There are many occasions in social work research when a standardized instrument appropriate for gathering data is not available. For example, a research area may be so new that no instrument has yet been developed. Additionally, researchers might need to integrate one or more standardized instruments in a larger survey that includes additional questions.

In these instances, researchers need to know how to create their own research instruments. Of primary concern are how the data will be analyzed and which statistical tests, if any, will be used to test the hypotheses and answer the research questions. We discuss the relationship between measurement and statistical testing in Chapters 11 and 12. The next sections provide a foundation for those chapters. Researchers can also use these principles to critique individual items as well as the overall quality of standardized instruments.

The basic principles of measurement design are essential to this process: level of measurement, response rate, measurement error, and pilot testing. Next we examine level of measurement, a concept that researchers must consider before they design specific questions. In the following sections we discuss how to design measuring instruments to maximize response rate and minimize error and then finish with some comments on the importance of pilot testing any instrument.

Level of Measurement

Before researchers can construct and critique questions, they must understand levels of measurement. Classifying variables according to their level of measurement is important to mastering measurement in social work research. Level of measurement is not only a consideration in minimizing measurement error but also has significant implications for data analysis.

Four levels of measurement can be distinguished and are generally presented in the form of a hierarchy:

> Ratio measurement
> Interval measurement
> Ordinal measurement
> Nominal measurement

On the bottom of the hierarchy is nominal measurement, with ratio measurement at the top. The higher we climb up the hierarchy, the more mathematical functions we can perform with the data.

A general rule in measurement is always to measure variables at the highest level of measurement possible. For instance, asking about income in dollar amounts represents a ration level of measurement, whereas asking about perceived income level represents an ordinal level of measurement. Seeking the highest level of measurement possible provides the most detailed information about the variable of interest. As we will see in Chapter 12, following this rule allows the researcher to conduct more powerful statistical analysis on the data.

Remember, too, that most variables are never inherently associated with a specific level of measurement. Rather, the way in which we operationally define them determines their level of measurement as demonstrated by the example on income represented as a dollar amount or an income category.

Nominal Measurement

When observations can be classified into mutually exclusive categories, a **nominal measurement** is used. Categories are mutually exclusive when each observation belongs to one and only one category. Variables such as gender, ethnicity, religion, and political party affiliation are examples of variables measured at the nominal level. The variable gender, for example, has two attributes, female and male, which is the minimum number of categories required to measure a variable. These two categories are mutually exclusive because if you belong to one category you cannot possibly belong to the other.

We could argue, however, that these categories are not **exhaustive**—another requirement of nominal measurement—meaning that there is an appropriate category for each response. Thus, depending on the nature of the study, the researcher may want to add the category transgender to make the categories exhaustive. When the researcher is not able to predetermine all of the categories, she or he has the option of using a category labeled other, with an option to write in the additional response.

In nominal measurement, the attributes are not numerical categories. The researcher, however, typically assigns a number or a code to each attribute solely for the purposes of tabulation and statistical testing. Using the variable gender as an example, the researcher could code all females as 1 and all males as 2. Significantly, the assignment of numbers to the attributes of nominal variables is purely arbitrary. In other words, the numeric codes associated with female and male have no quantitative meaning; they are simply category labels.

Because these numbers have no meaning, when researchers analyze the data from nominal variables, it makes no sense for them to perform mathematical operations such as addition, subtraction, multiplication, and division. Although the computer will perform any mathematical function it is programmed to run, the results will be nonsensical.

Ordinal Measurement

Ordinal measurement is common in social work and is often used in standardized scales and questionnaires. Variables can be measured at the ordinal level when the attributes of the variable can be rank-ordered from highest to lowest or most to least. Take the question "How satisfied are you with the level of involvement your family had in case planning?" The response categories could be listed as an ordinal variable with numeric codes as follows:

1. very dissatisfied
2. dissatisfied
3. neither satisfied nor dissatisfied
4. satisfied
5. very satisfied

As we can see from this example, the categories of ordinal variables have a fixed order. Like nominal variables, the categories must be exhaustive and mutually exclusive. In contrast to nominal variables, however, the numeric codes assigned to the categories of ordinal variables have a quantitative meaning.

Keep in mind that these numbers indicate only that one category is greater than or less than another. They cannot measure how much more or less one category is than another. Thus, in the above example, it does not make sense to claim that a score of 2 represents twice as much satisfaction as a 1, and so forth. The numbers assigned to represent the ordinal categories do not have the numerical properties necessary for arithmetic operations.

Another example is education: (1) less than high school degree, (2) high school graduate, (3) some college, (4) college graduate, and (5) postgraduate credit or degree. We cannot say how much more, in terms of education, one category is compared to another. All we can comment on is whether one category is greater than or less than another.

Interval Measurement

Interval measurement shares the same characteristics as ordinal measurement in that the categories have an inherent order and indicate whether each category is less or greater than the other categories. What separates interval from ordinal measures is that interval measures also have the feature of equal spacing between the categories—for example: IQ is one interval measure that may be used in social work research. Indexes and scales that combine the responses to a number of individual items measured at the ordinal level are treated as interval-level measures.

Interval measures are distinguished from ratio measures because they lack a true zero point. Therefore, the numbers can be added and subtracted but not multiplied or divided. For instance, some assessment scales that measure concepts such as self-esteem have scores that range from 0 to 100. A score of 0, however, does not imply a total absence of self-esteem. We cannot conceive of a situation in which there is a true absence of self-esteem.

Ratio Measurement

Highest on the measurement hierarchy is **ratio measurement**. On a ratio scale, each number represents a precise amount. Ratio scales also have a true or absolute zero where we can actually conceive of the absence of the attribute. Examples of ratio measures are age in years, years of military service, amount of debt, and number of out-of-home placements. Ratio-level data are suitable for all basic mathematical functions: addition, subtraction, multiplication, and division.

Researchers can convert ratio-level measures into ordinal categories where appropriate. For example, they can convert the full range of ages, from 0 to 120, into a number of ordinal categories (0–21, 22–45, 46–70, and so on). However, if age is measured at the ordinal level, the full range of information is lost because variables measured at the ordinal level cannot be converted to data that represents the ratio level of measurement. For example, if researchers know that 30 people are between the ages of 18 and 29 (ordinal), they do not know the exact age of each individual (ratio).

Sometimes placing values such as age and income that could be measured at the ratio level into ordinal categories is justified. For example, researchers might wish to avoid errors that often occur when they ask respondents to recall an exact number. In other cases, researchers attempt to soften an overly sensitive question that respondents may not answer. For example, many people are reluctant to state their exact income, but they will indicate the range into which their income falls. In most cases, though, researchers should keep ratio-level data as is rather than placing it in ordinal categories.

Response Rate

There are two basic principles of measurement:

1. Maximize response rate.
2. Minimize error.

The design of a questionnaire as well as the types of questions should all be developed or critiqued with these principles in mind. In an effort to maximize response rate and minimize error, social workers must pay attention both to formulating individual questions and, in the case of self-administered questionnaires and standardized instruments, to designing the layout, or look, of the instrument.

First impressions are important to achieving a good **response rate,** which is the number of responses compared with the number of questionnaires distributed. At first glance, respondents should perceive the questionnaire or self-administered instrument as professional and inviting. They also must be convinced

that completing the questionnaire or interview will not be either too time consuming or too boring. You can enhance the likelihood of conveying a good first
impression by adhering to the following 10 basic questionnaire design principles:

1. **The look.** Although an effective instrument maximizes the available space,
    try to avoid creating a cluttered look and using small type. If you are using
    a standardized instrument that is poorly formatted, you might want to
    spend time redesigning it. Although the instrument's weight can affect its
    mailing cost, respondents are less likely to fill out a cluttered instrument
    with small type than a longer, uncluttered instrument. Whenever possible,
    choose good design over a small cost saving.
2. **The purpose.** One way to boost the response rate is to explain clearly to
    respondents why you are conducting the research. You can counter
    respondents' feelings of being put upon by demonstrating that their par-
    ticipation will benefit them or the larger society. Exchange theory suggests
    that people weigh costs and benefits in making decisions about what to
    do. Be explicit in addressing "what's in it" for the respondent.
3. **The guarantee.** Assure respondents that the results will be kept confiden-
    tial and that no services will be withheld or denied even if they choose not
    to participate. In addition, reassure them that the questionnaire or instru-
    ment is not a test and there are no right or wrong answers. Be honest about
    how long it will take to complete the task and whether any follow-up
    contact will be required.
4. **Sensitivity.** If you plan to ask potentially sensitive questions, keep them to
    a minimum, make certain they are relevant, and position them later in the
    instrument. Also, keep in mind that sensitivity should be evaluated from
    the respondent's perspective, not yours.
5. **Knowledge.** Avoid asking questions that the target population is not likely
    to know anything about. This practice is not only demoralizing, but it will
    discourage participation. For example, do not ask questions about current
    events if you are not sure that respondents are familiar with them.
6. **Biased items.** Asking respondents to respond to biased items fits better
    with political campaigning or sales than with research. Consider, for
    example, the question "Do you believe that all forms of abortion, the kill-
    ing of preborn babies, should be illegal?" This question is biased because
    it defines abortion in a way that clearly is intended to elicit a negative
    response. To be less biased, the question does not need to include any
    definition of abortion. A better question would be "Do you believe that all
    forms of abortion should be illegal?"
7. **Open-ended questions.** The major disadvantage to open-ended questions is
    the burden they place on respondents. In a self-administered questionnaire,
    respondents may need a lot of time to write and structure their responses.

As a result, the responses may be illegible or incomprehensible. In addition, open-ended questions may discourage individuals who feel that they do not write or express themselves well. For these reasons, open-ended questions are most suitable in interviews. However, they should be used judiciously in all quantitative research. As a general rule, you should position closed-ended questions first.

8. **Response formats.** Two response formats that can help respondents complete the questionnaire or survey quickly and accurately are contingency questions and matrix questions. **Contingency questions** make the completion of a question contingent upon the response to a prior question. Use contingency questions to save the respondent time when not all questions may be relevant to all respondents. **Matrix questions** are used to display response categories across a number of questions when these categories are the same. Matrices use space efficiently and can reduce response time. See Exhibit 9.4 for an example of a contingency question and a matrix question.

EXHIBIT 9.4

Two Types of Response Formats: Contingency Questions and Matrix Questions

EXAMPLE CONTINGENCY QUESTION FROM AN INTERVIEW SCHEDULE

1. Hello, this is (interviewer), and I'm calling about a research study sponsored by the Department of Education. Are you a head of this household? ← question stem

response categories

Yes ....1 (go to question 4) ←

No .... 2 (go to question 3A) ← skip pattern

EXAMPLE MATRIX QUESTION FROM AN INTERVIEW SCHEDULE

10. Would you say that you are very satisfied, somewhat satisfied, somewhat dissatisfied, or very dissatisfied:

[1 = very satisfied; 2 = somewhat satisfied; 3 = somewhat dissatisfied; 4 = very dissatisfied]

a. with the school (child) attends this year? 1 2 3 4

b. with the teachers (child) has this year? 1 2 3 4

c. with the academic standards of the school? 1 2 3 4

d. with the discipline at the school? 1 2 3 4

9. **Question order.** The order in which you present the questions can affect the success of your research efforts. One valuable rule is to begin with questions that are likely to be interesting and engage the respondent. In addition, try to group questions according to content area so that respondents don't have to constantly switch their train of thought. Within each content area, order questions according to their response format. For instance, group questions that are closed-ended together and questions that are open-ended together. To the extent possible, place closed-ended questions with the same response categories together. In self-administered questionnaires, begin with non-threatening but interesting questions. In most cases, you should collect demographic information at the end to avoid making the survey appear like a routine information-collecting tool. The exception is interview schedules, where you may position demographic questions first to help you select the desired respondents and to establish rapport as quickly as possible.

10. **Transitional statements.** If a questionnaire is arranged into sections according to content area, you should introduce each section with a short statement that clearly explains its content and purpose. Transitional statements should sound natural and conversational. This transitional statement was part of a survey that sought to learn how nonprofit organizations develop, implement, and use the planning process:

The following items ask you some questions about factors related to your organization, its structure, and its daily functioning. The information you provide will allow us to describe the general character of the organizations represented in this study.

Measurement Error

Not only must you get the target population to respond, but you must get them to respond accurately. There is an old saying from computer programming known as GIGO—"garbage in, garbage out." This saying implies that no amount of fancy analysis is going to fix a study that is based on incorrect data. Computers will analyze the data, and researchers will interpret the computer output and write reports. The quality of the research, however, depends on the accuracy of the data.

The most important way to avoid measurement error is to remember that a measure is not necessarily the same as the attribute being measured. Thus, a bathroom scale may indicate that a person's weight is 140 pounds, but other, more accurate measures, such as the scale in the doctor's office, may report that the weight is 146.5 pounds. The difference between the actual attribute and the measurement of the attribute is measurement error.

In some research contexts, the amount of measurement error is critical. The consequences of measurement error can be quite obvious in the physical sciences. A classic example is the loss of a Mars orbiter in 1999. It occurred because one research team unknowingly used metric units while another was using the Imperial system.

Measurement error can have critical implications in social work as well. At times, an entire program is canceled as a result of a measurement error that fails to represent actual change in the target problem. Such an error leads to the inaccurate conclusion that the program had little or no effect on the population. Alternatively, a measure may erroneously show a positive effect and thus lend support to an ineffective program. In any case, social workers must attempt to minimize measurement error and maximize their ability to accurately represent what they are attempting to measure.

Measurement error can take two forms:

- **Random error:** measurement error that is neither consistent nor patterned. For instance, a respondent may misread a question and answer in a way that is contrary to her or his actual intent. Or an observer may lose concentration and fail to record an instance of the target behavior. Random error is the less worrisome kind of error because it has no specific direction. In the best-case scenario, a mistake in one direction will be counterbalanced by a mistake in the opposite direction. For example, an observer who misses one instance of the target behavior might subsequently record two incidents as opposed to the one that actually occurred. The net result of these two mistakes is no measurement error.

- **Systematic error**, also called **nonrandom error:** measurement error that has a definite pattern, unlike random error. It is therefore the more worrisome source of error for social work researchers. For example, if the majority of respondents misinterpret a question and thus answer in a particular way that does not reflect their experience, systematic error is being introduced. Unlike random errors, systematic errors do not balance out. Rather, they accumulate and bias the research findings.

Exhibit 9.5 illustrates the difference between random and systematic sources of error.

Following are 11 tips that can help you minimize error in the data:

1. **Audience.** Knowing the audience involves understanding respondents in a number of dimensions including language preferences and colloquialisms, age, culture, reading ability, mental status, and availability. Always try to avoid terms that respondents may not be familiar with, and consider if the language you use will be uniformly understood. A general rule is to write

EXHIBIT 9.5

Random and Systematic Sources of Error in Measurement

Measurement Situation	Type of Error
A person has a cold the day she takes a test and does a little worse than she normally would.	Random error—people's health or mood varies randomly.
The reading level of the scale is at ninth grade. Those with a lower reading level cannot understand it and skip many questions.	Systematic error—scores reflect reading level and not the variable being measured.

at the eighth-grade reading level, but this level may be too high for some populations. In addition, the age and life circumstances of the respondent group might have implications for the length of the instrument. If mental status or respondent burden is an issue, you might have to use a different form of measurement such as observation. Alternatively, you could choose different respondents who you believe can answer the questions accurately. For instance, in a study of elderly individuals with dementia, it may be preferable to survey caretakers or adult children.

2. **Clarity.** Check the instrument for spelling and grammatical errors that can change the intended meaning of the questions. Use simple language, and avoid abbreviations or slang, because someone is sure not to understand them. Always provide instructions for answering the questions.

3. **Length.** Keeping questions as short as possible increases the likelihood that respondents will read, understand, and complete them. Aim for a maximum of about 20 words per question. At the same time, if you need to shorten questions, make sure not to leave out important information. For example, state explicitly whether the question is referring to past or current behavior.

4. **Position.** Response categories should be positioned vertically underneath the question stem (the lead-in part of a multiple-choice question) rather than side-by-side, as illustrated in Exhibit 9.6. The respondent is more likely to be confused as to what to circle when the items are placed horizontally. Also, use a different labeling system for the question stem and the response categories. When you use the same labeling system, respondents sometimes mistakenly circle the label associated with the question stem. Present the number, symbol, or space for marking the answer to the left of the response categories rather than to the right. Indent the response

---

EXHIBIT 9.6

How to Position Response Categories in a Questionnaire

Recommended Layout and Labeling of Question Stem and Response Categories:

1. What grade are you currently in? (Please circle the letter corresponding to the correct response.)
    a.   6th grade
    b.   7th grade
    c.   8th grade

Poor Layout and Labeling of Question Stem and Response Categories:

1. What grade are you currently in?
    1 6th 2 7th 3 8th

1. What grade are you currently in?
    6th — 7th — 8th —

---

categories to distinguish them from the question stem. Unless the questionnaire is in a booklet format, avoid using the back of the page, because it might go unnoticed. Make certain to keep every question together on one page.

5. **Precision.** Precision clearly is essential to an effective instrument. As discussed earlier, some researchers sacrifice precision, for example, by moving from a ratio level of measurement to an ordinal level. As a general rule, you should take this step only if you believe that respondents will consider the question to be too sensitive and therefore will not answer it. In a trade-off between precision and response rate, go for response rate.

6. **Detail.** Avoid questions that ask for too much specificity or recall. No question should require respondents to remember excessive detail or specifics from so far in the past that they are not likely to answer with any accuracy. Confine your questions within a reasonable time frame. For instance, if you are interested in literacy activities in the home, asking respondents how many nights they have read to their children in the last month or more could prove difficult to answer. If you ask the same question within the time frame of the past week or less, they are more likely to respond accurately. If your interest is in the longer term, you could follow up with a second question asking whether their response is typical of the number of nights they read to their children on a regular basis.

7. **Double-barreled questions.** Avoid questions that ask respondents to give a single answer to a combination of questions. The following is an example of a double question: "Do you support abortion in the first, second, and third trimesters of pregnancy?" As a general rule, if the word *and* appears in the question, check to see if the item is a double question. The word *or* may also indicate a double-barreled question: "Do you support abortion, or are you a conservative?" If you want the answer to both parts of the question, use two separate questions.

8. **Negative wording.** Negatively worded items can be confusing and are easy to misread, thus contributing to error in the data. For example, the word *not* in the following question makes the item a negatively worded question: "Should the federal government not pay for children's school lunches?" It is easy to miss the word not in the question. The best remedy is simply to leave it out and ask "Should the federal government pay for children's school lunches?"

9. **Instructions.** All questionnaires should begin by providing clear instructions for completing the instrument. If the instrument is an interview schedule, you must clarify which instructions should be read to the interviewee and which instructions are for the data collector. You can differentiate instructions by the style or color of type or by the way the instructions are offset.

10. **Translation.** When you wish to translate a questionnaire either from or into a foreign language, if possible, secure the help of a native-language speaker whose background is similar to that of the majority of respondents. For instance, Spanish translations done in New York, where many Spanish speakers are from Puerto Rico, may differ from Spanish translations done in the Southwest, where the majority of Spanish speakers are from Mexico.

11. **Social desirability.** In the section on survey research, we discussed social desirability, that is, the tendency to answer sensitive questions based on what we believe we "ought to" do rather than what we actually do. One way to discourage socially desirable answers is to remind respondents that there is no right or wrong answer and that the value of the information depends on their open and honest responses.

Pilot Testing

The measure that is right for one situation may not be right for another. How do you know if you are using the right measure? The answer is to conduct a pilot test, one-on-one or in a group. In a **pilot test**, the researcher can strengthen a questionnaire by evaluating beforehand how clear the instructions are, how well respondents understand the measure, and how difficult the measure is to complete. Pilot tests also can help researchers estimate problems with response rate and error. In addition, they can indicate how long it will take to administer a measure. Pilot tests can be especially helpful in evaluating how accurately an instrument has been translated.

One technique for conducting pilot tests is to ask respondents to think out loud, and then you can tape or take notes on their comments, the expressions on their faces, and the speed with which they complete the questions. When you administer a pilot test in a group, you can conduct a discussion in which the respondents can interact and respond to the comments of other individuals. In addition, you can analyze pilot test data empirically. For instance, you can ask questions that attempt to elicit the same information in different ways and then compare the responses for consistency. This procedure can also help you to assess error in measurement. For example, you could administer three separate standardized instruments that measure depression. If the results of all three are not consistent, you can explore the reasons for the variability.

Some problems disclosed by the pilot test can be fixed; others cannot. If the problem relates to an instrument or question developed specifically for the study, such as a poorly worded question, you can simply fix it. However, if the problem stems from a standardized instrument, you may or may not be able to fix it. Some developers of standardized instruments explicitly state as a condition of use that the instrument may not be altered in any way. If a standardized instrument does not perform as it should and there are restrictions on changing it, you might have to drop it completely from the study.

THE QUALITY OF MEASURES

A quality measure is one that consistently and precisely measures what it is supposed to measure. If we measure weight, we want a bathroom scale that is accurate no matter who steps on it. We want it to tell us our weight, not our blood pressure. We want it to be sensitive to changes, for example, if we take off our shoes. We want to trust that it will give us the same reading over and over again, assuming that our weight does not change. Finally, we want to know that it still works that way with the passing of time.

Social workers must consider these same qualities of a good bathroom scale when they are using a standardized instrument for measurement in their research. When deciding whether to adopt a standardized measure for a particular research study, the social worker should consider four characteristics of the instrument: validity, reliability, utility, and past performance.

Validity and reliability are two of the most important characteristics of a high-quality measure. The degree to which the measure actually represents the concept of interest is referred to as its **validity**. Thus, validity exists when the researcher is actually measuring what he or she intends to measure. In contrast, **reliability** is the ability to find consistent results each time the measure is administered. A bathroom scale that measures the same person at 140 pounds at 10:00 a.m. and 150 pounds at 10:02 a.m., under the same circumstances, clearly is not reliable.

Good measures have both validity and reliability. Validity and reliability are not, however, absolutes. A measure can be valid and reliable in one research context and not in another. For example, a depression scale may accurately assess depression for college students in Nebraska but not for Native Americans on a reservation in New Mexico. For this reason, the researcher must also evaluate whether the measure is useful for the particular study in which he or she intends to use it.

Measurement Validity

A thermometer measures temperature. It does not measure weight. Therefore, if we are using a thermometer to measure weight, we are using an instrument that is not valid. A lack of validity represents a source of systematic error in the research study. Validity, however, is not an all-or-nothing proposition; rather, it is a matter of degree.

Researchers use four methods to assess an instrument's validity. Two of these methods—face validity and content validity—involve judgments by the researcher. The other two methods—construct validity and criterion-related validity—are empirical assessments of validity.

Face Validity

The first method, known as **face validity**, assesses the extent to which the measure appears to be valid to the people to whom it is being administered. That is, does the instrument appear "at face value" to measure the concept? For example, we would expect a depression scale to contain items about sadness, suicidal thoughts, grief, crying spells, and lack of energy. If the scale included items that asked about our hair color, favorite flavor of ice cream, and feelings regarding cats, it would not make sense on the face of it. Consequently, we would not take this scale seriously as a measure of depression. These negative feelings could affect our willingness to fill out the scale or the ways in which we answer the questions.

Some researchers argue that face validity is not a true form of validity because it is concerned only with whether the instrument appears to measure what it purports to measure. Face validity cannot determine whether the instrument is actually measuring the concept.

Technicalities aside, face validity is an important consideration in evaluating how a particular culture will respond to a specific measure. For instance, the concept of elder abuse discussed earlier can differ substantially from one culture to another. Items that measure elder abuse in one culture may be interpreted differently in another. These types of cultural differences can affect the respondents' willingness to cooperate, their ability to understand the questions, and the completeness of their responses.

Content Validity

The second method of judging a measure's validity, **content validity**, is concerned with both the choice of the items and the degree to which the measure has captured the entire domain of the concept. Content validity is concerned with why the researcher selected the items. The developers of the measuring instrument should provide information about the rationale for their selection of items. The content of the items is often based on theory, reports of practice experience, and experts' judgments. In addition, an instrument should address the full range of a concept. A test of parenting knowledge, for instance, that includes questions related to children's requirements for sleep, nutrition, and stimulation but does not address age-appropriate toileting expectations or social skills would not be considered content valid.

Whereas face validity is assessed from the perspective of the respondent, content validity is usually assessed from the perspective of people considered experts in the field.

Construct Validity

The assessment of **construct validity** is based on the way a measure is related to other variables within a system of theoretical relationships. For example, you would expect an individual's level of self-esteem to be related to depression but not to IQ or hair color. Basically, construct validity implies that the developers of standardized instruments form hypotheses regarding how the score on the instrument should relate to other concepts.

Construct validity involves two components:

■ **Convergent validity** is the degree to which the measure correlates highly with variables theoretically related to it. **Correlation** is a statistical test that provides a measure of the strength of the relationship between two sets of numbers or scores. Researchers use correlation as a means to test convergent validity. Chapter 12 explains correlation in greater detail. For now, it is enough to know that the **correlation coefficient**—the measure of the strength of the correlation—ranges from 0 to 1. The number 1 represents perfect correlation, and 0 represents no relationship. The closer the correlation coefficient is to 1, the stronger the relationship, and the greater the evidence of convergent validity. Thus, to validate the Index of Self-Esteem, a researcher might hypothesize that a respondent's score on this measure will be strongly correlated with a psychiatrist's rating of the client's level of depression.

■ **Discriminant validity** is the degree to which the measure does not correlate highly with variables that researchers hypothesize to be unrelated to it. For instance, the researcher may assume that self-esteem should be only weakly correlated with variables such as age, gender, geographic location, and ethnicity.

One way to assess convergent and discriminant validity is to administer a scale to a sizable group of people, say 100 or more, along with a background questionnaire on age, gender, income, ethnicity, and some other scale that measures a concept that is hypothesized to be correlated with the concept of interest. If the resulting pattern of correlations matches the hypothesized relationships, the instrument has evidence of construct validity.

If the pattern deviates from the hypothesized relationships, this is evidence that the instrument may be measuring something other than the concept it was developed to measure. For example, if you were testing a scale to measure depression, you would expect it to correlate highly (the hypothesized relationship) with other standardized measures of depression as well as with a measure of life satisfaction. In addition, you would not expect it to correlate highly (hypothesized relationship) with age, gender, ethnic group, or political party preference.

Criterion-Related Validity

Researchers also use **criterion-related validity**, which assesses a measuring instrument in relation to its ability to predict some external criterion. This method has two forms:

■ **Predictive validity** refers to the ability of the instrument to predict a future state on some external criterion. For example, if a preschool student's score on the Eyberg Child Behavior Inventory (ECBI) can predict academic success in first grade, the ECBI is said to have predictive validity. The external criterion in this example is the record of academic success.

■ **Concurrent validity**, in contrast, refers to the ability of a test to predict an external criterion as it concurrently exists. For example, the concurrent validity of the ECBI could be demonstrated by its ability to predict children's scores on the Perceived Self-Control Scale, another valid measure of child behavior.

Going further, criterion validity also maintains that the measure should be able to discriminate between groups based on the key variables. For example, a measure of depression should be able to discriminate between people who are in treatment for depression and those who are not. This form of criterion validity is referred to as **known groups validity**.

Measurement Reliability

As discussed earlier, reliability refers to how consistent the results are each time a measure is administered. In general, a good measuring instrument produces similar results under similar circumstances.

In contrast to validity, reliability is concerned with the introduction of random error into a research study. That is, the only time the outcome on a measure should fluctuate is when some real change has occurred in the target concept. For instance, a respondent's score on the Index of Self-Esteem should improve only if his or her self-esteem has actually increased. If there has not been any opportunity for real improvement in the person's self-esteem, the change in the score can be attributed to random error. Exhibit 9.7 illustrates the relationship between validity and reliability.

EXHIBIT 9.7

Relationship Between Validity and Reliability

Measurement Quality	Example
If Reliable, may not be Valid	A bathroom scale gives consistent measures but does not measure accurately.
If Reliable, may be Valid	A bathroom scale gives consistent measures and also measures accurately.
If not Reliable, never Valid	A bathroom scale gives inconsistent measures, so it cannot be accurate.
If Valid, then always Reliable	If the scale accurately measures your weight, it must be consistent.

There are several tests that researchers can use to assess an instrument's reliability. Five basic tests are

- interrater reliability
- test-retest reliability
- parallel forms reliability
- split-half reliability
- internal consistency

The test that the researcher selects will depend upon the type of measure being considered.

Interrater Reliability

For observational measures or existing records, when interpretations of information are to some extent subjective, **interrater reliability** is an appropriate test of reliability. To determine interrater reliability, two observers independently record their observations of the same incident or extract data from an existing record such as a case file. The results of the two observers are then compared for consistency, and a percentage of agreement is calculated. For example, if 10 instances of a behavior are recorded and the two observers agree on eight of them, the percentage of agreement would be calculated by 8/10 x 100 = 80%. Alternatively, a correlation coefficient could be calculated to measure the relationship between the data produced by the two raters.

Researchers can use the results from a test of interrater reliability to strengthen operational definitions and to formulate guidelines or decision rules to improve reliability. The level of reliability determined to be acceptable will vary depending on the degree of precision desired in the research study. In most cases, an agreement of 80%, or a correlation of approximately .80, would be considered acceptable. Researchers can reassess interrater reliability periodically to ensure that an adequate level is being maintained.

A related measure of reliability is **intrarater reliability**, which refers to the extent of agreement of ratings by the same observer at different points in time.

Test-Retest Reliability

If the measure is a standardized instrument or a survey instrument, **test-retest reliability** can provide a useful assessment. Test-retest reliability provides information on how consistent a measure is when it is administered twice in a relatively short time frame. The appropriate length for that time frame will vary with both the instrument and the target population. Generally, the time frame needs to be long enough so that the respondent cannot recall specific answers yet short enough to ensure that no real changes occur in the variable being measured.

If the scores between the two administrations are similar, the instrument is said to have good test-retest reliability. As with interrater reliability, researchers can calculate a correlation coefficient using the two sets of scores (O1 and O2) to represent the degree of consistency between the two administrations.

Parallel Forms Reliability

For standardized instruments that measure a single construct, the researcher can assess reliability through **parallel forms reliability**. In this test, the researcher correlates the scores from two versions of the same instrument. For example, a measure of mental health, the Mental Health Index, has two forms of psychological distress measures. Version 1 is based on the full battery of questions. To reduce the burden on respondents, the test developers created a new, shorter instrument by selecting a subset of Version 1 items.

To assess parallel forms reliability, the researcher would calculate a correlation coefficient to measure the strength of the relationship between the scores on the two versions. Scores of .80 or better are considered to show good parallel forms reliability.

Split-Half Reliability

A test related to parallel forms reliability, **split-half reliability** is used for standardized instruments that measure a single concept using several items. The instrument assesses split-half reliability by correlating one half of the items with the other half.

Because all of the items measure the same concept, the two halves should correlate highly. Consider, for example, a depression scale that contains 40 items. If all items measure aspects of depression, half of the items should correlate highly with the other half. As with parallel forms reliability, a correlation coefficient of .80 or higher would be expected.

Internal Consistency

Researchers use **internal consistency** as a test of reliability for standardized instruments that either measure a single concept or measure multiple concepts but calculate a score for each concept—also referred to as each subscale— separately. Internal consistency is concerned with the extent to which all of the items included in the index or scale for a single concept hold together, or how consistently the items are scored. In a reliable instrument, all of the items would be expected to correlate with one another because they measure the same concept. Those items that are not scored consistently serve to weaken the instrument.

Internal consistency is assessed by the magnitude of a statistic known as Cronbach's coefficient alpha, or the alpha coefficient, which measures the average correlation among all of the items. The alpha coefficient, is interpreted like a correlation coefficient in that it ranges from 0 to 1, with a 1 being a perfect correlation. An alpha coefficient greater than .80 suggests that all of the items are measuring the same concept.

Measurement Utility

Researchers must often select among the many standardized instruments that have demonstrated validity and reliability. One way to determine which will work best is to evaluate the utility of the instruments for the current purpose.

Determining Utility

The first step in making a decision is to ask *"What is the purpose of the measurement?"* Is the purpose to measure the current status of a variable (for example, level of assertiveness) or to screen for services based on a cutting score (for example, degree of risk for suicide)? If the purpose is screening, the researcher might require instruments with higher levels of validity and reliability. Moreover, if the researcher intends to use the measure for both screening and determining eligibility, the measure must be able to differentiate as accurately as possible between people who most need the service and people who do not.

In addition, the researcher must consider how long it will take respondents to complete the instrument. Some instruments can take more than an hour to complete. Others take five to 10 minutes.

Going further, is the purpose to evaluate practice with a single case, or is it to conduct research on a broader scale? If the former, the researcher should select a measure that is sensitive to small amounts of change in the target problem.

After the researcher identifies the purpose of the measurement, his or her next step is to ask *"How well does the measure fit with the program?"* For example, if the program is not designed or funded to increase readiness for preschool, it would be inappropriate to implement a measure of preschool readiness, even if this information would be "interesting." Similarly, self-esteem should not be included in a study simply because a valid and reliable measure of this variable is available.

As a general rule, the measures should not drive the program or pull it in a certain philosophical direction. Rather, the program objectives, or the intervention, should drive the selection of measures.

Another question to ask when evaluating utility is *"Who will be completing this assessment?"* If the measure will be used with an elderly population, the length and number of questions may be a barrier to completion. Similarly, if the mental status of the target population is in question, a self-report measure may not be the best choice.

In addition, the researcher needs to evaluate whether the language on the instrument is appropriate for the target population. For example, some standardized instruments specify a suggested reading level for comprehending the scale. Going further, the language used in some scales is biased toward a certain social class. For example, a test that measures problem-solving ability using subjects such as golf and sailing might be biased against low-income respondents.

Other instruments may have been developed a long time ago or in another country. In such cases, the vocabulary might not be familiar to contemporary respondents. For instance, the item "I feel downtrodden" may be difficult for young people to understand because the word downtrodden is not commonly used today. Finally, respondents may react to the titles of standardized instruments, especially titles that convey problems or deficits. For example, the Social Emotional Loneliness Scale sounds much more positive when it is referred to by its alternative title, the Goals Scale.

Measuring Change: Static and Dynamic Measures

Two important distinctions can be made regarding items used in measures to demonstrate change in a target problem. These distinctions also apply in instruments used to predict the risk of an event such as recidivism, or repeated criminal behavior. For example, a study may wish to investigate which factors are useful in preventing recidivism of juveniles currently in detention. In this case, some measures are more useful than others. Researchers use the terms static and dynamic to refer to items that relate to a changing state versus a non-changing state:

- **Static measures** are by their nature not amenable to change—for example, "previously arrested."
- **Dynamic measures** are amenable to change—for example, "lost job within the last 30 days."

In the case of items related to juvenile detention, a measure may be static or dynamic. If a question asks "Has the juvenile ever been detained?" the score on the item for juveniles who have been detained is never going to change. Clearly, once a juvenile has been detained, that fact can never change. This type of item is referred to as a static indicator. Static measures are limited in their ability to identify groups with vastly different probabilities of the outcome, in this instance, recidivism.

Dynamic indicators, in contrast, are able to show change. If the question asks "Has the juvenile been detained in the past six months?" the response is allowed to vary with the juvenile's change in status. In a measure designed to predict recidivism, dynamic indicators are more useful than static ones.

Measuring Personal Characteristics: Trait and State Measures

A second important distinction in measurement is the difference between trait and state measures. Whereas static and dynamic refer to the ability to show change, trait and state refer to measures that are related to personal characteristics, such as temperament and anxiety level.

- **Trait measures** are concerned with a relatively enduring or stable characteristic—for example, personality and temperament.
- **State measures** assesses a transitory condition or a condition amenable to change—for example, depression and anxiety.

When the goal of social work research is to predict risk or to evaluate the effectiveness of an intervention or treatment program, the researcher generally should select dynamic and state measures that are able to reflect change over time.

Measurement Performance

After the researcher has assessed the validity, reliability, and utility of the various measures, the final step in the decision process is to examine the literature to determine how the measure has performed in the past. If other researchers have used a standardized instrument, they likely have commented on its benefits and limitations in a published study.

It is advisable to use instruments that have shown conclusive results in previous studies. These studies provide some evidence that the instrument is able to make distinctions when it is used to measure the variables of interest. If the literature indicates that the instrument has never or seldom produced any conclusive results, the researcher should be very cautious about adopting it.

Note that when the results of a research study are inconclusive or negative, the recommendation is almost always to change the intervention or to attribute the lack of positive findings to some aspect of the research design. However, the problem may arise from the lack of sensitivity or accuracy of the measures themselves.

CONCLUSION

Social workers must have a clear understanding of measurement both in conducting their own research and in critically assessing the research of others. The results of a study are only as good as the measures used to obtain the results. Measurement is a representation of the object or phenomenon of concern, and it is not to be confused with the actual object or phenomenon. Thus, choices in measurement must be based on which measures will provide the most accurate representation.

Measuring instruments must be well designed with careful thought about the audience and the purpose for which they are intended. In addition, they must show evidence of validity and reliability. The choice of a research instrument is not an absolute; rather, it varies with the research context. No matter how valid and reliable a measure, it is only as good as the extent to which it has utility for the research context and the manner in which it is administered.

Once measuring instruments have been selected or designed, a researcher can begin to collect data. The next chapter on data collection focuses on the development and implementation of a data collection plan.

MAIN POINTS

- Measurement is the process of assigning numbers or other symbols to characteristics or attributes of a concept according to specified rules. It involves political decisions as well as methodological decisions.
- Three important sources of data for social work research are surveys (through self-administered questionnaires or interviews), standardized instruments, and existing records. The researcher's challenge is to pick the method that is feasible and will be the most accurate.
- Although it may seem like an easy task, question construction is complicated. The goal is to get the respondent to understand the question in the same way that the researcher intended it, and then to have the researcher understand the response in the same way that the respondent intended it.
- Many standardized measures have been developed for use in social work research. They may be used on their own or in conjunction with surveys and sometimes as a means of structuring observation.
- All measures are subject to error. Error may be introduced by chance, or it may be systematic. Social work researchers are most concerned with systematic error, as chance or random error can occur in either direction and has a way of balancing out.

■ Pilot testing measures is an essential step in preparing for measurement. The pilot test should be conducted with a small group of respondents who are similar to the target population.

■ Before choosing a measure or set of measures for a research study, we need to consider measurement validity and reliability. There is little point to conducting expensive data collection and analyses if the data are not valid and reliable.

■ Validity is the extent to which the researcher is measuring what she or he intended to measure. There are four different types of validity to consider when assessing the accuracy of a measure; two are empirical, and two require subjective judgments.

■ Reliability relates to the consistency of a measure—that is, whether all of the items are measuring the same thing in the same way each time. If a measure is reliable, it should produce the same results from one administration to another. There are a number of ways of assessing reliability, and the choice will depend on the form of the measure.

EXERCISES

1. Suppose that you wanted to conduct a study of community cohesion in Riverton using a survey.
   a. Write down the steps you would take to measure community cohesion, including how you would decide how to operationalize the concept.
   b. Write four questions that you could use in your study of community cohesion. In developing the questions, demonstrate your understanding of each level of measurement: nominal, ordinal, interval, and ratio.
   c. How might you pilot test your survey before rolling it out in Riverton?
   d. Are there any existing records that might complement your survey and increase your understanding of the concept of community cohesion in Riverton?

2. Consider the Sanchez family case. Construct questions to gather information on age, income, ethnicity/race, and sexual orientation for the adult individuals in the Sanchez family. For the age and income variables, construct two separate questions to measure each variable at the ordinal and ratio levels. Write questions related to the variables as they would appear on a questionnaire, with question stem, response categories, and instructions to individuals for responding. Then, conduct an Internet search to find how researchers are phrasing questions on ethnicity and sexual orientation. Evaluate different options using the two main principles of measurement: maximizing response rate and minimizing error. Based on what you have

learned, would you revise the questions you wrote? Why or why not? If you would revise them, how would the questions change? How could you use pilot testing to improve your measures?

3. Using the Carla Washburn case, develop 10 questions to help operationalize physical and emotional pain. Then, search the Internet and/or peer-reviewed literature for standardized measures of the same concepts. What do you notice about the questions contained in standardized instruments and the questions you developed? What are the similarities? What are the differences?

4. Using the Hudson City case, conduct a literature review to determine options for measuring disaster-related trauma among Hudson City residents. Comment on your preferred measure and provide a rationale for your choice. What are the risks of error—both chance and systematic—in seeking to measure disaster-related trauma in Hudson City? How can your instrument design reduce these risks? Be sure to use the concepts of validity and reliability as well as other desirable features of measures associated with utility as discussed in the chapter.

5. Considering the RAINN case, describe the approach used by the organization to measure consumer satisfaction among those utilizing the RAINN telephone and online hotline. Critically evaluate the approach. Using the concepts of measurement error, reliability, and validity, consider the strengths and weaknesses of this approach. What are the risks of error, and how could they be addressed? Considering consumer satisfaction more broadly, what are the roles for surveys, standardized instruments, and existing records? How can these sources be used, separately and together, to examine consumer satisfaction with a social work agency?

6. Conduct a literature review to find one or two peer-reviewed articles addressing efforts similar to the youth leadership group in Brickville. What are the important concepts mentioned in the articles? How are the important concepts operationalized and measured? Are there important concepts that remain unaddressed?

chapter
10

DATA COLLECTION AND DATA ENTRY

Man is a slow, sloppy, and brilliant thinker; computers are fast, accurate, and stupid.
Pfeiffer (n.d.)

Data collection marks the beginning of the implementation phase of the research study. Prior to data collection, a lot of time and thought has gone into identifying the research problem; specifying the research question; anticipating ethical considerations; choosing a research design that will enable the researcher to answer the research question with confidence; sampling; and deciding how to measure the variables. This chapter focuses on implementation of the research study, up to the point of analyzing the data.

The plan to carry out a study involves choices regarding the most appropriate data collection method; recruiting research participants; developing a data collection protocol; training and supervising data collectors; collecting the data; constructing a database; and entering the data into the database. This chapter pays special attention to two issues: recruiting participants for the research study and retaining them over the long term in longitudinal research studies. If researchers fail to anticipate and plan to avoid potential problems with participant recruitment and retention, these problems can derail the entire research study.

To help develop your research skills, this chapter will ask you to create a mini database from the *Riverton: A Community Conundrum* Youth Survey. This survey was administered as part of a community needs assessment. You will be expected to use Microsoft Excel and, if your educational institution supports it, IBM SPSS Statistics (SPSS). Microsoft Excel is a spreadsheet program that is part of the Microsoft package included with most computers. SPSS is a popular program for analyzing social science data. Many academic institutions have SPSS available for use by faculty and students, but many social service agencies and organizations where social workers are employed do not. Knowing how to enter and analyze data in both formats is a valuable skill for social workers. We encourage you to work with the data in both Excel and SPSS to expand your skills. Your academic institution or agency may also have a different spreadsheet or statistical analysis software program (such as SAS or MINITAB). Regardless of the program you use, the principles of data entry and analysis discussed in this and the next two chapters will still apply; only the details of using the software will vary. We have found that after we have mastered one spreadsheet or data analysis program, learning additional programs is relatively easy and is accomplished with the help of a basic manual, and online video, and sometimes a little help from a friend or technical support staff.

By the end of this chapter, you should be able to:

■ Describe the strengths and limitations of different data collection methods based on the research context.

■ Write a plan to recruit research participants.

■ Write a retention plan to limit attrition in longitudinal studies.

■ Write a data collection protocol that includes a training outline for data collection staff.

■ Administer a measurement instrument.

■ Create a database in SPSS and Excel, enter and save the data.

SELECTING A DATA COLLECTION METHOD

The previous chapters presented options for collecting primary data, including observation, in-depth interviewing, use of standardized instruments, and survey research. Obviously, observation and in-depth interviewing need to be conducted in person. However, within the broad category of surveys (including to some extent standardized instruments), there are a number of data collection options. As a result, a researcher who wishes to conduct a survey must decide which data collection option will best fit the research. How does the researcher decide whether a survey should be self-administered or, alternatively, administered by a trained data collector? If the survey is self-administered, will it be sent by mail or completed in person, either individually or in a group? Or will the survey be web based or sent by e-mail? Alternatively, if the survey is to be administered by a trained data collector, will this individual conduct the survey in person or by telephone? In answering these questions, the researcher must remember the two main objectives involved in all data collection tasks: minimize error and maximize response rate.

Methods for Administering Surveys

There are four main ways to administer surveys: by mail, over the telephone, in person, or by Internet. Previously there was a "known" hierarchy of survey response rates, with in-person administration producing the highest response rate, followed by telephone and then mail surveys (Dillman, 1978). Internet surveys were essentially unknown at the time. However, extensive work in survey research methods has challenged this belief. In fact, with proper attention to detail, all four survey methods have been shown to yield satisfactory response rates (Dillman, Smyth, & Christian, 2014). The challenge then becomes matching the method of survey administration to the research context. This section reviews basic requirements and guidelines for selecting the most appropriate method of survey administration.

Mail Surveys

To conduct a mail survey, a researcher needs a complete mailing list with current and accurate address information. The researcher who selects this method assumes that the target population is reasonably literate and is motivated to complete and return the questionnaire. The major costs involved in a mail survey are paper and envelopes, printing, and postage. Thus, it is a less expensive method than in-person administration.

Given the amount of junk mail people receive, one major concern associated with mail surveys is attracting enough attention so that the survey will not be thrown away or put aside and forgotten. Another concern is that the survey will get lost in the mail.

In a mail survey, the researcher gives up control over which individual in the household or the organization will respond to the survey. Even though the researcher may provide a preference as to who completes the survey—for example, the adult female householder, the CEO, or the director of human resources—he or she cannot be certain that this request will be honored.

Error can also be introduced in mail surveys, as the researcher has no control over respondents skipping parts of the survey, writing illegibly, marking answers other than those intended, and answering in a socially

---

EXHIBIT 10.1

Guidelines for Using A Mail Survey

Respondent characteristics	• Highly literate adult respondents with mailing addresses. • Motivated to respond thoroughly with attention to detail. • Suited to covering large geographic areas.
Survey questions and presentation	• Closed-ended questions that are simple and require no explanation, piloted on a similar population. • Attention to formatting and wording required. • Questionnaire short to moderate in length to minimize response burden and encourage motivation.
Resource requirements	• Accurate and complete mailing list. • Incentives provided in anticipation of response can improve response rates. Incentives are most commonly used when the survey is targeted to the general public or consumers of a service. • Cost of printing and mailing the questionnaire, follow-up requests, and return postage.

Skill requirements	• Design of the questionnaire.
	• Implementation of follow-up, including design of the follow-up, number of mailings, and response cards.
Examples of target groups	• Alumni of a university, staff of organizations and agencies, professionals, consumers of a service.

desirable manner. Exhibit 10.1 summarizes the research conditions that need to be considered when deciding whether the research is best suited to mail surveys.

Telephone Surveys

In order for a researcher to use a telephone survey, the potential research participants must have access to telephones, and the researcher must have access to a list of current telephone numbers. If the survey is targeted to the general public and the researcher does not have access to telephone numbers, he or she can generate telephone numbers using some form of **random digit dialing** in which the researcher selects a geographic area and then uses computers to generate phone numbers at random using the area codes and possibly the first three digits of a telephone number. Random digit dialing can include cell phone numbers, which solves a problem related to lists that only include landline telephones. Telephone surveys do not require a certain level of literacy in the respondent population as do mail surveys, and they are better suited than mail surveys to populations who are less motivated to respond. Telephone surveys are also better suited than mail surveys to young adult respondents.

Telephone surveys can be used to administer open-ended questions as well as questions with complicated skip patterns. Closed-ended and partially open-ended questions should be kept simple in a telephone survey so that the respondent does not have to remember too many response options in order to provide an answer.

Unfortunately, the use of the telephone for administering surveys precludes the use of any visual aids that can help the participant to respond. If the participant has difficulty understanding a question, the data collector can only repeat the question, offer clarification, and use prompts to encourage a response. Some researchers do not allow any prompts. Others do, although they prefer to standardize the prompts for uniformity throughout the data collection.

In a telephone survey, the researcher has greater control over which member of the household responds than in a mail survey. The researcher can also maintain greater control over the order in which the questions will be answered and the way in which the answers will be recorded. If the interviews are conducted in a room with several telephones, such as a call center, they can be monitored, and a supervisor can be present to provide oversight and answer questions as they arise.

The major cost in a telephone survey is the cost of data collection. Telephone surveys used to be the most efficient data collection method in terms of producing data quickly, although that has changed with the advent of Internet

EXHIBIT 10.2

Guidelines for Using A Telephone Survey

Respondent characteristics	• Any level of literacy, youth and adult. Must be able to concentrate and maintain focus. • Must have access to a telephone and be able to hear well and communicate orally. • Initial motivation to respond need not be as high as in a mail survey. • The researcher cannot provide immediate incentives. • Suitable for large geographic areas.
Survey questions and presentation	• Suitable for simple closed-ended (not too many response categories to choose from), partially closed, and open-ended questions. • The researcher can use prompts and clarification. • Skip patterns can be used. • Less attention to formatting, design, and quality of paper. • Can be administered electronically without paper copies. • Length of the survey will depend on the characteristics of the population surveyed. • Surveys can be longer than those administered by mail.
Resource requirements	• Telephone costs if long-distance calling involved. • Possibly data collection staff, training for data collectors. • The researcher must have access to telephone numbers or be able to generate telephone numbers. • Possibly supervision and support for data collection staff.
Skill requirements	• Excellent verbal interviewing skills. • Ability to record answers accurately and quickly.
Examples of target groups	• Alumni of a university, staff of organizations and agencies, professionals, consumers of a service, youth, general public.

surveys. Exhibit 10.2 summarizes the research conditions appropriate for tele-phone surveys.

In-Person Surveys

In an in-person or face-to-face survey, the data collector meets with the partic-ipants, either in a group or individually. An in-person survey can be self-administered in the sense that the participant completes the questionnaire while the data collector is present. Alternatively, the survey can be adminis-tered as a structured interview in which the data collector reads the questions to the participant and then records the participant's answers.

Whether the survey is self-administered or conducted as a structured inter-view will depend on the nature of the questions and the characteristics of the participant group. For instance, open-ended questions, skip patterns, and ques-tions requiring prompts are best suited to a structured interview. A structured interview is also preferred over self-administration if the researcher requires greater control and questions the participants' literacy or motivation to respond.

In-person survey administration is the preferred choice when the motiva-tion to complete and return a mail survey may be low. Moreover, in-person administration provides the researcher with access to populations that do not have telephones, computers, physical addresses, or postal boxes. In-person surveys are the preferred method when the respondents are either very young (pre-telephone age) or of advanced age. They are also recommended when respondents have certain disabilities related to hearing and mobility that would deter them from participating by telephone or in writing. Finally, in-person surveys are the most appropriate method of data collection for studies that deal with sensitive information such as grief and loss, violence, and illegal and devi-ant behavior. There is some question, however, as to the most effective method of survey administration for encouraging self-disclosure of sensitive, poten-tially embarrassing information and discouraging socially desirable responses. The Audio-Computer-Assisted Self Interview (A-CASI) is a methodology that allows respondents to listen to audio-recorded questions with headphones while the question is displayed on a screen. The respondent answers by touch-ing the chosen response on the screen. This technology improves the collection of sensitive information over traditional paper and pencil and in-person for-mats, without the need for high-level literacy skills (El-Khorazaty et al., 2007).

Of all the data collection methods associated with survey research, in-person surveys require the highest skill level. Unlike the telephone survey, in which only what is spoken is important, in in-person data collection, the entire demeanor, appearance, and body language of the data collector are important. In-person administration can also be the most expensive method of data collec-tion because it involves both travel time and transportation costs. It is also the most time consuming of all data collection methods. Exhibit 10.3 summarizes the research conditions conducive to in-person survey administration.

EXHIBIT 10.3

Guidelines for Using an In-Person Survey

Respondent characteristics	• Appropriate when literacy and motivation are questionable. If incentives are important to motivate participation, they can be provided immediately. • Suitable for all age groups. • Accommodates disabilities such as hearing and concentration as well as some physical disabilities that would prevent writing or talking on the telephone. • Allows the greatest control over who answers the questions and control over administration of the survey, including question order and recording responses. • Most feasible with small sample sizes and when respondents are located in a relatively small geographic area.
Survey questions and presentation	• Appropriate for closed-ended, partially closed, and open-ended questions. • Appropriate for long surveys; response burden not as much of a concern as with the other methods. • The ability to use visual aids allows for the inclusion of complex questions. • Can include observational questions. • Appropriate for asking sensitive information. • Formatting and presentation not as important, unless the participant will be given a copy of the interview schedule.
Resource requirements	• Transportation. • Training, paying, and supervising data collection staff. • Incentives if applicable. • Formatting and printing of questionnaires.
Skill requirements	• Excellent interviewing skills and attending behavior; attention to speed and accuracy in recording data. • Appearance and attire are added considerations and must be appropriate for the target population. • Attention to safety while interviewing.
Examples of target groups	• Incarcerated populations, homeless individuals, children and youths, elderly and disabled, and parents of preschool children.

Internet Surveys

The use of the Internet as a data collection tool is a relatively recent development. As computer literacy has increased and computer technology has evolved and become more affordable, the use of the Internet as a vehicle of survey administration has expanded dramatically. The flow of communication in an Internet survey is from machine to machine, whether that is a smart phone or computer.

By using the Internet, the researcher can avoid the mailing and transportation costs associated with mail and in-person survey administration. Similarly, the researcher can avoid the labor costs associated with telephone and in-person interviews. Internet surveys have the potential to provide data quickly and cheaply.

The major disadvantage to Internet surveys—albeit one that is likely to lessen over time—is access. Some nonprofessionals still do not know how to use a computer, others do not have access to a computer outside of work, and not everyone with a computer has access to the Internet. All three of these aspects—knowledge, access, and connectivity—are required of the participant in an Internet survey.

There are two types of Internet surveys: Web and e-mail. Web surveys have several advantages over e-mail surveys, one of which is presentation. Web surveys can employ color, graphics, audio, video, and other interactive features, as well as automatic skip patterns, scoring, and response features. E-mail surveys, in contrast, are basically text messages that are either included in an e-mail message or attached to it as a separate word processing or spreadsheet document. Another advantage of web surveys over e-mail is the simplified submission process. The respondent needs only to click on the Submit Survey button, and the survey is delivered. In contrast, e-mail surveys do not always make it back to the intended destination, either because they are returned to the wrong e-mail address or they are not sent at all.

Although e-mail surveys do not require a great deal of skill or cost to design and distribute, web surveys require researchers to be technologically savvy or to include discretionary funds in the research budget. However, web-based survey programs such as Qualtrics and SurveyMonkey have greatly simplified the Internet survey process.

Three key factors affect the respondent's ability to view web surveys as intended by the researcher: the respondent's computer operating system, the speed and type of the respondent's Internet connection, and the respondent's degree of computer literacy. Tracking survey responses and conducting follow-up requests is much easier with Internet than email surveys. Tracking, however, has to be built into the design of web surveys, otherwise it is impossible to know who has responded and where to focus follow-up efforts.

One issue the researcher will have to deal with in an Internet survey is getting through devices that are set up to block spam and being recognized as legitimate before being sent to the trash folder. Many legitimate communications are blocked because they are mistakenly identified as spam. Firewall security is often set up to block unknown Internet access in schools and courts. Exhibit 10.4 presents a summary of the research conditions suitable for Internet surveys.

EXHIBIT 10.4

Guidelines for Using an Internet Survey

Respondent characteristics	• Professionals in businesses, organizations, and government departments where computer use is expected and access is assured. • Inability to provide advance incentives to increase motivation.
Survey questions and presentation	• Closed-ended questions, attention to formatting and wording. • Short to moderate in length to minimize response burden.
Resource requirements	• Web survey design requires specialized knowledge and time spent in development, but once developed, both web and e-mail surveys are low cost.
Skill requirements	• Design of the survey. • Implementation and follow-up.
Examples of target groups	• Staff of organizations, agencies, government departments, and universities, members of professional organizations.

Survey Methods and the Objectives of Research

In some instances, the choice of a data collection method may be self-evident. For instance, if the purpose of the research is to evaluate a school-based abstinence education program, it makes sense to administer the survey to participants in an in-person, self-administered, group format both before and at the end of the delivery of the curriculum. Mailing surveys to students' homes or trying to contact them by telephone would only increase the cost of the research and would contribute to nonresponse error.

In contrast, a lengthy survey involving several open-ended questions would probably be best administered in person in a structured individual interview format, unless the target participants are spread across an expansive geographic area, in which case a telephone survey would work best. Finally, a large national survey of professionals is probably best carried out using a combination of methods, including the Internet and regular mail or telephone. Conducting the first round of the survey using the Internet would significantly reduce printing and mailing costs. The researcher could then follow up using regular mail surveys if addresses are available, and even telephone surveys if phone numbers are available and there are resources to call and administer the survey questions.

The decision of what data collection method to use should always involve answering the following two questions in this order:

1.   Which method would most minimize measurement error?
2.   Which method would yield the best response rate?

Measurement error was discussed in Chapter 9. The next section discusses nonresponse. Regardless of the selected method of survey administration, all researchers need to concern themselves with nonresponse.

Nonresponse

Nonresponse is a problem when it follows a pattern that introduces bias into the study. This type of bias, called **nonresponse error**, occurs when those who do not respond, i.e., the nonrespondents, share certain characteristics that differentiate them from the respondents. For example, the respondent group may include a higher percentage of participants who have more free time to fill out the survey because they are retired, unemployed, or do not have children.

There is no consensus among researchers as to what constitutes a satisfactory response rate. This is because the relationship between response rate and nonresponse error varies. In some surveys, it may be possible to have only a 50% response rate and yet have very little response error. In contrast, it is possible to have a high response rate, for example, 80%, and have substantial nonresponse error. A low response rate does not necessarily lead to nonresponse error, just as a high response rate cannot always eliminate or avoid nonresponse error. Rather, the size of the nonresponse error depends on how well the respondents reflect the total population of those surveyed and the variability within that population.

Opinion polls illustrate this phenomenon. For example, if the proportion of voters in the population who favor one candidate over another is very uneven, say 80% in favor of Candidate A compared to 20% in favor of Candidate B, then a response rate of 50% will not be problematic in terms of accurately predicting the winner. In this instance, a prediction can be made fairly accurately based on a moderate rate of response.

In contrast, if the split in the population is fairly even—for example, 48% in favor of Candidate A and 52% in favor of Candidate B—then a high response rate will be critical to reducing nonresponse error and accurately predicting the outcome.

The size of the nonresponse error is a function of both

- response rate and
- the extent to which respondents differ from nonrespondents.

Thus, in addition to reporting the response rate, researchers should compare respondents with nonrespondents on variables that might reasonably impact the dependent variable or what is being studied. In studying community members' attitudes about developing additional group homes for people with mental illness, for example, the researcher needs to know whether homeowners are equally represented among responders and nonresponders because homeowners often oppose group homes based on the fear that their property values will decline.

A report of survey research results should always include a statement of the response rate, as well as a description of how it was calculated and the decision rules used. A useful lesson in survey research, therefore, is how to calculate response rates. It would seem logical to do so by taking the total number of complete responses, dividing by the total number of possible respondents (the number of sampling units included on the sampling frame), and then multiplying by 100 to arrive at the overall response rate. For example, if you mailed 300 surveys and 240 were returned to you, your response rate could be calculated as 240/300 x100 = 80%. You might conclude that your nonresponse rate is 20%. This method can, however, substantially inflate the rate of nonresponse.

QUICK GUIDE 5 CALCULATING RESPONSE RATES

1. Determine the number of units in the sampling frame and the number of responses, whether they come from individuals, families, groups, agencies, organizations, or any other aggregate.
2. Determine the number of nonrespondents or nonresponse units. That is not the same as the number of surveys that have not been returned. Those who can legitimately be counted in the calculation of nonrespondents or nonresponse units are:

   - Those who could not possibly have responded because, for all practical purposes, they do not exist (for example, deceased individuals, vacant households and empty lots, sampling units with out-of-service or misclassified telephone numbers)
   - Those who refuse to participate
   - Those who terminate their participation partway into the survey (the definition of complete should be defined by the researcher)

- ■ Those who cannot be contacted because they are not available when they are called or do not answer or send back the survey
- ■ Those who are unavailable due to death that occurred after the survey start date
- ■ Those who are unavailable due to physical or mental inability, language problems, and miscellaneous other reasons
- ■ Those who cannot be verified as either nonrespondents or nonresponse units

3. Reduce the total number of sampling units by first subtracting the number of nonresponse units from the total number of units in the sampling frame, then dividing the number of complete responses by that number, and then multiplying by 100:

$$\text{Response rate} = \frac{\text{Number of complete responses}}{(\text{Number of sampling units} - \text{Number of nonresponse units})} \times 100$$

Example:

1. surveys sent out, 240 responses received
2. 39 legitimate nonresponse units:

- ■ 34 surveys returned unopened, marked "not at this address and no forwarding address"
- ■ 5 survey units determined to be deceased prior to survey date

3. Response rate = 240/(300 - 39) x 100 = 240/261 x 100 = 92 %.

In reality, even though only 240 of 300 surveys were returned, the true number of nonrespondents may not total 60. Nonrespondents are not necessarily all the sampling units to whom you sent the survey but who never returned it to you. The procedure for determining how many nonresponses are actually involved and for properly calculating response rate is outlined in Quick Guide 5 above. This calculation can significantly increase the response rate. With this calculation, the response rate in the example is 92% and the nonresponse rate is 8%.

Feasibility

The decision about which survey method to use will also be based to a large degree on feasibility. For example, if the budget does not include funds for travel or for hiring data collection staff, in-person data collection may not be feasible. As another example, if the period is short, a telephone or Internet survey may be a better alternative than a mail survey.

When the original plan for administering the survey is not feasible, the research study may be scaled back to include a smaller sample; restricted in terms of geographic area; or shortened to include fewer questions, fewer focus groups, or fewer follow-up points. In some instances, the researcher might target a different group of respondents in order to fit the research with the budget. For example, instead of surveying children by using in-person individual interviews, the researcher might decide to survey parents by mail or interview teachers in a focus group. In some instances, the researcher might have to modify the research question.

RECRUITING RESEARCH PARTICIPANTS

As discussed in Chapter 2, in order for the research to be considered ethical, participation must be a voluntary and informed activity. This fact does not prohibit researchers from taking reasonable steps to convince people to participate. The challenge for the researcher is to motivate respondents to comply without being coercive.

Failure to achieve broad participation can result in a major source of error due to nonresponse. Further, it can lead to delays in starting the research study, and, in some cases, it can cause an entire study or evaluation to be canceled.

Researchers will be well served by developing a recruitment strategy for participants before the research begins. The next section identifies six "triggers" that can be used to influence those in the sampling frame to participate.

Using Six "Triggers" of Influence

One way to encourage broad participation is to use Robert Cialdini's (2006) theory of influence. Cialdini, an experimental social psychologist, describes six major tactics that researchers can use to encourage people to participate in survey research. Each tactic is governed by a fundamental psychological principle that directs human behavior.

According to Cialdini, technological advances in modern society have led to changes in the ways that people make decisions. The fast pace of modern life and the abundance of available information lead people to adopt a shortcut approach to decision making. Instead of rationally weighing the pros and cons of each decision, people often make decisions quickly on the basis of a single piece of information called a **trigger,** which, as the word implies, is something that leads people to choose one response over another. Cialdini claims that people make all kinds of decisions based on triggers: decisions to give, to buy, to believe, and even to participate in research. He predicts that the tendency toward shortcut decision making will only increase in the future, thereby escalating the importance of understanding and using triggers in recruiting participants.

The following sections present a discussion of the six triggers and the principle on which each is based. The implications for the recruitment of research participants are also summarized.

Reciprocity

Cialdini asserts that one of the most widespread and basic norms of human culture is embodied in the principle of reciprocity. The *principle of reciprocity* implies that we should try to repay in some form what another person has provided to us. According to Cialdini, this trigger is so effective it can overwhelm the influence of the other five principles.

People who take and make no effort to give in return are generally viewed negatively. People go to enormous lengths to avoid being viewed this way. Marketers and other persuaders often offer "gifts" to activate this response. Undoubtedly, you have witnessed this principle in operation. Examples are supermarkets that give free samples to consumers to encourage them to buy, real estate agents who leave magnets on the door in the hope of gaining clients, and organizations that send nickels and address labels in the mail to encourage donations. Why do we see these types of examples so frequently? The answer to that question is simply "Because it works." This principle is so effective that it even works when the gift has little to no value to the recipient. This is good news for the social work researcher, who can use this principle to encourage participation in research on even the slimmest of budgets. The implications of this principle for increasing recruitment in a research study are the following:

- Provide advance incentives to increase response rates.
- Along with the request to participate, include small incentives, which are even more effective than the promise of larger incentives.

Incentives may be monetary or nonmonetary, such as a one-dollar bill, special parking privileges, a gift certificate, or drawings for an iPad, cash prize, or electronics.

Commitment and Consistency

This principle refers to the desire in most people to think and act in a steady or similar manner across different situations (Cialdini, 2006). Inconsistency is generally considered an undesirable trait, hypocritical at least, and at worst a sign of mental confusion. In recent political discourse, the term *flip-flopper* has emerged as a derogatory label for someone accused of being inconsistent.

To apply the principle of commitment and consistency to research, the researcher begins recruitment by encouraging potential participants to make a small commitment that is consistent with a behavior that the researcher will later request of them. Consider, for example, a study focused on a campaign to recruit blood donors. Making a small initial request for permission simply to add a person's name to a list of potential blood donors and then calling the person seven to 10 days later will be a more effective means of recruitment than a straightforward request to donate.

Significantly, not all commitments are equally effective at inducing compliance. Commitments generally are most effective when they are active, such as signing an agreement to be contacted or to receive more information; made in the public eye; and viewed as internally motivated (Cialdini, 2006).

This last point requires further explanation. For an example we will use a campaign to encourage people to join a bone-marrow registry, a list of volunteers ready and willing to donate bone marrow if identified as a match with someone in need. People who already donated blood to the organization were sent a letter praising them for being donors. The letter was accompanied by a questionnaire on their altruism, commitments, and social support. Of those who received the letter, 13% subsequently joined the registry. In contrast, only 6% of a control group who received only a brochure on the registry and 6% of a second control group who received a brochure with a letter asking them to join the registry actually joined. The letter sent to the experimental group was designed to influence and reinforce their self-perception as donors, and the questionnaire was sent to actively reinforce that perception (Sarason et al., 1993).

The implications of this principle for recruitment to participate in a research study are the following:

■ Create or build on an identity that is consistent with the later request to participate in the research.
■ Attempt a smaller, easier-to-achieve commitment before asking for a larger commitment that is consistent with the first.

Social Proof

The principle of social proof implies that we determine what is correct by finding out what others think is correct. That is, we perceive a particular behavior as correct in a given situation to the extent that we observe other people performing the same behavior. This principle is particularly relevant in a context of uncertainty, when the decision is unclear or ambiguous. In addition, the more we consider the people we observe to be similar to ourselves, the more likely we are to imitate their behavior. According to Cialdini (2006), powerful imitative effects have been found among children and adults and in such diverse activities as purchase decisions and contributions to charity.

The implications of this trigger for social work research include the following:

■ People are likely to respond positively to a request to participate if they perceive that others, especially others who are similar to themselves, have also responded positively.
■ Social proof is not an appropriate tactic to use when the subject matter of the research may be perceived as too personal or embarrassing to discuss in a group context.

Liking

The principle of liking has implications for the characteristics of the people conducting the recruitment as well as for the manner in which the study is titled and framed. People prefer to comply with the requests of individuals they know and like. One feature that influences liking is physical attractiveness. A second factor is perceived similarity: people tend to like people whom they view as similar to themselves.

Here are a few ways to employ the trigger of liking and thereby encourage participation in a survey:

■ Praise, compliment, and demonstrate interest and concern toward potential participants.
■ Foster increased familiarity through repeated contact, especially contact under positive circumstances.
■ Connect yourself with an association perceived as positive, such as a child's school or basketball camp.

Authority

Society exerts strong pressure to comply with the requests of people in positions of authority. This tendency to obey authority figures originates in socialization practices that teach obedience as the correct mode of conduct. This principle is continuously reinforced because authority figures generally have the ability to reward and to punish.

Psychologist Stanley Milgram (1963) demonstrated the strength of the authority principle in his classic studies of obedience at Yale University. Milgram found that normal and psychologically healthy individuals were often willing to administer what they thought were dangerous levels of electric shocks to another person, based simply on the order to do so by an experimental scientist.

Not only do individuals tend to comply with the requests of people in authority, but they also tend to react to mere symbols of authority in an automatic way. For example, titles such as Dr. or Reverend; clothing, including police uniforms, badges, and pastoral robes; and automobiles, including fire trucks, police cars, and ambulances, tend to command respect and attract immediate attention. Think about how you react when you are driving and you notice a police car in the rearview mirror. Does your foot automatically lift off the gas pedal while your eyes shift nervously to the speedometer? What other authority figures or symbols do you tend to react to in an automatic way?

Here are a couple of tactics that can draw on the authority trigger to encourage participation:

- A letter to parents and caregivers from a teacher encouraging their participation in a research study.
- An appeal from local fireman to participate in a research study on water safety practices.

Scarcity

According to the scarcity principle, people assign more value to an opportunity when it is considered rare, in short supply, or available only for a limited time. The scarcity principle works because people typically place greater value on things that are difficult to attain. There are plenty of everyday examples of this principle. Perhaps the most obvious cases occur as the holiday season approaches. During the 2016 Christmas season, for instance, the Smart R2D2 from the Star Wars movie, worth about $99, was in such high demand that it was being sold on the secondary market for over $200.

In the case of participant recruitment, the scarcity trigger can be employed in a variety of ways:

- Frame the request so it can be perceived as consisting of exclusive information.
- Direct requests to a specific name instead of using a general reference like "Dear Friend" or "Current Resident" or no reference at all.
- Inform potential participants that they are among a select number of individuals who have been offered the opportunity to participate and that their decision is time limited.

An example of this last suggestion was used effectively in an experimental study to examine the effectiveness of a child abuse and neglect prevention program. Potential participants were told that they were among 200 local families being contacted and that they would be contacted within three days for their decision to participate.

Tailoring Recruitment to the Target Participant

The previous section discussed the application of six general principles that can influence the research recruitment process. This section develops that discussion by presenting a framework that researchers can use to tailor the recruitment strategy to the target participant. Two key objectives of any recruitment strategy are to anticipate and remove any obstacles and to increase people's motivation to participate. The parallel to these objectives in social work practice is "beginning where the client is."

Social workers are generally familiar with thinking in terms of a **systems framework** (Bronfenbrenner, 1977). When designing an effective recruitment strategy, it is helpful to view the target participant as operating within a system. This system includes the micro level of individual and family, which is grounded in the mesosystem comprising the participant's neighborhood, employer, church, schools, and recreation facilities. Beyond the mesosystem are the macro system and the exo systems, which include the local economy, the social service and educational systems, the media and the government.

Exhibit 10.5 presents a systems framework for tailoring participant recruitment strategies. The framework in Exhibit 10.5 can also be used for strategically planning recruitment when a gatekeeper, such as a parent, caretaker, or

---

EXHIBIT 10.5

Systems Framework for Tailoring Recruitment Strategies

- **Participant**: Participants can be defined in terms of gender, age, ethnicity, sexual orientation, group, income, life experience, and so on.
- **Goal**: The purpose of the research should be evaluated in terms of its relevance for the target participant. Take into account that the appeal of certain goals may vary among participants in the same target group.
- **Contract**: The contract or agreement to participate should be evaluated in terms of the target group.
- **Meeting place**: Is the meeting place for recruitment and later participation considered safe, accessible, and comfortable for the target group? Is it associated with a positive experience?
- **Use of time**: The time commitment and scheduling should be evaluated in terms of the target group.
- **Relationship**: The desired relationship between the research staff and the participant should be considered as well as the style of communication.
- **Outside resources**: The provision of outside resources may be necessary to remove barriers to participation. Childcare, transportation, food, and referral to other resources may be required.

administrative assistant, stands between the researcher and the participant. The process of "gaining entry" through gatekeepers is discussed further in Chapter 6.

Define the Participant

The first step in this framework is to define the target participant. In performing this task, researchers can consider a multitude of variables, including gender, age, ethnicity, income, preferred language, literacy, and experience. The more carefully the researcher defines the target participant, the more precisely he or she can tailor the recruitment strategy.

Targeted recruitment strategies are especially important to recruit low-income and minority populations. El-Khorazaty et al. (2007) demonstrated how such efforts could be used to recruit and retain African American and Latina women for a randomized clinical trial to reduce smoking, depression, and intimate partner violence during pregnancy. In addition to financial and other incentives, and regular updates of contact information, attention to cultural competence was considered key to successful recruitment. Women were first recruited for a screening interview. The recruitment process was flexible, and when women were reluctant to participate due to time constraints they were invited back at a later time. Data collection staff were matched by gender and ethnicity with the target population, and were trained in how to build rapport including being respectful and culturally sensitive. This tailored approach was effective in recruiting ethnic minority and low-income women at high rates in both the intervention and control groups.

Define the Study in the Participant's Terms

After the researchers have defined the target participant, the remaining steps in the framework are tailored to fit with the life circumstances of the target participant.

- *Clarify goals.* The goals of the research. These goals should be clear and should be evaluated in terms of their relevance for the target participant. The key is to ask potential recruits to participate in something they want to do, as opposed to persuading them to do something they don't want to do.
- *Tailor the contract.* The contract or agreement to participate should be tailored to the target participants. Is the language clear and understandable to the participants? Does it share important information that will motivate the participants and inform them of the expected role they will have in the research as well as the potential impact on their lives?
- *Offer a meeting place.* To improve success rates, recruitment efforts and activities should be located in a place that is easily accessible and considered safe

by the participants. Safety could also refer to space to conduct private interviews and to answer participants' questions in confidence.

■ *Respect time.* A major consideration in any recruitment effort is that the research must be responsive to the complexities of the participants' lives. Recruiters should evaluate time frames to determine when they should ask individuals to participate. They should consider the season, day of the week, time of day, and overall time required for recruitment. For instance, if the research targets farmers, the strategy might be to contact them in the evening, during fall or winter, once harvesting is complete. If the research study involves parents of preschool children, early morning and evening may not be the best times to attempt contact, as they coincide with eating, dressing, and bedtime routines. Also, contacts with the parents of young children should be kept relatively short. If the research setting is a school, the researcher must plan around testing cycles. In an agency that receives public funds, contract renewal is a bad time to approach the administration with data requests.

■ *Enhance the relationship.* Another responsibility of the recruiter is to assess whether the approach is sensitive to differences in culture, age, and gender or whether it needs to be modified along those lines. A related issue is whether the characteristics of the recruiter will appeal to the target participants. For instance, if the target population is youths who congregate at the mall, it may not be best if the recruiter is female and near the age of the youths' mothers. These youths may respond best to someone younger and not associated with authority. The recruiter should also consider which relational style fits best with target participants. Would potential participants respond best to someone they perceive as passive or to someone more directive and extroverted, for example?

■ *Offer outside resources.* The recruiter should use available outside resources to reduce the barriers to participation as perceived by the participants. For example, if the participants are caring for children or elders, the offer of outside resources should take into account the participants' roles as caretakers. Similarly, some low-income participants may have basic needs such as food, transportation, and safety. In addition or as an alternative to providing basic goods and services, providing information on community resources can be an incentive to participate. A list of local resources could include information on where to ask for food boxes, free or low-cost city bus tickets, and recreational programs for children from low-income families.

Planning for Retention

The success of many research studies with more than one round of measurement— for example, a pretest/posttest or longitudinal research design—depends on

retention, that is, the ability to retain participation of the same individuals over time.

The opposite of retention is attrition, which can be characterized by permanent or intermittent loss. Permanent loss results when a participant withdraws from a study, dies, or cannot be accessed due to long-term incarceration or relocation without notice. Intermittent loss includes temporary difficulty contacting a participant, participant inability or refusal to participate on a particular occasion, inaccurate location information, and other factors that result in missed appointments. Both intermittent and permanent loss of research participants are problematic, but permanent loss is by far the worst.

We know from Chapter 7 that attrition in longitudinal research is to be expected. In fact, considerable attrition should be expected. This section presents techniques that can enhance participant retention, even with populations that are prone to attrition. Strategies to enhance retention should begin at recruitment, when impressions are made, relationships are developed, and participants establish an image of the research study or evaluation.

Not all strategies will work with all participants. Therefore, researchers should develop a multifaceted retention plan. Whatever the specific plan, persistence, ingenuity, and flexibility are essential to achieving good retention rates.

Develop Rapport

Retention involves many of the same principles and considerations as participant recruitment. One common principle in recruitment and retention is liking. If the research participant does not experience a positive rapport with the data collector, does not trust the data collector or the study, or does not find participation interesting or enjoyable, he or she is not likely to continue to participate, even if incentives are provided.

Strategies for developing rapport with participants include the following:

- Matching the qualities of the data collection staff to the characteristics of the participant. Personal attributes that can reduce attrition include perceived similarity to the participant.
- Training, supporting, and supervising data collection staff in establishing rapport (for example, adopting a nonjudgmental attitude, showing interest, listening attentively, being punctual, and adhering to procedures such as maintaining confidentiality).
- Maintaining contact with the participant between data collection periods if contact is otherwise infrequent, for example, intervals of six months or greater. Strategies for staying in touch include phone calls, personal visits, birthday/holiday cards, and periodic mailings. Reminder cards should be mailed to participants a couple of weeks before the scheduled contact.

■ Providing continuity by limiting turnover in data collection staff.

■ Conducting data collection in person whenever possible.

■ Emphasizing the confidentiality of the data and respect for participants.

■ Stressing the importance of the participant's contributions.

■ Emphasizing the benefits of participation.

■ Being accommodating and flexible with regard to the time and place of data collection.

■ Adding a personal touch to all project communications. For example, you can create a project logo for all correspondence so that participants will recognize the communication and open it instead of discarding it.

Develop a Tracking System

Research suggests that failure to locate participants is the greatest cause of attrition. Not surprisingly, then, persistence in trying to find participants is a key factor in retention. Recruiters need to develop tracking systems for recording and updating contact information, providing reminders to contact participants intermittently, and recording the outcome of each attempt to establish contact. Tracking systems can be manual or automated, sophisticated or simple. Moreover, researchers can now use contact management software programs to help manage tracking efforts.

A participant tracking system might include the following data:

■ Information on as many ways of contacting the participant as possible (all telephone numbers, mailing address, postal box, e-mail, employer contact).

■ Contact information for at least two friends or relatives who are the most likely to have stable residences and know the participant's whereabouts.

■ Schedule of when to contact participants between data collection periods by sending birthday or holiday cards along with scheduled phone calls. Automated contact reminders can be built into computerized tracking systems.

■ The outcome of all attempts to make contact.

■ Updates of information at every data collection point, including changes in employment, outside contacts, and future relocation plans.

■ List of community agencies that may have contact with the participant (educational institutions, treatment programs, criminal justice systems).

■ List of places the participant likes to frequent.

Employers or agencies that serve the participant will generally not provide the researcher with information on any participant's whereabouts. Nevertheless, these contacts are often willing to deliver a message to the participant to make contact with the researcher. In addition, the participant can fill out a release-of-information form that grants family members, friends, and others permission to give the researcher information about the participant's whereabouts.

In addition to collecting contact information, the researcher should inquire as to the best times to contact the participant. She or he should also consider cultural factors with regard to how, where, and when to contact participants.

Another strategy to improve the retention rate of research participants is to give the participants the researcher's contact information. This information can include a business card, a magnet with contact information, a card with the date of the next scheduled contact, and a request to call if any contact information changes. Setting up a toll-free number or encouraging participants to place a collect call to the project office is another useful technique for managing attrition.

If a respondent has moved, the project staff can send a letter with "Do not forward, address correction requested" written on the envelope to obtain the respondent's new address from the postal service. Resources for locating participants include directory assistance, phone books, Internet locator sites, and relatives, friends, and other contacts.

Minimize the Research Burden

One source of participant attrition is the perceived burden of the research. Several strategies can be used to reduce response burden:

- Reduce the length of the interview or questionnaire.
- Make the task fun as opposed to boring.
- Ask only relevant questions.
- Keep sensitive items to a minimum and place them near the middle to the end of the instrument. Consider the use of A-CASI for sensitive information.
- Make the location for data collection convenient and accessible.
- Reduce the frequency of data collection.
- Be flexible in scheduling times and locations and rescheduling.
- Facilitate communication by providing participants with a toll-free telephone number, business cards, magnets with project contact information, and stamped change-of-address cards.

Provide Incentives

One method of encouraging participation is to reward participants for their initial and continued participation. Providing incentives can convey the sentiment that participation is important and can help motivate participation in follow-up contacts. The use and value of incentives will ultimately depend on the research budget.

It is common to provide incentives to private individuals but not to organizational participants, elected officials, or employees of a social service agency. The participation of these groups in research is usually viewed as a function of their employment or an extension of their civic duty.

When planning for incentives, the researcher can use the following strategies:

- Make the incentive large enough to be meaningful but not so large that it may be considered coercive.
- Increase the value of the incentive over time to reflect the increasing value and importance of participation.
- Provide a schedule of incentives to participants at recruitment and at each data collection period thereafter reminding them of the timetable and the requirements of the research.
- Provide small incentives to participants who inform the researcher of changes in contact information.
- Consider the type of incentive and its appeal to the participant. Some researchers do not like to use cash incentives because of concerns about the safety of data collectors in the field. Checks are useful in the sense that they can be mailed and tracked if they are lost, but they are not as flexible as cash. Gift cards restrict how participants can use the incentive and may require participants to make arrangements for transportation. Nonmonetary forms of incentives, such as food, diapers, and toiletries, may also be considered and should be tailored to the characteristics of the respondent.
- Identify alternative sources of funding if the research budget is too tight to afford incentives. For example, researchers can elicit donations from local businesses and organizations. Examples of donated incentives include movie tickets, restaurant coupons, and sports items.
- Substitute a drawing—in which only one or a few participants win a prize—if incentives cannot be provided to everyone. Drawings are not a good idea when the participants are young children or very needy individuals. In these instances, researchers should make an effort to provide each participant with an incentive.
- Remember that incentives alone are not enough to encourage participation.

PREPARING FOR DATA COLLECTION

Long intervals between participant recruitment and data collection will lead to problems with retention. Thus, the plan for collecting data and for hiring and training data collectors must be developed before participant recruitment begins. The goal is to begin data collection immediately as participants come forward.

Developing a Data Collection Protocol

To prepare for data collection, the researcher must develop a **data collection protocol**, a set of written instructions and policies that outlines the specific rules governing contact with participants and guides data collection. Similar to recruitment and retention plans, data collection protocols are a proactive step to prevent problems before they occur.

The researcher views the protocol as a work in progress. He or she completes the protocol to the maximum extent possible in advance of the study and subsequently updates it as questions arise, decisions are made, and problems are resolved.

The information that goes into the data collection protocol will vary with the context and scope of the research. The following 18 items may be considered as a useful framework for designing a data collection protocol.

- *Schedule of measures.* This is a list that documents what data collection instruments will be administered in which observation periods, assuming there is more than one data collection point.
- *Policy for participant contact.* This section of the protocol outlines the general guidelines for contacting participants. It includes such information as how far in advance and by what methods participants are to be contacted, the minimum and maximum number of attempts to contact a participant, the interval or schedule for contact attempts, and the procedure to follow in the event of a missed appointment. It can also include the specifics of what the researcher needs to do before making contact, e.g., mailing out a pre-notice letter, printing a map of directions, and gathering the forms and instruments that will be used.
- *Tracking procedures.* The protocol must specify the data needed for tracking, when to use the tracking procedure, and the appropriate sequence of tracking (for instance, the researcher would attempt personal contacts before contacting an employer).
- *Equipment.* An effective protocol specifies the equipment needed to conduct an interview or observation. An example would be a tape recorder with set of spare batteries. The protocol also outlines the testing procedures that must be conducted before using the equipment. Finally, it can list the equipment the researcher considers necessary for contact and safety, for instance, a cell phone.

■ *Answers to frequently asked questions (FAQs).* This section of the protocol consists of a one-page summary of answers to frequently asked questions, such as who is sponsoring the study, what the perceived benefits of the study are, when the study results will be available and how they can be accessed, and whom to contact to answer further questions or address concerns regarding the study. The one page of FAQs may be prepared as a handout to be distributed to participants and gatekeepers who want more information about the research.

■ *Incentive policy.* The incentive policy states when, and in what form, incentives will be provided. It also indicates how the data collector will access the incentives and which accounting procedure will be used for tracking the incentives. For instance, when cash or gift card incentives are provided in person, participants should be asked to initial a receipt. In such cases, the protocol should specify the procedures for recording and filing initialed receipts.

■ *Safety protocols.* An important feature of the protocol is the description of potential safety concerns with advice on what to do in the event the data collector encounters a problem. For instance, if the research requires home visits, the data collector may encounter situations in which he or she becomes aware of domestic violence, child abuse, drug use, or other illegal behavior. If the data collector must go into the field to collect data, the protocol should specify the requirements for reporting his or her where-abouts at all times. The collector should also be provided with a working cell phone and encouraged to dial 911 if a safety concern arises. All data collection staff should be outfitted with official identification tags that they can show participants when making home visits or in-person contacts.

■ *Standards for administration.* The protocol should include rules about administering the data collection instrument. In structured interviews, for example, interviewers should always read the questions exactly as they are written in each interview. Interviewers also must appear neutral at all times and never offer to the participant any indication, verbally or otherwise, of whether she or he feels that the answer given is "right" or "acceptable." In questions in which the level of measurement is nominal or ordinal, interviewers must read the entire scale before the participant provides an answer, at least for the first few items in a series of questions where the response categories are the same.

■ *Supervision policy.* The protocol should contain a policy for randomly checking the accuracy of the data and performance of the data collector in the field. This policy may involve observing data collection activities and eliciting participants' impressions of these activities. It is much better for researchers to discover a problem with data collection and take steps to correct it than to have problems brought to their attention by a participant or gatekeeper after data collection has been ongoing for some time. The protocol should also outline the policy on how data collectors can access a researcher or supervisor when they are in the field.

■ *Policies on probing.* The protocol should include examples of how to probe "don't know" answers. It should also contain responses to help participants say all they have to say about an open-ended question.

■ *Communication standards.* The protocol should outline the terminology both to use and to avoid when discussing the study. For example, the study may be referred to as a project rather than a study. This section of the protocol should also provide guidelines concerning any specific letterhead, paper, header, or footer that must be included on all project correspondence. If there is a project logo, the protocol might state that it will appear on all correspondence. Also included is the procedure for proofreading all correspondence before it leaves the office. The protocol should explicitly state the project expectations for participants regarding punctuality, politeness, and return communication.

■ *Record keeping.* The protocol should specify the records that the data collectors must keep during data collection: mileage, hotel, food, and other travel receipts. It should also indicate the time frame within which the data collectors must submit all of their receipts, to whom, and how.

■ *Data security rules.* The rules governing data storage—for example, do not leave data in the car, do not carry data on external drives, do not take data home—should be included in the protocol. In addition, the protocol should develop rules for the transfer of data if they pass between people or offices. The disposal of data—both hard copy and electronic formats— must be outlined in advance of the study.

■ *Data recording rules.* The protocol should also include rules regarding how the data are to be recorded, including the use of pen or pencil, when and how to record, and procedures for checking the recording for completeness and accuracy.

■ *Analytical plan.* Researchers conducting quantitative analysis will want to plan the analysis in advance of implementing the study. This procedure serves a couple of purposes. First, it can help researchers to collect only those data that they believe are relevant and have a chance of being used. Second, it helps them determine whether they have considered all of the variables needed for the analysis. In contrast, for researchers engaged in qualitative research, analysis is a process that is conducted concurrently with data collection. Transcripts of interviews and observations should leave room for comments, tentative interpretations, and emerging hypotheses. Notes are important in describing how researchers analyzed the data and arrived at the conclusions. The protocol should remind researchers of these necessary steps.

- *Ethical standards.* Most ethical rules seem like common sense. Even so, the protocol should explicitly state the rules to prevent unfortunate ethical breaches from occurring. Rules of ethical conduct may be specific, such as "You do not approach or request contact with any participant outside the research context or for any purpose other than data collection." Rules of ethical conduct can also address less concrete situations such as the differences between a data collection interview and a therapeutic interview. There is no one set of ethical guidelines that will be appropriate for all research contexts. For instance, in ethnographic research in which the researcher often participates in the everyday activities of participants over an extended period, the rules of ethical conduct may differ from those governing in-person survey research.
- *Journaling requirements.* In qualitative research, the rules and decisions made as the research is conducted should also be recorded. This process is called journaling, and it becomes a crucial piece of the data in a qualitative study. The qualitative journal can include notes about research scheduling and logistics as well as reflections on self, research participants, and the data that are being collected. Journaling is also a helpful tool for quantitative research studies.
- *Decision rules.* Once data collection begins, questions and problems will arise for which decisions must be made. Keep track of all decision rules (rules regarding how decisions are made) in writing, and make certain that the information is shared with all project staff through the data collection protocol. These steps will help ensure the integrity of the research project.

The challenge of clear communication increases with the number of research staff and the division of labor, making the role of the data collection protocol even more important.

Preparing Data Collectors

Unless the study is small, the research participants may never actually meet the social work researcher who has designed and carefully crafted the study or evaluation. The data collection staff represent the research project to the participant. This point illustrates the importance of hiring and training data collectors who will represent the study in a professional and positive manner.

Hiring

Advertising for data collection staff can include considerations of education, language skills, and requirements such as a valid driver's license, the use of a car, and proof of insurance. When advertising for staff, distinguish between what you require and what you desire in potential candidates. For example, if the research involves asking the data collectors to go into people's homes in economically disadvantaged areas, or to meet with certain population sub-groups, you probably desire staff with experience with these types of settings or people. If the work requires the data collector to speak, read, and write fluently in Spanish, you should state this fact as a requirement.

Actual decisions related to hiring should take into account the concepts discussed under participant recruitment, including factors related to liking. The ultimate decision will be based on a reference check and possibly a criminal records check and drug screen. The final decision on hiring will be contingent on the candidate's signing a statement of confidentiality and agreement with a code of ethical conduct. These extra steps are warranted when data collectors will be going into participants' homes and meeting with children or other vulnerable populations.

Training

The researcher may want to set aside several days or even a week for training data collection staff. The data collection protocol can be used as the training manual, or, depending on the scope of the research project, the researcher may want to develop a separate manual.

Here are suggestions for items to be included in the training manual:

- Orientation to the employing agency.
- Agency policies and procedures.
- Overview of the research study.
- Suggestions for self-awareness, including voice, posture, facial expressions, body language, and attire.
- Principles of participant motivation and rapport building.
- Suggestions for time management and control of the interview process. Data collectors must know how to redirect and avoid getting caught up in chitchat and joking. Pacing is important to give participants time to think and respond without distracting them from answering.
- Other interviewing basics similar to what would be covered in a social work interviewing course. Among the most basic interviewing skills are speaking in complete sentences, clarity, speed, avoiding utterances and nervous gestures, conveying interest, asking for clarification, and maintaining neutrality.

The training of data collectors should include plenty of opportunities to observe and practice. Practice should include introducing oneself and the study to participants, administering the interview, and closing the interview. The success or failure of data collection will depend on how the task is presented.

Before data collection begins, the data collectors need to familiarize themselves with each data collection instrument by completing it and administering it to one or more individuals. They must know the wording of each data collection instrument and approximately how long it takes to complete.

They must also be able to assure the participant of the importance of the data collected and to describe how the data will be used. An apologetic attitude on the part of the data collector immediately conveys to the participant the sense that the data collection is unnecessary and unwarranted.

The data collector must repeatedly stress the importance of answering accurately and honestly. The research will not benefit anyone if the information is error ridden.

Finally, the data collector must be sensitive to literacy problems. One way to avoid embarrassment over literacy is to offer to read the instrument to anyone who so desires.

As a final training requirement, the data collection staff should be required to enter the practice data that they collect into the project database. The purpose of this exercise is to illustrate the need for accuracy and completeness in data recording. Unless the data collection staff have an opportunity to actually use the database, they may have little understanding of the relevance or importance of the data that they collect. We discuss databases in the next section.

DEVELOPING THE DATABASE

A **database** is a grid that specifies all of the variables in the study. The structures of all databases are similar, regardless of the particular data analysis, spreadsheet, or data management program used. Databases can be constructed manually, but this is seldom the case anymore, thanks to computers. Exhibit 10.6 provides an example of a typical database with the parts labeled. These are the key features:

■ *Columns:* Typically the variables in the database are positioned in the columns beginning on the left and progressing to the right. If there are 90 variables, there will be 90 columns in the database.

■ *Rows:* The data for each sampling unit are entered in the rows. The totality of data for each sampling unit (person or otherwise) is called a **record**. Thus, if there are 50 participants in the study, there will be 50 records or rows of data in the database. The rows are numbered consecutively, with the numbers appearing on the left side of the grid, starting with 1.

■   *Cells:* In the database, the data on each variable for each sampling unit are recorded in spaces called cells. The number of cells in a record matches the number of variables.

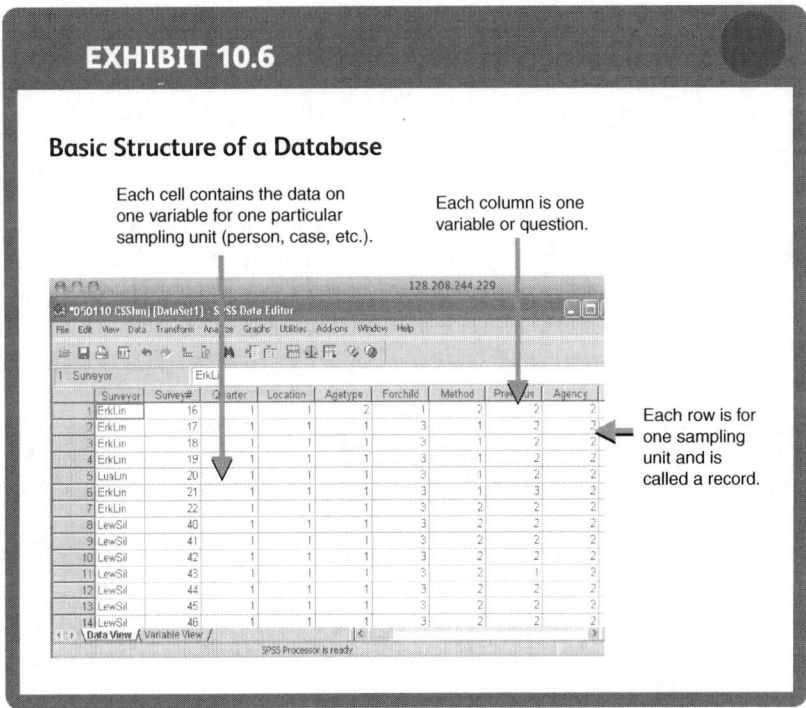

EXHIBIT 10.6

Basic Structure of a Database

It is good practice to develop the database before collecting any data. Constructing the database can help you identify and correct errors on the measures before you begin the study. There are several steps to setting up a database:

1.   Determine the order of variables.
2.   Decide on a unique case identifier.
3.   Develop the data codebook.
4.   Specify missing data.
5.   Enter the data.

These steps are discussed in the following sections.

Determining the Order of Variables

The first step is to determine the order in which the variables will be displayed in the database. The order of the variables should be consistent with the order of the variables on the data collection instruments. Following this rule will make data entry easier.

Note that each question on the data collection instrument requires a column to record the response in the database. A question that involves either more than one part or more than one answer requires as many columns in the database as there are parts or possible answers to the question.

To illustrate the construction of a database, we will refer to the first four questions from the Riverton Youth Survey. These questions are shown in Exhibit 10.7. A column in the database will represent each of the questions as in Exhibit 10.6. The order of the variables in the database will correspond to the order of the items on the questionnaire. For instance, question 1 will be positioned before question 2, question 2 between questions 1 and 3, and so on. The first variable in the database, however, is always reserved for the unique case identifier, explained in the next section.

EXHIBIT 10.7

Example of Database Construction: First Four Questions in the Riverton Youth Survey Questionnaire

Youth Survey Questionnaire	Strongly Disagree	Disagree	Neither	Agree	Strongly Agree
1. When I get older, I plan to live in the same community as I currently live.	1	2	3	4	5
2. When I get older, I plan to get a job in this community.	1	2	3	4	5
3. When I get older, I plan to graduate from high school.	1	2	3	4	5
4. When I get older, I plan to go to the doctor for regular checkups.	1	2	3	4	5

Deciding on a Unique Identifier

The first variable to be specified in a database will be the **unique case identifier**, which identifies the sampling unit for each particular record. The researcher must decide which system to use to assign unique case identifiers. Both SPSS and Excel allow you to use either string data or numeric data. As their names suggest, **string data** consist of letters or words, whereas **numeric data** are numbers.

It is possible to use participants' names (string data) when you enter data, but this might not be a good practice for reasons of confidentiality. The preferred method is to store participants' names separately from their other data, even if you encrypt the file. **Encryption** is the translation of data into a secret code. It is the most effective way to ensure that the data are secure. To read the encrypted file, a person must have access to a key or password that enables him or her to *decrypt* the file, that is, to restore it to the original text. Another good reason not to use names is because two or more individuals often have the same name.

An alternative to using names is to use the participant's Social Security number (SSN). However, using SSNs could violate participants' privacy and possibly lead to identity theft. As a rule, unless it is necessary to collect SSNs, do not do it.

A third option is to assign each participant a number. This number may be recorded on the hard-copy questionnaire or measures, or it may be associated with the participant's name in a file stored separately from the database.

Using a unique case identifier can help researchers avoid several common errors. For example, well-intentioned social workers who want to evaluate their programs sometimes administer a pretest to participants before an intervention and a posttest following the intervention. They then enter the data into a database without assigning any unique case identifiers to the data that will enable them to match the pretests and posttests of the individual participants.

Mistakenly, some social workers think that calculating the average pretest and posttest scores for *all* participants and examining the differences will provide insight into changes that occurred over the course of the intervention. Clearly this assumption is false. In most interventions, some participants inevitably improve, some show no change, and some might even deteriorate. Generally speaking, when you analyze aggregate or group data rather than the data for individual cases, these variations remain invisible, and the scores come out looking "pretty average."

Another advantage to using a unique case identifier is that the researcher can easily go back to the original data if there appears to be an error in data entry. Sometimes the data that should be in a record are either left out of the database by mistake or entered incorrectly. The unique identifier allows the researcher to access the original data. If the researcher does not use a unique identifier, he or she has no way of going back to the original data and verifying the information or of gathering additional information from the sampling unit to correct the error.

Developing the Data Codebook

A **data codebook** is a listing of each variable in the order in which it appears in the database. The variables should be listed in the same order as they appear on the data collection tool (the interview schedule, questionnaire, or observational recording form, for example).

The more variables included in the study, the more work will be required to develop the codebook. Fortunately, data analysis programs such as SPSS can develop the codebook directly in the program as the database is being created. In contrast, spreadsheet programs such as Microsoft Excel require the researcher to develop a separate codebook using either a different sheet in Excel or a word processing program such as Microsoft Word.

As its name implies, a codebook requires the researcher to develop a system of numeric codes that will be used to represent qualitative answers as numbers in the database. Codes are necessary for the response categories of variables measured at the nominal and ordinal levels. Take, for example, the four questions listed in Exhibit 10.7. These questions are measured at the ordinal level. The possible responses to each question are really labels that represent degrees of agreement with a statement. In this case, developing the numeric codes for these labels is easy because the participant is asked to respond to the questions using a continuum of numbers from 1 through 5. Thus, the code for the label "strongly disagree" would logically be the same as the response, that is, the number 1. Similarly, the code for "disagree" would be 2, and so on. Another, rather simple option for developing a codebook is to use a blank measurement instrument (such as the questionnaire or interview schedule) and write or type in the codes for the different responses to variables at the ordinal and nominal levels.

Responses to partially closed questions that leave a space for "other" with a request to specify the response can be treated either numerically as an additional response category or as a string variable. Data analysis programs like SPSS and Excel are not suited to managing long string responses, however. Unless the response is treated numerically and assigned a mutually exclusive code, the answers to partially closed questions are best compiled in a word processing program.

Variables measured at the interval and ratio levels have numeric responses that have a quantitative meaning. In these instances, a code does not need to be specified, although some researchers use the word *actual* to clarify that they are entering the actual values.

In addition to developing codes for response categories, the creation of a database requires the researcher to assign a name to each variable so that it can be identified. Many data analysis programs like SPSS have certain conventions for naming variables. For instance, in SPSS, **variable names** cannot be more than eight characters long and may not start with a number or include any spaces.

Next to the abbreviated variable name, the researcher will want to specify a **variable label**, a short description of the variable. Variable labels may also have certain restrictions in terms of the number of characters that can be specified. For example, the restriction in recent versions of SPSS for variable labels is 120 characters. Thus, a variable label for a variable named ID could be "Identification number." A variable label for question 1 in Exhibit 10.7 could be "plans to live in the community as an adult." Variable labels should be short and descriptive.

Without variable labels, a researcher who uses a variable naming convention such as Q1, Q2, Q3 might not know what the variable names mean. In this regard, SPSS is more user-friendly than Excel because it prints out the variable labels associated with the variables included in the analysis. In contrast, Excel requires users to refer back and forth between the analysis and the data codebook. For this reason, Excel users may want to avoid using variable names like Q1 and Q2 in favor of short, descriptive variable names such as "plnlive" for Q1, which refers to plans to live in the community, and "plnjob" for Q2, which refers to plans to get a job in the community.

Accounting for Missing Data

When using SPSS or other data analysis programs, the researcher will want to specify a code for each variable to represent **missing data**—those responses that are not provided, are illegible, or are out of range and an obvious error. Although specifying a value for missing data in the database is not required, it is strongly advised. The advantage of entering codes for missing data is that the researcher will know whether the otherwise blank space is a data entry error as opposed to a true missing value.

Often the code specified for missing data will be the same across many variables. Remember, though, that the codes used for missing data cannot be the same as any valid numeric response for that variable. For instance, on an ordinal scale ranging from 1 through 5, the code for missing data could not include any numerals from 1 through 5. It could, however, be any other numeric value of one or more digits, for example, a 9 or a 99.

If numeric codes are used in the database for missing data, they must be specified in the program as the value for missing data. If they are not, the computer will simply treat them as numeric values. This happens by error from time to time, often with major consequences for the analysis. For example, in predicting risk of recidivism for juvenile offenders, a zero might be entered into the database to represent missing data. If the value of zero is being treated as a numerical value as opposed to missing data, however, it will lower the score for risk of recidivism by juveniles with missing data.

SPSS has the flexibility to treat numeric values as missing data, whereas Excel does not. In Excel, missing data can be entered with a nonnumeric symbol such as the pound sign (#), or the cell can be left blank.

Exhibit 10.8 displays the SPSS codebook for the first question in the Riverton Youth Survey. Notice that in an SPSS codebook, the variable name is positioned at the far left (ID, for example) and the variable label is located to the right of the variable name (ID number, for example). Note also that the codebook does not begin with question 1 but rather with the unique participant identifier variable, labeled ID.

The second variable in the codebook corresponds with question 1 on the survey and is labeled Q1. This is the variable that refers to the participant's plans to live in the same community as she or he gets older. The response categories of the variable are listed as variable values under the heading "Value," and the corresponding value labels are listed to the right of each value. The variable is measured at the ordinal level in that the numerical values are ranked in order but do not have any quantitative meaning and are not suitable to be manipulated mathematically. Note that the ordinal variable values need to be listed in

EXHIBIT 10.8

Example of SPSS Codebook: First Question in the Riverton Youth Survey

Name		Position
ID	ID number	1
	Measurement Level: Scale	
	Column Width: 8 Alignment: Right	
Q1	Live in the same community when you get older	2
	Measurement Level: Ordinal	
	Column Width: 8 Alignment: Right	
	Missing Values: 9	

Value	Label
1	Strongly disagree
2	Disagree
3	Neither agree or disagree
4	Agree
5	Strongly disagree

order from highest to smallest or most to least; they cannot be listed at random. The numbers under the heading "Position" close to the far right margin in the codebook are the columns in which the data for that variable are located.

Entering the Data

Once the researcher has collected all or at least some of the data, she or he will begin entering the data into the database. Quantitative data are typically entered directly from the questionnaire, interview schedule, or observational recording device. The researcher or data entry assistant proceeds through each data collection tool systematically from start to finish, keying in the responses for each variable. It may be useful to set the number pad on the computer keyboard in the lock position and use it for data entry. Data entry, however, is a matter of personal preference, and the objectives in order of priority are first accuracy and then speed.

Regardless of the process the researcher uses to enter the data, there are bound to be a few **data entry errors**: a wrong value entered here or there, a skipped question, transposed digits. Depending on the size of the database and the number of eligible sampling units, the researcher may need to check all or a portion of the data collection instruments against the database to look for data entry errors. Any errors that he or she detects should be corrected. If the researcher is checking only a sample of the questionnaires and finds very few errors, he or she may be reasonably confident that the entered data are accurate. Conversely, if the researcher discovers a number of errors, he or she should continue checking.

Certain data entry programs—some of which are available free of charge—enable researchers to set limits on the values that they can enter into a specific field. For example, if the valid responses to a variable such as Q1 on the Riverton Youth Survey range from 1 to 5, with 9 specified as the value for missing data, the program will alert the researcher if she or he has entered any number outside that range in that particular field. The next chapter discusses checking the data for errors on a variable-by-variable basis.

The completion of data entry and error checking represents a major achievement in the research process. The data are now recorded in a format that will enable the researcher to begin analyzing them.

WORKING WITHIN A BUDGET

Although the budget is certainly not the final consideration in preparing for data collection, we present it as the final topic in this chapter in order to provide an overview of the many different items that must be considered in a

EXHIBIT 10.9

Checklist for Items in a Research Budget

1. **Labor**
   - ☐ Time for the researcher
   - ☐ Data collectors
   - ☐ Data entry
   - ☐ Office support

2. **Preliminary Research on the Problem Area**
   - ☐ Literature review
   - ☐ Analysis of secondary data
   - ☐ Primary data collection activities

3. **Development of the Sample**
   - ☐ Access to a sampling frame
   - ☐ Recruitment of sample

4. **Measurement**
   - ☐ Measures, manuals, and scoring sheets
   - ☐ Development of measures: constructing questions, pretesting, translating, formatting, printing
   - ☐ Translation: measures, cover letters, informed consent documents, project correspondence
   - ☐ Preparation of mailed packets and follow-up packets
   - ☐ Internet surveys preparation

5. **Data Collection**
   - ☐ Hiring of data collection staff (advertising, criminal record check, drug screen)
   - ☐ Training of data collection staff (development of written materials, in-person training, and observation)
   - ☐ Supervision and intra- and interrater reliability testing
   - ☐ In-person expenses (mileage, cell phones, rental cars, insurance)
   - ☐ Mail survey expenses (paper, envelopes, postage, preparation of address labels)
   - ☐ Telephone survey expenses (long-distance charges, toll-free telephone line)
   - ☐ Tracking system (computerized or manual)
   - ☐ Interim contact (cards, postcards, postage)

6. **Incentives**
   - ☐ Number and value of incentives
   - ☐ Incentives to report change of contact information

7. **Data Preparation**
   - ☐ Transcription
   - ☐ Setting up the filing system for storing data as hard copy and electronically
   - ☐ Database development
   - ☐ Data entry (optical scanning)
   - ☐ Verification of data

8. Equipment and Supplies

- ☐ Data recording equipment (audio/video recorders, laptops)
- ☐ Pens, markers, paper, stapler
- ☐ Poster paper (focus groups)
- ☐ Devices and applications for tracking schedules
- ☐ Cell phones

9. Data Analysis

- ☐ Database development
- ☐ Data entry
- ☐ Data analysis
- ☐ Report writing
- ☐ Consultants

10. Research Dissemination

- ☐ Report editing
- ☐ Report formatting
- ☐ Printing (extra for color)
- ☐ Posting on the web
- ☐ Equipment rental (overhead projector)
- ☐ Conference registration
- ☐ Conference travel

11. Overheads

- ☐ Hardware (computers, scanners, copier, fax, overhead projector)
- ☐ Furniture (desks, telephones, filing cabinets)
- ☐ Space rental (office space, interview space)
- ☐ Software (word processing, database, tracking, data analysis, spreadsheet, presentation)
- ☐ University overhead (a percentage of the grant, often between 35 % and 60 %, if research is conducted by university faculty or institute on university time)

research or evaluation study. Exhibit 10.9 presents potential line items in a research budget. As you can infer from the number of items, research can be a costly and time-consuming endeavor. Research is not to be undertaken and then abandoned midway through because of a failure to budget adequately.

The items a researcher includes in the budget will ultimately depend on the requirements of the funding source or sponsoring agency and the type of research design to be implemented. For multiyear projects, the budget may be developed by calendar or fiscal year as well as for the entire project. You can use the line items listed in Exhibit 10.9 as a guide for preparing a budget.

CONCLUSION

Preparing for data collection is a busy time for the social work researcher. A lot of planning and development has to go into managing the task of implementation. All steps in planning and implementing the research study are carried out with two main objectives in mind: minimizing error and maximizing response rate.

The research project's success depends on such steps as being strategic in planning for participant recruitment and retention. Development work requires writing a data collection protocol, a manual for training data collectors, and constructing a database and codebook. Even though data will not be entered in the database until after it is collected, developing the database before data collection begins can help pinpoint potential problems in the research or evaluation study.

Depending on the scope of the research or evaluation, the data collection staff may be the face of the research to the participant. This makes hiring, training, and supervising data collectors of key importance to the success of the study.

This chapter concludes discussion of the implementation phase of the research process. With data in hand and entered in the database, the social work researcher is set to begin the process of data analysis. The analysis of quantitative data is the subject of Chapters 11 and 12.

MAIN POINTS

- The researcher's choice of data collection method will depend on several factors, including characteristics of the research participants; size of the geographic area; requirements of the measures used; subject matter; and the research budget.
- The researcher must be explicit in reporting the method she or he has used to calculate a response rate, and, when possible, examine the differences between respondents and nonrespondents. To avoid reporting inflated calculations of nonresponse, the researcher should subtract the number of nonsampling units from the original number of sampling units.
- In long-term research and evaluation studies, failure to recruit and retain target participants can lead to the failure of the entire research project and at times cancellation of entire programs.
- Incentives may be used to encourage participation but should only be one part of a multifaceted recruitment and retention plan.
- Before participant recruitment begins, the researcher should develop a data collection protocol that will outline such items as the schedule of measures, the requirements for contacting participants, tracking procedures, the provision of incentives, recording requirements, data storage, and ethical considerations. The data collection protocol is a work in progress and will be updated as questions arise and decision rules are made with regard to data collection.

- Training and practice opportunities must be provided for data collectors so that they can assure participants of the importance of the data collected and describe its eventual use.
- Spreadsheet and data analysis computer software programs, such as Microsoft Excel and IBM SPSS, are available for analyzing and displaying quantitative data. Knowing how to use these programs is a valuable skill for social workers.
- Developing the database before data collection begins can help identify errors in the measures that can be corrected before implementation. The researcher should always develop a unique identifier for each record in the database.

EXERCISES

1. In the Riverton case, the following results were obtained in a randomized telephone survey of adults in the community. Use the numbers provided to calculate the response rate for the survey. Write the response rate in narrative form as you would in a research report. Explain how you arrived at your answer.
    - ☐ Disconnected/nonworking numbers = 47
    - ☐ Household refusal = 173
    - ☐ No answer, not home = 35
    - ☐ Unable to answer due to disability or language problem = 37
    - ☐ Respondent did not complete the interview = 52
    - ☐ Completed interviews = 656
2. Using Cialdini's six triggers of influence, design a recruitment plan for a research study on the impact of the Hudson City disaster on city residents. Be specific about the tactics you would use for each principle. In designing your plan, assume that you have a limited budget and need to be efficient in your use of resources.
3. What data collection method(s) would you use in a survey of individuals who call the RAINN hotline? Would your recommendation change for those who contact RAINN online? Justify your choices. How might retention of subjects be a particular challenge in this context?
4. Create a database in SPSS that includes the four questions and data from the Riverton case Youth Survey found in Exhibit 10.7. To help with this task, search for a tutorial on the Internet on how to create a database in SPSS. Create a codebook by performing the following tasks for each of the four questions:
    a. Develop a variable name.
    b. Develop a variable label.

    c.   Define the variable values as appropriate given the level of measurement.

    d.   Specify a value for missing data.

        Remember that the first variable in your database should be a unique student identifier. When you have created your database, name it and save it to a disk.

5.   Create a database in Excel for the first four questions from the Riverton Youth Survey (found in Exhibit 10.7). If you need help getting started, search for a tutorial on the Internet on how to create a database in Excel.

    a.   Create the database.

    b.   Name and save the database.

    c.   Create a codebook using a word processing program of your choice.

6.   Once you have completed questions 4 and 5, explain how SPSS and Excel differ in the steps required to create a database. How do the two programs compare for database creation? What do you prefer about either of the programs; what don't you like about either program?

7.   How does cultural competence come into play in designing a data collection protocol within a community of ethnic or racial minorities? For example, if you wanted to conduct a longitudinal analysis of the effects of early childhood intervention on Latino adolescents in a community such as the one the Sanchez family lives in, what data collection methods may help with recruitment and retention of participants? What approaches could you use in order to select culturally competent methods?

8.   What factors do you think might affect response rates in a changing community such as Brickville? How could you, as a researcher, design a data collection approach in order to increase the chance of getting sufficient response from all of the subcommunities of interest?

DESCRIPTIONS OF QUANTITATIVE DATA

Science is facts; just as houses are made of stones, so is science made of facts; but a pile of stones is not a house and a collection of facts is not necessarily science.
Henri Poincare, French mathematician & physicist (1854–1912)

What do data have to offer? The answer to that question is not much. Raw data do not convey meaning, tell a story, or paint a picture. To illustrate this point, Exhibit 11.1 shows raw data as they appear in an Excel file.

In order to fulfill the purpose of research, we have to turn the raw data into information. Information consists of the meaningful conclusions formulated by ordering, summarizing, and analyzing the data. Information, not data, helps to guide social work practice. **Data analysis,** the focus of this chapter, is the process by which researchers turn data into information that can be used to determine the nature or cause of something in order to improve social work practice.

EXHIBIT 11.1

Raw Quantitative Data

Id	Q1	Q2	Q3	Q4	Q5
1	4	3	5	4	4
2	2	2	5	4	3
3	3	1	3	4	4
4	1	1	5	5	5
5		4	5	4	4
6	3	3	4	5	5
7	5	4	2	4	5
8	1	1	1	5	4
9	2	2	5	4	5
10	1	1	1	5	5
11	4	5	5	2	3
12	2	4	5	3	3
13	3	4	5	3	3
14	2	2	4	4	4
15	3	1	5	3	4

To analyze data effectively, the researcher must act like a detective and ask the right questions. There are two important questions the researcher will try to answer through data analysis:

■ What is typical or common in the data?
■ What is the extent of difference or variation in the data?

For example, in a quantitative data set we may find that all of the respondents are teenagers. This is something they all have in common, and this is probably something useful to know. We may also find variation in the data, noting that the teenagers come from diverse economic backgrounds, with gross annual household incomes ranging from as low as $2,300 to as high as $56,000. These are examples of the useful information we can extract from quantitative data.

These two questions—"What is common in the data?" and "How do the data vary?"—help guide the analysis of quantitative data. The researcher often answers these questions by using descriptive statistics. We explain and illustrate these processes in this chapter.

Some students experience considerable anxiety when they think about *statistics*. If you are clutching your chest and feeling short of breath right now, take a moment, breathe deeply, and prepare to enjoy your journey. Remember that computers do most data analysis. If you understand the logic of data analysis, the computer will then do the math for you.

The information in this chapter and Chapter 12 may seem a little like learning a foreign language at first, but once you read the explanations, scrutinize the examples, and then try it for yourself, it will become much clearer. This chapter uses quantitative data from the Riverton Youth Survey and RAINN for the purposes of illustration and practice.

Can you do this? Yes, you can; and like many others before you, the authors included, you may find yourself excited about being able to derive meaning and draw conclusions from data, because you will use the information to improve social work services and social conditions.

Chapter 10 concluded at the point in the research process in which the researcher entered quantitative data into a database. Although data collection and preparation are major achievements, the true value of the research comes in the form of analysis and reporting. This chapter addresses the kinds of information that quantitative data have to offer. It also explains how to condense and extract this information from the quantitative database. In addition, it focuses on how to tell the story of the data—that is, to extract and describe the information that emerges from data analysis in a concise and meaningful way.

By the end of this chapter you should be able to:

■ Critique a frequency table.
■ Conduct a preliminary analysis of quantitative data.

■ Discuss how to select descriptive statistics based on level of measurement and distribution.

■ Develop charts to visually show your data.

VERIFYING QUANTITATIVE DATA

Once you have entered the data in the database, it is important to engage in **data verification**—checking to see that the data have been entered and coded correctly. This process not only helps to prevent errors in analysis but also serves the useful purpose of making the researcher more familiar with the data.

Data verification may sound tedious because it has to be done variable by variable. The use of computer software programs such as SPSS (Statistical Package for the Social Sciences) and Excel, however, has made the procedure much simpler than in the past. This chapter presents the process of data verification as a series of four logically ordered steps:

■ Ordering the data
■ Examining the data graphically
■ Recoding data
■ Computing scales by combining multiple variables

Before we examine these four steps in detail, let's look at one example of what can happen when errors are not corrected before analysis.

CASE-IN-POINT: CODING ERRORS PRODUCE FALSE PICTURE OF GIRLS' PREGNANCIES

Perhaps you have heard the expression "Garbage in, garbage out" (GIGO). GIGO is used it to highlight the fact that data that start out faulty are not fixed by running them through a computer. An experimental study to determine the effectiveness of an integrated case management program for children with multiple agency involvement is a good illustration of GIGO.

A researcher reported that 12 months into the study all 11 girls in the control group were pregnant compared to none in the intervention group. When presenting that finding to a group of stakeholders, the results suddenly struck the researcher as odd. What were the chances that 100 % of the girls in one group would be pregnant? When the researcher checked the original data, she found that the results were indeed false due to errors that had been made in coding. In this case, "pregnant" was coded as "1" but "1" was labeled "not pregnant" in the computer program. In reality, none of the girls in the control group was pregnant—a very different story than what she had presented.

The moral of this unfortunate story is that databases almost always have errors: errors in recording, coding, and data entry. Researchers must take time to verify the data before analysis, not only to avoid drawing erroneous, embarrassing, and even damaging conclusions, but also because they have an ethical responsibility to ensure that their research is accurate.

Ordering the Data

You can order data sets by having the computer arrange the data in an **array,** that is, in ascending or descending order column by column. You can then browse each column to spot possible errors. For example the number six should never be found in a variable that is coded on a scale from one to five. It would be important to correct any observed errors.

A much more efficient means of ordering data is to construct a **frequency distribution** for each variable, which provides a count of how many times each variable value is represented in the database. It answers the question: With what frequency does each value of a variable occur? A frequency distribution can be constructed for variables at all levels of measurement: nominal, ordinal, interval, and ratio. By using a computer program such as SPSS or Excel, you can accomplish this task in very little time.

Frequency Distributions at the Nominal Level

For a variable measured at the nominal level, such as ethnicity, the frequency distribution shows how many different ethnic categories are represented in the dataset and the frequency with which each category is represented. Exhibit 11.2 shows a frequency distribution in SPSS for the variable Gender from the Riverton Youth Survey. When we examine the first two columns of the frequency distribution, we see that the variable value of male has a count, or frequency, of 89, and the variable value female has a count of 99. That is, of the 190 respondents, 89 (46.8%) were coded as male and 99 (52.1%) were coded as female.

We also see variable values 3 and 4, each with a count of 1. Returning to our database or our codebook, we check the valid codes for Gender and note only three codes: 1-male, 2-female and 9-missing data. This means that variable values 3 and 4 are not valid codes. In order to determine what the correct values are, we need to find the two errors in the database. If the invalid responses

EXHIBIT 11.2

Frequency Distribution for a Variable Measured at the Nominal Level: Gender

Gender

	Frequency	Percent	Valid Percent	Cumulative Percent
Valid Male	89	46.8	46.8	46.8
Female	99	52.1	52.1	98.9
3	1	.5	.5	99.5
4	1	.5	.5	100.0
Total	190	100.0	100.0	

occur more than once, as indicated by a frequency greater than 1, we need to find each occurrence of the error.

Once we locate the errors in the database or codebook, we look for the identification number associated with each record (usually found in the first cell in the row), and we use it to look up the original hard-copy data collection instrument. We may find that the values were data entry errors; if so, we can fix them by typing the correct values into the database and saving the file. Alternatively, we may find that the questionnaires did not have valid responses. If we cannot determine the correct values, we would change the incorrect values to 9s to indicate missing data.

Do not forget to save the corrected file, and always use the corrected version for your analysis.

Frequency Distributions at the Ordinal Level

In the case of a variable measured at the ordinal level, the frequency distribution shows the range of values represented on an ordered continuum of responses. Exhibit 11.3 displays a frequency distribution created in SPSS for the Riverton Youth Survey variable q9. This variable represents responses to the statement, "I feel safe in my community." (Notice that the frequency distribution table is titled with the variable label rather than with the variable name q9. This is a useful feature in SPSS.) Examining Exhibit 11.2, we observe that the responses of the 190 youths spanned the entire range of responses from Strongly Disagree to Strongly Agree. In contrast to Exhibit 11.2, there are no apparent out-of-range values in this frequency distribution.

EXHIBIT 11.3

Frequency Distribution for a Variable Measured at the Ordinal Level: Degree to Which Respondent Feels Safe in Community

I Feel Safe in my Community

		Frequency	Per-cent	Valid Percent	Cumulative Percent
Valid	Strongly Disagree	18	9.5	9.5	9.5
	Disagree	25	13.2	13.2	22.7
	Neither	51	26.8	26.8	49.5
	Agree	62	32.6	32.6	82.1
	Strongly Agree	34	17.9	17.9	100.0
	Total	190	100.0	100.0	

When you report the percentage of respondents in one category—for example, 9.5% of the 190 youths strongly disagreed with the statement that they feel safe in their community—use the percentages in the fourth column labeled "Valid Percent." The third column, "Percent," happens to be identical to the "Valid Percent" column in Exhibits 11.2 and 11.3 because there are no missing data. The percentages in the "Percent" column, however, are calculated from the total number of cases, whereas the valid percentages are calculated from the total number of valid responses; they do not include cases with missing responses. Valid percentage represents the percentage of all cases for those where the value is known on that variable.

For an example of a frequency distribution with missing data see the upcoming Exhibit 11.5. The frequency of Race shows that there are 14 African American youth. This is 6.3% of the 221 youth who completed the survey, but the Valid Percent is 6.6% of the 213 youth who answered this particular question.

Given that the data in Exhibit 11.3 are ordered in a frequency distribution, the column Cumulative Percent calculates the total percentage up to that particular point. For example, the cumulative frequency distribution indicates that 22.7 percent of respondents answered either Strongly Disagree or Disagree. Thus, we could legitimately offer the following conclusion: Of the 190 youth surveyed, 22.7 percent disagreed with the statement, "I feel safe in my community." This type of information is useful when considering data at the ordinal level and the ratio level as well.

When examining frequency distributions for each variable, we should always ask, "Does the information from the data make sense given what I know about the population or sample?" This is often the only way to identify coding errors such as those described in the Case-in-Point about the erroneous reporting of the control group as 100% pregnant.

Frequency Distributions at the Interval and Ratio Levels

Whereas frequency distributions are useful for verifying nominal- and ordinal-level data, they have limited utility when used with interval- and ratio-level data. This is especially true in large studies that have many records and many values represented for each variable. To illustrate this point, consider a hypothetical frequency distribution for the variable Ethnicity (nominal-level data). The frequency distribution will have the same number of categories represented regardless of whether the study includes 200 or 1 million individuals. The same observation holds true for a variable measured at the ordinal level, such as the statement "I feel safe in my community," that has a set number of responses.

Now consider a frequency distribution for the variable Gross Annual Income, which is measured at the ratio level. The frequency distribution for 200 individuals would have a maximum of 200 different values. Although this number is not concise, it is manageable. The frequency distribution for 3,000 individuals, in contrast, could literally have as many as 3,000 different values in an ordered list. This number certainly would be unmanageable. Conversely, if we were to examine the age of the freshman class at a large university, there might be little variation even though there are thousands of students.

Clearly, then, we must decide variable by variable, based on the number of records in the database and the expected variability in the data, whether a frequency distribution is appropriate for interval-level and ratio-level data.

Examining the Data Graphically

As the old saying goes, "A picture is worth a thousand words." In the case of interval and ratio data, we might say, "A picture is worth a thousand data points." Each value entered in the database is a data point. When frequency distributions are inappropriate for verifying interval and ratio data, as described previously, a graphic representation may be a useful alternative.

Programs such as SPSS and Excel can produce plots to illustrate the types of information that a frequency distribution offers. There are different kinds of plots, but we will present the scatterplot because it is frequently used with variables measured at the interval and ratio levels of measurement. A **scatterplot** is a graphic representation of the values of one or two variables. In this chapter, we deal with only one variable at a time; in Chapter 12 we deal with two variables.

We can draw an analogy between scatterplots and stargazing. Each data point on the plot is analogous to a star in the night sky. In examining scatterplots, we look for patterns in the data similar to constellations we might search for. We can glean a great deal of information from examining a scatterplot.

For the purpose of verifying data, however, we are interested primarily in detecting the presence of **outliers**: data points that are off by themselves, isolated from the other data points. If you think that this definition sounds rather arbitrary, you are right. Later in this chapter we will present a mathematical method for judging whether an outlier should be excluded from the analysis. Take a minute to examine Exhibit 11.4, which is a scatterplot of data for the age variable. Which data points would you consider outliers?

Sometimes a data point that appears to be an outlier is actually an error. For this reason, we should verify the values of all outliers. For example, in the context of Exhibit 11.4 an outlier that shows age to be 143 is most likely an

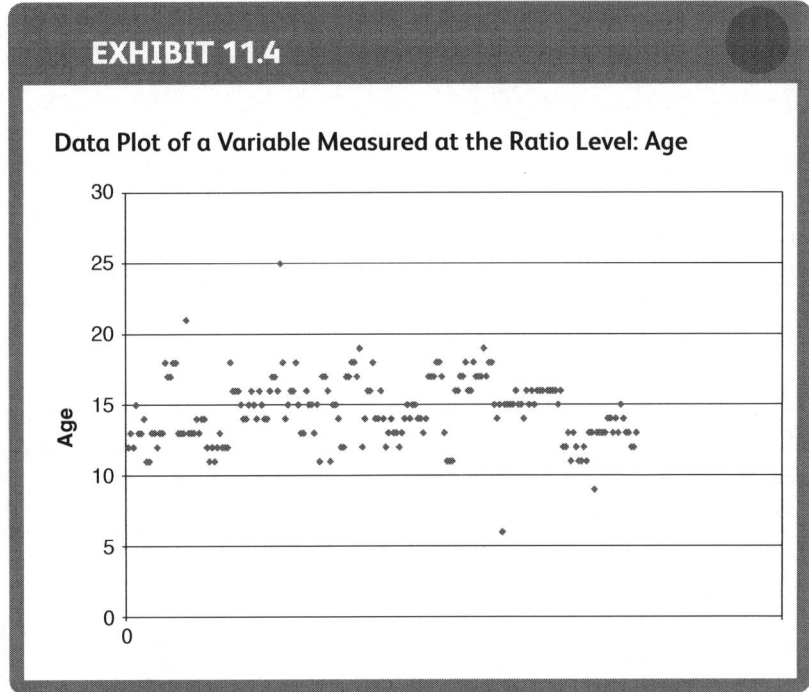

EXHIBIT 11.4

Data Plot of a Variable Measured at the Ratio Level: Age

error. We use the same process of verifying suspect values detected in a scatter-plot as for out-of-range values:

1.   Locate the value in the database.
2.   Find the associated record identification number.
3.   Go back to the original questionnaire to determine whether the data were entered correctly.

In some cases, we may even return to the source of the data, as the error may have been introduced in data collection rather than data entry.

If we verify that the extreme data points are not errors, we still want to make note of them. As you will see later in this chapter, true outliers will require us to be selective about how we report our analysis.

Whether we are examining data in the form of frequency distributions or graphically, we should adhere to the same process. Step back from the plot and ask: Based on what I know about the research, population, and sample, does this story make sense? Sometimes when we are immersed in the process of verifying data, it is difficult for us to "see the forest for the trees." It is vitally important, then, to take time to reflect on the meaning suggested by the data. If the meaning does not make sense, there is probably a reason. At that point, we need to search a little deeper for possible sources of error.

Recoding Data

In the process of ordering the data and presenting them graphically, we may notice that some categories of certain variables do not have many cases in them. One explanation is that the categories were not well conceptualized. Another possibility is that in retrospect some categories either were not mutually exclusive or had little relevance to respondents. In such circumstances, we may decide to collapse some of the categories, that is, to combine two or more categories into a smaller number of categories. Collapsing categories has the effect of increasing the number of cases represented in a given category.

To illustrate the process of collapsing categories, consider the variable of ethnicity. The frequency distribution presented in Exhibit 11.5 was generated from one question in the Riverton Youth Survey. The youth were asked, "What do you consider yourself to be?" They were then provided with seven responses to describe their ethnicity. The value labels listed in the codebook for this variable were as follows:

1.   African American
2.   Asian American, Pacific Islander

3. White, Non-Hispanic
4. Hispanic, Latino, Spanish
5. Native American, American Indian
6. Multiracial
7. Other

As we can see in Exhibit 11.5, four youth, approximately 1.9% of the 221 respondents, selected the "Other" category to represent their ethnicity. These respondents subsequently were asked to specify what they meant. Their responses include four variations of Irish including Irish, Irish American, Irish descent, and Irish full blood.

Based on the respondents' descriptions of their ethnicity, the researcher's next step is to create some decision rules about changing some of the responses

EXHIBIT 11.5

Frequency Distribution Requiring Recoding: Ethnicity

Race

		Frequency	Percent	Valid Percent	Cumulative Percent
Valid	African American	14	6.3	6.6	6.6
	Asian American, Pacific Islander	37	16.7	17.4	23.9
	White, Non-Hispanic	133	60.2	62.4	86.4
	Hispanic, Latino, Spanish	6	2.7	2.8	89.2
	Native American, American Indian	5	2.3	2.3	91.5
	Multiracial	14	6.3	6.6	98.1
	Other	4	1.8	1.9	100.0
	Total	213	96.4	100.0	
Missing	999	7	3.2		
	System	1	.5		
	Total	8	3.6		
Total		221	100.0		

coded as Other. One decision rule might be to code as 3 all responses that specify any variation of Irish. Similarly, the researcher might later create a new category, Non-Majority, by combining all ethnic groups other than White, Non-Hispanic into one large group.

One purpose of creating new categories is to reduce the ambiguity within the categories. Another purpose is to create groups large enough for data analysis using statistics requiring a minimum number of cases in each category. Changing a respondent's answers or grouping categories is acceptable, as long as the decision rule (what was done) and the justification for doing so (why it was done) are made clear when reporting the results.

The researcher considering the frequency distribution in Exhibit 11.5 might note two potential ethical dilemmas regarding the low frequency in the category American Indian/Native American ($n = 5$). If the researcher's plan is to present data by ethnic category, she or he may want to collapse this category into Other. There are two reasons:

- To protect the confidentiality of the five American Indian youth represented in the sample because in a small geographic area some people reading a summary of the research could reasonably guess the identity of the individuals from such a small subgroup
- To discourage readers from drawing conclusions from the data based on such a small subgroup

This process of changing one value to another—for example, changing 5s representing American Indian / Native American to 7s representing Other, is referred to as **recoding**. Although recoding could be a tedious process and subject to error if it were done manually, it is easily accomplished using available routines in computer programs such as SPSS and Excel.

Statistical programs usually offer users the choice to create a new variable with the recoded results or to overwrite the existing variable. Recoding the variable into a new variable with a new name is always better than writing over the old variable. Otherwise, we will be unable to refer back to the original data. Finally, it is important to keep notes on decision rules made with regard to recoding in a file or a journal.

Computing Scales by Combining Multiple Variables

In Chapter 9 we discussed scales as one option in measurement. For many concepts—depression, for example—measurement using a single item would be unreliable. For this reason, researchers prefer to use a combination of items that, when combined, are represented by a single score. Sometimes researchers use a standardized scale; at other times they create a scale from questions they develop.

The 31 items listed in Exhibit 11.6 represent the items included on the Riverton Youth Survey. Notice that the response categories for each question are identical. Therefore, the questions can be easily combined into a scale.

If we examine the list of items carefully, we might conclude that it would make theoretical sense to construct a number of one-dimensional scales, or scales that measure only one concept. For instance, 10 items on the question-naire relate to perceptions of crime in the community (items 15, 16, 18, 21, 22, 23, 26, 27, 28, and 31). These 10 items could be combined to produce a single "perceptions of crime" subscale score. Other subscales could be developed from the survey items to include future health plans, future community plans, sense of connection, satisfaction with community services, and so on.

A scale or subscales are only useful if they are demonstrated reliable and valid measures of the concepts they are intended to measure. One indicator of the reliability of a measure is **internal consistency**, the degree to which the items show similar measurement, that is, positively correlate with each other.

Assessing Internal Consistency

Chapter 9 introduced the concepts of measurement validity and reliability. The section on reliability included a discussion of **Cronbach's alpha,** or **alpha coefficient,** a statistic used to assess the internal consistency of the items included in a scale. If items in a scale are measuring the same variable, then it is expected that the items would show a high positive correlation with each other. The alpha coefficient is a measure of the extent to which scale items correlate with each other.

Scales in which the items are not scored consistently will have a relatively low alpha coefficient. Conversely, scales in which the items are scored consis-tently will have a relatively high alpha coefficient. A general guideline is that a scale used for research should have an alpha coefficient of .60 or greater (Hudson, 1991).

In the case of a poorly performing scale, the researcher may want to change the scale by using different or fewer items and then recompute the alpha coef-ficient, aiming for .60 or greater. A statistical computer program will identify items that do not correlate highly with other items in the scale. These items can then be eliminated from the scale. Extensive testing of the internal consistency of a scale should be done *before* using a scale in a research project, practice context, or program evaluation.

The first step in computing an alpha coefficient may be **reverse scoring**. Reverse scoring is only necessary if some of the items are worded positively and some negatively. For example, questions 11 and 13 in Exhibit 11.6 are part of

EXHIBIT 11.6

Riverton Youth Survey

Youth Survey Questionnaire	Strongly Disagree	Disagree	Neither	Agree	Strongly Agree
1. When I get older I plan to live in the same community as I currently live.	1	2	3	4	5
2. When I get older I plan to get a job in this community.	1	2	3	4	5
3. When I get older I plan to graduate from high school.	1	2	3	4	5
4. When I get older I plan to go to the doctor for regular checkups.	1	2	3	4	5
5. When I get older I plan to go to the dentist for regular checkups.	1	2	3	4	5
6. When I get older I plan to seek counseling if I have a personal or family problem.	1	2	3	4	5
7. When I get older I plan to seek counseling if I have a drug or alcohol problem.	1	2	3	4	5
8. When I get older I plan to go to the doctor if I feel sick.	1	2	3	4	5
9. I feel safe in my community.	1	2	3	4	5
10. If I have a health problem I feel that I have someone I can talk to about it.	1	2	3	4	5
11. I don't feel respected by the adults in my community.	1	2	3	4	5
12. I feel connected to my community.	1	2	3	4	5
13. I trust the teachers at my school.	1	2	3	4	5
14. I feel connected to my family.	1	2	3	4	5
15. The police do a good job of preventing crime in this community.	1	2	3	4	5

Youth Survey Questionnaire	Strongly Disagree	Disagree	Neither	Agree	Strongly Agree
16. I feel that I cannot talk to the police if there is a problem.	1	2	3	4	5
17. Parents are not involved with their kids in this community.	1	2	3	4	5
18. There is too much crime in this community.	1	2	3	4	5
19. When I grow up I feel that I can get a good education in this community.	1	2	3	4	5
20. There is nothing to do for fun in this community.	1	2	3	4	5
21. There are too many drug dealers in this community.	1	2	3	4	5
22. Gangs are a problem in this community.	1	2	3	4	5
23. Family violence is a problem in this community.	1	2	3	4	5
24. Teen pregnancy is a problem in this community.	1	2	3	4	5
25. There is a lack of health care services in this community.	1	2	3	4	5
26. A lot of parents are using illegal drugs in this community.	1	2	3	4	5
27. I worry about being a victim of crime in this community.	1	2	3	4	5
28. A lot of teens are using illegal drugs in this community.	1	2	3	4	5
29. There is a lack of counseling services in this community.	1	2	3	4	5
30. There is a lack of good schools in this community.	1	2	3	4	5
31 There are not enough police officers in this community.	1	2	3	4	5

a subscale that measures Relationship with Adults. High scores should indicate positive feelings about adults. If items are inversely worded—that is, low scores indicate high levels of positive feelings—the researcher would need to reverse score the data for those items so that high scores are positive and low scores are negative. As you can see, question 11 states "I don't feel respected by the adults in my community," and question 13 states "I trust the teachers at my school." In order to combine these two variables into a single scale, the researcher would have to reverse score the responses of question 11 to be consistent with the direction of the responses on question 13. Thus, if she or he wished to reverse score the items in a positive direction, the values of question 11 would be recoded as follows:

1. (strongly disagree) would become 5
2. (disagree) would become 4
3. (neither) = 3 (neither) (no recoding necessary)
4. (agree) would become 2
5. (strongly agree) would become 1

Once the researcher has completed reverse scoring the data, she or he should save the data file under a new file name—for example, YSrecode—in order to differentiate it from the original data file. Once the researcher has saved the recoded file, there is no need to repeat the process, unless additional recoding is required. Again, useful tutorials can be found on the Internet.

Calculating a Total Scale Score

Each item in a scale should be represented in the database as a separate variable. If only total scale scores are entered, testing for internal reliability cannot be accomplished, nor can recoding. To avoid error, it is best to let the computer do the calculations rather than conduct them manually. Total scale scores are computed by combining the values of the individual variables that make up the scale. There are many ways to calculate a total scale score. If the scale is standardized, the scale's author undoubtedly will provide instructions for scoring.

If instructions are not available, one way to calculate the total scale score is simply to add the responses to the different items in the scale. However, simply adding the values can produce misleading results if there are missing data for some of the items. For instance, one individual with a score of 30 may have failed to respond to 4 of the 10 items on the scale. Another individual with a score of 30 may have answered every item. It is unlikely that these two individuals are actually equivalent on the concept measured by the scale, even though their scores may sum to the same value.

For situations such as this one, the researcher might want to create a decision rule concerning the minimum number of responses that must be present for a total scale score to be calculated or considered in any analysis. If the scale is a published scale, the author may already have recommended such a rule. An example of such a rule is that at least 80% of the total number of items on the scale must be completed, or the total scale score will be calculated as missing.

Another way to deal with missing values is to use the **mean**, or average value, as a substitute for the missing score on an item. (We discuss the calculation of the mean later in this chapter.) For example, if the mean score for question 11 were 2.35, anyone missing data for question 11 would be assigned 2.35 in place of the missing data value. If the researcher inserts the mean for the missing data, the group mean for question 11 will not change, and there will be no missing values. Again, the researcher must explain this decision rule, in writing, in the research report.

Another problem with simply adding the value of the individual items is that the distribution of possible values on the scale may not permit easy comparison to other scale scores. Scale scores that can vary from 18 to 73 are more difficult to interpret and visualize than scores from 0 to 100.

Fortunately, social work researchers have already figured out how to accommodate missing data and create total scale scores with a common metric of 0 to 100. One formula to accomplish this task is as follows:

1. Count the number of completed items in the scale (a).
2. Add the response values for all items (b).
3. Subtract 1 from the highest possible score on the response scale (c).
4. Calculate the total scale score: $[(b - a) * (100)] / a * c$.

Exhibit 11.7 uses data from the Riverton Youth Survey to illustrate this equation. Ten items on the scale relate to "perception of crime." If we add the responses to these items for any individual, the total subscale score could range from a low of 10 (10 items x 1, the minimum response) to a high of 50 (10 items x 5, the highest response). To create a common metric for this subscale for all the individuals who have taken the survey, we would begin by summing the item responses for one individual (b), subtracting from that sum the number of completed items (a), and then multiplying by 100. The resulting number is the numerator, the top number in the equation. The denominator, the bottom number in the equation, is calculated by multiplying the number of completed items (a) by the highest possible value on the response scale minus 1 (c). The final step is to divide the numerator by the denominator (Hudson, 1991). For this individual, the total subscale score would be 62.5. Computing this equation by hand for each sampling unit would be laborious,

EXHIBIT 11.7

How to Compute a Total Score Scale That Ranges From 0 To 100: Riverton Youth Survey

The item numbers for a subscale within the Riverton Youth Survey are listed in the left column, and the responses to each item from one person are listed in the right column. Any inverse or negative items have already been recoded. The computation is shown step-by-step on the right.

Item	Score
15	3
16	4
18	4
21	5
22	3
23	(missing)
26	2
27	(missing)
28	4
31	3

Variables in the equation:

a   There are 8 completed items.

b   The sum of the responses = 28 (without items 23 & 27).

c   The highest possible item response is 5, and $(5 - 1) = 4$.

Compute the equation:

Total scale score = $[(b - a) * (100)] / (a * c)$

$= (28 - 8) * 100 / (8 \times 4)$

$= 20 * 100 / 32$

$= 2{,}000 / 32$

$= 62.5$

but the equation can be computed simultaneously for each case using a computer program such as SPSS or Excel.

Once we have completed the four steps in data verification, we are ready to begin the analysis of our dataset. The next section examines how we can use descriptive statistics to describe the data.

DESCRIBING QUANTITATIVE DATA

The goal in describing quantitative data is to present as complete a picture of the data as possible in a concise and informative manner. To accomplish this, we use descriptive statistics. **Descriptive statistics** are measures used to consolidate the many numbers included in the database into fewer numbers that are descriptive of the entire set of data. Descriptive statistics provide information for the aggregate data, rather than for each individual case or record included in the data. This is why descriptive statistics are commonly referred to as *data-reduction devices*.

The role of descriptive statistics is to communicate about the data, one variable at a time, without attempting to generalize. **Univariate analysis** refers to this examination of data one variable at a time. As we will see, the choice of univariate statistic is based on the level at which the variable is measured.

Descriptive statistics are often categorized into two types: *measures of central tendency* and *measures of variability*. When these two types are used together, they are powerful statistical tools for describing what is common and what varies in the data.

Central Tendency

Central tendency refers to analysis that summarizes or represents all of the data related to a variable. It shows the degree to which the data are similar. There are three measures of central tendency, and they are probably very familiar to you, even though you may not recognize them by name. They are the mode, median, and mean. Each of these measures can convey important and distinctive information about the **distribution,** defined as the range of values for a particular variable.

Mode

The **mode** specifies the value that occurs most frequently in the entire distribution. We are referring to the mode when we ask questions of the data such as: Do boys or girls constitute the majority of the sample? And: What was the most frequently visited domestic violence shelter in the city?

At times, more than one value in a distribution occurs with relative frequency. For example, three shelters may have topped the list of "the most frequently visited" in 2016. If so, we have more than one mode to describe what is common in the data. When two values occur with the greatest relative frequency, the distribution of the data is said to be **bimodal**. When more than two values occur with greatest relative frequency, the distribution is **multimodal**. A distribution with only one mode is **unimodal**. Note that the modes do not have to be equal to be considered the most frequent, there will likely be some variation between or among them.

We can use the mode to help describe the data at all four levels of measurement: nominal, ordinal, interval, and ratio. Exhibit 11.8 depicts a

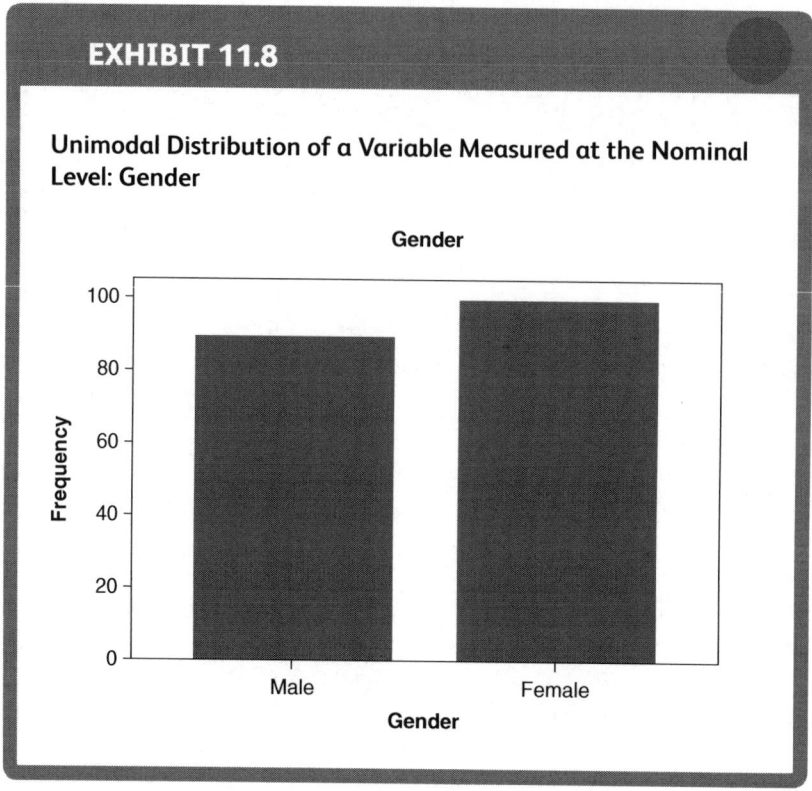

EXHIBIT 11.8

Unimodal Distribution of a Variable Measured at the Nominal Level: Gender

unimodal distribution for the variable "Gender." In this example, the count on the y axis (the vertical axis labeled "Frequency") indicates that there are 90 males and 100 females in the distribution. Therefore, the mode is female. To graphically represent the mode of nominal data we use a bar chart. The bar chart presented in Exhibit 11.8 was created in SPSS.

Exhibit 11.9 illustrates a multimodal distribution for the variable Gross Household Income. The data for this variable are continuous and are measured at the ratio level. A **histogram** is the graphic tool of choice to represent the distribution of continuous data. The histogram, a graph of a frequency distribution in which vertical bars of different heights are proportionate to corresponding frequencies, is shown in Exhibit 11.9. It was created using SPSS and shows several distinct peaks in the data, which are the modes.

Median

Several variables of concern to social workers including wages, rent, and housing prices are typically reported as median values. The **median** represents the 50% mark, or the value that divides a distribution in half so that 50% of the

EXHIBIT 11.9

Multimodal Distribution of a Variable Measured at the Ratio Level: Gross Household Income

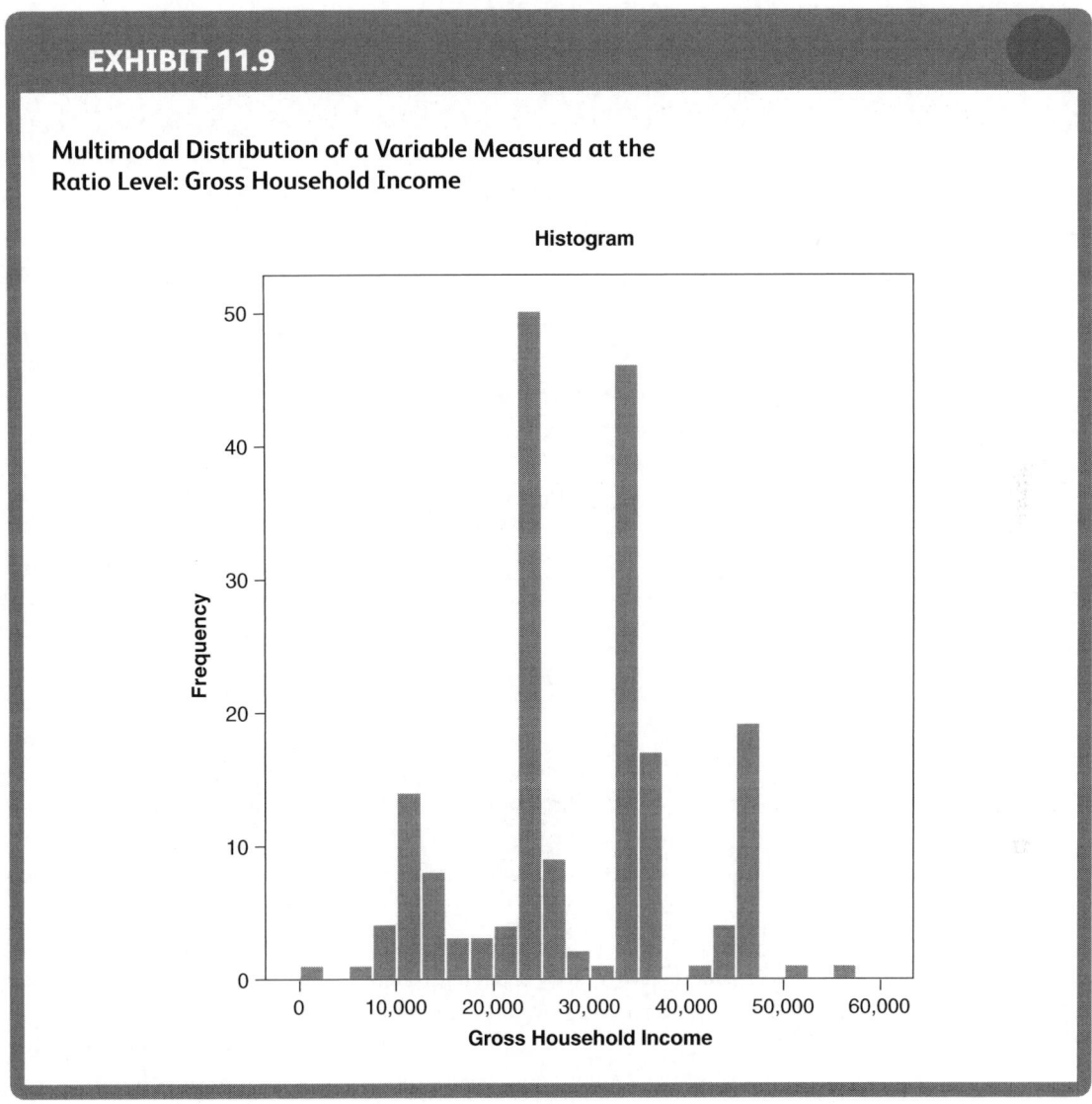

data points fall below this value and 50% above it. The median is meaningful only for data at the interval or ratio levels.

For example, the in-child welfare research median days to permanency (e.g., adoption, reunification, guardianship) can be reported for yearly cohorts of children entering out of home care as soon as 50% of the cohort has achieved permanency. Reporting the mean would require waiting until all of the children had achieved permanency, significantly delaying the report.

A preliminary step in determining the median for any distribution is to order the data. If the distribution has an odd number of values, the median is the number at the center of the distribution. If the distribution has an even number of values, we compute the median by calculating the average of the two most central values (adding them and dividing by 2). For example, consider the following distribution of values for the variable Years of Age:

10, 10, 11, 13, 14, 15, 15, 15, 16, 17, 18

The median in this example is 15 because it is the sixth of 11 values in the ordered distribution. Note that in this example the median and the mode are the same. In many other cases this will not be true. Now consider an even number of values (10) for Years of Age:

10, 10, 11, 13, 14, 15, 15, 15, 16, 17, 18

In this case, the median is 14.5, which is the 5th and 6th values (14 and 15) divided by 2.

Mean

The **mean,** or the average as it is typically referred to, is probably the most commonly used and broadly familiar measure of central tendency. To calculate the mean, we sum all of the values in a distribution and then divide that sum by the total number of values. We use the mean to answer questions such as: What is the average cost of childcare in South Tucson? And: What is the average life expectancy of African American males in the United States?

Like the median, the mean is intended for use with interval- or ratio-level data. Sometimes it is also acceptable to calculate a mean for ordinal-level data; other times it is not. For example, reporting the average response to the item "I feel safe in my community" with a 1 representing Strongly Disagree and a 5 representing Strongly Agree would make sense. Reporting a mean of 2.5, however, for a variable that rank-orders income categories such as 1 (0 to $10,000), 2 ($10,001 to $20,000), 3 ($20,001 to $30,000), and so on, would not be meaningful. Means computed for nominal data are always meaningless, even though SPSS and Excel will easily produce them. If data are coded with a 1 for male and 2 for female, the average value for Gender might be 1.6, a meaningless value.

A special feature of the mean is that it is the only measure of central tendency that uses every value in the distribution in its calculation. This is why calculating the median days to permanency as in the previous example is a better option than waiting to calculate the mean. This property of including each value makes the mean sensitive to extreme values. If the distribution is heavily weighted at both ends as in the example below, the mean value may not be a good representation of what is common. Take a minute to examine the following test scores, and answer the following questions.

1,1,1,1,1,3,100,100,100,100,100

What is the mode? What is the median? What is the mean? Which seems to be the best measure of central tendency in this case?

After you have tried to answer the questions yourself, you can look here for the answers: The mode is 1 and 100. The median is 3. The mean is 46.2. If you wanted to give a true picture of the test scores in this case, it would be best to use the mode.

Variability

If we were limited to measures of central tendency to describe data, our descriptions would be incomplete and sometimes misleading. However, if we combine measures of central tendency with **measures of variability**, also referred to as *measures of dispersion*, we can provide a much more thorough description of the data. The words *variability* and *dispersion* imply the opposite of the word *central*. Measures of variability enable us to describe how the data differ or vary from what is common.

There are four commonly used measures of variability: minimum, maximum, range, and standard deviation. As with the median and the mean, measures of variability are intended for use with interval- and ratio-level data, although sometimes they are appropriately used with ordinal data as well.

Minimum, Maximum, and Range

The **minimum value** is the lowest value represented in a distribution. Conversely, the **maximum value** is the highest value in a distribution. The **range** is the spread between the minimum and the maximum values. We calculate the range by subtracting the minimum value from the maximum value and adding 1 (one). To illustrate these concepts, use this distribution of ages:

25, 26, 27, 28, 30, 31, 32, 32, 33, 86

- Minimum age in the distribution = 25 years.
- Maximum age in the distribution = 86 years.
- Range in age ([86 – 25] + 1) = 62 years.

Any distribution with values that are similar would be described as slightly variable or containing limited variation. A distribution in which all of the values are the same displays no variation, and is described as constant. We would characterize the distribution of age above as variable.

A common application of these three measures of variability is their use in describing the distribution of scores on a standardized scale. If a researcher were describing the results of a pretest of a depression scale, the researcher might report, "The minimum score on the pretest was 14 points and the maximum score was 68, a range of 55 points between the lowest and highest scores."

Standard Deviation

The measure of variability known as the **standard deviation** is not widely used in everyday life, but it has a great deal of utility in statistical analysis. The standard deviation is a statistical measure of the amount that a set of values differs from the mean, that is, the extent to which the data show variability. For example, in a classroom, a high standard deviation on a test means that student scores are spread out, implying that there is a great range in their mastery of the subject. Conversely, test scores with a low standard deviation means that students scored within a narrow range and imply that students have similar mastery of the material. As with the mean, the calculation of standard deviation requires us to include every value in a distribution.

The formula for calculating the standard deviation is presented in Exhibit 11.10. You will probably never manually calculate a standard deviation, however, because you will use the computer to do it for you. The book's web site provides instructions for how to calculate the standard deviation in SPSS and Excel.

Standard deviation has three important uses:

■ It enables us to compare the variability in different distributions.
■ It is used in the calculation of many statistics, including the correlation coefficient, which is discussed in Chapter 12.
■ It helps us to interpret the scores within a normal distribution.

This section discusses the first function; the third is addressed in a later section titled "Normal Distribution." The use of the standard deviation in calculating statistical tests can be found in many statistical textbooks and is beyond the scope of this book.

Standard deviation reflects the variation in the scores so that we can compare different distributions. The size of the standard deviation is directly related to the variability in the data. That is, the greater the value of the standard

EXHIBIT 11.10

Formula for Calculating the Standard Deviation

$$SD = \sqrt{\dfrac{\sum (\bar{X} - x)^2}{N}}$$

$\sum$ is the mathematical symbol for summation
$\bar{X}$ is the mathematical symbol for the mean
x represents each value in the distribution

To calculate *SD*:

1. Subtract each value in a distribution from the mean of that distribution.
2. Compute the square of each of these numbers.
3. Add the squares. The resulting number is called the *sum of squared deviations from the mean*, and it is the numerator in the equation.
4. Divide the sum by the total number of data points in the distribution (*N*). (Note: When calculating the *SD* for a sample rather than a population, the denominator is N-1 rather than N.)
5. Calculate the square root of this number to produce the standard deviation (*SD*).

deviation, the greater the variation in the distribution. The smaller the value of the standard deviation, the less the variability in the distribution, and the more clustered the data are about the mean.

To illustrate these points, consider the following two distributions of age, which are identical except for the 10th values.

■ Distribution A: 25, 26, 27, 28, 30, 31, 32, 32, 33, 86
■ Distribution B: 25, 26, 27, 28, 30, 31, 32, 32, 33, 34

The mean of Distribution A is 35 years, not much different than the mean of Distribution B, which is 29.8 years. However, the standard deviation of Distribution A is 18.1 years, compared to the standard deviation of 3.12 years for

Distribution B. By comparing the sizes of the standard deviations, we can conclude that the values are much closer to the mean in Distribution B, and we might assume that there is much more variability in Distribution A.

What we do not know from these summary statistics about Distribution A is that an outlier is responsible for distorting the mean and the standard deviation. In fact, the values are actually quite clustered around the mean in Distribution A, with the single exception of the value 86. Clearly, then, combining information on the mean and standard deviation with the minimum and maximum values provides us with a clearer picture of the two distributions, even if we do not review the raw data. We can use the standard deviation, together with the mean, minimum, maximum, and number of data points (N), to describe a small-to-large number of data points.

Shapes of Distributions

Graphically displaying continuous data (such as the range of ages used in previous examples) allows us to see at a glance how the data are distributed over the entire range of values. The shape of the distribution gives us an idea about what kind of distribution the data conform to. The data associated with many variables that are of interest to social workers are consistent with a type of distribution known as the normal distribution, the topic to which we now turn.

Normal Distribution

The **normal distribution,** an example of which appears in Exhibit 11.11, is a theoretical distribution of data that has several distinctive features:

- It is symmetric, meaning that one half is a mirror image of the other half.
- Because it is symmetric, it is also unimodal. The data are distributed symmetrically about a single peak or mode.
- 50% of the data points fall on either side of the peak, indicating that the value of the median is the same as the value of the mode.
- The mean value of the distribution is precisely half way between the ordered data points, indicating that it is also equal to the values of the mode and the median.

Therefore, in a normal distribution, mean = mode = median. If the mean, median, and mode are approximately equal, the data fit the profile of the normal distribution. Of course, the mean, median, and mode are precisely the same only when we have a very large number of data points; for small samples they will differ slightly.

EXHIBIT 11.11

Normal Distribution

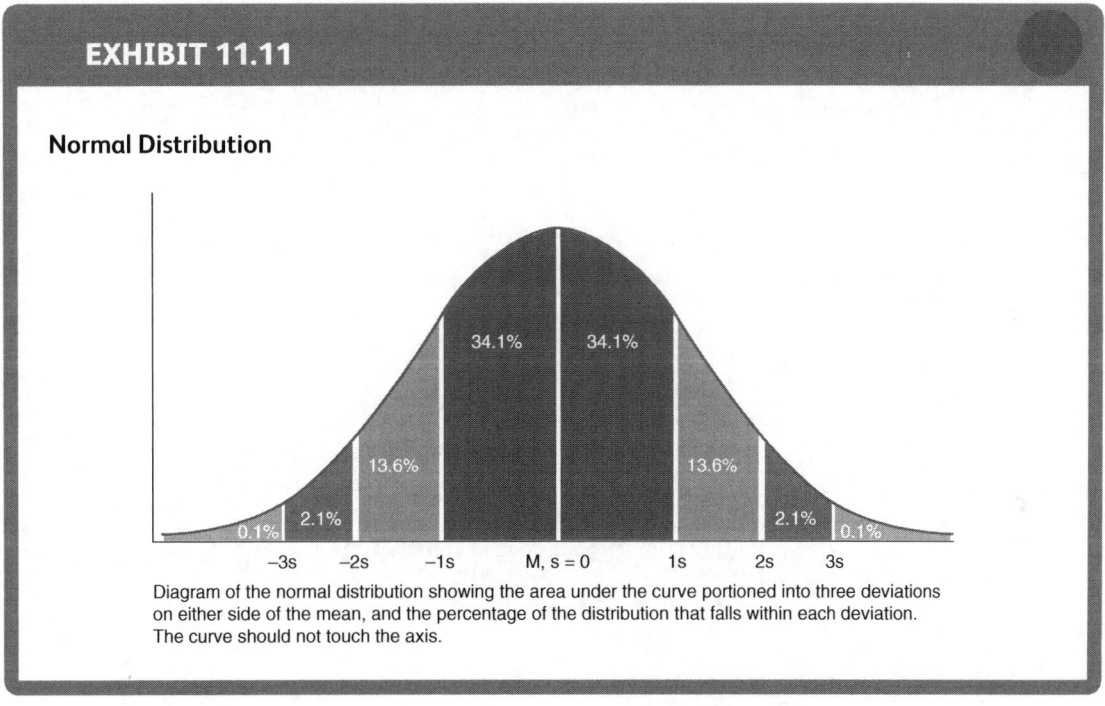

Diagram of the normal distribution showing the area under the curve portioned into three deviations on either side of the mean, and the percentage of the distribution that falls within each deviation. The curve should not touch the axis.

Many things in life appear to have the characteristics of a normal distribution, perhaps accounting for its name. A normal distribution can be seen in a pile of raked leaves, the distribution of height and weight in the population, the age at which youth reach puberty, and most human talents and abilities.

Other things do not have a normal distribution. Grades in graduate school are usually not normally distributed; they cluster at the high end. Wealth in the United States is not normally distributed; households are clustered at the low end of the wealth continuum.

This brings us to the third important use of standard deviation. When the data are consistent with the shape of the normal distribution, we can apply the mathematical properties of the normal distribution to the data to interpret them with greater precision. These mathematical properties are summarized in Quick Guide 6. We usually report the standard deviation together with the mean so that the reader can get a better picture of how the data are distributed about the mean. Presenting the mean and the standard deviation together also indicates where a given score falls relative to other scores in the distribution.

For example, Exhibit 11.12 presents a histogram showing the distribution of scores on a posttest of Life Skills. The data are from the Riverton Youth

QUICK GUIDE 6 MATHEMATICAL PROPERTIES OF THE NORMAL DISTRIBUTION

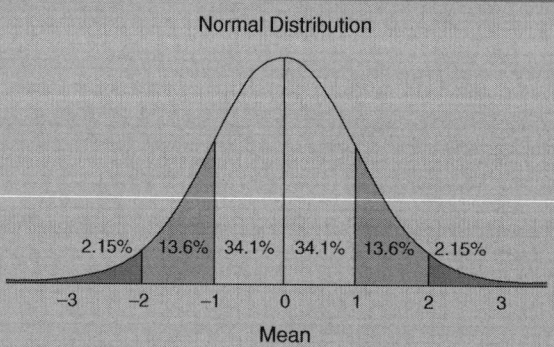

Normal Distribution

- The total area underneath the curve of the normal distribution, or any distribution for that matter, is always equal to 1, or 100 %.
- The fact that the normal distribution is symmetric means that 50 % of the distribution is found on either side of the mean (μ).
- The distance of 1 SD to the left of the mean is the same as the distance of 1 SD to the right of the mean, and so on.
- If we partition the area under the curve, 34.13 % of the distribution of scores will fall within 1 SD of the mean, and 68.26 % of the distribution will fall within plus or minus 1 SD of the mean (±1 SD).
- Another 13.59 % of the distribution will fall between 1 and 2 SDs from the mean. This means that approximately 95 % of the scores in the distribution will fall within ±2 SDs on either side of the mean. Thus scores falling outside of two standard deviations is a fairly rare event that happens only 5 % of the time.
- Another 2.15 % of the distribution will fall between 2 and 3 SDs. Thus, a total of 99.72 % of the area under the curve is accounted for within ±3 SDs from the mean.
- The curve does not touch the horizontal axis, or x axis at ±3 SDs from the mean.
- Even though 99.7 % of the distribution will be accounted for within 3 SDs on either side of the mean, the remaining .0014 % of the scores will fall outside the lowermost and uppermost deviations.

Survey, and they represent the scores of 187 youth ($N = 187$). By considering the way the histogram conforms to the shape of the curve and comparing the mean, median, and mode, we could reasonably conclude that the distribution approximates the normal distribution. The mean and the median are equal at 64, and the mode is slightly lower at 58. The scores on the posttest ranged from a low of 17 to a high of 98.

Knowing that the distribution approximates normal, the mean equals 64.11, and the SD equals 14.91, we can draw certain conclusions about how the values are distributed around the mean. For example, because the mean

EXHIBIT 11.12

Example of Distribution That Approximates the Normal Distribution: Riverton Youth Survey

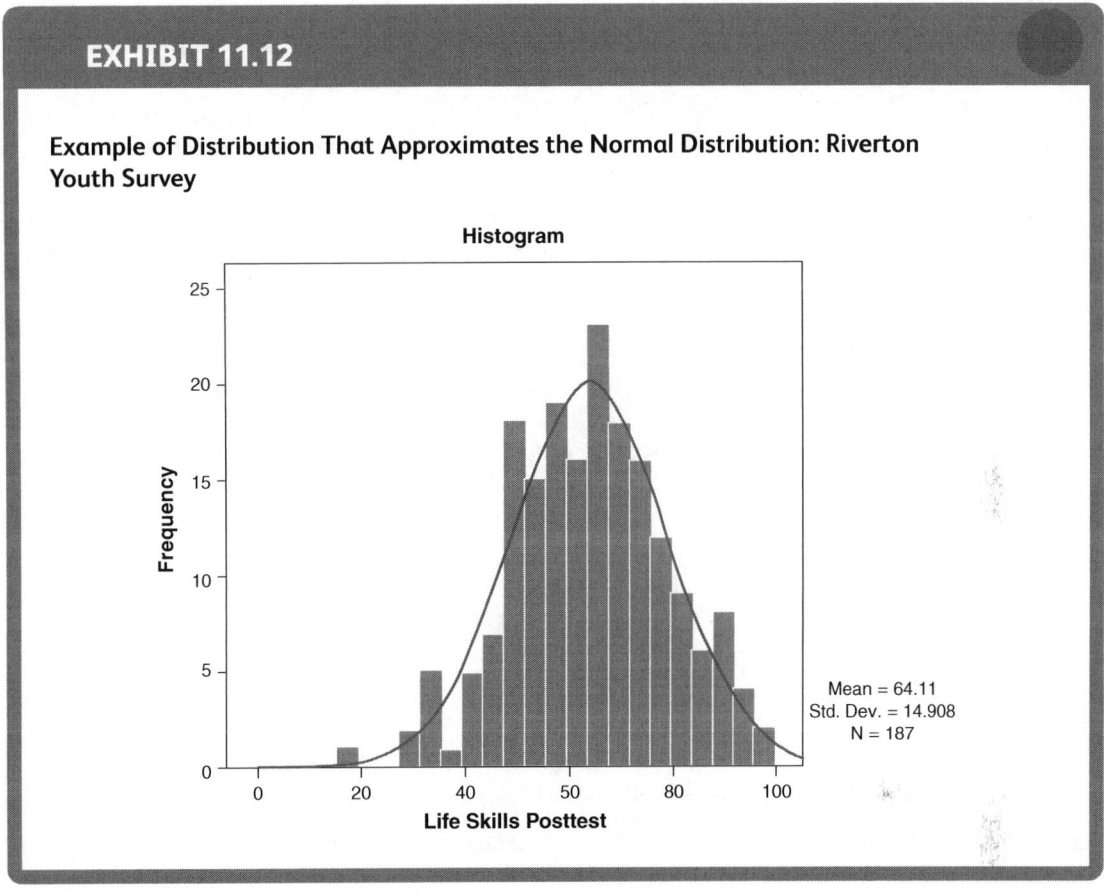

posttest score was 64, we know that approximately 50% of the scores were below that number and 50% were above it. We also know that approximately 68% of the scores in the distribution fell within one standard deviation from the mean—specifically, between the scores of 49.20 (64.11 – 14.91) and 79.02 (64.11 + 14.91).

Knowing that a distribution is normal can also help us determine whether a certain value is likely or unlikely to occur. Similarly, we can use the properties of the normal distribution to objectively judge whether an outlier should be excluded from the descriptive analysis. The presence of outliers can severely distort the mean and standard deviation of a distribution. The social work researcher is likely to encounter at least one or two true outliers in her or his career, so the question becomes how to handle them. Sometimes the data that are outliers seem obvious, but the data analysis is more trustworthy if the reasoning for eliminating the outliers can be shown through statistics.

EXHIBIT 11.13

Using the Properties of the Normal Distribution to Decide Whether to Exclude an Outlier

The application of Chauvenet's criterion is one technique for objectively assessing whether an outlier is so unlikely to occur in a sample that it should be excluded (Taylor, 1997). Chauvenet's criterion uses the properties of the normal distribution to evaluate the likelihood that a data point of a certain magnitude is an unlikely occurrence. The probability that a data point will fall beyond 2 *SD*s on either side of the mean is roughly 5 %, or .05.

To apply Chauvenet's criterion, we multiply the total number of data points (*N*) by .05. If the result is less than .5, then we can exclude the outlier.

For example, consider the following distribution for age:

25, 26, 27, 28, 30, 31, 86

The value of 86 appears to be an obvious outlier. There are seven data points in this distribution (*N* = 7), so the probability that the outlier (86) should be so far from the mean is calculated as .05 * 7 = .35. Applying Chauvenet's criterion, .35 is less than .5, so the outlier of 86 should be excluded from the analysis.

The revised distribution (25, 26, 27, 28, 30, 31) has a mean of 27.83 and a *SD* of 2.32. These summary statistics are much more representative of the central tendency and variability in the data than the summary statistics calculated with the inclusion of the outlier ($\bar{X}$ = 35, *SD* = 18.13).

Exhibit 11.13 describes one method for objectively deciding whether or not to exclude an outlier from the data.

Skewed Distributions

If a distribution does not appear symmetric when we plot it—that is, one half of the distribution is not a mirror image of the other half—we describe the distribution as **skewed** or **non-normal**. The term *skewed* simply means that it deviates from the normal distribution.

We can judge the direction in which the data are skewed, positive or negative, by examining a histogram or by determining where the mean and mode fall on the distribution:

■ **Positive skew:** The scores cluster around the low end of the distribution or the left side of the curve. Visually, the mode of a positively skewed distribution is to the left of the mean, and the curve extends to the right as if it had a longer tail on that side.

■ **Negative skew:** The scores are clustered on the high end of the distribution. Visually, if the long tail is to the left of the mean and the mode is to the right of the mean, the distribution is negatively skewed.

Exhibit 11.14 presents examples of positively and negatively skewed distributions.

Determining the type of distribution is necessary because, as we will see in Chapter 12, the types of statistical tests that can be used to analyze the data depend on the distribution of the data.

Descriptive Analyses in Reports

Once you have analyzed the data in terms of central tendency and variability, you will want to report it to individuals and groups who have an interest in the results. This step represents the culmination of your work in executing the research process. To do your research justice and to ensure that it has the desired impact on social work practice, you must report the results clearly and accurately.

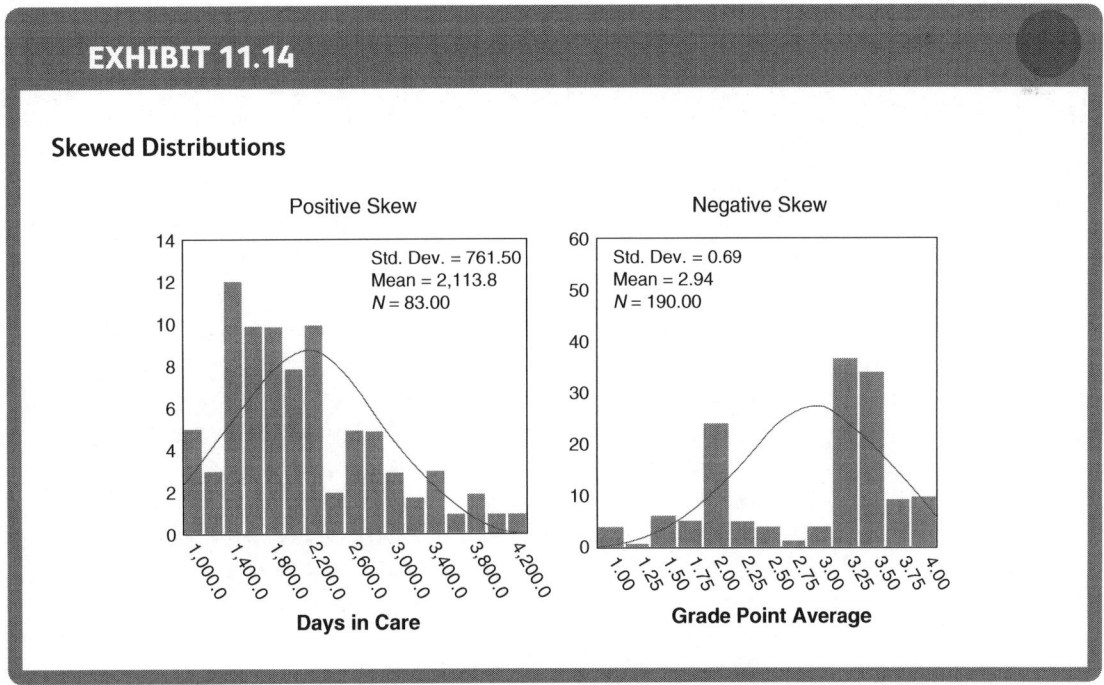

EXHIBIT 11.14

Skewed Distributions

One goal in this chapter is to provide you with some general tips and alert you to some common errors in reporting descriptive analysis. Chapter 13 outlines the various options for presenting research results, including conference and poster presentations, reports, and writing for publication. In addition, there are many books and style guides that describe how to communicate research results. The information we provide here serves two functions: to help you present and describe data effectively, and to read and critique the presentation of descriptive analyses by other researchers.

There are three ways to present descriptive analyses:

■ displayed in a table
■ graphically in bar charts, histograms, line graphs, and so on
■ in narrative or written form

A combination of these methods is often the most effective approach, and it serves as a guided visual tour through the results.

It is unlikely that you will report every single finding from your study. Instead, you must choose carefully among the results that best fulfill the objectives of the research and that lead the intended audience to the conclusion revealed by the analysis. For this reason, you will want to begin the writing process by first designing the tables and graphics and then developing the written or spoken narrative around the presentation of the analysis.

Designing Effective Tables

A frequency table, like the one shown in Exhibit 11.15, is one of the simplest ways to organize and display data. The following guidelines will assist you in designing effective tables:

■ Nominal and ordinal variables naturally order themselves into groups that lend themselves to frequency tables.
■ To present interval and ratio data in a frequency table, you can divide the data into six to 15 equally spaced and mutually exclusive intervals.
■ Tables should be labeled as tables in the report and numbered consecutively (e.g., Table 1, Table 2, and so on.). In addition, they should be titled in a way that clearly describes the tables' contents.
■ Each row and column in a table must have a heading.
■ Some core information is standard and expected in the table. The variables go into the rows and the frequencies or other statistics in the columns. If you report percentages in the table, you must also report Ns, usually in the heading. Use horizontal lines to break up the sections of the table. An alternative is to present the table as a grid.

EXHIBIT 11.15

Sample Frequency Table

Characteristics of Youths in Residential and Detention Programs

	Detention (N = 116)		Residential (N = 145)	
Variable	Number	Percentage	Number	Percentage
Race				
White	71	61%	92	63%
Nonwhite	45	39%	53	37%
Gender				
Male	90	78%	102	70%
Female	26	22%	43	30%

Source: Roe-Sepowitz, 2005. Adapted with permission from the author.

- Use statistical symbols and abbreviations in tables to conserve space: "%" for percent, $\bar{X}$ for Mean, *Mdn.* for Median, *Mo.* for Mode, *SD* for standard deviation, and Min. and Max. for minimum and maximum. Use an uppercase, italicized *N* for the entire sample or population and a lowercase, italicized *n* to report the size of subgroups such as male and female.
- Always report valid percentages rather than absolute percentages in the tables. Remember that valid percentages are calculated without the inclusion of missing data in the Ns.
- Use notes at the end of the table for explanation, such as presenting operational definitions, decision rules, and documentation of sources.

Developing Graphics

Most word processing programs can help you create graphics that you can integrate into the text with ease. You can also import graphics from Excel and SPSS. When you incorporate graphics into the text, you should refer to them to as figures, number them consecutively, and describe each in a caption.

Interval and ratio data should be displayed in histograms and line graphs. Line graphs, such as the one shown in Exhibit 11.16, are recommended for displaying trend data, or data over time. This graph illustrates how

EXHIBIT 11.16

Sample Line Graph

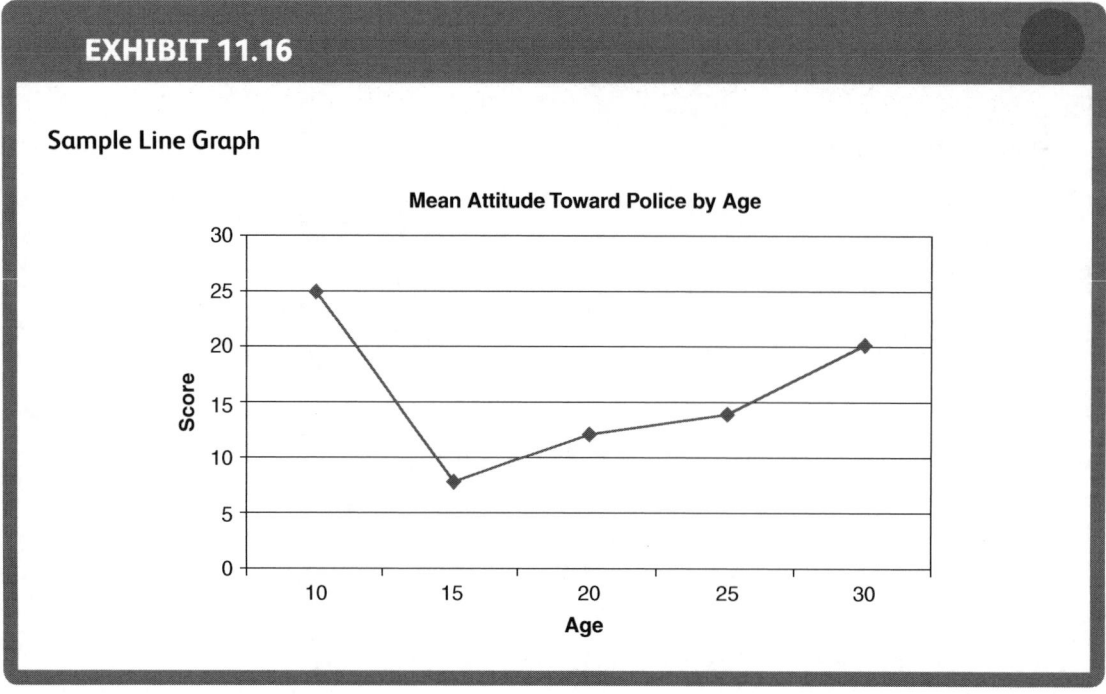

attitudes towards police change over time. It represents a longitudinal study in which scores on an attitude scale were measured every five years from age 10 to age 30. Higher scores represent more favorable attitudes. What patterns do you notice in the line graph?

In contrast, nominal and ordinal data are best displayed in pie charts, like the one shown in Exhibit 11.17, or bar charts. Always report valid percentages (which leave out missing data in the total sample) in the charts. A table can handle many variables at a time, whereas a chart is restricted to a single variable. Published articles often present categorical data in tables rather than charts due to space restrictions. In contrast, research reports and presentations generally do not have the same space limitations.

Finally, if the research report will be printed in black and white, avoid using graphics that require the reader to distinguish between too many shades of gray. The graphics should be large enough that all type is easy to read. A common size for a typical graphic is about half a page.

Writing the Narrative

Most of the descriptive analysis will be presented in the results section of the research report or presentation. The results section should include only the

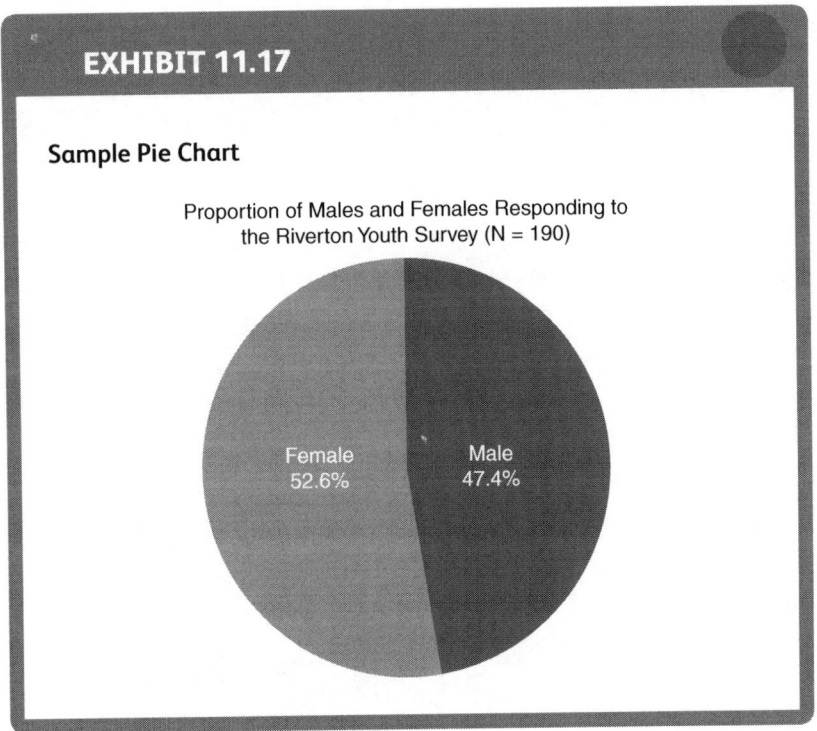

EXHIBIT 11.17

Sample Pie Chart

Proportion of Males and Females Responding to
the Riverton Youth Survey (N = 190)

Female
52.6%

Male
47.4%

presentation of the results. The results section is not the appropriate place to introduce theories or discuss implications of the research.

When you are writing the narrative, consider the following points:

- If the objective of the research is to compare two or more groups, instead of presenting aggregate information for the group as a whole, provide only the descriptive information for each group.
- The narrative should always address the data contained in the tables, but it should avoid discussing every detail. It is best to pick out the two or three most salient points in each table and discuss each one for emphasis.
- The tables and graphics should be placed near the location in the narrative where they are mentioned. Otherwise the reader has to flip back and forth between the text and the visuals.
- Interval and ratio data should be described with means, standard deviations, and Ns (total numbers in the sample). If the distribution of the data does not conform to the normal distribution, the median, minimum, and maximum values should be reported as alternatives.

- When reporting percentages always report the corresponding *N*s.
- Use percentages only to compare groups that are similar in size. Otherwise, they can be misleading.
- Avoid reporting percentages for small groups. For instance, if 50% of the sample is less than 10 cases, reporting percentages can be misleading. Report actual numbers for small samples.

CONCLUSION

The use of personal computers has made the analysis and presentation of quantitative data much easier than in the past. The social work researcher, however, must tell the computer what to do. This requires knowledge of the different statistics and graphical formats that are right for each level of data and for the way that the data are distributed.

This chapter examined the use of descriptive statistics to evaluate data and to summarize and describe it one variable at a time. The next chapter looks at using statistical tests to examine the relationship between two or more variables at a time.

MAIN POINTS

- Data are not useful in raw form. To have utility for social work practice, data have to be analyzed and turned into information. This requires social workers with sound research skills. Data analysis software cannot turn data into information.
- An outlier is a value that is out of range relative to most of the data. In quantitative data analysis, we look for outliers by examining scatterplots or by developing frequency distributions for interval and ratio data. All outliers should be verified as to whether they are true extreme values or errors.
- Descriptive statistics are useful in providing an overview of the research to the reader.
- There are two types of descriptive statistics, central tendency and variability. Used in conjunction, they are powerful tools for describing data.
- The value of the entire research process will be judged by the quality of the analysis as reported in the final report or presentation. If the report is not well conceptualized, accurate, or effectively written, the research will not have the desired impact: To improve social work practice.

EXERCISES

1. Using the RAINN case Visitor Feedback data file, locate two variables: one measured at the nominal level and one representing ordinal measurement. For each of the variables, describe the appropriate descriptive statistics that you would use to describe the data in narrative and graphic form.

2. Using the RAINN case, verify the data in the Visitor Feedback data file for *Date* of session. Do you detect any plausible errors or outliers? List these and explain what leads you to this conclusion and what you believe might explain these points.

3. Using the RAINN case, describe how you would create a "total satisfaction" score that includes the five consumer satisfaction variables. What descriptive statistics would you use to describe the data on satisfaction? Explain why you would select these and how they would shed insight on the question of satisfaction.

4. Your graduate school of social work conducts a salary survey and finds that the average salary among MSW alumni in 2016 was $70,620. Since the mean salary for graduate social workers nationally is approximately $53,000, how might you explain the higher mean salary associated with your program? List all of the possible explanations you can think of, and then identify at least one research approach you could use in order to test this possible explanation.

5. The Latino population in the United States is a diverse one, with substantial differences in country of origin, immigration/citizenship status, and other dimensions, which may affect individuals' experiences and outcomes. Write a paragraph explaining how you could use measures of central tendency and variability to explore an outcome such as educational attainment or household income in this diverse community, as well as some of the limitations of these descriptive statistics, in this case.

6. The test scores on the social work research mid-term for two different sections of a research class each have a mean of 87. The professor, however, argues that the sections are actually very different in their research competence. Can the professor be correct when the means are identical? Explain.

7. None of the measures of central tendency is the best; rather, selecting the best measure depends on how the data are distributed. For example, assume that we asked a sample of 10 individuals their age in years. Their responses were as follows:

    25, 26, 27, 28, 30, 31, 32, 32, 33, 86

The sum of the 10 numbers is 350. Answer the following seven questions:

a. What is the mode of the distribution?

b. What is the median of the distribution?

c. What is the mean of the distribution?

d. Which of the 10 values, if any, would you consider an outlier?

e. How does the outlier influence the calculation of each measure of central tendency?

f. Which of the three measures of central tendency best represents the typical age in this distribution?

g. What did you learn from this exercise?

8. Using the Riverton case, locate the age variable in the Youth Survey data file.

a. Plot the age variable using Excel.

b. Calculate measures of central tendency and dispersion using SPSS if it is available to you, or Excel.

c. Remove case #14, and rerun the measures of central tendency. What measures of central tendency and dispersion are sensitive to extreme values? What measures of central tendency and dispersion are relatively unchanged by the deletion of case #14?

BIVARIATE STATISTICS AND STATISTICAL INFERENCE

A point of view can be a dangerous luxury when substituted for insight and understanding.

Marshall McLuhan, Canadian Communications Professor

Making inferences comes so naturally that most of the time we are not even consciously aware that we are engaged in the process. We make inferences when we mentally calculate the odds of a certain outcome based on prior knowledge and experience. For instance, what are the chances that this will be a good restaurant based on my friends' recommendations? What are my chances of crossing a busy intersection without getting hit by a car? When the consequences are serious, we accept very low risk, as in crossing a busy intersection. Other times, we may have a higher risk tolerance, as in choosing a potentially bad restaurant.

Similarly, in social work practice we make decisions based on inferences about the odds of a particular outcome. Sometimes the consequences of making an error are serious. For example, what are the chances that a child will be safe if left in a home with a parent who has previously been abusive? At other times, the consequences of making the wrong decision are less serious. For example, what are the chances that shortening a parent education program from 16 to 12 sessions will reduce the program's effectiveness? This process of mentally calculating the odds is referred to as making a **logical inference**.

Statistical inference is similar in that it involves making a calculated decision based on the results of an observation. Instead of making a judgment based on how we feel or think about the odds, as we do in logical inference, statistical inference relies on a mathematical calculation of the odds. Statistical inference is based on **probability**—the odds or chances that something will happen based on the ratio of the number of favorable outcomes to the total number of possible outcomes.

The previous chapter discussed ways to describe quantitative data one variable at a time using frequency tables, measures of central tendency, and measures of variability. In this chapter we discuss **bivariate analysis**, statistical methods that enable us to go beyond consideration of one variable to consider two or more variables at one time. Much of social work research is concerned with how two or more variables are related.

By the end of this chapter you should be able to:

- Explain hypothesis testing by statistical inference, including the concepts *p*-level, rejection level, and statistical significance.
- Explain what is meant by Type I and Type II errors in hypothesis testing.
- Explain when to use parametric and nonparametric statistics.
- Explain the use of specific statistical tests for hypothesis testing, including Pearson's r, chi-square, various t-tests, and one-way analysis of variance (ANOVA), including how to interpret and report them.

- Explain the difference between a statistically significant result and a meaningful result.
- Given a quantitative research study using the statistical tests described in this chapter, explain what conclusions we can and cannot reasonably draw from the data.

PROBABILITY

If someone tossed a coin and correctly predicted that it would land heads up, we might not be too impressed because we know there is a 50/50 chance of that person being right. Getting about 50% heads and 50% tails is the typical, or expected, variation in tossing coins. If the person correctly predicted the outcome of a coin toss 70 times in a row, however, we might be either very impressed or very suspicious that the coin was not a regularly minted coin.

We all have an intuitive sense of probability. For example, if the average height of men is 5 feet 9 inches and the average height of women is 5 feet 5 inches, which of the following groups do you believe is all female?

- Group 1: 5'8", 5'6", 5'4", 5'2", 5'4", 5'5", 5'6", 5'1"
- Group 2: 5'9", 6'1", 5'8", 5'7", 5'8", 5'9", 6'2", 5'6"
- Group 3: 5'6", 5'8", 6'0", 5'2", 5'7", 5'5", 5'7", 5'4"

You probably guessed that Group 1 is female, Group 2 is male, and Group 3 is hard to tell. You based your decision on your intuitive knowledge of probability.

In contrast, in making inferences about the outcomes of research, we use the science of probability to assess the likelihood that our finding is the result of chance or typical variation in our object of study. This is statistical inference. We use a mathematical method called **inferential statistics** to estimate whether a sample reflects the characteristics of a population or whether the observed differences between the sample and the population are the likely result of chance—the chance that a particular sample is not representative of the population.

STATISTICAL SIGNIFICANCE TESTING

For most human attributes there is variation; that is, there is a range of possibilities. People vary in height, in level of self-esteem, in political attitudes, in parenting skills, and so on. We assume that there is variation in any population. Thus, when we study a sample, it should also exhibit variation. We hope that the variation in the sample reflects the variation in the population from which the sample was drawn, especially if the sample selection was random and of sufficient size.

In order to make judgments about the certainty of our findings, we must know not only the extent to which differences occur but also the extent to which they occur more frequently than we would expect by chance variation. For example, in a truancy prevention program, we not only need to know whether the number of days of truancy has been reduced, but also whether it has been reduced more than normal variation for those who did not attend the program. Similarly, for a group of people with depression, we need to know if a program lessened depression more than chance or typical variation in their level of depression. **Statistical significance testing** is the process of determining the probability that the findings from sample data are likely to be due to chance. We say a result is statistically significant when, based on probability, it is unlikely to occur by chance.

Statistical significance is influenced by two factors: the representativeness of the sample and the degree of variability within the sample. In this section we discuss some of the methods and pitfalls of statistical significance testing. We also examine the utility of statistical significance testing in nonexperimental research.

Sampling Error

As discussed in Chapter 8, selecting a sample that does not accurately reflect the true level of variation in the population is referred to as **sampling error**. Let's say that, in a hypothetical population of 500 students, 350 (70%) support same-sex marriage and 150 (30%) do not. It is possible, but unlikely, to draw a random sample of 100 students who are all against same-sex marriage. If we accepted this nonrepresentative sample as representative, we would wrongly conclude that all students in the population are against same-sex marriage.

We can never be entirely certain that a finding is *not* the result of sample error. After all, strange samples do happen. The odds of winning the lottery are 40 million to 1, but someone still wins.

However, we can assess the likelihood that we have drawn a sample that accurately reflects the population. That determination depends on two factors:

■ *Size of the sample.* It is intuitive that if you have a population of 1,000 people and you randomly sample 990, the sample will very closely reflect the population. If you sample 800 people, the sample will still closely reflect the population. But if you sample only 50 people, then the sample will be far less likely to accurately reflect the characteristics or views of the other 950 people.

■ *Degree of variability within the sample.* The lower the variability in the population, the smaller the sample size required to be representative of the population. Conversely, the greater the variability, the larger the sample needs to be.

One way to judge whether a finding is real or a product of sample error is through **replication**, repeating the study and drawing multiple random samples from the population. If we get the same results using several samples, we then gain confidence that the results actually reflect the population. Replication is an important means of advancing knowledge, but it requires time and resources. It is more efficient to use inferential statistics to assess the likelihood of sample error.

Calculating p-Value

Statistical significance testing relies on probability to tell us the likelihood that the findings from the sample are the result of sampling error. For example, the probability of drawing one of the four aces from a full deck of cards is 4 out of 52, or $4/52 = .07$ (7%). If someone consistently draws an ace 50% of the time, we might conclude that there are more than four aces in the deck (sample) and that the sample does not reflect the population (true decks of playing cards).

The probability that a relationship between variables or a mean difference found in a sample is a result of sample error is represented by the *p*-**value**. The *p*-value ranges from 0 (almost certain that the results are not based on sample error) to 1 (almost certain that the results are from sample error). Note that we are never completely certain that the results are the product of sample error. The only certainty in research is that the results will always have some uncertainty. Our question is whether that uncertainty is at an acceptable level.

As Chapter 3 explains, we begin any research project by assuming that the **null hypothesis (H_0)** is true; that is, we assume that no relationship between or among the variables exists unless the evidence indicates otherwise. In statistical terms, the null hypothesis is a statement that there is no difference or relationship between variables. The alternative hypothesis or **research hypothesis (H_1)** is a statement that there is a relationship between variables or difference between the variables. We use statistical tests to support or not support the null hypothesis.

Because we can never be 100% certain that there is no relationship between two variables, we need to determine the statistical level, or *p*-value, at which we can reject the null hypothesis and say that there is a relationship between the variables. That level, called the **rejection level**, depends on how willing we are to make a mistake in rejecting the null hypothesis. The decision of where to set the rejection level is arbitrary and is based on logic. In a drug study when someone's life is at stake, we may be willing to tolerate only a 1 in 10 million chance of being wrong. Most social science research, by contrast, uses a less stringent rejection level, generally .05. That is, there is only a 5% chance that the relationship found in the sample is due to sample error or chance. When the p-value is below the rejection level, we refer to the result as "statistically significant." For example, we have a program to reduce truancy among teens. We divide a group of truant teens randomly into two groups, those who were given the program and those who were not. We can then compare the mean number of days truant for each group. The results show that the teens in the program had a mean truancy of five days compared with a mean of 12 days truant for the teens not in the program. If the difference in means is likely to occur less than 5% (the rejection level) of the time, we conclude that the difference is statistically significant.

Because it is not possible to be 100% certain that the results of a study are not due to sample error, we should avoid using the term *prove* in relation to hypothesis testing. Instead we refute, reject, or fail to reject the null hypothesis. The statistical significance test is always a test of the null hypothesis; it is never a test of the research hypothesis.

Assessing the Impact of Sample Size

When considering the results of statistical significance testing, we need to take sample size into account. The larger the sample size, the more likely that we will find statistical significance—that is, that the p-value will fall below .05. The reason for this rule is that large sample sizes are more likely to be representative of the population, whereas smaller sample sizes have a greater likelihood of being skewed. As a result, whereas we might reject the null hypothesis at the .05 probability level with a sample of 250 ($N = 250$), we might not do so with a sample size of only 25 ($N = 25$).

This conclusion holds true even when the observed relationship between the variables or the difference between the means in both samples is the same. As you might imagine, it makes interpreting the results of any one study more difficult. However, if we replicate the results in other studies with different sample sizes, we can have greater confidence that the relationship between the variables actually exists in the population. When the results of small sample studies are not significant but all point in the same direction—that is, they show a similar relationship between the variables—we also can have more confidence in the findings.

Errors of Statistical Inference

There are two kinds of error associated with making statistical inference

- **Type I error** occurs when we mistakenly reject the null hypothesis, thereby inferring that a relationship that is observed in the sample actually exists in the population, when, in fact, it does not. Going back to a previous example, we concluded that a relationship exists between income and mental health because the *p*-value is less than .05. It is possible, however, that there is no such relationship in the population because we drew an unrepresentative sample.
- **Type II error**, conversely, occurs when we mistakenly support the null hypothesis and conclude that there is no real relationship between the variables in the population when, in fact, there is such a relationship. For example, we test the relationship between income and mental health and conclude from a *p*-value of .16 (or any level greater than .05) that no relationship exists. It is still possible that income and mental health are related in the population but that the sample did not show the relationship because it was not representative.

These relationships are shown in Exhibit 12.1.

To put it another way, the higher the *p*-value (or rejection level), the greater the likelihood of making a Type 1 error. Conversely, the lower the *p*-value (or rejection level), the greater the likelihood of making a Type II error.

Small sample sizes increase the likelihood of making a Type II error, which is failing to reject the null hypothesis when it is false. For this reason, the

---

EXHIBIT 12.1

Type I and Type II Errors of Statistical Inference and Their Effect on Hypothesis Testing

	Statistically Significant Relationship Shown in Sample	Actual Relationship in Population	Erroneous Decision
Type 1 Error	Yes	No	Reject H_0, accept H_1
Type 2 Error	No	Yes	Accept H_0, reject H_1

H_0 = null hypothesis
H_1 = research hypothesis

researcher with a small sample size may decide before the study begins to set a higher rejection level, for example, .10 instead of the conventional .05.

Statistical Significance Testing in Nonexperimental Research

From the preceding discussion, you might conclude that statistical significance testing is appropriate only when the data are from true experimental research that includes a random sample. What if the data are from a convenience sample, or what if they represent an entire population? Recall from Chapter 8 that research with nonrandom samples and narrowly defined populations (population subgroups) is the norm in social work research. In contrast, research designs that involve randomization are rare in social work because they are often objectionable on ethical grounds and because they are difficult to implement, especially in small geographic areas where contamination between samples is more likely.

If the sample is not truly random, the significance test can overstate the accuracy of the results because it considers only random sampling error and cannot assess the biases that result from other, nonrandom sources of error. In the absence of random sampling, how do we interpret the p-value?

The appropriate use of statistical significance testing is a research issue that has long been debated by social work researchers (Cowger, 1984; Glisson, 1985). To get a sense of where the profession stands on this issue today, browse through any number of research articles in recently published social work journals. What you are likely to find is many instances of statistical significance testing in studies employing quasi-experimental and even pre-experimental research designs. The consensus in social work seems to be that statistical significance testing is a formal and objective way of evaluating whether the strength of an observed relationship or the difference between means was small enough that it was likely a chance occurrence or large enough to suggest the possibility of systematic variation.

Statistical inference with nonexperimental designs does have some usefulness as long as the conclusions and recommendations based on the study are appropriate. For instance, generalization of the findings and claims of causation are not defensible in nonexperimental research. If the findings are statistically significant, the researcher could reasonably claim that further research is warranted that involves at best, a more rigorous research design, and, at minimum, replication.

COMMON BIVARIATE STATISTICAL TESTS

Let's take another look at a previous example. Assume that we have drawn a sample of 300 people at random from a community. We then collect data pertaining to the income and mental health of the people in the sample. After examining the data, we find that a relationship exists between income and mental health. Specifically, people with lower incomes have poorer mental health, and people with higher incomes have better mental health. We are faced with two possibilities:

■ There is a "real" relationship between income and mental health.
■ The sample does not reflect the population, in other words, we have a case of sample error. That is, even though the relationship is true for the 300 people in the sample, it is not true of the population from which it is drawn.

How do we decide between these two possibilities? We use statistical tests to determine the probability that sampling error or chance is responsible for the observed relationship and thus to support or reject hypotheses. To examine the relationship between two variables we use **bivariate statistics**. Exhibit 12.2 provides examples of the different types of bivariate hypotheses.

In Chapter 11, we saw that the choice of univariate statistics was based on the level at which the variable was measured. Similarly, the choice of bivariate statistics also depends on level of measurement, as well as a few additional considerations. There are two classes of bivariate statistical tests:

■ **Parametric statistics** are used when at least one of the two variables being analyzed is measured at the interval or ratio level and is normally distributed in the population. We saw in Chapter 11 that when data are normally distributed they have certain mathematical properties: (a) the mean,

---

EXHIBIT 12.2

Types of Bivariate Hypotheses

Type	Example
Null hypothesis (H_0)—No relationship	There is no relationship between income and mental health.
Two-tailed (nondirectional) hypothesis (H_1)—There is a relationship	There is a relationship between income and mental health.
One-tailed hypothesis (H_1)—Directional relationship	The greater the income, the greater the mental health.

median, and mode are roughly equal; (b) when plotted, they approximate a normal curve; and (c) they can be shown to have come from a random sample. The use of parametric statistics is the most common form of analysis in quantitative social science research.

■ **Nonparametric statistics** are used for analyzing data that are not normally distributed, are nominal or ordinal variables, were not randomly selected, and were selected from a very small sample.

Demonstrating or describing how to manually compute the bivariate statistical tests is not an objective of this book. Rather, this chapter is aimed at developing a conceptual understanding of select statistical tests, including the use, misuse, and interpretation of each test. The computation of the statistics presented in this chapter and additional statistical tests are addressed in courses focused on statistics, and they can be found in a variety of books on statistical analysis for the social sciences. Also, more complex statistics such as multiple regression analysis are available for examining the relationship among a larger number of variables. Many of these statistical tests are the subject of advanced courses in statistics.

You can easily perform the statistical tests presented in this chapter, however, with the aid of a computer program such as SPSS or Excel. To this end, tutorials for both SPSS and Excel are easily accessed from the Internet.

The remainder of this chapter presents the most common parametric statistical tests used in social science research: Pearson's Product Moment Correlation Coefficient, three types of t-test, and one-way analysis of variance. There are more bivariate statistical tests available than those presented here, but these are commonly used. In addition, this chapter discusses one very common nonparametric test, chi-square. The chapter then concludes with a discussion of common pitfalls to avoid in tests of statistical significance and conventions for reporting statistical findings.

Linear Correlation

Linear correlation is the degree to which two variables measured at the interval or ratio levels of measurement are related, or co-vary. Linear correlation is concerned with how the values of the two variables vary in unison:

■ **Positive correlation:** the two variable values move in the same direction. For example, what is the relationship between education and income? Generally speaking, the more years of education people have, the greater their income. Of course, sometimes, for a variety of reasons, people who are highly educated do not earn a good income. Overall, though, the relationship holds true.

- **Negative correlation**, or **inverse correlation:** the variables relate in an opposite way— low scores on one variable co-vary with high scores on the other. For example, in most cases, the higher the income adults have, the lower their health risks.
- *Little or no correlation:* the variables appear to be unrelated. Height and IQ, for instance, do not co-vary. It would not be true that "the greater the height, the higher (or lower) the IQ."

Chapter 11 discussed the use of scatterplots to verify data. A scatterplot is also a useful tool to visually show the relationship between two linear variables:

- *x* **axis** (horizontal axis): represents one variable, customarily the variable we are using to make the prediction (the independent variable).
- *y* **axis** (vertical axis): represents the variable being predicted (the dependent variable).

For example, we can plot the relationship between self-esteem and marital satisfaction, both of which are measured on an interval-level scale. We may hypothesize the relationship between these two variables as, H_o: there is no relationship between marital satisfaction and self-esteem, and H_1: the greater the marital satisfaction, the greater the self-esteem (in other words, there is a relationship between marital satisfaction and self-esteem). To test our null hypothesis, we administer a self-esteem scale that can range from 0 to 30 points to a random sample of married individuals. We also administer a marital satisfaction scale that varies from 0 to 12 points to each individual.

Exhibit 12.3 displays three scatterplots. Each scatterplot displays how the scores of the 36 individuals who participated in our study might be distributed. Each point on any of the scatterplots represents one individual's score on both of the scales. In this example, scores on the self-esteem scale are plotted on the *y* axis and scores on the marital satisfaction scale on the *x* axis.

Correlation Direction and Line of Best Fit

Examining the first scatterplot in Exhibit 12.3 (labeled Positive Correlation) we see that the first point on the left side of the scatterplot represents an individual with a score of 2 on the marital satisfaction scale and 8 on the self-esteem scale. From examining the pattern of data points on the scatterplot, it can be seen that there is generally a positive correlation between self-esteem and marital satisfaction: the higher one's marital satisfaction score, the higher his or her self-esteem score.

As you can see in the exhibit, a straight line has been drawn though the points on the scatterplot so that one half of the points is above the line and one

EXHIBIT 12.3

Scatterplots Showing Correlation

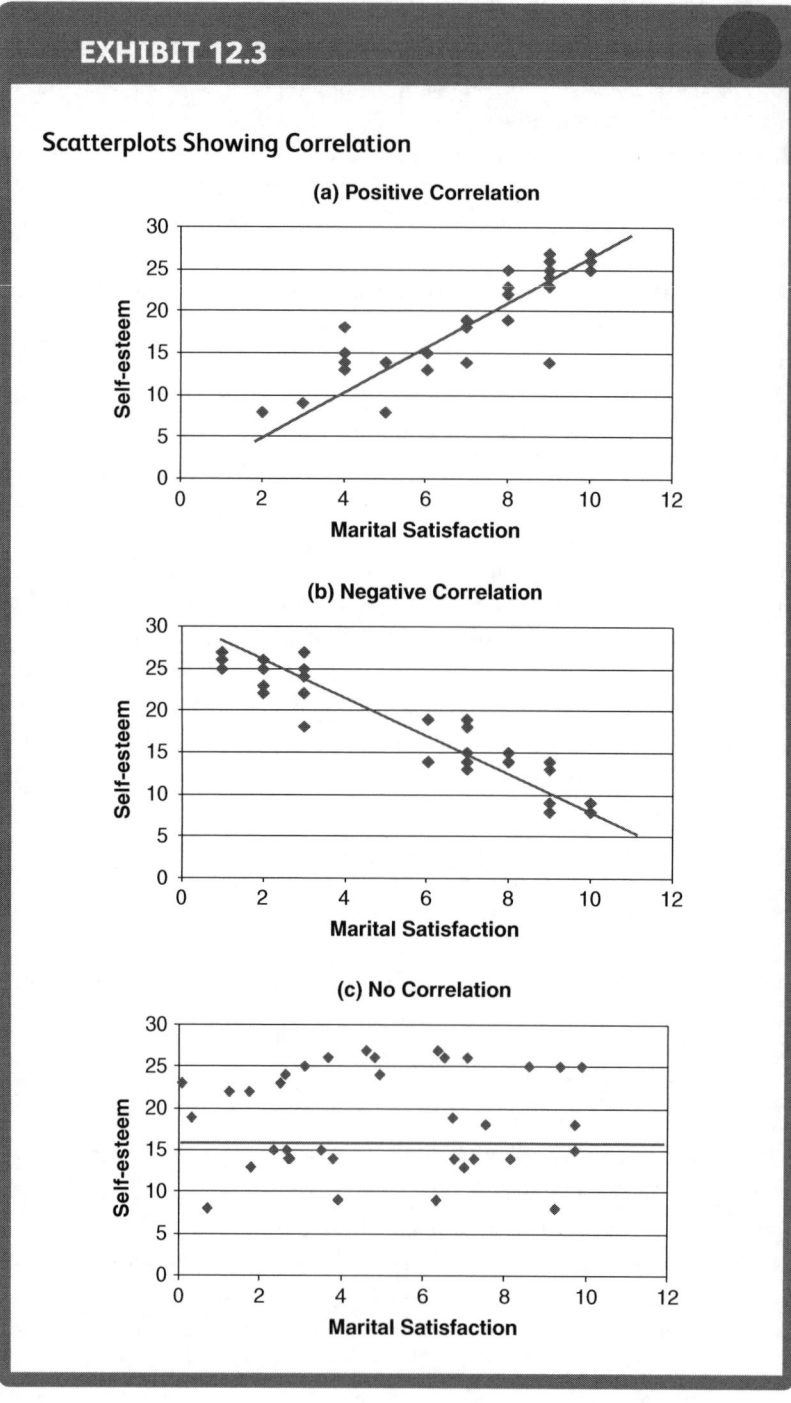

half is below it. This is called the **line of best fit**. The slope of the line varies with the type of correlation, as Exhibit 12.3 demonstrates:

- *Positive correlation* (first scatterplot): the slope of the line will rise from left to right.
- *Negative correlation* (second scatterplot): the line of best fit will slope downward from left to right.
- *Little or no correlation* (third scatterplot): the slope of the line of best fit will be approximately horizontal and the points will not form any pattern.

Determining the direction of the correlation is just one step in describing linear correlation. It is also important to test the strength of the correlation.

Curvilinear Relationships

Keep in mind that correlation is useful only when the relationship between two variables is linear. A **linear relationship** is one that continues in the same direction over the entire range of data points and can be represented by a straight line. A person's height and age, for example, have a linear relationship from birth until about age 20.

In contrast, correlation is not useful when the relationship is **curvilinear**, in which two values do not continue in the same direction over the entire range of values. The relationship between income and age over a lifetime, for example, is curvilinear, because people tend to have less money in their early years and after they retire.

You can determine whether the data are linear by using a scatterplot. If the pattern in the data reveals a consistent direction, either positive or negative, the data are linear. If the pattern curves markedly, the relationship is curvilinear, as illustrated in Exhibit 12.4. In the case of a curvilinear relationship you should not use a correlation coefficient.

Correlation Strength and Pearson's r

As we discussed in Chapter 9, a correlation coefficient is a number that represents the strength and direction of the relationship between two variables measured at the interval or ratio level. The most common statistical computation of correlation is the Pearson's Product Moment Correlation Coefficient, called **Pearson's r** for short. By convention, the correlation coefficient is expressed as a lower case, italicized **r**. It ranges from 1 (a perfect positive correlation) to -1 (a perfect negative correlation), with 0 indicating no relationship. In a perfect correlation, which seldom occurs in real life, all of the points on the scatterplot would fall on the line of best fit. In a research report the

EXHIBIT 12.4

Scatterplot Illustrating a Curvilinear Relationship

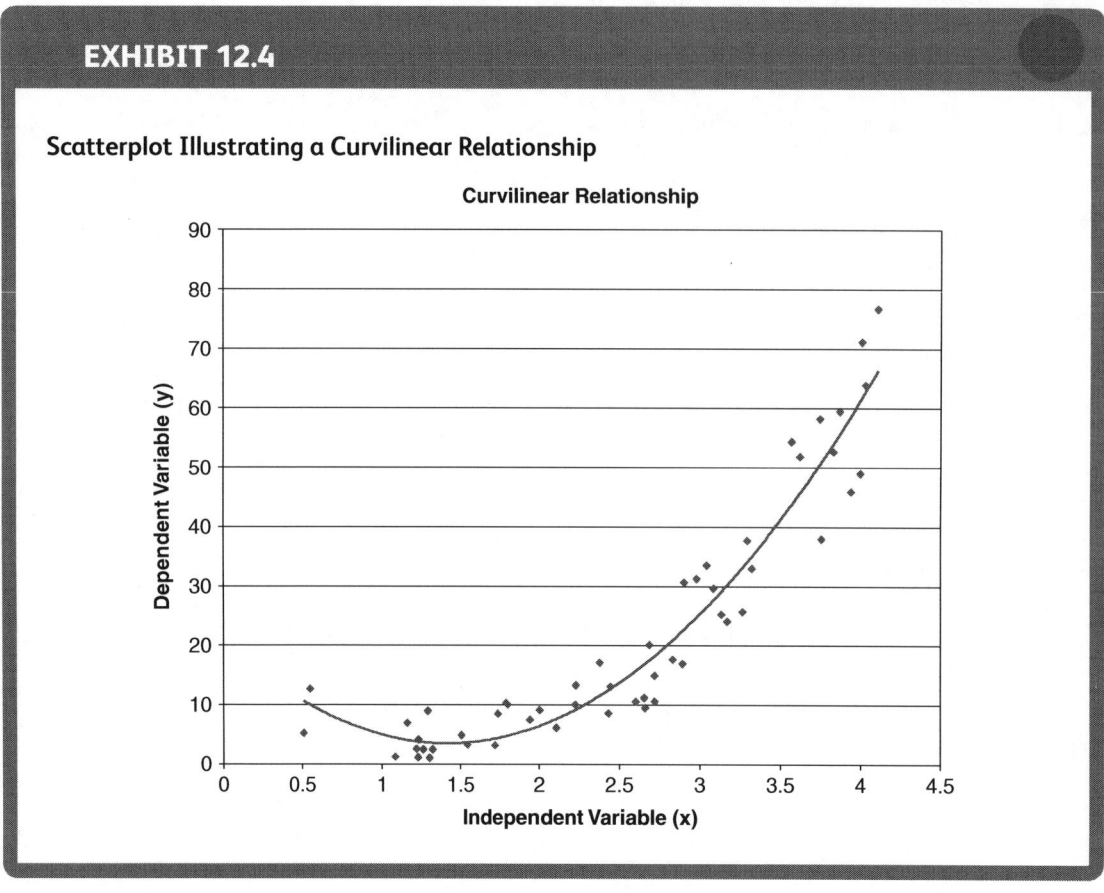

findings of a correlation would be written as follows: "In a random sample of 250 community members there was a statistically significant moderate correlation found between income and mental health ($r = .47$, $p < .02$)."

The magnitude of the correlation coefficient indicates the strength of the relationship. The sign of the correlation coefficient indicates the direction of the relationship, that is, whether it is positive or negative. Positive numbers (which do not include a plus sign) indicate a positive correlation, and negative numbers indicate a negative correlation. In the correlation between two linear variables, the correlation coefficient summarizes in one number what we can observe in a scatterplot. The correlation coefficient is a good illustration of the utility of statistics—the succinct summary of raw data.

When can you say that a correlation is strong? Social work researchers often use the guidelines in Quick Guide 7 for describing the strength of a correlation coefficient in a research report (Guilford & Fruchter, 1973).

**QUICK GUIDE 7 GUIDELINES FOR DESCRIBING THE STRENGTH
OF A CORRELATION COEFFICIENT**

Correlation Coefficient	Strength of Relationship Between Variables
Less than .20	Slight, almost negligible
.20 – .40	Low correlation; relationship definite but weak.
.40 – .70	Moderate correlation; substantial relationship
.70 – .90	High correlation; marked relationship
.90 – 1.00	Very high correlation; very dependable relationship

---

Coefficient of Determination

The strength of a correlation coefficient cannot be considered to have ratio-level properties. For instance, a correlation coefficient of .60 cannot accurately be described as being twice as strong as a correlation coefficient of .30. To compare the relative strength of correlation coefficients, we use the **coefficient of determination** (r^2). We calculate the coefficient of determination simply by squaring the correlation coefficient. For example, if $r = .50$, $r^2 = (.50 * .50). = .25$.

The coefficient of determination measures how much of the variance in one variable is explained by variance in the other variable. For example, if a student's grade point average (GPA) and score on the Scholastic Aptitude Test (SAT) produce a correlation of .50 ($r = .50$), then GPA explains 25% of the variance in SAT. The remaining 75% of the variance is explained by other factors such as motivation, number of hours studying, academic preparation, previous course work, language skills, health, knowledge of the culture, and so on.

Hypothesis Testing with Pearson's r

When you use a program such as SPSS or Excel to calculate a correlation coefficient, it also calculates a *p*-value. The general statement of null hypothesis for a test of correlation is represented by $H_o: r = 0$. The null hypothesis indicates that in the population, there is no actual relationship between the two variables.

If we set the rejection level at .05 ($p < 0.05$), we state that there is no more than a 5% chance that the correlation between the two variables is really equal to zero in the population, and we describe the findings as "statistically significant." A *p*-value greater than .05 ($p \geq .05$) suggests that there is more than a 5% chance that the true correlation in the population is equal to zero. In this case, we conclude that the correlation is not statistically significant.

Correlation Matrix

A research report that identifies more than a few correlations often presents the findings in a **correlation matrix**, in which each variable is listed in the rows down the left hand side of the matrix as well as in the columns across the top of the matrix. The correlation between any two variables is found in the cell at the intersection of the row and column.

For example, in the correlation matrix presented in Exhibit 12.5, the correlation (*r*) between age and income is .384, and the correlation between depression level and income is -684. In a research report you might read this finding as "There is a moderate inverse correlation between income and level of depression (r = -.68, p < .001)." Notice in Exhibit 12.5 that a correlation between a variable and itself is always 1.00, a perfect correlation. This is why the cells along the diagonal of a correlation matrix are always 1.00.

Crosstabulation

Another common bivariate statistical test used in social science research is **crosstabulation**. We often want to determine if there is an association between two variables measured at the nominal or ordinal level. For example, your community group is considering whether to build a new youth center, so it undertakes a survey to assess how the community members feel about this issue. In your survey of a random sample of 200 people, you find that 40% are in favor of the center and 60% are not. You would like to target an advertising

EXHIBIT 12.5

Sample Correlation Matrix

n = 120		Age	Income	Depression Level
Age	*r*	1.00		
	p			
Income	*r*	0.384	1.00	
	p	0.043		
Depression level	*r*	0.025	-0.684	1.00
	p	0.913	0.001	

EXHIBIT 12.6

Sample Frequency Distribution: Gender and Attitude Toward Youth Center

Attitude About the Youth Center		Gender
In favor	105 (52.5%)	Female = 125 (62.5%)
Not in favor	95 (47.5%)	Male = 75 (37.5%)

campaign at the 60% who are not in favor in hopes of changing their position. It might be useful to know whether being male or female affects an individual's attitude toward the youth center. In other words, does someone's attitude depend on his or her gender? In this case, attitude is called the dependent variable because it depends on the value of another variable, called the independent variable, which in this case is gender.

It is possible to describe the sample one variable at a time. For instance, you can use a frequency distribution (see Exhibit 12.6). Data in this form, however, do not tell us whether males or females differ in their attitudes regarding the center. In order to find out whether attitudes differ by gender, it is necessary to conduct bivariate analysis for the community by **crosstabulation**—tabulating one variable against the other in a table commonly referred to as a **crosstab**, or **contingency table**. The first table in Exhibit 12.7 explains the content of each cell and the second table shows the related data. For example, we can see in the first cell that 80 (64%) of 105 females have positive attitudes about the youth center.

In the crosstab, the dependent variable (attitude) is shown in the columns, and the independent variable (gender) is shown in the rows. The table could have just as easily been organized with the dependent variable in rows and the independent variable in the columns.

In order to see if women and men differ in their attitudes, we compare the percentages in the columns labeled "in favor" for females (64%) and for males (33%). From examining the table, we determine that proportionately more women than men are in favor of the new youth center. It is important, however, to know the likelihood that this finding is a result of sample error. If we believe that this is a true finding, we might target our limited advertising dollars at men in order to increase their support.

EXHIBIT 12.7

Sample Crosstabulation: Gender and Attitude Toward Youth Center

(a) Crosstabulation Table

	In Favor	Not in Favor	Total
Female	Female, in favor (% of row)	Female, not in favor (% of row)	Row total (% of total)
Male	Male, in favor (% of row)	Male, not in favor (% of row)	Row total (% of total)
Total	Column total (% of total)	Column total (% of total)	Grand total

(b) Data for Crosstabulation Table

	In Favor	Not in Favor	Total
Female	80 (0.64)	45 (0.36)	125 (0.625)
Male	25 (0.33)	50 (0.67)	75 (0.375)
Total	105 (0.525)	95 (0.475)	200

Hypothesis Testing with Chi-square

Chi-square (χ^2) is one commonly used statistic to test the association between two variables measured at the nominal or ordinal level. It is pronounced "kī" (rhymes with "pie") square. The variables tested by chi-square may have two or more categories. Many independent variables of interest to social work researchers are measured at these levels, including demographic variables such as gender, marital status, race, and type of disability. We also measure many dependent variables at the nominal or ordinal level—for example, recidivism (yes/no), level of improvement (none, some, a great deal), and type of placement (shelter, foster care, group home).

Although the chi-square test can be used with ordinal data, most statistical textbooks claim that it is preferred practice to reserve chi-square for nominal data because the test does not make use of the rank-order information in ordinal data. Nonparametric alternatives to chi-square for use with ordinal level data are the Mann-Whitney U, the Median test, the Kruskal-Wallis test, and the Kolmogorov-Smirnov test. These tests are not discussed in this chapter, but they can be found in most general statistics texts.

Chi-square is a nonparametric statistical test and thus does not assume that the data are normally distributed. It does, however, require a sufficient sample size so that most of the expected frequencies in the table are at least 5. The more categories in the data, the larger the sample size must be in order to meet this requirement.

If it makes sense theoretically, then the data for a table that is larger than 2 × 2 (2 rows × 2 columns) can be collapsed into a smaller number of rows and columns. The table cannot be any smaller than a 2 × 2, however. For example, consider a study that examines the relationship between *satisfaction with an after-school program* and *grade level*. The frequencies for each combination of variable values are presented in Exhibit 12.8.

Expected Frequencies and Observed Frequencies

An assumption of the chi-square test is that no more than 20% of the cells will have an expected frequency of less than 5. **Expected frequencies** are those numbers that we expect to observe in each cell if there is no association between the variables. We calculate expected frequencies by multiplying the row total

---

EXHIBIT 12.8

Sample Crosstabulation: Grade Level by Satisfaction with After-School Program

	High Satisfaction	Low Satisfaction	Total
7th Grade	8	2	10
8th Grade	6	5	11
9th Grade	3	5	8
10th Grade	2	3	5
Total	19	15	34

with the column total for any one cell and then dividing by the total N. Programs such as SPSS automatically calculate this information for us.

In Exhibit 12.8, because the number of 9th graders and 10th graders is small, we might collapse the data by combining 7th and 8th graders into a "Junior Students" category and 9th and 10th graders into a "Senior Students" category. Theoretically this move makes sense because grades 7 and 8 are normally considered middle school or junior high, whereas grades 9 and 10 are considered high school.

In the absence of a theoretical justification we must avoid collapsing the data simply to meet the assumptions of the chi-square test. Other statistical tests—for example, the Fisher exact test—are useful alternatives to the chi-square when the expected frequencies are small.

The table in Exhibit 12.9 combines 7th- and 8th-grade students and 9th- and 10th-grade students into two categories. Now each of the four main cells in this 2 × 2 table has an expected frequency of at least 5. Comparing the percentages in the columns, we see that 67% of junior students report high satisfaction with the after-school program, compared to only 38% of senior school students.

The p-value associated with the chi-square statistic indicates whether the observed frequencies differ from those we would expect if there were no association between the variables. In addition, it indicates the likelihood that the observed association is the result of sampling error. In effect, the chi-square statistic uses mathematics to do what we do on an intuitive basis. For example, if we tossed a coin 100 times, we would expect to get 50 heads, the expected

EXHIBIT 12.9

Sample Crosstab Illustrating Collapsed Categories, Frequencies, and Row Percentages: Student Grade Level by Satisfaction with the After-School Program

	High Satisfaction	Low Satisfaction	Total
Junior Students	14 (0.67)	7 (0.22)	21 (100%)
Senior Students	5 (0.38)	8 (0.62)	13 (100%)
Total	19 (0.56)	15 (0.37)	34 (100%)

frequency. If the result was only 48 heads, the **observed frequency**, we might not think that it was an unlikely result or much different from what we expected. However, if we observed only 3 heads, we might think that the observed frequency was much different than the expected frequency and was a very unlikely result.

Similarly, consider the example of a social work research project that tests the effectiveness of two different interventions to prevent further child abuse. Intervention A uses in-home coaching, and Intervention B uses group parent education classes. If the success rate—defined as no additional reports of child abuse for six months—for Method A is 70%, you would expect the success rate for method B to be 70% (expected frequency) if there was no difference in the treatment outcomes. If Intervention B, however, has a success rate of only 30%, you might conclude that there is a meaningful difference between the two treatments because the observed frequency (30%) is much different than the expected frequency (70%).

As with other tests of statistical inference, we predetermine a rejection level and then test the null hypothesis at that level. In the case of this example:

■ Null hypothesis (H_0): There is no difference between Home Visitation and Parent Education in a subsequent report of child abuse at six months post intervention.
■ Research hypothesis (H_1): There is a difference between Home Visitation and Parent Education in a subsequent report of child abuse at six months post intervention.
■ One-tailed hypothesis (H_1) (if you believe that one intervention is better): Intervention A is associated with a lower rate of reported child abuse than Intervention B at six months post intervention.

Chi-square Statistic and Degrees of Freedom

An additional value that helps to read the results of a chi-square analysis is **degrees of freedom** (*df*), which represents the number of values in the final calculation of a statistic that are free to vary. *Degrees of freedom* are calculated from the size of the sample. This section will focus on reading the results of a chi-square analysis and on the meaning of those results.

In the example of the child abuse prevention program, 50 parents were randomly assigned to either Group A or Group B. The data were analyzed using SPSS and produced the 2 × 2 crosstab table shown in Exhibit 12.10. (To compute a chi-square statistic in SPSS or Excel use the step-by-step tutorial found on the course web site.)

The numbers included in the table are the observed frequencies and the associated percentages. The organization of the variables in the crosstab permits

EXHIBIT 12.10

Sample Crosstabulation: Parent Intervention Group by Success of Intervention

		SUCCESS		TOTAL
		NO	YES	
Group A	Count	8	18	26
	% within Group	30.8%	69.2%	100%
Group B	Count	19	5	24
	% within Group	79.2%	20.8%	100%
Total	Count	27	24	50
	% within Group	54%	46%	100.0%

us to compare the success rate between the rows. From the table we see the following results:

- Group A has a success rate of 69.2% ($n = 26$) compared with only 20.8% ($n = 24$) for Group B.
- Looking at the bottom row, both groups combined have a success rate of 46%.

Researchers generally produce crosstabulation tables and calculate the chi-square statistic with the help of a statistical program such as SPSS or Excel. The table in Exhibit 12.11 presents SPSS output for the chi-square test of the data in Exhibit 12.10. It allows us to determine if the results are statistically significant at the preset rejection level of .05. The calculation we are interested in is shown in the top row that reads "Pearson Chi-square." The columns to the right show the output used to determine whether the chi-square test finds an association between the type of intervention and program success.

- Value (of Chi-Square) = 11.768. This is the value computed using a formula based on the difference between the observed and the expected values and the degrees of freedom. The larger the value of the chi-square statistic, the greater the association between the variables.

EXHIBIT 12.11

Chi-Square Tests of the Success Rate for Two Interventions

	Value	df	Asymp. Sig. (2-Sided)	Exact Sig. (2-Sided)	Exact Sig. (1-Sided)
Pearson Chi-square	11.768[1]	1	0.001		
Likelihood Ratio	12.334	1	0.000		
Fisher's Exact Test				0.001	0.001
Linear-by-Linear Association	11.533	1	0.001		
N of Valid Cases	50				

[1] 0 cells (0.0%) have expected count less than 5. The minimum expected count is 11.04.

- Degrees of freedom (df) = 1. Df is computed from the number of rows minus one (R–1) multiplied by the number of columns minus 1 (C–1). Using the example shown in Exhibit 12.10, that number is 2–1 × 2–1, or 1 × 2 = 1. For any 2 × 2 table, the degrees of freedom is equal to (2–1)(2–1) = 1.
- Asymp. Sig. 2 sided: = .001. This number is the p-value for rejecting the null hypothesis in a two-tailed test.

The formula for computing the chi-square statistic and a more detailed discussion of degrees of freedom can be found in many statistics books and on the internet.

In a research report these results might be written as follows: "The association between the type of intervention and a subsequent report of child abuse at 6-months post treatment was statistically significant ($\chi^2(1)$ 11.8, p < .001). Approximately two-thirds (69.2%) of the 26 parents in Intervention A had no further report of child abuse, compared with only 20.8% of the 24 parents in Intervention B. Intervention A appears to be more successful than Intervention B in reducing further child abuse." The way to read the formula in the first sentence of this description is "Chi-square with one degree of freedom equals 11.8; the probability that this result is due to sample error is less than 0.1 percent."

The following Case-in-Point describes an example of the use of Chi-square to test hypotheses.

CASE-IN-POINT: USER DIFFERENCES IN AN ONLINE RAPE CRISIS HOTLINE

As part of their 2011 annual evaluation, RAINN wished to examine differences by gender in the experiences of their users. Among other variables, RAINN collected information from counselors about the gender of the users of the online hotline and the timeframe of assault. Using crosstabulation, the evaluation found that with regard to timeframe, of 924 sessions, females (27%) are more likely than males (16%) to deal with issues within the past month, and males (26%) are more likely than females (13%) to deal with issues occurring more than 5 years ago. (χ^2 (9) 29.02, p < .001). (This statistical expression should be read as: *Chi-square with nine degrees of freedom equals 29.02. The probability that this result is due to sample error is less than .1%*).

RAINN prepared counselors to deal with crisis intervention and short-term issues related to rape. These findings are important because they highlight the need for counselor training to also deal with long-term unresolved rape issues, especially for men. Further research is needed to better understand the similarities and differences in the rape experiences and help-seeking behavior of women and men.

In considering this report it is necessary to keep in mind that:

- This is an exploratory study at one point in time.
- The representativeness of the sample in terms of rape victims is unknown.
- The data are based on the counselor's impression of gender from written transcripts, and not the user's statement of gender.

---

t -Tests: Comparing the Difference Between Two Means

As we have seen, crosstabulation enables us to measure the relationship between nominal and ordinal variables. However, social work researchers are often interested in differences both between and within groups that are measured at the interval and ratio levels. Regarding differences between groups, we may ask: Is sixteen weeks of services more effective than 10 weeks? Or, do men and women differ in their benefit from parenting classes? Within-group differences are conveyed by questions such as: Do people behave differently at the end of an intervention program than they did at the beginning? A **t-test** is used to assess group differences that are expressed in either interval or ratio data.

The t-test is a parametric statistic that assesses (a) whether group differences are greater than what we would expect based on chance and (b) whether sample error might account for the observed differences. Because the t-test is a parametric statistic, the assumptions of normality in the population and random sampling apply. The t-test, however, is a robust test, so it can be used when the data vary somewhat from a normal distribution. If the data are not normally distributed, we could consider a nonparametric test or some sort of transformation of the data. These topics are covered in more advanced statistical textbooks.

There are three different kinds of t-tests discussed below, each of which has a particular use:

- **Independent samples t-test:** compares the means of two independent groups. It assesses the likelihood that the means of two groups are equal or that they come from the same population. For example, an independent t-test would be used to test whether a treatment and a control group differed in their level of depression as measured by a depression scale following an intervention program. In addition to the assumptions of normality and random selection, the groups must be independent; that is, each member can belong to only one of the categories of the nominal level variable (to only one group).

- **Paired samples t-test**, also known as **dependent samples t-test**: measures changes in the same individuals at two points in time. We would use a paired samples t-test to compare the pretest and posttest scores of the participants in a program designed to teach assertiveness skills to a group of shy teens. The test is based not on the overall group mean and variance but on the difference between the pretest and posttest scores for each individual.

- **One sample t-test:** estimates the likelihood that a single sample comes from a given population. In other words, is the sample typical of the population? We would use a one sample t-test to test whether a group of children in a specific neighborhood had health problems similar to other children their age in the population.

At the course web site you can find step-by-step tutorials in computing the independent samples t-test, paired samples t-test, and one sample t-test in SPSS and Excel. Below are more detailed descriptions of each test.

Independent Samples t-Test

The independent samples t-test compares the mean scores and the degree of variation on the dependent variable in two independent groups. (The calculation of the t-test can be found in many statistics books and is beyond the scope of this chapter.) The degrees of freedom (df) are also considered in the calculation. In the case of the independent samples t-test, degrees of freedom are equal to $n - 2$, and as such they are a function of the sample size. Statistical programs will produce the t-statistic, degrees of freedom, and the corresponding p-value. As with other tests of statistical inference, a rejection level is specified in advance of conducting the test, usually .05. The following example illustrates the use and interpretation of the independent samples t-test.

A study of satisfaction among consumers of mental health services in Pennsylvania used two different methods of survey administration: telephone and in-person. The administrators wondered, "Do these two methods produce the same results?" In both methods the interviewer read a list of 25 items to consumers and recorded their responses. The items covered areas such as satisfaction with appointment times, relationship with the therapist, and knowledge of grievance procedures. For example, one item was: "My service provider spends enough time with me."

The interviewer asked consumers to rate their level of agreement with each item from 1 (strongly disagree) to 5 (strongly agree). The researcher then summed the item scores to produce a total satisfaction score that could range from 25 to 125.

The null hypothesis was that there is no difference in reported satisfaction between those consumers who were interviewed by telephone and those who were interviewed in person. Conversely, the research hypothesis was that there is a difference between the two groups in reported satisfaction. Because the independent variable (method of interview) is measured at the nominal level with only two categories and the dependent variable (satisfaction) is an interval measure, the researcher used an independent samples t-test to test the null hypothesis.

The results are summarized in Exhibit 12.12. The first table shows a difference in the means of the groups (118.5 and 108.1). It appears that consumers surveyed in person averaged higher satisfaction scores than those surveyed by telephone.

The second table in Exhibit 12.12 is part of the SPSS output. It indicates that there was a statistically significant mean difference in satisfaction based on the method of survey administration. The results would be reported as, (t (72) 2.64, $p < .01$). Note that:

- The t-test, or t, is 2.64.
- The degrees of freedom, or df, is 72, calculated as $N - 2$.
- The probability that the result is due to sample error or chance is $p < .01$.

How should the social work researcher interpret these findings? The following are all viable explanations.

1. There are real differences in consumer satisfaction based on the interview method. The agency should use only one interview method.
2. There are real differences between interview methods. In-person interviews are likely to show higher satisfaction because of social desirability;

EXHIBIT 12.12

Sample Independent Samples t-Test: Satisfaction with Services by Survey Method

Consumer Satisfaction for Telephone Versus In-Person Interviewing

	Method of Interview	N	Mean	Standard Deviation
Total Satisfaction	In-person	14	118.5	3.0
	Phone	60	108.1	3.3

Independent Samples t-Test

		t-Test For Equality of Means		
		t	df	Sig. (2-Tailed)
Total Satisfaction	Equal variances assumed	2.641	72	0.01

that is, people are afraid to be critical in-person. The agency should only use telephone interviews.

3. There are real differences between interview methods. These differences might result from the ways in which the survey was administered. The agency should investigate whether the interviewers administer the questions the same in-person as they do on the telephone.

4. Even though the mean differences were statistically significant, the average amount of difference was small and relatively meaningless. Nothing need be done.

5. The result could be a Type I error, that is, a result of sample error. The study should be replicated to see if the results are the same.

Which of these interpretations would you support, and why?

Paired Samples t-Test

A paired samples t-test is used to determine whether there is a statistically significant difference between the mean values of the same measurement on each person made under two different conditions. The test is based on the differences in scores for each person at two points in time. As with the independent samples t-test, statistical programs will produce the t-statistic and *p*-value and calculate the degrees of freedom. The null hypothesis is that the difference in the mean values is zero. The research hypothesis is that the difference in the means is not zero. The following example illustrates the use and interpretation of the paired sample t-test.

A preliminary study of foster youth aged 7 to 17 years found that they were less likely to learn computer skills than other youth of comparable age (Finn, Kerman, & leCornec, 2003). In response to this finding, Casey Family Services began a unique program in which they gave foster families a computer and Internet connection to improve the children's computer skills. The study involved a pretest in which the participants rated their own computer skills on a scale ranging from 1—very few or no computer skills—to 5—very skilled. Approximately one year later the evaluators administered a posttest using the same measure. The results from the analysis of the paired means are presented in Exhibit 12.13.

The null hypothesis is that there is no difference between the pretest and posttest scores for the youths. The research hypothesis is that there is a difference. The mean pretest score—2.595—is located on the top row of the SPSS

EXHIBIT 12.13

Sample Paired (or Dependent) Samples t-Test: Changes in Perceived Computer Skills of Foster Youth

	Mean	N	Std. Deviation	Std. Error Mean
Pretest: Rate computer skills	2.595	37	1.1170	0.1836
Posttest: Rate computer skills	3.459	37	0.90045	0.1480

	Paired Differences					t	df	Sig. (2 Tailed)
	Mean	Std. Deviation	Std. Error	95% Interval of Confidence				
				lower	Upper			
Pretest: Rate computer skills Posttest: Rate computer skills	-0.8649	0.85512	0.14058	-1.1499	-0.57975	-6.152	36	0.000

output, and the mean for the posttest—found on the second row—is 3.459. The results of the t-test are written, (t(36) 6.15, p = .00). Note in the SPSS output that the p-value is written as .000. This is due to rounding the actual value. When the p-value is .00, an equal sign (=) is used since the probability cannot be less than zero. The findings indicate a statistically significant increase in the ratings of foster care youths regarding their computer skills between pretest and posttest.

We can drop the minus sign from the t-test statistic in reporting. We always check the statistical output to verify the direction of the mean difference. For instance, did the youths' ratings of their computer skills increase or decrease from pretest to posttest? There have been cases in which researchers reported a certain direction of change that was consistent with their expectations, when the data suggested a statistically significant finding in the opposite direction.

How should we interpret these results? Consider the following possibilities.

1. The youth improved their computer skills after one year in the program. This is one indicator of program success.
2. The result is a Type I error and no real difference exists. This is always possible. The p-value, however, suggests that this is highly unlikely.
3. The youth have come to like the staff over a year in the program and gave higher rating just to "be nice." Thus, the difference in the scores is a result of social desirability and not real program change.
4. Some other factor accounts for the change in scores. For example, the schools may have begun a new computer training initiative just as the program was beginning. Without a control group, this cannot be ruled out.

How would you interpret the findings? Can you think of alternative explanations for the results?

One Sample t-Test

We use the one sample t-test to compare the mean of a variable measured at the interval or ratio level in a sample with the known or estimated mean in the population. This test helps us to evaluate whether the sample is typical, or representative, of the population. The known mean of the population is called the test value. The null hypothesis is that there is no difference between the sample mean and the test value. The research hypothesis is that there is a difference between the means.

For example, we know that the mean IQ in the United States is 100. We would like to determine if the IQ in a sample of 10 youths is different than the population mean. A one sample t-test using SPSS produced the results in Exhibit 12.14.

EXHIBIT 12.14

Sample One Sample t-Test: Mean IQ of Youths in Sample Compared with Mean IQ of Population

One-Sample Statistics

	N	Mean	Std. Deviation	Std. Error Mean
IQ	10	106.00	10.274	3.249

One-Sample Test

	Test Value = 100					
	t	df	Sig. (2-tailed)	Mean Difference	95% Confidence Interval of the Difference	
					Lower	Upper
IQ	1.847	9	0.098	6.00	-1.35	13.35

The table indicates that the mean IQ for the 10 youths is 106, which is slightly higher than the national average. The t-test, however, indicates that the difference is not statistically significant at the .05 level (t (9) 1.85, $p < .098$). Therefore, we cannot reject the null hypothesis. Instead we must conclude that there is no difference in IQ between the youths as a group and other youths in the population. Because the one sample t-test is based on the mean and standard deviation, it is possible that some of the youths have IQ scores that are significantly above or below the test value. As a group, however, they do not.

How should we interpret these results? The following are possibilities to consider.

1. There is no difference between these youths as a group and other youths in the population.
2. The sample size is small. If we had set the rejection level at .10, these youths would show a significantly higher IQ than the population.
3. The results may be due to sample error, especially given the small sample size.
4. Whether or not the youths differ significantly in IQ, the difference, 6 points, is relatively small and without much meaning.

How would you interpret the results?

Analysis of Variance

One-way Analysis of Variance (ANOVA) is a parametric statistical test that compares the means of more than two groups. For example, we might wish to test three treatment conditions or analyze certain behaviors among four different socioeconomic groups. In this way ANOVA is very similar to the independent samples t-test. In addition, it has the same requirements, except for the number of groups. In fact, an ANOVA calculated to assess the difference between two groups provides results consistent with the t-test.

ANOVA produces an F statistic that serves the same purpose as the t value. The computation of F can be found in advanced statistics textbooks. A statistical program such as SPSS will produce the F statistic, degrees of freedom, and the p-value needed for hypothesis testing. To compute a one-way ANOVA in SPSS or Excel use the step-by-step tutorials found on the course web site.

The null hypothesis in the ANOVA test is that the means of the dependent measure do not differ between the groups. The research hypothesis is that there is a statistically significant difference between at least two of the group means. The one-way ANOVA tests the mean differences between each of the groups as well as the difference between the mean of each group and the *grand mean* (or overall mean) of the combined groups.

The F statistic indicates only that there is a statistically significant difference among the groups. **Post-hoc analysis** compares the means of each of the groups two at a time in order to determine which groups differ. If the F statistic is associated with a p-value that is less than the rejection level, typically .05, then the means of at least two of the groups differ at a level that is statistically significant. If the p-value of the F statistic is greater than .05, then none of the groups will be significantly different, and the post-hoc analysis is unnecessary. Many post-hoc tests are available, some of which are included in SPSS. A full discussion of post-hoc analysis can be found in many statistics texts.

The following example illustrates the use of one-way ANOVA. A study examined the leadership style of three categories of agency personnel: administrators, supervisors, and direct service workers. Thus, Agency Personnel is the independent variable, measured at the nominal level. High scores on the dependent variable, the *Leadership Scale*, indicate a preference for authoritarian leadership. Exhibit 12.15 was produced using the ANOVA function in SPSS.

The result would be written: $F (3,294)$ 4.01, $p < .008$. The numbers in the parentheses are the degrees of freedom, calculated from the number of categories of the independent variable (3), and N minus the number of categories (297–3). Since the p-value of F is less than .05, the results suggest that there is a difference in leadership style among administrators, supervisors, and direct service workers.

Having accumulated these data, we need to employ post-hoc analysis to determine which of the groups actually differ. Exhibit 12.16 shows the

EXHIBIT 12.15

Sample One-Way Analysis of Variance (ANOVA): Differences in Leadership Style Among Agency Personnel

ANOVA

Leadership

	Sum of Squares	df	Mean Square	F	Sig.
Between Groups	1355.072	3	451.691	4.051	0.008
Within Groups	32779.559	29.4	111.495		
Total	34134.631	29.7			

EXHIBIT 12.16

Sample Post-Hoc Analysis Comparing the Means of More Than Two Groups: Differences in Leadership Style Among Agency Personnel

Multiple Comparisons

Dependent Variable Leadership Least Significant Difference

(I) Primary Job Responsibility	(J) Primary Job Responsibility	Mean Difference (I – J)	Std. Error	Sig	95% confidence Interval	
					Lower Bound	Upper Bound
Direct Services	Supervision	-4.938*	1.925	0.011	-8.73	-1.15
	Administration	-5.159*	1.949	0.009	-8.99	-1.32
	Other	2.566	2.912	0.379	-8.30	3.17
Supervision	Supervision	4.938*	1.925	0.011	1.15	8.73
	Administration	-0.221	2.543	0.931	-5.23	4.78
	Other	2.371	3.339	0.478	-4.20	8.94
Administration	Supervision	5.159*	1.949	0.009	1.32	8.99
	Administration	0.221	2.543	0.931	4.78	5.23
	Other	2.592	3.353	0.440	-4.01	9.19

*Group differences that are statistically different at the 0.05 level.

post-hoc analysis using the Least Significant Difference (LSD) test, one of several post-hoc tests available in SPSS. Note that the mean difference between groups is presented in the second column. For example, the mean difference between direct service workers and supervisors is 4.94, which is slightly less than the mean difference of 5.16 between direct service workers and administrators. In contrast, the mean difference between supervisors and administrators is much smaller: .22. The *p*-value is given in the column labeled "Sig."

What can we conclude from this study? The following are possibilities to consider.

1. Social workers in different positions have different preferences for leadership style. The statistically significant differences are between direct service workers and administrators and between direct service workers and supervisors, but not between administrators and supervisors.
2. Given the *p*-value of .008, it is unlikely that the result is from sample error.
3. Although the differences are statistically significant, they may not be meaningful. All groups may have a preference for non-authoritarian leadership, but the preference of direct service workers is stronger. To know if the results are meaningful, we would need to know the norms for leadership scores and whether outcomes in the real world conform to a particular level of leadership score.
4. The results indicate that more research is needed. While there is a difference in leadership style preference, we don't know why this preference exists or whether this difference has consequences in the real world.

Six Common Pitfalls to Avoid in Significance Testing

You can use the information in this section whether you are engaged in producing research or critiquing research to be alert to six common pitfalls in statistical significance testing.

Equating Statistical Significance with Importance

Statistical significance is not synonymous with importance. We may find, for example, that, compared to children living in a group home arrangement, more foster children prefer chocolate over vanilla ice cream. Moreover, the difference is statistically significant at the $p < .05$ level. Nevertheless, that finding is not very important in terms of helping us provide services. Ultimately, we must judge the importance of the results.

Similarly, an alcohol treatment program may find that participants reduce their alcohol consumption from 25 to 20 drinks per day. Although the difference may be statistically significant, it has little meaning in terms of real-life health consequences.

Inferring the Magnitude of the Results from the Size of the p-Value

When the sample size is large, even small differences and weak relationships will be statistically significant. Sometimes even small differences may be important; other times, however, they will not. Therefore, we must be careful not to automatically interpret a small p-value as a strong relationship between variables or a large difference between independent or related groups. A weak correlation is still a weak correlation, whether the associated p-value is .1 or .0001.

As we mentioned earlier in the chapter, the size of the p-value is related to the size of the sample, regardless of the strength of the relationship. The magnitude of the result should be described through the coefficient of determination for r, the presentation of mean differences and standard deviations for t and F, and percentage differences for X^2.

In addition to these techniques, the researcher can calculate a statistic known as the **effect size**. Calculating the effect size (ES) statistic allows the researcher to compare the magnitude of effects across studies. Effect size can be calculated with the formula: *(Experimental group Mean − Control group Mean) / Control group standard deviation*. For example, in a study to increase self-esteem, the mean for the Experimental group is 50 and standard deviation is 2.2. The mean for the Control group is 46 and standard deviation is 2. Using the formula for ES, (50-46)/2 = 2. An ES of 0 would indicate no effect (no difference between the groups). ES scores greater than 0 indicate greater change in the experimental group than in the control group.

The ES can be used to compare studies using different methodologies. For example, a second study of self-esteem using a different intervention and different measure for self-esteem was found to have an effect size of .65. If both these studies were methodologically sound, the ES indicates a stronger effect for the first study (ES=2) than for the second study (ES=.65). Although both studies were found to show significant improvement in the experimental group at the .05 level, social workers using evidence-based practice would give greater consideration to the first method rather than the second when considering which self-esteem program to use in their practice since it has a stronger effect size. For further explanation of effect size see an advanced statistic textbook such as Cohen (1977).

Mistaking Rejection of Null Hypothesis for Confirmation of Research Hypothesis

Rejection of the null hypothesis simply means that it is unlikely that the observed findings are the result of sample error. The null hypothesis deals only with chance as a possible explanation for the findings. It does not rule out other sources of error in measurement or interpretation. Thus, it does not lead to blind confirmation of the research hypothesis.

Support for the research hypothesis must also take into account the research design, the quality of the measurement and data collection, theoretical support, and the findings of related research.

Fishing for Statistically Significant Relationships

Beware of the study that reports a large number of statistical tests. When the rejection level is set at .05, 1 in every 20 statistical tests (5%) is statistically significant by chance alone. In a study with many variables, if 100 statistical tests are computed, 5 of those are likely to produce false results, and there is no way of telling "real" differences from chance.

To avoid this pitfall, plan statistical analyses in advance based on theoretical considerations, and then run only the minimum number of tests necessary.

Inferring Causation from Statistical Significance

It is important to understand that statistically significant results do not imply a cause-and-effect relationship. For example, if we find a positive correlation between self-esteem and marital satisfaction, we cannot conclude that one causes the other. We know only that the two variables tend to vary together.

To prove causation we must use a true experimental design in which threats to interval validity and extraneous variables are controlled.

Failing to Consider Statistical Power

Statistical power relates to the ability of a statistical test to detect a true relationship when one exists—in other words, to correctly reject the null hypothesis. Statistical power analysis involves calculating the probability of committing a Type II error based on the type of test, the sample size, and an estimate of the strength of the relationship.

Significantly, some statistical tests are considered more powerful than others because of the way they are calculated. For instance, some tests make use of each value in the data set for their calculation rather than relying on summary statistics. Another factor in the power of a test is level of measurement.

Parametric statistics, for example, are more powerful than nonparametric statistics because they rely on variables measured at the interval or ratio level rather than categorical data.

Because statistical power is related to the type of statistical test, there are multiple statistical power tables. For example, if we were using Pearson's r, we would consult a statistical power table for linear correlation. Thanks to pioneering work by Jacob Cohen (1977), social workers can make a judgment about the power of a statistical test by consulting the appropriate statistical power table in his book.

Ideally, researchers should consider statistical power during the planning stages of a research study so that they can ensure that they have an adequate sample size to correctly reject the null hypothesis if a true relationship exists. If researchers do not consider statistical power during the planning stages, then they should conduct a statistical power analysis following any study that failed to reject the null hypothesis. Performing this analysis allows researchers to comment on the adequacy of the sample size, given the magnitude of the relationship. Many studies that report null findings fail to consider the impact of sample size on the significance of the results.

CONVENTIONS FOR REPORTING STATISTICAL FINDINGS

The reporting of statistical results tends to follow certain conventions, some of which are summarized here:

- It is customary to include the symbol for the statistical test, for example, r, t, F or X^2, along with the actual value achieved (such as, $r = .60$), and the degrees of freedom if applicable to the test. The degrees of freedom are placed in parentheses after the test symbol, for example, t (24) 5.11, $p < .001$. Note the statistical symbols that are italicized and the use of parentheses and punctuation.
- The value of the statistic is reported to two decimal places, and the entire p-value is presented.
- The rejection level used to test the null hypothesis should also be reported. If the same rejection level is used for all analyses, it should be reported near the beginning of the results section—for example: *A rejection level of .05 was used for all analyses*. Rejection levels are also correctly referred to as *alpha levels*.
- It is also important to explain whether the reported p-value is associated with a one-tail or two-tailed test of the hypothesis.

QUICK GUIDE 8 SUMMARY OF SELECT BIVARIATE STATISTICAL TESTS

Statistical Test	Research Question	Level of Measurement
Pearson's correlation (r)	Is there a relationship between two variables? *Is there a relationship between income and longevity?*	Two variables, each measured at the interval or ratio level.
Chi-square (χ^2)	Do observed values differ from those expected if there is no association between the variables? *Do men and women differ in their support of group homes in their community?*	Independent variable: nominal or ordinal. Dependent variable: nominal or ordinal. Typically at least one of the variables is nominal. Not a preferred test for ordinal data.
Independent samples t-test (t)	Do two groups come from the same population? Do their means differ? *Is intervention A better than intervention B in reducing the number of missed school days?*	Independent variable: measured at the nominal level with only two categories. Dependent variable: interval or ratio.
Dependent sample t-test (t)	Does the average value of two measurements of the same dependent variable differ? *Do the pretest and posttest scores differ?*	Independent variable: nominal. Dependent variable: interval or ratio.
One-sample t-test (t)	Does a single sample come from a specific population? Is a sample typical of the population? *Is the level of ADHD in the community similar to the level in the rest of the state?*	The test value is measured at the interval or ratio level.
One-way analysis of variance (ANOVA) (F)	Are the means equal, or do the means of three or more groups differ? *Is there a difference between 7th, 8th and 9th grade in number of missed school days?*	Independent variable: nominal with more than two categories. Dependent variable: interval or ratio.

■ In addition to reporting the statistical significance of the findings, comment on the importance of the findings, for example, by calculating and interpreting a coefficient of determination for r, and presenting means and standard deviations for t and F.

Additional information on reporting research is provided in Chapter 13 and in style manuals such as the *Publication Manual of the American Psychological Association* (APA, 2009). Different style guides will use slightly different conventions. It is important to be consistent, and if writing for publication to check the style of the journal in which you would like to publish your manuscript.

CONCLUSION

As consumers of social work research, we need to understand and critically assess the statistical information presented in research articles and other forms of research presentations. In addition, the credibility of your own research will depend on your ability to use scientific methods and the appropriate use of statistical procedures when conducting your research and describing your findings. Stating and testing hypotheses using the correct statistical tests for the types of questions you wish to examine and the types of data used to answer the questions are integral to the development of evidence-based practice. Quick Guide 8 summarizes the six statistical tests reviewed in this chapter, provides an example of the type of question that the test is suitable to address, and lists the level of measurement of the variables that each test requires.

Statistical tests when used correctly are wonderfully useful. When applied in conjunction with appropriate research designs, they tell us the likelihood that a finding is "real" rather than based on chance. They allow us to test our theories and notions about what is important and what works in social work practice, effectively allowing us to advance our knowledge base. They allow us to present evidence that others can understand and attempt to replicate.

On the other hand, the computer adage GIGO (garbage in, garbage out) applies to statistical tests. It is especially important to remember this adage when evaluating conclusions about social problems or program effectiveness based on statistics. Others who do not share social work's goals may seek to use statistics to misrepresent the facts or draw unfounded conclusions. Knowledge of statistics empowers social workers to critique the evidence presented by others in a rational and professional manner.

Statistics do not exist in a vacuum. They are based on data from research projects and program evaluations related to social work practice, however imperfect. The next chapter discusses how to present research findings in various formats.

MAIN POINTS

■ The choice of statistical test will depend largely on the level at which the variables to be considered are measured. Other requirements of statistical tests can involve normality—how well the data in the population conform to the normal distribution, random sampling, and sample size.

■ Parametric statistics are used to analyze data that meet certain assumptions including normal distribution in the population from which the sample was drawn, random sampling, and at least one of the two variables being considered must be measured at the interval or ratio level. Common parametric statistical tests include Pearson's r, the t-test, and ANOVA.

■ Nonparametric statistics represent a good alternative to parametric statistics when the assumptions of parametric tests cannot be met, or when the sample size is very small. For instance, when both variables in a bivariate analysis are measured at the nominal or ordinal levels we have no choice but to use nonparametric statistics. Chi-square is a popular example of a nonparametric test.

■ Tests of statistical significance provide us with the likelihood that relationships between variables or differences between means are the result of sample error. They are a test of the null hypothesis, and not a test of the research hypothesis.

■ Hypotheses are rejected or supported on the basis of statistical significance testing, as well as through the replication of research studies. Both statistical significance testing and replication are important ways of advancing the knowledge base of social work.

■ Bivariate statistics consider the relationship between two variables at a time. This is in contrast to univariate statistics that focus on one variable at a time, and multivariate statistics that are used to analyze more than two variables at a time.

■ The informed social work researcher will be careful to avoid the following errors in conducting and interpreting tests of statistical significance, for example: equating statistical significance with importance, conducting "fishing" expeditions to try find statistically significant results, inferring causation on the basis of statistically significant results, and failing to consider statistical power.

■ The power of a test to correctly accept or reject the null hypothesis is based on a number of factors including the type of test used, sample size, and the level of measurement of the data. Researchers should make certain to examine statistical power when the null hypothesis is accepted.

■ There are conventions in reporting tests of statistical significance that include always reporting the test, the test statistic, the degrees of freedom if applicable, and the exact p-value available in the statistical output when a computer program such as SPSS is used in the calculation.

EXERCISES

Note: To expand your repertoire of research skills, we encourage you to use both SPSS and Excel to complete the practice exercises using the Riverton Youth Survey and RAINN data, which are found at www.routledgesw.com/cases.

1. Using the *Riverton: A Community Conundrum* case, develop a health-related research question and bivariate hypothesis based the Riverton Youth Survey questions. What statistical test would you use to answer your question and test your hypothesis? Justify your choice.

2. Assume you gave a random sample of 100 social work research students a pretest similar to their final exam and then a final exam. Their scores ranged from 30 to 100 on the pretest and from 30 to 100 on the final, with 100 being the maximum possible score. You also collect demographic data: age, sex, hair color, and eye color. Which statistical test would you use to answer the research questions below? Justify your answers.

    a. Is age associated with test scores?

    b. Is there a difference in score by hair color (blonde, brunette, red-head)?

    c. Did students improve from the pretest to the posttest?

3. You want to test the relative effectiveness of couple counseling with and without a spouse included in the intervention. You notice that about one-half of the couples at the agency are in individual counseling and one-half are seen as couples. You sample 20 clients, with 10 in each condition. The dependent variable is the individual's score on a marital satisfaction scale. You do both a pretest and posttest.

    a. Write a null hypothesis for this study.

    b. Write the research hypothesis. Would you use a one-tailed or two-tailed hypothesis? Why?

    c. Would you use a parametric or nonparametric statistic? Why?

    d. Which statistic would you use to test group differences at posttest?

    e. How would you check to see if marital satisfaction is related to length of marriage?

    f. If you had to make either a Type I error or a Type II error, which would it be? Why?

4. Using the *Riverton: A Community Conundrum* case answer the following questions relating gender differences to attitudes about crime. If you do not have SPSS or Excel, explain how you would set up the analyses.

    a. Find all of the questions on the Riverton Youth Survey related to crime, gangs, or violence. Recode the data to each question so that Agree and Strongly Agree are combined into one category and Disagree and

Strongly Disagree are combined into another. Recode the "neither" category as missing data.

b. Use chi-square to test for gender differences related to crime. What do you conclude?

c. Add the scores for items related to crime to create a scale with a single total score. For this question, you will want to use the data as entered (not recoded). Use an independent samples t-test to examine gender differences related to crime. What do you conclude?

d. Using the scale you created in (c), are attitudes about crime correlated with age?

5. Using the *Riverton: A Community Conundrum* case create a scale that combines the scores of items related to drugs or alcohol. Test the null hypothesis: females and males feel the same way about drugs and alcohol based on their answers to the Riverton Youth Survey. What do you conclude? What alternate explanations can you think of for your results?

6. Using the *Riverton: A Community Conundrum* case calculate a Pearson's r to examine the relationship between income and GPA. Plot the data including a line of best fit.

7. Using the *Riverton: A Community Conundrum* case use the paired samples t-test to examine if there are any differences in the pretest and posttest scores for the Life Skills Program. Examine the differences between males and females. Write up your results as you would if you were writing a research report. Along with the findings, report your interpretation and conclusions.

8. Use the RAINN interactive case to consider the data regarding consumer satisfaction with the RAINN online service.

a. In a study of 5,000 RAINN consumers, you find that there is a significant relationship between consumer satisfaction and age of consumer: $r = .15$, $p < .04$. Is age important in predicting consumer satisfaction? HINT: how much of the variance in satisfaction is explained by age?

b. A study of 40 RAINN consumers finds that consumer satisfaction is greater when women are providing services. What conclusions might staff reach based on this finding?

c. A random sample of 500 RAINN consumers found that consumer satisfaction was higher for white consumers than for Latino or African American consumers based on One-Way Analysis of Variance (ANOVA). What steps should be taken because of this finding?

9. Use the RAINN interactive case to examine program information for the online hotline.

a. Is there a relationship between overall satisfaction and satisfaction with Volunteer's Knowledge and Skills? Use Pearson's *r*. Report your findings as you would in a research report.

b. Do volunteers believe their sessions are more helpful with women than men? Use Independent Samples t-test to examine gender differences in Perceived Helpfulness of Session.

c. Do women and men differ in their frequency of being assaulted? Use crosstabulation to answer the question. What are your null and alternative hypotheses?

A RESEARCHER'S WRITING AND PRESENTATION TOOLS

In the Communication Age, we must learn to extract the knowledge from the information, put it into a dynamic "digital" form, and communicate it to cause action.

Daniel Burrus, Technology Speaker, Futurist and Author of *Technotrends*.

Social work is a practice profession. Not surprisingly, then, social work research focuses on improving processes and outcomes for those we serve. Research accomplishes this task by testing theories, developing measurement instruments that improve understanding and help assess change, evaluating interventions, and providing information about social conditions. Research, however, is a resource-intensive process—it is costly in terms of people's time and effort. The value of doing research can be realized only when the results of studies are presented in a way that impacts knowledge, and social work practice and social policy.

Fortunately, social work researchers have many options for sharing their research findings. Specifically, they may engage in any or all of the following activities:

- Write a grant application for funding new or existing programs.
- Justify the need for policy change or new services through reports and public testimony.
- Contribute to the profession's knowledge base by publishing articles in professional journals and presenting papers at national and local conferences.
- Educate community groups about social issues, and help to secure support for services through reports in newsletters, reports, and webinars.
- Support accountability to board members of organizations through written reports.
- Support the administration in program planning and the evaluation process through reports of process, outcome, and cost studies.
- Document the outcomes of practice at the worker level to enhance individual practice.

Writing and presenting research are creative acts. Similar to other creative acts, it requires putting together what you know and wish to convey with considerations about the purposes you wish to achieve and the audience to whom you will communicate. In this chapter, we discuss how to communicate the findings of research in a way that will be best received by the intended audience. We focus on the types of research presentations that are common in social work practice, the style and format for writing and presenting research reports, and ethical and political issues to consider. In addition, we present evaluative criteria to help you produce your own research and critique the research of others.

By the end of this chapter you should be able to:

- List and describe the sections of a research proposal.
- List and describe the sections of a research article.
- Describe the design elements of a research presentation.
- Critique a research report or presentation.
- Explain what is meant by plagiarism and how to avoid it.

RESEARCH PROPOSALS

A **research proposal** describes why a research project should be done, and it outlines the plan for how it will be done. It is written for a specific purpose and often for a specific audience. The purpose and the requirements of the audience will dictate the format of the proposal. Some proposals are limited to a few pages, whereas others are hundreds of pages in length, including supporting documentation.

Research proposals may be written for a variety of purposes:

- To secure funding. The proposal may be directed to a government agency such as a federal grant program, a private agency such as the United Way, or a philanthropic foundation. Funding proposals are discussed at greater length in an upcoming section.
- To help agency board members and/or administrators decide whether to approve a research project within their agency.
- To obtain permission from an institutional review board (IRB) for carrying out funded research. When the federal government or other organization requires IRB permission, then the sections of the proposal that discuss the purpose, research design, confidentiality procedures, informed consent, and qualification of the researchers must be submitted as part of the application.
- To help the researcher clarify in her or his mind why and how the study is to be conducted.

Goals of a Research Proposal

Regardless of the purpose in writing a research proposal, the author has two primary goals. The first is *to convince the audience such as the funding agency or board that the research is important and worth doing.* To accomplish this goal, the proposal must:

- Explain the importance of the research.
- Include a literature review that provides background about the extent and nature of the issue to be addressed.

■ Include information about pilot studies that were done in preparation for the current project, if there were any.

■ Explicitly state the benefits or outcomes of the research. These benefits can include improved social conditions, improved interventions or programs, additional information for policy development, and theory development.

■ Highlight the interests of the audience. For example, a Request for Proposals (RFP) may focus on improving substance abuse prevention for adolescents through training programs for school social workers. In this case the proposal would need to focus on program description and evaluation rather than policy or theory, although the research may have implications for all of these areas.

The second primary goal of a research proposal is *to convince the audience that the author possesses the expertise to conduct the research*. The intended audience must believe that the author has the necessary knowledge and skills to do the proposed research. To accomplish this goal, the author must:

■ Include an introduction and a literature review, in which he or she demonstrates knowledge of the area.

■ Describe the conceptualization and method of the research.

■ Document his or her credentials and experience. Research proposals often have a section that explicitly states the author's qualifications. This section includes educational background, current position, and previous research experience.

■ Attach a résumé.

Sections of a Research Proposal

A research proposal generally has the following sections in the following order, although this list varies with the requirements of the funding or approving organization:

■ *Abstract.* A one- or two-paragraph summary of the research purpose and method.

■ *Executive Summary.* Brief but detailed summary of the purpose, method, benefits, and limitations of the proposed study.

■ *Introduction.* Statement of the purpose and benefits of the study that includes a literature review of previous research. This section is similar to the introduction of a research manuscript for publication.

■ *Method.* Description of the proposed research in terms of methodology, similar to the method section of a research manuscript for publication.

EXHIBIT 13.1

Guidelines for Qualitative Research

Sufficient Data

Although length and intensity of time in the field are certainly not the sole determinants of good qualitative research, I am uneasy when researchers call their research "qualitative" or "ethnographic" and then reveal that they have spent only a few days or a week or two collecting data. I want to know that the researcher has taken the time needed to gain entry to a classroom or program or workplace, has taken the time needed to understand it in its complexity and totality, and has taken the time needed to collect sufficient data to answer the questions that were posed. All this will make findings more credible.

Sufficient Accounts of Data and Analysis

Typically, qualitative researchers face formidable space problems in writing about their projects, which don't lend themselves to pithy summaries or representation in tables or charts, and are hampered by the page restrictions imposed in journals. Qualitative research is best described discursively and at length, so that readers can get a sense of the types of data that were collected and the ways in which those data were analyzed.

Ideally, enough data should be included in a report so that a reader can examine them and compare his or her own conclusions with those of the author.

Acknowledging Dilemmas

Most qualitative researchers experience various dilemmas in the field whether with gaining entry to a site or establishing a relationship with participants or negotiating the extent of the study or even with some of many possible ethical problems. It is always helpful and honorable for researchers to come clean about such issues, in either the body of their paper or an appendix, to represent their research honestly and to provide helpful road maps for future field workers.

Representing Others

Since at its heart qualitative research is an up-close look at other lives, I am always interested in how well those other lives are represented on the page. I look for representations that are grounded, being built from actual data; that are always respectful, yet not romanticized; that reveal complex human beings rather than cartoonish stick figures; and that situate people's choices, values, and activities in a larger socio-cultural, political, and historical context.

Source: Glynda Hull, Professor of Education, University of California, Berkeley (Hull, 2005). Used with permission

■ *Data Analysis*. Analysis of the research questions and/or hypotheses to be studied that specifies the data analysis that will be performed to determine the outcomes of the research. In *quantitative research*, the types of data that will be presented, the statistical tests to be used, and the justification for using these tests are presented. In *qualitative studies,* the types of analyses (such as data coding) and the justifications for these methods are specified. Other reporting standards appropriate to qualitative research are presented in Exhibit 13.1.

■ *Administrative methods*. Explanation of how the research project will be administered, including the responsibility for overall management of the project, the availability of necessary resources, the location of the study, and organizational context in which the study will take place. The administrative section also includes a budget, a timeline, and an organizational chart. The budget essentially describes the costs of the research project in terms of personnel, equipment, supplies, communications, stipends for subjects or participants, consultants, travel, and any other expenses encountered by the project. Funders generally set a maximum amount they will fund for a specific project. The timeline shows in outline form the sequence of events that will take place and how long each phase of the project is expected to last. The outline should specify which activities are to take place and by what dates. Finally, an organizational chart should highlight the administrative structure of the organization conducting the research, including the lines of responsibility for managing the project.

■ *References*. A list of all references used in the introduction, literature review, or other sections of the proposal. Authors should use the APA format unless they are otherwise instructed by the organization for which the report is intended. All references found in the text should be in the reference section. Similarly, all references in the reference section should be found in the document.

■ *Supporting documents*. A research proposal, especially one directed to a funding organization, may include letters from other organizations or important community members that support the need for the research, describe areas of collaboration, and generally endorse the project. Supporting documents may also include an organizational chart, an annual report, reports of pilot projects, and any other materials that demonstrate the need for the research and the capabilities of the researchers to accomplish their goals.

Grant Funding Proposal

All social work programs, whether new or continuing, require funding. Funding may pay for facilities, personnel, equipment, transportation, or other needed resources. Many programs, especially those provided by private nonprofit organizations, depend on funding from federal, state, city, or private organizations. This funding often involves social workers in the process of finding, writing, and submitting a grant to a funding organization. Major components of a grant-funding proposal that can be prepared in advance include:

■ An agency mission statement and explanation of how the proposed program fits with the agency mission.

■ Specified goals and objectives for the proposed program. This should include a logic model showing the relationship between the social problem to be addressed and the program objectives and outcomes. Other visual aids such as a timeline and organizational chart are also useful.

■ Description of the history and current organizational capacity of the agency. This should include brief descriptions of agency leadership and key staff, physical resources, current agency financing, previous record with grants, and current goals and programs.

■ Documentation of collaborations. Many funders will ask for documentation of community support and collaborations as part of the project. Community collaborators should understand how they may be of help (for example, writing a letter of support) and be aware that the agency will seek funding using their help.

Once the background materials are prepared, an organization can find funding opportunities from a variety of sources. These include federal, state, and city web sites, foundation and corporate RFPs, and for-profit and nonprofit organizations that offer grant finding services. For example, the Foundation Center, a nonprofit organization, provides a searchable database of over 100,000 U.S. foundations and corporate donors.

Success in grant funding will depend on the match between the funder's priorities and the proposed program, the quality of the written proposal, and the relationship between the funder and the requesting organization. These are some hallmarks of successful proposals—in other words, those that get funded:

■ *Address the funder's priorities:* In order to receive funding, there must be a good fit between the values and goals of the funder and the agency seeking funding. An agency can learn about the funder's values and goals through the request for proposals document (RFP), funder's web site and written materials, and research about previously funded projects. The agency will then need to demonstrate how their proposed program fits the values and goals of the funder.

■ *Follow instructions:* A funder will specify the format in which a grant should be written, including length, descriptions and documentation to be included, submission format (e.g., online or in print), and deadline for submission. Grants that do not follow the funder's guidelines are unlikely to be considered.

- *Understand the scoring system:* Many funders provide a system by which they score the merits of a grant, usually a point system based on percentages. For example, the program description of the grant may count for 35% of the total score and the budget for 15%. In this case, approximately 35% of the length of the proposal should address the program description. No section assigned a point value should be left out.

- *Address the need:* Grant seekers need to describe the problem that their program addresses and the benefits to consumers and the community if the program is funded. In addition, describe the negative consequences of what could happen if it is not funded. For example, for a proposal to address the consequences of untreated PTSD in cases of rape, the proposal should include research from the literature showing charts, graphs, and detailed facts about the extent of need. The focus of the grant should be on meeting the needs of consumers, not on the agency's need for personnel or equipment.

- *Include a detailed budget:* Funders will want to understand the expenditures related to a proposed program as well as the rationale for these expenses. The budget should include both direct costs (e.g., salary, equipment, transportation) and indirect costs (the cost of administering the grant). The budget should only include costs allowed by the funder. For example, some funders do not fund indirect costs or equipment.

- *Include an evaluation plan:* Funders generally request that programs be evaluated to determine the outcomes and impact of the program. The evaluation should be specified in terms of objectives, measures, and research methods.

- *Include a plan to disseminate the results:* Funders generally look favorably on programs that plan to disseminate the results of their project. This provides information to other organizations working on similar issues and publicity for the funder. Dissemination may include describing the project on an agency web site and newsletter, presenting the project at a local or national conference, or writing a research or descriptive article about the project for a refereed journal.

- *Get feedback first:* Once a draft of the grant proposal is written, people outside of the project should review it. It is best to have two types of readers: lay and expert. Lay readers can provide feedback about whether they understand what is being written. Expert readers know the field and can give feedback on missing research, research design problems, or a discrepancy in organizational plans. Feedback is especially useful if a team of individuals whose writing style and sense of the proposal may differ. Quick Guide 9 is a checklist used to evaluate grant proposals.

QUICK GUIDE 9 RATING SHEET FOR EVALUATING GRANT PROPOSALS

Checklist for Evaluating Grant Proposals

- ☑ The proposal recognizes needs and proposes solutions consistent with the purpose of the funding.
- ☑ There is evidence of ability to plan, arrange, and control tasks to ensure success.
- ☑ The research will make a significant contribution to the field and has clear implications for practice and/or policy.
- ☑ The study is based on good research design principles.
- ☑ The research methods fit the study questions.
- ☑ The proposal has enough flexibility to ensure success.
- ☑ The proposal addresses issues of the appropriateness and accuracy of the measures.
- ☑ The researcher has the education, knowledge, and experience to carry out the research.
- ☑ The proposal has a realistic budget, plan, and timelines.
- ☑ The researcher has sufficient resources to carry out the project.
- ☑ There is evidence of support for the project by important constituencies.
- ☑ Ethical guidelines have been addressed and followed.

RESEARCH REPORTS

Research reports may be written for a variety of reasons in a variety of formats, depending on the purpose of the report and the nature of the intended audience. The following sections describe traditional research reports as well as the more flexible research briefs and infographics. The last section is about creating manuscripts for publication in professional journals.

Reports to Stakeholders

At times, the funders of research will require regular reports of progress, every three, six, or 12 months. A final report to funders detailing all aspects of the project is also generally required. This report may be lengthy, often 100 pages or longer.

The format, contents, and writing style of the report vary depending on its audience and purpose. At times, the completed report may be written in lay terms so that the board or the general community can understand it. Research presentations in annual reports often serve this purpose. At other times, the audience may be composed of research reviewers at funding agencies that require considerable detail and statistical analyses. In any case, keeping in mind the general sections of a research manuscript—introduction, method, results, discussion, and conclusion—will serve as a useful guide to organizing the report.

Another key part of such reports is an executive summary that describes upfront the important results and implications of the study. Often a board or committee at the funding agency wants a concise version of the report to save time and focus their review. An executive summary might be one page and organized along the same lines as the report is presented.

Research Briefs

Research briefs are an increasingly popular way of bringing research to the practice and consumer communities. Authors can find templates for briefs or newsletters online, making publishing relatively easy and cost efficient. Further, by distributing the brief electronically and posting it on a web site, authors can avoid printing and mailing costs.

Briefs can be organized thematically. They usually include four or five short sections that are written in a focused area. Infographics are shorter in length and intersperse text with graphics or easy-to-read tables. The use of color and pictures help to make these short publications stand out to the reader. The briefs can be the focus of webinars or mini seminars. In dissemination of research, sometimes less can be more, as the audience can easily become lost in the details. Programs that facilitate the development of research-based infographics are also available at low or no cost on the Internet.

Manuscripts for Publication in Professional Journals

The core knowledge of the social work profession is disseminated through professional journals. Social work publications can be found in a wide variety of social work and social science journals. Lists of social work journals can be found through an Internet search and have been compiled by various libraries and academics from schools of social work. When looking for a journal an author might consider information about the journal's mission or focus, acceptance rate, review process, and procedures for submitting manuscripts for publication. Journals vary in their focus, and they generally have a fairly narrow area of interest. Before you submit a manuscript for publication, you should know the focus of the journal because even an excellent manuscript will be rejected if it does not match the journal's mission.

One purpose of publishing in professional journals is to "get the word out" to practitioners and researchers. Thus, publishing is a strategy for informing the professional community and other interested readers about new theories or evidence to support or reject theories, new interventions, results of the evaluations of programs, and other information that increases the knowledge of the profession. Publication is a way to inform others of new developments as well as to suggest needed research to build the knowledge base.

Publication Process

As both a producer and a consumer of research, it is important to understand the publication process. Some journals are **refereed,** meaning that experts determine whether or not the manuscript is worthy of publication. In most cases, manuscripts submitted to refereed journals undergo **blind review**, meaning that reviewers do not see any identifying information about the author(s). In other journals or special editions of refereed journals, the reviewers know the identity of the author(s). Journals with blind review processes are believed to set a higher standard because the identity of the author is not a factor in judging the quality of the manuscript.

You should also be aware that journals vary in their acceptance rates. Some journals accept only a small proportion of the manuscripts that are submitted to them. Authors make decisions about where to submit a manuscript for publication based on a number of factors including the journal's mission, reputation, target audience, circulation, and acceptance rate. The convention is to send a manuscript to only one journal at a time to prevent wasting the reviewers' time and to make the publication process more manageable.

There are many steps in the publication process, as Exhibit 13.2 indicates. The time from review to publication may be lengthy. In order to reduce this time lag, some journals publish their work online following acceptance. Some journals are completely online. Online journals often use the same blind review process as print journals. The use of the web for publication can reduce the lag time from review to publication to only a few weeks. For an example of an online journal visit the web site of *Journal of Social Work Values and Ethics* (http://www.socialworker.com/jswve/).

Formatting

A **research manuscript** describes a completed research study. Writing a research manuscript for publication in a professional journal is a matter of both substance and form. The manuscript must contribute something new and useful to the literature in a specific area. In addition, it must be written in a format that is acceptable both to the journal and to the professional community.

The majority of social work journals and many social science journals use the format required by the journals of the American Psychological Association

EXHIBIT 13.2

Journal Publication Process

- An author writes a manuscript for publication and sends it to a journal editor.
- The editor sends the manuscript to between two and four reviewers with recognized expertise in their field. At this point, the manuscript contains no names or identifying information in order to prevent possible bias in the review (blind review).
- The reviewers provide a critique of the manuscript and make a judgment about its merit based on the author's contribution of new knowledge to the field, his or her use of appropriate methodology, and the overall writing style.
- The reviewers return the manuscript to the editor. The editor then makes a judgment based on the reviews. The judgment will usually be one of the following:
  - ☐ *Accept:* The manuscript is accepted.
  - ☐ *Accept with revisions:* The manuscript is accepted, but the author must make minor revisions before it can be published.
  - ☐ *Revise and resubmit:* The manuscript is not accepted, but will be re-reviewed if the changes suggested by the reviewers are satisfactorily made.
  - ☐ *Reject:* The manuscript is not accepted for publication in the journal.
- If a manuscript is not accepted for publication, an author generally has three options: (1) make the suggested changes and resubmit the manuscript, (2) send the manuscript to a different journal with little or no change, or (3) give up on publishing the manuscript.
- If the author chooses to revise and resubmit the manuscript, the editor and/or reviewers re-review the manuscript to see if it now warrants publication. This process can occur several times.

(APA). **APA format** provides specific rules about the structure of the paper such as heading style, margins, spacing, and reference format (American Psychological Association, 2009). Guidelines to APA format can also be found on some web sites, for example The OWL at Purdue. What happens when a manuscript does not follow the APA format? In some cases, the journal editor will ask the author to reformat the work into APA style. In other cases, the manuscript will be immediately rejected.

A research manuscript traditionally has the following sections:

- *Title:* A descriptive title stating the theme of the research report.
- *Affiliation:* The affiliation of all authors including university or organization of employment.
- *Abstract:* A summary of the purpose, methods, and major finding of the article.
- *Key Words:* Approximately five key words describing the focus of the article. These words help researchers find the article in key word searches of bibliographic databases.

■ *Introduction:* The background for the research study. The introduction states the purpose of the study and explains why the research is important. It also reviews the theory and research on which the study is based. (See the discussion of literature review in Chapter 3.) In addition, the introduction defines the terms and variables used in the study. It leads the reader from a summary of relevant previous research to the research questions and hypotheses in the study to be presented. In this way the introduction serves both to educate the reader and to establish the author's credibility and expertise.

■ *Method:* Describes the methodology used in the study so that an informed reader can judge the validity of the research. In addition, the method section should provide enough detail so that a different researcher could replicate the research in another study. This section includes descriptions of the research design (for example, pretest-posttest with random assignment) as well as the rationale for using that design. It should specify the research procedures in terms of who did what, with whom, when, and where. The method section also describes the demographics of the sample and population from which it was drawn, as well as the sampling method. It explains which data were collected, and it identifies the measuring instruments or procedures that were used, with information about their source, reliability, and validity. Finally, this section describes any methodological issues that might have impacted the results of the study. For example, in a study of parent education groups, if group leaders needed to be changed half way through the study, then the methods section should report this fact. It should also point out any detail that might produce bias in the results. If the age, race, or gender of the interviewer might have affected the results, for example, this possibility should be reported.

■ *Results:* The results section describes the major findings of the study. It generally progresses from simple to more complex findings. This section includes descriptive statistics about the sample and the major variables. It also presents the analysis of the information, both quantitative and qualitative, that is needed to answer the research question(s). The results section may contain tables and graphs to help summarize and clarify the results. If the study used statistical tests, then the results section could indicate the types of tests and the rationale for using them. One key point to remember is that the results section should be strictly descriptive and factual. In other words, it should not make any attempt to interpret the meaning of the results.

■ *Discussion:* This section summarizes the major findings and considers their meaning, importance, and implications. The discussion may include implications for theory development, practice, program development, education and training, policy, and further research. It may also consider the extent to which the study corroborates or contradicts the findings from previous research. Finally, it can include a description of the limitations of the study and how they might be addressed in future research. This information can be quite useful to readers. These limitations may be related to any aspect of the research method such as the lack of generalizability of the sample, limited knowledge of the validity of the measuring instruments, low return rate or high dropout rate, or the inability to collect certain data. In addition, the discussion should report any intervening variables that may have affected the study. For example, in a study of student attitudes towards alcohol use, a drunk-driving death involving several students of the school just prior to the study should be reported, as it almost certainly will have influenced students' responses.

■ *Conclusion:* Although not always a standard part of all manuscripts, the conclusion can be useful when the discussion is long and complex. The conclusion briefly summarizes the main findings of the study and highlights the implications of the study for practice, policy, and future research.

■ *References:* All literature and other references reviewed in the article should be cited in the format required by the journal. See the section titled "Plagiarism" later in this chapter for more information about citing references.

■ *Tables and figures:* These summarize data, provide detailed information about statistical test results, and represent concepts in a graphical format. References to the tables and figures appear in the text, and the tables and figures are placed at the end of the manuscript.

You can use the checklists in Quick Guide 10 to evaluate the merits of each section of a research manuscript.

QUICK GUIDE 10 CHECKLIST FOR EVALUATING A RESEARCH MANUSCRIPT

Ethical Considerations

☑ Author's affiliation is stated.
☑ Funding sources are acknowledged and values made explicit.
☑ Potential bias or conflict of interest is acknowledged.
☑ Research proposal was reviewed by IRB or other appropriate research review entity.
☑ Language is free of bias, stereotypes, or other cultural insensitivity.

Introduction Section

☑ Purpose of paper is stated clearly.
☑ Importance of study is justified.
☑ Linkage to previous literature is sufficient to provide rationale and context for study.
☑ Literature review includes the most recent and relevant studies.
☑ Concepts and variables are clearly defined.

☑ Research questions and hypotheses are clearly stated.
☑ There are no ethical violations.

Method Section

☑ Type of study is specified (for example, qualitative, quantitative, cross-sectional, longitudinal).
☑ Research design is specified and appropriate for questions or hypotheses.
☑ Study could be replicated based on its description.

Measurement

☑ Variables are clearly and logically operationalized.
☑ Unit of analysis is specified and logical.
☑ Measuring instruments or methods are specified, and there is evidence of their reliability and validity.
☑ Research procedures do not affect measures.
☑ Threats to internal validity are controlled or acknowledged.
☑ Conditions of study are like real-world conditions (external validity).

Sample

☑ Sample and population are specified.
☑ Sampling rationale and procedure are specified.
☑ Sampling frame is specified and logical.
☑ Sample is representative of population.
☑ Sample size is specified and is large enough for generalization and analyses.
☑ Information is provided about return rate and attrition rate in study.
☑ Sampling error is specified.
☑ Limits of generalization, given sample, are specified.

Pre-experimental and Experimental Design

☑ Independent and dependent variables are specified.
☑ Type of experimental design is specified and logical for purpose.
☑ Assignment of subjects to comparison and experimental groups is specified and justified.
☑ Equivalence of comparison and experimental groups is specified.
☑ Periods of measurement are specified and logical for purpose.
☑ Threats to internal validity are controlled or explained (history, testing, maturation, instrumentation, statistical regression, selection, attrition).
☑ Issues related to placebo effect or "Hawthorne" effect are explained.
☑ Any deception is explained and justified.

Survey Research

☑ Type of survey (mail, telephone, in-person, Internet) is specified.
☑ Exact questions (or where to find them) are specified.
☑ Questions are clear and understandable by intended respondents.
☑ Questions cover only one idea at a time.

☑ Closed questions provide all mutually exclusive categories.
☑ Categorization or coding of open-ended questions is specified and logical for purpose.
☑ Social desirability can be ruled out as contributing to responses.
☑ Return rate is specified and high enough to warrant generalization.

Qualitative and Field Research

☑ Selection of observations or interviewees is specified and justified.
☑ Classifying or coding system for observations or interview analysis is specified and appropriate for purpose.
☑ There is evidence or justification that another researcher observing same events would classify them the same way.
☑ Impact of researcher on observations and coding is explained and justified.
☑ Impact of researcher's own gender and cultural identity on interpretation of observations is explained.
☑ Field notes or recordings are available for review.
☑ Generalizability of study is explained.

Results Section

☑ Methods of data collection are specified.
☑ Statistical tests are appropriate for type of data collected.
☑ Difference between statistical and meaningful findings is clear.
☑ All relevant analyses were performed.
☑ No logical flaws appear in analysis and interpretation of data.
☑ Tables and graphs summarize results when appropriate.
☑ Tables and graphs are appropriately labeled with headings and necessary detail.
☑ Statistical significance and effect size (ES) are reported.
☑ If qualitative data, enough examples are presented to allow reader to understand or replicate coding or analysis.
☑ Data are recent enough to be relevant.
☑ Results are reported as factual without interpretation.

Discussion and Conclusion Sections

☑ Major findings are summarized and their significance is discussed.
☑ Discussion includes how topic adds to, modifies, replicates, or contradicts previous research.
☑ Research flaws, shortcomings, and other plausible reasons for results of study are explained.
☑ Implications of results for practice and policy are discussed.
☑ Specific suggestions are provided for further research.
☑ Conclusions are warranted by the research design and analyses.

PRESENTATIONS AT CONFERENCES AND PROFESSIONAL MEETINGS

Presentations at research conferences or other professional meetings, like journal publications, are sometimes refereed and sometimes invited. There are several formats for research presentations at professional meetings: research papers, poster sessions, and workshops. At times, a presentation may report on a completed research project. At other times, a conference may allow a researcher to present ideas for a project, works in progress, or a completed project that has not been formally written up.

Research presentations at professional meetings may be the most cutting-edge research because the researcher often presents the study shortly after completing it rather than waiting several months for the findings to be published in a journal. On the negative side, however, conferences often accept a research presentation based on an abstract of the proposal rather than a completed manuscript. In these cases, professionals in the field may not have reviewed the entire presentation.

Unlike journal articles or research proposals, a research presentation at a professional meeting is not meant to be a one-way presentation of the project. Rather, it is intended to inform an audience as well as to provide a forum for two-way interaction involving questions and comments from the audience.

As with a research paper, the presenter must take into account the knowledge level and expertise of the intended audience. The nature of the audience should determine:

- the extent to which the presenter needs to define and clarify the key concepts
- the appropriate level of methodological detail
- the types of statistics, charts, and tables that the presenter should use

Presentations of Research Papers

The content of research paper presentations is similar to that of research papers and proposals. The presentation should discuss the traditional areas of introduction, method, results, and discussion in about 20 to 30 minutes, although the presenter can place more emphasis on some areas than others depending on the focus of the conference and the interests of the audience.

Research presentations vary in style and format. Some presenters read their papers. Generally speaking, however, unless the paper is especially well written and of great interest to the audience, the audience is likely to tune out to the reading of a paper. Other presenters use an outline and discuss the research, often involving the audience by inviting questions and comments. Presenters increasingly use presentation software such as Microsoft PowerPoint as well as multimedia such as music, graphics, and embedded video. Exhibit 13.3 provides some useful guidelines for developing slides for presentation.

EXHIBIT 13.3

Guidelines for Presentation Slides

■ Prepare about one slide for each minute of your speaking, leaving time for questions and comments.

■ Select a background theme that suits the theme of your research. For example, don't use a farm scene if your research is about urban issues.

■ Use the same theme for each slide.

■ Use light text with dark backgrounds for projecting slides with an overhead or computer projector. Use dark text and light backgrounds for printing.

■ Limit the material on each slide. Don't let the slide look cluttered. Blank space is useful and easier on the eyes.

■ Use fonts no smaller than 24 points if possible.

■ Use the 1 by 1 and 6 by 6 rules: 1 idea per page; 1 idea per line. No more than 6 words per line; no more than 6 lines per page.

■ Use color to enhance the organization. For example, if the first level of an outline is orange, then consider printing the second level in green to distinguish it.

■ Use graphics that relate to your presentation: an informative chart or table or an interesting graphic or picture that relates to the information you are conveying.

■ Look for free graphics on the Internet—for example, by typing key words into the Google search engine. Be very careful not to use images that have a copyright. If you are not certain whether an image has a copyright, you can e-mail the contact person on the web site and ask for permission to use the image.

■ Copy an image from the web by right clicking on the image then clicking **Save image as** and saving the image to your hard drive. You can also copy and paste the image directly into PowerPoint. Right click on the image and click **Copy**. Then move to your slide in PowerPoint and click **Edit/Paste**.

■ Don't use too many "fancy tricks" on one slide. It is distracting. PowerPoint allows you to use many different features, including blinking and flying text, sounds, graphics, and music. Using too many of these features will encourage the audience to focus on the technology rather than the material being presented.

The following are some pointers for presenting research papers at professional conferences.

■ Always have a backup of your presentation. If possible, come to the room early to make certain that the equipment is working.

■ Make available electronic handouts of slides and other supporting printed material so that the listeners do not need to take notes. Handouts also provide listeners with your name and contact information. Finally, they help the audience remember the important points of your presentation.

- If possible, move from behind a podium during your presentation in order to interact with the audience. Involve the audience by asking questions if you have time.
- Don't read your slides or notes. It puts people to sleep. Use the slides as an outline and organizing mechanism, and freely discuss the main points.
- Use humor when appropriate and possible.
- Be sure that people can hear you. Ask someone in the back of the room to confirm that you are speaking loud enough before you begin your presentation. Use a microphone when necessary.
- Make certain that the entire audience can see the screen. Never block the screen yourself by standing in front of it. Do not speak facing the screen rather than your audience.
- Acknowledge input from the audience.
- Do not get into a disagreement with audience members over research issues. Simply thank them for their thoughts or suggestions. Remember that criticism (critique) of research is part of the scientific culture and should not be taken personally.
- Do not correct your co-presenter in front of the audience.
- If possible, watch a videotape of yourself doing a presentation. Check your posture, gestures, movements, and voice tone for any changes you might want to make.
- After a presentation, analyze what did and didn't work. Keep notes for future presentations.
- Do not worry about feeling nervous. Many people are nervous presenting in front of groups. It is possible to do a fine presentation when you are nervous. Nervousness usually disappears after the first few minutes.
- Avoid utterances like "uh," "um," and "mm."
- Practice, practice, practice.
- Finally, remember to have fun!

Poster Sessions

Poster sessions are a format commonly used at professional meetings in which a number of people present their research projects at the same time. Usually poster sessions are held in a large, open space. The presenters each have an area and use a printed poster or a digital display on a computer to exhibit the highlights of their research. The audience moves from poster to poster, reading the material and interacting with the presenter. Exhibit 13.4 presents guidelines for developing posters.

EXHIBIT 13.4

Guidelines for Poster Presentations

- Organize the material with the title at the top and the printed material placed in three or four columns.
- Format the printed material so that people will read it moving down the columns and then left to right. Place the introduction in the upper left corner and the Conclusion in the lower right corner.
- Do not use too much text. Graphics and tables should be the primary focus of the poster.
- Because not all people will discuss the poster with you, they should be able to understand the poster without verbal explanation.
- Use bullet points where possible.
- Use colors and fonts that are easily readable from about three feet and that help distinguish among sections.
- Detail is not necessary. It can be kept for discussion with participants who visit the poster.

Workshops

Workshops are designed to actively involve the audience in learning new information or skills. For example, a workshop may present recent research about the financial abuse of elders and teach participants about new ways to assess and intervene when they suspect financial abuse. Workshops may last from an hour and a half to three hours or longer, leaving time for the audience to practice new skills, discuss their experiences, and ask questions. Presenters often use active learning techniques such as role-playing, group discussions, and structured exercises to enhance skill development among the participants.

Workshops should be developed with specific objectives to be accomplished by the end of the workshop. For example, in the elder abuse workshop, the objectives might be stated as follows:

By the end of this workshop, participants should be able to:

- Describe the research that suggests the extent of financial abuse of elders.
- Define financial abuse of elders, and explain the difficulties involved in operationalizing the definition.
- List and describe three types of financial abuse of elders.

- Describe the role of police, social services, and family court with regard to financial abuse of elders.
- Conduct an assessment interview with an elder to determine whether elder abuse warrants further investigation.

Presenters should also develop an agenda that specifies the approximate time that will be allocated for each section of the workshop. In addition, they should provide handouts and other materials to participants to reinforce learning. Finally, presenters should incorporate some procedure for evaluating their workshops for both content and process. Frequently, these procedures involve simply eliciting feedback from participants for improving the workshop the next time it is given.

THE ETHICS AND POLITICS OF RESEARCH REPORTS

Research reports are written to increase knowledge and perhaps influence organizational or social change. They involve not only scientific considerations but ethical and political considerations, including these:

- Should the results be made public?
- If so, how and to whom will the results be distributed, and in which languages?
- Which data will be included and which will be left out of a research report?
- What interpretation will be given to the results?
- Who will be given credit for authorship of the report?

These decisions and guidelines for making them are discussed next.

Research reports must follow the ethical standards of the social work profession. Results must be reported truthfully and accurately. Furthermore, the report must never violate client confidentiality. No one should be identified or quoted without giving his or her permission. In addition, the report should not reinforce stereotypes or disparage any group by presenting or interpreting the results in a biased manner.

Plagiarism

A major ethical responsibility that all researchers must respect whether they are writing or presenting research reports is to avoid plagiarism. **Plagiarize** is defined in Merriam-Webster's Collegiate Dictionary as "to steal and pass off (the ideas or words of another) as one's own: use (another's production) without crediting the source"; "to commit literary theft: present as new and original an idea or product derived from an existing source" (2012). Plagiarism is considered intellectual property theft, and theft is a serious ethical violation.

All of the actions listed below are defined as acts of plagiarism (Swales & Feak, 2004):

- Intentionally using another's person's words or ideas in your writing without properly citing them (i.e., giving credit through referencing the material)
- Paraphrasing someone's work without giving proper credit
- Using facts, statistics, graphs, drawings, music, or anything that is not considered common knowledge without giving proper credit through citation
- Using someone's exact words without using quotation marks, even if you have cited the source
- Using someone's ideas or words that you received in oral communication or by e-mail without attributing them to the source
- "Forgetting" to cite the source of ideas or words taken directly from another person's work
- Using another person's work because you "did not know" the rules and conventions regarding plagiarism

Knowing what is not plagiarism is also useful. It is not plagiarism to write your own ideas, thoughts, experiences, observations, or research findings. In addition, you may state "common knowledge" without including a citation. For example, you may state that George Washington was the first president of the United States without referencing it. In addition, citing sources improperly is not plagiarism. In general, a good rule to avoid plagiarism is: when in doubt, cite your source. Computer programs have been developed that can check for plagiarism by comparing a document to a database.

Language

Ethics and politics are also considerations in the use of language in research reports. Being "politically correct" is also being ethically correct.

Use gender-neutral terms whenever possible—use *letter carrier* rather than *postman*—and avoid using *he* as an exclusive pronoun when referring to both genders. Conversely, avoid using *she* exclusively when referring to social workers.

In addition, you should strive to use terms that are ethnically and culturally sensitive to the groups under discussion. For example, the word *Indian* may be insulting to people who define themselves as American Indian or First

Nation Peoples. When you are doing research on diverse groups, consult with community members about their preferred terms of reference.

Values and Bias

Funding organizations decide what research to spend their money on and who to give the money to. These decisions are, at least in part, politically based. Research may provide evidence to support or contradict a particular theory or practice method.

Research related to politically divisive topics such as abortion, sex education, or same-sex foster parents will be especially vulnerable to political influences. A research report can be expected to come under attack from individuals or groups who oppose the findings for scientific or political reasons. Interest groups may criticize the value of the research, the methods used, the data collected, or the interpretation of the findings. Such criticisms should be anticipated. The report should address any limitations dealing with the scientific basis of the study in the discussion section.

The authors should also acknowledge any value biases that might have influenced the research. It is better to acknowledge any weaknesses of the study in a report than to have others do so publicly or in print. Keep in mind that there is no "perfect study." All studies have some limitations and are therefore open to criticism.

Authorship

Authorship is another "political" issue in research reports, especially reports done by university-based researchers that are published in professional journals. Many universities and colleges are "publish or perish" institutions. Publication can be an important factor in receiving tenure, promotions, and merit rises. Therefore, claiming or assigning authorship of a report is a significant issue.

In research publications, authorship is given to the individuals who are responsible for the concepts, data, and interpretation of results for the project. Authorship includes the people who do the actual writing as well as other individuals who have made substantial scientific contributions to the study. In general, the person most responsible for conceptualizing, managing, and writing the project is listed as the first author, the next most involved is second author, and so on.

It is important for members of a research team to be clear on authorship before they undertake the research project. In some cases, authors may note that the work was shared equally. In such cases authorship generally is listed alphabetically.

Organizational Politics

Organizations usually dislike surprises, especially those that may be problematic for the organization. As we saw in Chapter 5, research reports, especially those involving the evaluation of programs, have the potential to embarrass an organization or jeopardize its funding. To avoid these problems, before publishing or presenting a report, the researcher should share the results with the organization or program that has been the focus of the research. The organization and the researcher can then discuss the best ways to present the findings in a positive light. Even when the report has negative results, it can focus on the lessons learned and directions for change.

Publishing research findings can also be a political issue that requires negotiation and compromise. A research project often includes a "Memorandum of Understanding" that details the responsibilities of all parties. There is generally a section in the memorandum that discusses publication. Some organizations include a clause that specifies who "owns" the results of the research and under what circumstances the research can be published. Funders may insist that they control the decision about whether to publish the research and where to publish it as a condition for their support. In other cases, an organization may have the right to refuse publication of research for any reason (including negative findings). A researcher should be clear about the publication agreements before beginning the project. She or he should then work collaboratively with the organization concerning distribution of the results.

CONCLUSION

All researchers owe a debt to those who came before them in that current research is based on the theory and research methods previously developed by others. The practice of writing research reports, manuscripts, and newsletters and presenting research is a way of sharing information with the professional community. By doing so, others can use the evidence as a basis for practice and can build on the work already done.

Human beings and social conditions are too complex for any one study to provide definitive answers to social problems. Science is a process of research, replication, and incremental knowledge development. This could not happen without formal and somewhat standardized mechanisms for sharing research studies. Writing and presenting research reports in social work is a way of becoming part of the scientific process and contributing to the generation of new knowledge for the improvement of social work practice and ultimately for the benefit of those we serve.

MAIN POINTS

■ Research proposals describe why a research project is needed and how the research project will be conducted. It is written in order to specify the details of the project, obtain funding for the project, and obtain permission to engage in the project. The format varies with the purpose and audience of the report.

■ Research should be shared in order to build the knowledge base and improve practice. Presenting research through journal articles, conference presentations, reports, and newsletters requires good written and oral communication skills.

■ A research report or manuscript generally contains the following sections: Introduction, Method, Results, Discussion, and Conclusion. Manuscripts sent to journals for publication must have a specific focus and format in order to be accepted.

■ Conference presentations often present the latest research in an area. Good presentations require consideration of the audience and purpose of the presentation as well as practice and preparation.

■ Presentation software can enhance a presentation by helping to make the presentation well organized and visually appealing.

■ Plagiarism involves using other people's ideas, words, and intellectual work without giving due credit though appropriate citation. Plagiarism is unethical.

■ Research reports involve ethical and political as well as scientific considerations. They must be written within the values of the profession and in cooperation with all parties involved in the research. Political struggles over resources or values may affect both the content of research reports and the way they are received by various interest groups.

EXERCISES

1. You submit a grant proposal for the RAINN online hotline to a federal agency, but it is rejected because, "It does not include a control group in the evaluation of the program." Because participants in the online hotline are anonymous, you cannot use a control group. How can you improve your chances of being funded the next time you submit a grant proposal for the RAINN program?

2. Using the RAINN case, create a set of slides that describe the methods, results, and implications of the RAINN Visitor Satisfaction survey.

3. You have done a survey on the need for a youth center in your community. In which section of a research report would you put the following information—Introduction, Methods, Results, or Discussion?

a.   The number of people who were interviewed.

b.   The percentage of people who would like to see sex education at the youth center.

c.   A table showing the level of support for the center by age of respondent.

d.   Data from a report of the impact of youth centers on delinquency rates in a similar community.

e.   Your thoughts about why males say they would attend the center more than females.

f.   Explanation of theories about why youth become delinquent and why a center would help.

g.   An explanation of how the survey was developed.

h.   An explanation of how the needs assessment could be improved in the future.

4.   For each of the following scenarios, first specify whether or not you would need to provide a citation and explain your answer. Then describe what you would need to do to avoid plagiarism.

a.   You are writing about your experiences using play therapy.

b.   You are writing to disagree with an editorial in the newspaper.

c.   You quote Jane Addams in the introduction of your paper.

d.   You contrast your findings with previous research findings.

e.   You state that NASW provides a Code of Ethics for social workers.

f.   You begin your paper with an anecdote that a board member told you.

g.   You copy a message from an online self-help group and use it as an example in your paper.

h.   You use a map you found on the Internet that shows high poverty areas in your state.

i.   You want to use a famous quotation but you can't remember who said it.

5.   An evaluator gave a draft of a final evaluation report on a child abuse and neglect prevention program to the Agency Director. After reviewing the draft the Director asked the evaluator to "downplay" some sections of the evaluation report that described operational problems within the program. The Director cautioned the evaluator that the findings in this section of the report were stated in such a way that could cause readers to overlook the success of the program's implementation. The primary client of the evaluation is the state legislature, which makes major funding decisions regarding the program. The evaluator concludes that the findings have been reported in a fair and balanced nature. Despite this assessment, the evaluator revises the section in question, mainly by deleting detailed quotes made by staff and program participants that concern operational problems in the program. Did the evaluator act ethically? Justify your response.

6. Using the *Riverton: A Community Conundrum* case, list the ethical and political issues that might be involved in writing a report of the results of the Riverton Youth Survey.

7. In order to obtain a grant, you are asked to accept a clause in the funding foundation's contract that states, "No publication without consultation and approval." In other words, you cannot publish the results of your evaluation without permission of the foundation. What ethical issues are involved in your decision to accept or reject the grant based on this clause?

References

Abbott, R., Barber, K. R., Taylor, D. K., & Pendel, D. (1999). Utilization of early detection services: A recruitment and screening program for African American women. *Journal of Health Care for the Poor and Underserved, 10*, 269–280.

Allen, J., & Boettcher, R. (2000). Passing a mental health levy: Lessons for the community practice professional. *Journal of Community Practice, 7*, 21–36.

American Academy of Social Work and Social Welfare (n.d.). Grand challenges for social work: Social progress powered by science. Author.

Americans with Disabilities Act (2010). *Definition of disability*. Retrieved from https://www.ada.gov/2010_regs.html.

Anderson, E. (1999). *Code of the street: Decency, violence, and the moral life of the inner city*. New York: Norton.

APA (American Psychological Association) (2009). *Publication manual of the American Psychological Association* (6th ed.). Washington, DC: Author.

Arnett, J. (2000). Emerging adulthood. *The American Psychologist, 55*(5), 469–480.

Barnes, P. M., Adams, P. F., & Powell-Griner, E. (2005). Health characteristics of the American Indian and Alaska Native adult population: United States, 1999–2003. Advance data from vital and health statistics; No 356. Hyattsville, MD: National Center for Health Statistics. Retrieved December 29, 2005 from www.cdc.gov/nchs/data/ad/ad356.pdf.

Barsky, A. E. (2010). 'The virtuous social work researcher', *Journal of Social Work Values and Ethics, 7*(10). Retrieved April 20, 2010 from http://www.socialworker.com/jswve/spring2010/6virtuoussw.pdf.

Bloom, M. (2010). Client centered evaluation: Ethics for 21st century practitioners. *Journal of Social Work Values and Ethics, 7*(1), 34–40. Retrieved from http://www.socialworker.com/jswve/content/view/140/70/.

Bloom, M., Fischer, J., & Orme, J. G. (2009). *Evaluating practice: Guidelines for the accountable professional* (6th ed.). Boston: Allyn & Bacon.

Bonifas, R. P. (2015). Resident-to-resident aggression in nursing homes: Social worker involvement and collaboration with nursing colleagues. *Health and Social Work*. DOI: 10.1093/hsw/hlv040.

Bonifas, R. P., Simons, K., Biel, B., & Kramer, C. (2014). Aging and place in long-term care settings: Influences on social relationships. *Journal of Aging and Health, 26*(8), 1320–1339.

Bosman, J., Davey, M., & Smith, M. (2016, January 21). As water problems grew, officials belittled complaints from Flint. *New York Times*, p A1.

Bronfenbrenner, U. (1977). Toward an experimental ecology of human development. *American Psychologist, 32*, 513–531.

Buchanan, E. A., & Zimmer, M. (2016). Internet research ethics. *The Stanford encyclopedia of philosophy* http://plato.stanford.edu/archives/spr2016/entries/ethics-internet-research/>.

Burnette, D. (1994). Managing chronic illness alone in late life: Sisyphus at work. In C. K. Reissman (Ed.) *Qualitative studies in social work research*, pp. 5–27. Thousand Oaks, CA: Sage Publications.

Bynum, T. W. (2006). Flourishing ethics. *Ethics and Information Technology*, *8*(4), 157–173.

Campbell, H. S. (1883/1970). *Prisoners of poverty: Women wage-workers, their trades and their lives*. New York: Garrett.

Campbell, D. T., & Stanley, J. C. (1963). *Experimental and quasi-experimental designs for research*. Chicago: Rand McNally.

Carey, B. (2015v May 29). Study on attitudes toward same-sex marriage is retracted by a scientific journal. *New York Times*, p. A16.

Casselman, B. (1972). On the practitioner's orientation toward research. *Smith College Studies in Social Work*, *42*, 211–233.

Chasnoff, G. (2016, Spring). How are FASDs and Zika virus similar? *NTI Upstream*.

Cialdini, R. B. (2006). *Influence: The psychology of persuasion* (4th ed.). New York: Harper Business.

Clayton, R. R., Cattarello A. M., & Johnstone B. M. (1996). The effectiveness of Drug Abuse Resistance Education (Project DARE): 5-year follow-up results. *Preventive-Medicine*, *25*, pp. 307–318.

Cohen, J. (1977). *Statistical power analysis for the behavioral sciences*. New York: Academic Press.

Community Health Works (2001). *A community needs assessment of Lower Manhattan following the World Trade Center attack*. New York: NYC Department of Health.

Cowger, C. D. (1984). Statistical significance tests: Scientific ritualism or scientific method? *Social Service Review*, *58*, 358–372.

Creswell, J. W. (1998). *Qualitative inquiry and research design: Choosing among five traditions*. Thousand Oaks, CA: Sage.

Creswell, J. W., Plano Clark, V. L., Gutmann, M. L., & Hanson, W. E. (2003). Advanced mixed methods research designs. In A. Tashakkori & C. Teddlie (Eds.), *Handbook of mixed methods in social and behavioral research* (pp. 209–240). Thousand Oaks, CA: Sage.

Cross, T. L., Bazron, B. J., Dennis, K. W., & Issacs, M. R. (1989). The cultural competence continuum. In *Toward a culturally competent system of care: A monograph on effective services for minority children who are severely emotionally disturbed* (p. 13). Washington, DC: Child and Adolescent Service System Program, Technical Assistance Center, Center for Child Health and Mental Health Policy, Georgetown University Child Development Center.

CSWE (2015). 2015 EPAS. https://www.cswe.org/Accreditation/Standards-and-Policies/2015-EPAS.

Dillman, D. A. (1978). *Mail and telephone surveys: The total design method*. New York: Wiley-Interscience.

Dillman, D. A., Smyth, J. D., & Christian, M. L. (2014). *Internet, phone, mail, and mixed-mode surveys: The tailored design method* (4th ed.). New York: Wiley.

Duggan, A., Fuddy, L., Burrell, L., Higman, S. M., McFarlane, E., Windham, A., & Sia, C. (2004a). Randomized trial of a statewide home visiting program to prevent child abuse: Impact in reducing parental risk factors. *Child Abuse and Neglect*, *28*, 623–643.

Duggan, A., McFarlane, E., Fuddy, L., Burrell, L., Higman, S. M., Windham, A., & Sia, C. (2004b). Randomized trial of a statewide home visiting program: Impact in preventing child abuse and neglect. *Child Abuse and Neglect*, *28*, 597–622.

El-Khorazaty, N. M., Johnson, A.A., Kiely, M., El Mohandes, A., Subramanian, S., Laryea, H. A., Murray, K. B., Thornberry, J. S., & Joseph, J. G. (2007). Recruitment and retention of low-income minority women in a behavioral intervention to reduce smoking, depression, and intimate partner violence during pregnancy. *BMC Public Health 7*, 233, DOI :10.1186/1471-2458-7-233.

Elo, S., & Kyngäs, H. (2008). The qualitative content analysis process. *Journal of Advanced Nursing, 52*(1), 107–115.

Federal Register (2016). Annual update of the HHS poverty guidelines. U.S. Department of Health and Human Services. Retrieved July 23, 2016 from https://www.federalregister.gov/articles/2016/01/25/2016-01450/annual-update-of-the-hhs-poverty-guidelines#t-1.

Fehr-Snyder, K., Nichols, J., & Slivka, J. (2004, March 18). ASU vows to fight Havasupai lawsuits. www.azcentral.com/families/education/articles/0318genes18.htm.

Figueira-McDonough, J. (1993). Policy practice: The neglected side of social work intervention. *Social Work, 38*(2), 179–188.

Finn, J. (2002). MSW student perception of the ethics and efficacy of online therapy. *Journal of Social Work Education, 38*, 403–420.

Finn, J. (2004). A survey of online harassment at a university campus. *Journal of Interpersonal Violence, 19*, 468–483.

Finn, J., Kerman, B. & LeCornec, J. (2003). *Providing technology to foster families: First year evaluation of the Building Skills–Building Futures Program*. Hartford, CT: Casey Family Services.

Fischer, J. & Corcoran, K. (2007). *Measures for clinical practice: A sourcebook* (4th ed.) (2 vols). New York, NY: Oxford.

Fitz-Gibbon, C. T., & Morris, L. L. (1987). *How to design a program evaluation*. Beverly Hills, CA: Sage.

Fletcher, A. C., & Hunter, A. G. (2003). Strategies for obtaining parental consent to participate in research. *Family Relations, 52*(3), 216–221.

Foner, N. (1995). Relatives as trouble: Nursing home aides and patients' families. In J. Neil Henderson & M. D. Vesperi (Eds.) *The culture of long term care: Nursing Home Ethnography*, pp. 165–177. Westport, CT: Greenwood.

Gao, X. (2015). *Prevalence and risk factors of elder maltreatment among Chinese Americans*. Unpublished doctoral dissertation. Arizona State University.

Glisson, C. (1985). In defense of statistical tests of significance. *Social Service Review, 59*, 377–386.

Goliszek, A. (2003). *In the name of science*. New York: St. Martin's Press.

Gould, S. J. (1981). *The mismeasure of man*. New York: W. W. Norton.

Gould, R. L., Coulson, M. C., & Howard, R. J. (2012). Cognitive behavioral therapy for depression in older people: A meta-analysis and meta-regression of randomized controlled trials. *Journal of the American Geriatrics Society, 60*(10), 1817–1830.

Guilford, J. P., & Fruchter, B. (1973). *Fundamental statistics in psychology and education* (5th ed.). New York: McGraw-Hill.

Haas, A. P., Rodgers, P. L., & Herman, J. L. (2014). *Suicide attempts among transgender and gender non-conforming adults: Findings of the national transgender discrimination survey*. New York: American Foundation for Suicide Prevention.

Harmon M. A. (1993). *Reducing the risk of drug involvement among early adolescents: An evaluation of Drug Abuse Resistance Education (DARE)*. College Park, MD: Center for Substance Abuse Research (CESAR), University of Maryland.

Harmon, A. (2010, April 21). Indian tribe wins fight to limit research of its DNA. *The New York Times*, http://www.nytimes.com/2010/04/22/us/22dna.html.

Herrenkohl, T. I., Hill, K. G., Chung, I., Guo, J., Abbott, R. D., & Hawkins, J. D. (2003). Protective factors against serious violent behavior in adolescence: A prospective study of aggressive children. *Social Work Research*, 27(3), 179–191.

Hite, S. (1989). *The Hite report: Women and love: A cultural revolution in progress*. New York: Alfred A. Knopf.

Hsieh, H-F., & Shannon, S. E. (2005). Three approaches to qualitative content analysis. *Qualitative Health Research*, 15(9), 1277–1288.

Hudson, W. W. (1991). *MPSI technical manual*. Tempe, AZ: WALMYR.

Hudson, W. W., & Nurius, P. S. (1994). *Controversial issues in social work research*. Needham Heights, MA: Allyn & Bacon.

Hull, G. (2005). Research with words: Qualitative inquiry. National Center for the Study of Adult Learning and Literacy. Retrieved September 19, 2005 from www.ncsall. net/?id=468.

Jenkins, L. (2016, April 3). The four letters more dangerous than Zika. https://medium. com/@digital_dad/the-four-letters-more-dangerous-than-zika-255b29f85c03#. u3yzskq3b.

Jenson, J. M., & Fraser, M. (2016). *Social policy for children and families: A risk and resilience perspective*. Thousand Oaks, CA: Sage.

Johnson, S., Pion, C., & Jennings, V. (2013). Current methods and attitudes of women towards contraception in Europe and America. *Reproductive Health*, 10(7).

Kang, H. K., Bullman, T. A., Smolenski, D. J., Skopp, N. A., Gahm, G. A., & Reger, M. A. (2015). Suicide risk among 1.3 million veterans who were on active duty during the Iraq and Afghanistan wars. *Ann Epidemiol*. 25(2), 96–100. DOI: 10.1016/j. annepidem.2014.11.020.

Kansas Foundation for Medical Care (2010). *An effectiveness based approach* (5th ed.). Newbury Park, CA: Sage.

Kettner, P., Moroney, R., & Martin, L. (2017) *Designing and managing programs: An effectiveness-based approach* (5th ed.). Newbury Park, CA: Sage.

Kirk, S. A., & Fischer, J. (1976). Do social workers understand research? *Journal of Education for Social Workers*, 12, 63–70.

Kirk, S. A., & Reid, W. J. (2002). *Science and social work: A critical appraisal*. New York: Columbia University Press.

Krysik, J., & LeCroy, C. W. (2002). The empirical validation of an instrument to predict risk of recidivism among juvenile offenders. *Research on Social Work Practice*, 12(1), 71–81.

Kyhle Westermark, P., Hansson, K., & Olsson, M. (2011). Multidimensional treatment foster care (MTFC): Results from an independent replication. *Journal of Family Therapy*, 33, 20–41. DOI: 10.1111/j.1467.2010.000515.x.

LaFree, G., Birkbeck, C., & Wilson, N. C. (1995). *Policemen in the classroom: Albuquerque adolescents' opinions about the Drug Awareness and Resistance Education program*. Albuquerque, NM: New Mexico Criminal Justice Statistical Analysis Center.

Lanigan, J. (2014). Physical activity for young children: A quantitative study of child care providers' knowledge, attitudes, and health promotion practices. *Early Childhood Education Journal*, 42, 11–18.

LeCompte, M. D., & Schensul, J. J. (1999). Designing and conducting ethnographic research. In J. J. Schensul & M. D. LeCompte (Eds.) *Ethnographer's Toolkit*, Vol. 1. Walnut Creek, CA: Altamira.

LeCroy, C. W., & Krysik, J. (2011). Randomized trial of the Healthy Families Arizona home visiting program. *Children and Youth Services Review*. DOI: 10.1016/j.childyouth.2011.04.036.

Lehman, A. F. (1998). Public health policy, community services, and outcomes for patients with schizophrenia. *Psychiatric Clinics of North America, 21*, 221–231.

Lenhart, A., Madden, M., & Hitlin, P. (2005). *Teens and technology: Youth are leading the transition to a fully wired and mobile nation*. Pew Internet & American Life Project.

Lewinson, T. (2010). Residents' coping strategies in an extended-stay hotel home. *Journal of Ethnographic & Qualitative Research, 4*, 180–196.

Lundahl, B. W., Nimer, J., & Parsons, B. (2006). Preventing child abuse: A meta-analysis of parent training programs. *Research on Social Work Practice, 16*, 251–262.

Lynam, D. R., Milich, R., Zimmerman, R., Novak, S. P., Logan, T. K., Martin, C., Leukefeld, C., & Clayton, R. (1999). Project DARE: No effects at 10-year follow-up. *Journal of Consulting and Clinical Psychology, 67*, 590–593. Available at www.apa.org/journals/features/ccp674590.pdf.

March of Dimes (2009). Study: Average preemie costs $49,000 in first year. Retrieved July 24, 2016 from http://www.cnn.com/2009/HEALTH/03/17/premature.babies/index.html?eref=rss_us.

Marcus, A., & Oransky, I. (2015, May 22). What's behind big science frauds? *The Opinion Pages, New York Times*. http://www.nytimes.com/2015/05/23/opinion/whats-behind-big-science-frauds.html?action=click&contentCollection=Science&region=Footer&module=WhatsNext&version=WhatsNext&contentID=WhatsNext&moduleDetail=undefined&pgtype=Multimedia.

Marsiglia, F. F., & Kulis, S. (2015). *Diversity, oppression, and change* (2nd ed.). Oxford: Lyceum.

McMurchie, M. (2013–2014). Dustbin of quackery Senate Bill 1172 and the legal implications of banning reparative therapy for homosexual minors, *Southern California Law Review, 87*(6), 1519–1548.

Mendes, E., & McGeeney, K. (2012, August 16). In U. S., majority overweight or obese in all 50 states. Gallup Well-Being. Retrieved from http://www.gallup.com/poll/156707/majority-overweight-obese-states.aspx.

Miles, M. B., & Huberman, A. M. (1994). *Qualitative data analysis: A sourcebook of new methods* (2nd ed.). Thousand Oaks, CA: Sage Publications.

Milgram, S. (1963). Behavioral study of obedience. *Journal of Abnormal and Social Psychology, 67*, 371–378.

Moore, D. (2005, January). *The elusive truth*. Retrieved www.gallup.com/poll/content/print.aspx?ci=14656.

Morse, J. M., & Richards, L. (2002). *Readme first for a user's guide to qualitative methods*. Thousand Oaks, CA: Sage.

Munford, R., & Sanders, J. (2016). Understanding service engagement: Young people's experience of service use. *Journal of Social Work, 16*(3), 283–302.

Murphy, D. E. (2004, March 18). San Francisco married 4,037 same-sex pairs from 46 states. *New York Times*, p. A26.

National Coalition for Homeless Veterans (2010) The 2010 National Homeless Assessment Report to Congress. https://www.hudexchange.info/resources/documents/2010homelessassessmentreport.pdf.

NASW (2016). https://www.socialworkers.org/join.asp.

NASW (2017). *Code of Ethics*. Revised and adopted by the Delegate Assembly of the National Association of Social Workers. Washington, DC: NASW Press.

Nordrum, A. (2014, September). The new D.A.R.E. Program: This one works. *Scientific American*. Retrieved July 24, 2016 from http://www.scientificamerican.com/article/the-new-d-a-r-e-program-this-one-works/.

NPR (2014, April 25). Blood victory in medical research dispute. NR. Retrieved http://www.npr.org/2014/04/25/306832661/blood-victory-in-medical-research-disp.

NTI Upstream (2016, Spring). *Spring Newsletter*. How are FASDs and the Zika virus similar? Author.

Office of Management and Budget (1993). Government performance results act. Office of Management and Budget. Washington, DC. Retrieved 19 September, 2005 from www.whitehouse.gov/omb/mgmtgpra/gplaw2m.html#h1.

Olson, H. C., Ohlemiller, M. M., O'Connor, M. J., Brown, C. W., Morris, C. A., & Damus, K. (2009). National task force on fetal alcohol syndrome and fetal alcohol effect. A call to action. U.S. Department of Health and Human Services.

Patton, M. Q. (1980). *Qualitative evaluation methods*. Beverly Hills, CA: Sage.

Patton, M. Q. (2005). Misuse of evaluation. In *Encyclopedia of evaluation* (pp. 255–256). Sage: Thousand Oaks, CA.

Pence, G. E. (2000). *Classic cases in medical ethics: Accounts of cases that have shaped medical ethics, with philosophical, legal, and historical backgrounds* (3rd ed.). New York: McGraw-Hill.

Pew Internet & American Life Project (2013). Health online 2013. Retrieved July 23, 2016 from http://www.pewinternet.org/2013/01/15/health-online-2013/.

Pfeiffer, J. (nd). https://www.goodreads.com/quotes/488215-man-is-a-slow-sloppy-and-brilliant-thinker-computers-are.

Picard, R. (1997). *Affective computing*. Cambridge, MA: Cambridge University Press.

President's Commission on Mental Health (1978). *Report to the president from the U.S. President's Commission on Mental Health* (Vol. 1). Washington, DC: Superintendent of Documents, U.S. Government Printing Office.

Proctor, E. (2001). Social work research: Asking relevant questions and answering them well. *Social Work Research*, 25(1), 3–4.

RAINN (2016). National sexual assault hotline: Statistics. Retrieved July 23, 2016 from https://www.rainn.org/statistics/people-helped-through-national-sexual-assault-hotline.

Reid, W. J., & Fortune, A. E. (1992). Research utilization in direct social work practice. In A. Grasso & I. Epstein (Eds.), *Research utilization in the social services* (pp. 97–115). New York: Haworth.

Reynolds, C., & Picard, R. (2005). Evaluation of affective computing systems from a dimensional metaethical position, 1st Augmented Cognition International Conference, In Conjunction with the 11th International Conference on Human-Computer Interaction. July 22–27, 2005, Las Vegas, Nevada, U.S.A. Appears in: *Foundations of augmented cognition*. Lawrence Erlbaum Associates Publishers, Mahwah, NJ, pp. 899–907.

Roe-Sepowitz, D. (2005). Indicators of self-mutilation: Youth in custody. Unpublished doctoral dissertation. Florida State University, Tallahassee, FL.

Rosenblatt, A. (1968). The practitioner's use and evaluation of research. *Social Work*, 13, 53–59.

Saint-Exupéry, A. (1943/2000). *The little prince*. (R. Howard, Trans.) Orlando, FL: Harcourt.

Saltzburg, S. (2004). Learning that an adolescent child is gay or lesbian: The parent experience. *Social Work*, 49, 109–118.

Sarason, I. G., Sarason, B. R., Slichter, S. J., Beatty, P. G., Meyer, D. M., & Bolgiano, D. C. (1993). Increasing participation of blood donors in a bone-marrow registry. *Health Psychology*, *12*, 272–276.

Sheehan, N. W., & Donorfio, L. M. (1999). Efforts to create meaning in the relationship between aging mothers and their caregiving daughters. *Journal of Aging Studies*, *13*(2), 161–176.

Short, K. (2011, November). The research supplemental poverty measure: 2010. Consumer Income. United States Census Bureau.

Smith, S. J. (1992). Operating on a child's heart: A pedagogical view of hospitalization. In J. M. Morse (Ed.), *Qualitative Health Research* (pp. 104–122). Newbury Park, CA: Sage.

Spence, S., White, M. Adamson A. J., et al. (2014). Does the use of passive or active consent affect consent or completion rates or dietary data quality? Repeat cross-sectional survey among school children 11–12 years. *BMJ Open*, *4*. DOI: 10.1136/bmjopen-2014-006457.

Steckler, A., McLeroy, K. R., Goodman, R. M., Bird, S. T., & McCormick, L. (1992). Toward integrating qualitative and quantitative methods: An introduction. *Health Education Quarterly*, *19*(1), 1–8.

Stein, L. I., & Test, M. A. (1980). Alternative to mental hospital treatment. I. Conceptual model, treatment program, and clinical evaluation. *Archives of General Psychiatry*, *37*, 392–397.

Strauss, A., & Corbin, J. (1998). *Basics of qualitative research: Techniques and procedures for developing grounded theory* (2nd ed.). Thousand Oaks, CA: Sage Publications.

Swales, J., & Feak, C. B. (2004). *Academic writing for graduate students*. Ann Arbor, MI: University of Michigan Press.

Taylor, J. R. (1997) *An introduction to error analysis* (2nd ed.). Sausalito, CA: University Science Books.

Tenkku, L. E., Mengel, M. B., Nicholson, R. A., Hile, M. G., Morris, D. S., & Salas, J. (2011). A web-based intervention to reduce alcohol-exposed pregnancies in the community. *Health Education and Behavior*, *38*, 563–573.

The Data Center (2011). Research Reports. http://www.datacenter.org/publications/#New%20Research%20Reports.

Trochim, W. M. K. (2006). Types of designs. Retrieved August 1, 2016 from http://www.socialresearchmethods.net/kb/destypes.php.

U.S. Census Bureau (2012). Profile America facts for features. Retrieved from https://www.census.gov/newsroom/releases/archives/facts_for_features_special_editions/cb12-.

U.S. Social Security Administration (2016). Social Security benefits for children with disabilities. Retrieved August 7, 2016 from https://www.ssa.gov/pubs/EN-05-10026.pdf.

U.S. Department of Justice, Federal Bureau of Investigation (2015). 2014 Crime in the United States. Author. Chapter 1 exhibit 1.2.

U.S. Department of Health and Human Services (2016). Poverty thresholds 2015. http://www.census.gov/data/tables/time-series/demo/income-poverty/historical-poverty-thresholds.html.

Van Noorden, R. (2011). The trouble with retractions. *Nature*, *478*, 26–28.

Wakefield, J. C. (1988). Psychotherapy, distributive justices, and social work. Part I. Distributive justice as a conceptual framework for social work. *Social Service Review*, *62*, 187–210.

Walther, J. (1996). Computer-mediated communication: Impersonal, interpersonal, and hyperpersonal interaction. *Communication Research, 23*(1), 3–43.

Webster's encyclopedic unabridged dictionary of the English language. (2012). New York: Random House.

West, S. L., & O'Neal, K. K. (2004). Project D.A.R.E. outcome effectiveness revisited. *American Journal of Public Health, 94*(6), 1027–1029.

Westerfelt, A. (2004). A qualitative investigation of adherence issues for men who are HIV positive. *Social Work, 49*, 231–239.

Woodyatt, C. R., Finneran, C. A., & Stephenson, R. (2016). In-person versus online focus group discussions: A comparative analysis of data quality. *Qualitative Health Research, 26*, 741–749.

Zalmanowitz, S. J., Babins-Wagner, R., Rodger, S., Corbett, B. A., & Leschied, A. (2013). The association of readiness to change and motivational interviewing with treatment outcomes in males involved in domestic violence group therapy. *Journal of Interpersonal Violence, 28*, 956–974.

Zayas, L. E., Wisniewski, A. M., & Kennedy, T. (2013). Instrumental activity of daily living limitations and supports in a clinic population of low-income Puerto Rican elderly adults with chronic diseases. *Journal of the American Geriatrics Society, 61*, 1789–1795.

Glossary

AB design: In single subject research, measurement of the dependent variable during the baseline (A) and intervention (B) phases

ABC design: In single subject research, a design in which the dependent variable is measured at the baseline (A), intervention (B), and follow-up (C) phases

abstract: A brief statement of approximately 100 words that summarizes the objectives, methods, results, and conclusions of a research article or proposal

active consent: A form of informed consent that requires the parent or legal guardian to sign an informed consent form, agency case records, newspaper accounts, and even suggestion boxes

alternative hypothesis: A hypothesis stating that a relationship exists between two or more variables

American Psychological Association (APA) format: The manuscript style and reference format of the American Psychological Association used in many social science and social work journals

anecdotal information: Based on casual observations rather than research which puts the reliability of such information in doubt

anonymity: The agreement not to record a participant's name or other identifying information such as address or social security number. This does not guarantee confidentiality

applied knowledge: The use of research to develop knowledge that will inform social work practice

array: A set of data arranged in ascending or descending order column by column

assent: A form or verbal statement stating that a minor or disabled person is aware that his or her parent or guardian has consented to his or her participation in a research study and that the minor or disabled person voluntarily agrees to participate

attributes: In measurement, the options that a variable may take, for example, the attributes of the variable *political party* may be *Democrat, Republican, independent,* or *other*

attrition: Tendency of participants to withdraw prematurely from a research study

baseline: In single subject design, this phase involves repeated measures of the dependent variable prior to the introduction of the intervention

before-and-after research design: A term for research that includes a pretest and posttest

beneficence: A moral principle stating that one's first consideration (in research) should be to "Do no harm"

bimodal: When two values occur in a distribution with the greatest relative frequency

bivariate analysis: Examination of the relationship between two variables at a time

bivariate statistics: Statistical tests that examine the relationship between two variables at a time, for example, t-tests and Pearson correlation

blind review: In the process of publication of research articles, reviewers do not see any identifying information about the author when reviewing the manuscript

bracket: To suspend all judgments about what is "real" because, in the phenomenological tradition, reality can only be understood in the context of the meaning assigned to it by an individual

case-level research designs: Research designs that are appropriate for an N of 1

case study: A research strategy that seeks to examine a single unit of analysis, be it an event, person, family, group, organization, or company, in order to generate an in-depth understanding of that unit

central tendency: How the data are similar or what is typical of a data set. In univariate analysis, the mean, median, and mode are typically reported measures of central tendency

changing criterion design (changing intensity design): A single subject research design in which the criterion for changing the level of performance is gradually increased (or decreased) until a specified goal is reached

Chi-square (χ^2): A commonly used statistic to test the association between two nominal- or ordinal-level variables

closed-ended question: Survey question that forces the respondent to choose from a limited number of predefined responses

cluster sampling: A random sampling method in which aggregates of elements called clusters are randomly sampled first, and then the elements of the population are either all included (cluster sampling) or are randomly sampled (multistage random sampling) from the selected clusters

coding: In qualitative analysis, a method of categorizing nonnumeric data so that themes and common elements can be grouped to make them manageable for analysis

coefficient of determination (r^2): The square of the correlation coefficient

cohort study: Longitudinal research that follows a group of individuals over time but that is not concerned that they be the same individuals from one time to the next

comparison group: In experimental research, the group that is not subject to the independent variable when group assignment is not based on randomization

computer-assisted telephone interviewing (CATI): A telephone survey in which the computer asks the questions and records the responses

concept: An abstract or general idea; a symbol for some observable attribute or phenomenon

concurrent validity: The ability of a measure to predict an external criterion, as it concurrently exists

confidence interval: A statistical range with a specified probability that a given sample lies within the range

confidence level: In sampling, the degree to which we can be sure that the results from a sample represent the population

constant: Something that does not vary; represented by only one numeric value or category

constant comparison: In qualitative research, a method in which the researcher first identifies codes of meaning within the data and combines these codes to form categories. The researcher then continually compares subsequent data with those categories to describe them completely in terms of their properties and dimensions

construct validity: The extent that a measure is related to other measures to which it is theoretically related and not related to those to which it is not theoretically related

content validity: The extent that the measure has captured the entire domain of the concept

contingency questions: aka filter questions, direct the respondent in a survey to questions based on their response to a previous question. For example, those who answer yes to a question on smoking behavior would be directed to a particular set of questions, different from questions for those who respond no to the question. Contingency questions allow some respondents to skip some questions

contingency table: A table showing the joint or compound frequencies of occurrence of two or more variables or attributes. Frequency and/or percentages placed in the cells of the table, giving the proportion that each cell contributes to the sum of particular rows or columns, are helpful in detecting the strength and direction of relationships

control group: In experimental research, the group not receiving the experimental condition

convenience sample: A nonprobability sample in which the selection of sampling elements is based on the most available elements to constitute the sample

convergent validity: The extent that the measure correlates highly with variables theoretically related to it

correlation: A statistical test that provides a measure of the strength of the relationship between two sets of interval or ratio level numbers or scores

correlation coefficient: A number that represents the strength and direction of the relationship between two interval or ratio level variables

correlation matrix: A way to present the findings of the correlation between several variables; each variable is listed in the rows down the left-hand side of the matrix as well as in the columns across the top of the matrix. The correlation between any two variables is found in the cell at the intersection of the row and column

cost/benefit analysis: An estimate of all costs and benefits of a program expressed in monetary units

cost-effectiveness analysis: Estimates the net costs and effects of an intervention compared with some alternative

cost minimization analysis: A form of cost-effectiveness analysis that assesses the costs of two alternative methods of producing the same outcome

Council on Social Work Education (CSWE): Develops educational policy and accreditation standards for social work education programs on the baccalaureate and master's levels. CSWE provides accreditation, continuing education, publications, and advocacy related to social work education

criterion-related validity: Extent to which the measurement correlates with an external criterion of the phenomenon under study

critical thinking: The process of analyzing and applying evidence to arrive at a reasoned course of action or decision

Cronbach's alpha: A measure of the internal consistency of a group of items that make up a scale. A high alpha suggests the items measure the same concept

cross-sectional design: A research design in which subjects are assessed at a single point in time

cross-sectional study: Research that involves observation at one point in time

crosstabulation: Expressing the association between two or more nominal or ordinal measured variables through a contingency table or crosstab whereas the frequencies of each variable value are displayed

cultural competence: The ability to perform effectively in multicultural settings based on an understanding of one's own and other's language, customs, values, and beliefs

cultural proficiency: The culmination or end-point on the continuum of cultural competence. It is characterized by knowledge, attitudes, and behavior that hold culture in high esteem

curvilinear relationship: The relationship between two variables does not continue in the same direction over the entire range of values and can be represented by a curved line

cutting scores: On a scale, a measure that sets the difference between two levels of a condition or performance

data analysis: The process in which researchers turn data into information that can be used to determine the nature or cause of something

database: A grid that specifies all of the variables in the study, and has a space called a cell to record the data on each variable for each sampling unit

data codebook: A listing of each variable in the order it appears in the database along with associated attributes and codes and labels

data collection protocol: A set of written instructions and policies that outline the specifics of contact with participants and guide data collection

data display: In qualitative research, a visual representation of the data such as a matrix or chart to make it easier to see themes, patterns, and hypotheses

data entry error: A wrong value entered in the statistical program due to a skipped question, transposed digits, or other typing mistake

data reduction: The analysis of something into simpler elements or organized systems, especially with a view to explaining or understanding it; generally associated with the quantitative research approach and the opposite of an approach that is holistic

data verification: The process of checking to see that the data has been entered and coded correctly

deductive reasoning: An approach to research in which hypotheses are logically derived from a theoretical framework prior to beginning a research study

degrees of freedom: In statistical tests, the number of values in the final calculation of a statistic that are free to vary

delayed pretest: The second of two pretests administered prior to the administration of an independent variable

dependent samples t-test: A parametric test that assesses the likelihood that the means of two measures from dependent samples taken at two points in time come from the same population or are statistically the same

dependent variable: The variable that changes its values according to the value of other elements that are present (the independent variable)

descriptive research: Research in which the purpose is to describe the characteristics of the problem and the characteristics of those affected by the problem. This involves questions such as: How many people are affected and with what consequences? How does the problem differ by demographic and cultural characteristics?

descriptive statistics: Measures used to summarize the numbers included in the database into fewer numbers that are descriptive of the entire set of data. These often include the mean, standard deviation, median, and mode

deviant cases: In qualitative research, those cases that do not follow a pattern similar to the majority of cases

dimensions: In qualitative research, the range of properties within a category, its extremes and variability

directional (one-tailed) hypothesis: A research hypothesis that specifies the nature of the relationship between variables, that is, either positive or negative

discriminant validity: The degree to which the measure does not correlate highly with variables hypothesized to be unrelated to it

disproportionate sampling: The proportion of each stratum in the sample does not correspond to the respective proportion in the population; small strata may be over-sampled

distribution: The values for a particular variable

double-blind: A research study in which neither the researcher nor the participant knows to which group a participant is assigned

dynamic measure: Measures that are amenable to change over time, e.g. number of days of attendance in the past month

ecological fallacy: An error in interpretation of research data that occurs when a statement related to one unit of analysis is made on the basis of data collected from a different unit of analysis

effect size (ES): A measure of the strength of the relationship between two variables independent of sample size, often used in meta-analysis to compare the strength of treatment effects

element: Each member or entity in the population

emic: The participant's perspective in qualitative analysis

encryption: The translation of data into a secret code; the most effective way to achieve data security

ethnography: Qualitative research methods involving interview and observation aimed at describing the culture of a group

etic: The researcher's perspective in qualitative analysis

evaluability assessment: Analysis of a program to determine whether the goals and objectives are stated clearly enough to permit program evaluation

evidence-based practice (EBP): Use of interventions based on the research literature or clinical expertise that have shown consistent scientific evidence of being related to preferred client outcomes

exhaustive: In measurement, there is a category appropriate for each response

existing records: Include paper and electronic documents, databases, and other non-document artifacts of human behavior, often used for secondary data analysis

expected frequency: The expected number of occurrences of an event based on the probability of its occurrence. For example, the expected frequency of heads on a coin flip is 0.5

experimental conditions: In social work, the interventions used to produce positive changes; the independent variable(s)

experimental design (this is the same as experimental research design)

experimental group: In experimental research, the group receiving the experimental condition

experimental mortality: A threat to internal validity; the danger that an observed effect is due to the different kinds of persons who dropped out of a particular group and so were not observed at posttest

experimental research design: A research design in which there is random assignment to two or more groups, introduction of an independent variable to the experimental group, and measurement of the dependent variable following introduction of the independent variable

experimental success: The intervention has resulted in clear improvement in target objectives, but not all goals have been fully reached

explanatory research: Research in which the purpose is to explain how and why things happen. Questions are targeted at generating an in-depth understanding of the problem area. It often seeks to establish cause-and-effect relationships that allow the prediction of events

exploratory research: Research in which the purpose is to gain an initial understanding of the general nature of an area; to identify relevant variables. This is needed when little is known about an area of research

expressed need: An expression of need based on concrete evidence such as waiting lists, documented agency records, or program attendance

external validity: The degree that the research findings can be generalized to other cases not studied

face validity: The extent that a measure appears to be valid to those being administered the measure

fidelity (this is the same as treatment fidelity)

focus group: A method of data collection that requires in-person interviewing of about five to 10 people per group by a skilled moderator in an environment that is conducive to sharing information

follow-up observation: In experimental research, subsequent measurement of the dependent variable following the initial measurement of dependent variable after the introduction of the independent variable; a measurement to assess the longer-term impact of the independent variable

formative (process) evaluation: Research to determine whether the program is being delivered as intended

frequency distribution: A summary of variable that provides a count of how many times each variable value is represented in the database

gaining entry: In qualitative research, gaining access to the target participants

gatekeepers: In qualitative research, those who are key in providing access to the research participants

generalizability: The extent to which the results of research based on a sample can be generalized to the entire population

generalization: Applying results based on a sample to the entire population

Government Performance and Results Act (GPRA): Federal legislation in 1993 intended to hold agencies accountable for achieving program results through measurement and public reporting. Updated in 2010 by the Government Performance as people, organizations, and agencies

group research designs: Research designs that are appropriate for answering research questions that deal with groups of elements, such as people, organizations, and agencies

grounded theory: A process for theory development based on constant comparison of the actual data collected during the process of qualitative research and the emerging theory based on the data. The theory is emergent—it is discovered in the data

heterogeneous: Consisting of dissimilar parts. In research, a sample or population with considerable variation

histogram: A graphical display of data in which frequencies are shown as bars with no space between categories

history effects: A threat to internal validity; the observed effect in a research study is influenced by an event that takes place between the pretest and the posttest

homogeneous: Consisting of similar parts. In research, a sample or population with little variation

human subjects: Human participants in research studies

hypothesis: A tentative answer to a research question written as a statement and used as a basis for further investigation

impact: In program evaluation, the changes in the larger community or social system as a result, at least in part, of program activities

implementation evaluation: A type of formative evaluation that focuses on the processes and activities that are established to implement the program

inference: In sampling, the researcher's claim that what is true of the sample is likely true of the population from which the sample was drawn

inferential statistics: Statistical tests that use probability theory for inferring the properties of a population from the analysis of the properties of a data sample drawn from it. Read more at: *http://www.businessdictionary.com/definition/inferentialstatistics.html# ixzz27fVmL6Ey*

informal conversation: A casual conversation without a specific agenda, used in qualitative analysis as one source of data

independent samples t-test: A parametric test that assesses the likelihood that the means of two groups come from the same population or are statistically the same

independent variable: The variable assumed to be responsible for change in the dependent variable

inductive approach: An approach to research in which observations are collected and analyzed prior to theory development, and tentative conclusions are reached based on those observations

informed consent: A procedure whereby subjects agree in writing to participate in a research study under specific conditions; in which rights and responsibilities of subjects and the researcher are specified

institutional review board (IRB): A peer/community review committee who volunteer their time to review research proposals and monitor ongoing research studies to ensure the protection of the people participating in the research

instrumentation: A threat to internal validity; the unintended changes in the way the dependent variable is measured over time

internal consistency: The extent that the items in an index measure a single concept; the extent that all items correlate with each other; represented by Cronbach's alpha coefficient, which can range from 0 to 1.0

internal validity: The extent of evidence that changes in the dependent variable are the result of the independent variable and not some other factor

interpretivism: A philosophical paradigm concerned with understanding social conditions through the meaning individuals ascribe to their personal experiences as interpreted by the researcher. It forms the basis for qualitative research

interrater reliability: For observational measures or existing records, the extent of agreement of ratings between two different raters

interval measurement: The attributes of the variable have order and equally spaced categories, but there is no true zero point for the measure

interview schedule: A measurement tool in which questions are asked of respondents in face-to-face or telephone interviews

intrarater reliability: For observational measures or existing records, the extent of agreement of ratings between the same rater at different points in time

intrasession history: A source of internal invalidity when an event that influences the outcome occurs in one group and not the other

item: A single indicator of a variable

key informants: Community members with known expertise about the history, needs, culture, power structure, and reactions of the community; interviews with key informants are often useful in needs assessment and program planning

known groups validity: A form of criterion validity in which it is shown that a measure can discriminate between groups based on the key variables, for example, a depression scale should be able to discriminate between those in treatment for depression and those not in treatment

linear correlation: The degree to which two variables measured at the interval or ratio levels are related or co-vary

linear relationship: The relationship between two variables continues in the same direction over the entire range of values and can be represented by a straight line

line of best fit: In linear correlation, a straight line drawn though the points so that one half of the points is

literature review: A summary of what has been previously published on a problem area by scholars and researchers

logical positivism: A philosophical paradigm that uses empirical analysis through observation and measurement as the way of knowing. It forms the basis for quantitative research

logical inference: An estimation of the probability that a decision is correct based on logic or beliefs rather than mathematical calculations

logic model: In program evaluation, a diagrammatic summary of goals, objectives, and measures used to chart the path from the social conditions that necessitate the program to the evaluation of the program benefits

longitudinal design: Uses three or more observations over an extended time period

longitudinal studies: Research in which the measurement of a phenomenon is conducted at multiple points in time; research requiring multiple observations

margin of error: In sampling, an estimation of the extent to which a sample's reported percentages would vary if the same sample were taken multiple times

matrix questions: Multiple questions presented in a grid with the same set of response choices. Presenting questions with the same set of response in a matrix format saves overall space and time to respond

maturation: A threat to internal validity; an observed effect is due to the respondent's growing older, wiser, stronger, and more experienced between the pretest and posttest

mean: The average value for a set of data calculated by dividing the total of the values by the number of values

measurement: The process of assigning numbers or other symbols to characteristics or attributes of a concept according to specified rules

measures of variability: Describe how the data differ or vary from what is common

median: The value that divides a distribution in half—the point at which 50 percent of the data points fall below and 50% are above the value

memoing: The process of keeping a running log of thoughts, concerns, and questions regarding the coding process and the use of certain codes

methodology: How the research was carried out, including the research design, sampling, and measurement

minimum value: The value that is the lowest value relative to all of the other values in a distribution

missing data: Responses that are not provided or are illegible, out of range, or are an obvious error

mixed-methods approach: Use of a combination of qualitative and quantitative research approaches in which the limitations of one approach are offset by the benefits of the other

mode: The most frequently occurring response

multigroup, posttest-only research design: A research design with more than two groups and in which there is no pretest but rather the measurement/observation occurs after the administration of the intervention in the treatment group and at a comparable time in the comparison or control group. This design may test more than one intervention or variations of an intervention resulting in the need for more than one intervention group

multimodal: When more than two values occur with greatest relative frequency in the distribution

multiple group time series research design: A research design with more than two groups and in which multiple measurements/observations are taken over time of the same variables, typically at defined periods such as every six months

multigroup research designs: Research designs that include more than two groups, for example a treatment group, a comparison group, and a comparison group with a delayed pretest

multiple baseline design: In single subject research, two or more dependent variables are measured. This is useful in showing the effect of the intervention on two or more related areas

multistage cluster sampling: A variation of cluster sampling in which the researcher repeats the random sampling at increasingly targeted levels until the sample population is reached

multiple component design: In single subject research (sometimes known as an ABC design), involves the use of sequential interventions or changes in the amount or intensity of the same intervention

multiple treatment interference: A threat to external validity; occurs when the effects of two or more treatments cannot be separated

National Association of Social Workers (NASW): The largest organization of professional social workers in the world, having approximately 150,000 members. NASW works to enhance the professional growth and development of its members and to create and maintain professional standards

NASW Code of Ethics: A set of ethical principles for the practice of social work developed by the National Association of Social Workers

needs assessment: Research to provide evidence about whether a current or proposed program is needed

negative or inverse correlation: The extent to which two variables co-vary in the opposite direction

nominal definition: A definition that describes a concept in ways similar to a dictionary definition. It provides the meaning of the term, but does not define to the degree that it is measurable

nominal measurement: Classifies observations into mutually exclusive and exhaustive categories

nondirectional (two-tailed) hypothesis: A research hypothesis that does not specify the proposed direction of a relationship between variables

non-normal distribution: A distribution that does not meet the requirements of a normal distribution; that does not appear symmetric when plotted

nonparametric statistics: Statistical tests used with data that do not meet the assumptions of parametric statistics

nonprobability sampling: A sampling procedure in which all of the elements in the population have an unknown and usually different probability of being included in the sample

nonrespondents: In sampling, those who did not respond for any reason to a request for research participation

nonresponse error: In survey research, when nonresponse to mail survey follows a certain pattern that may introduce bias into the study

nonsampling error: Sampling error that is not related to the actual sampling procedure and includes inadequate sampling frames, high levels of attrition or nonresponse, and measurement and data entry errors

normal distribution: A theoretical distribution with these properties: Symmetric, unimodal distributed symmetrically about the peak or mode; 50% of the data points fall on either side of the peak, indicating that the value of the median is the same as the value of the mode; the mean value of the distribution is precisely halfway between the ordered data points indicating that it is also equal to the values of the mode and the median

normative need: An expression of need defined by experts based on a set of data or criteria

norms: In a standardized instrument, there is information available about the distribution of the range of scores that can be expected of members of a particular population

null hypothesis: A hypothesis that asserts that no relationship exists between two or more variables

numeric data: Data that are numbers

objective: Specific, measurable statements about what is to be accomplished

observed frequency: The actual frequency of occurrences of an event. For example, obtaining nine of 10 heads on flips of a coin

observer inference: Measurement error caused when an observer explains or understands a behavior, or feeling differently than the way that the person being observed intended

one-group, pretest-posttest research design: A group research design in which there is only one group and that group has an initial measurement or observation, an intervention, and then a second measurement or observation following administration of the intervention. The objective of having two measures/observations is to assess change from the initial measure or observation to the second

one-group, posttest-only research design: A group research design in which there is only one group, and the measurement or observation is only applied after the administration of the intervention. There is no measurement or observation prior to the intervention

one sample t-test: A parametric test that estimates the likelihood that a single sample comes from a given population; that the sample is typical of the population

one-shot case study: A research design employed to answer a research question from observation at one point in time and that is not concerned with an independent variable

one-way analysis of variance (ANOVA): A parametric statistical test used to compare the means of more than two groups

open coding: In qualitative research, a method in which there are no predetermined codes for data analysis—rather, codes emerge from the data

open-ended questions: A form of question in which no present response is required and discourse is encouraged

open interviews: An interview format in which there are no predetermined questions or time limits

operational definition: Defining a concept in terms of the procedures used to manipulate or measure it

operationalize: To define a concept in a measurable way

order bias: When selecting a sample, the ordering in the sampling frame corresponds with the random start and the sampling interval to create an under- or over-representation of subgroups within the population

ordinal measurement: The attributes of the variable can be rank-ordered from highest to lowest or most to least

outcome (outcome objectives): Objectives of the program stated in terms of changes in the target system

outcome evaluation: Evaluation of the extent to which the intended changes in people or systems actually take place

outliers: Values that are extreme in any direction from the mean

oversampled: In stratified sampling, the strata are sampled in greater proportion than their proportion in the population

panel study: Longitudinal research that follows the same individuals referred to as the panel over time

parallel forms reliability: The extent that two versions of the same instrument are correlated

parametric statistics: Statistical tests based on assumptions that the data are normally distributed in the population, the sample is randomly selected, and at least one of the variables being analyzed is continuous

participant observation: In observational research, the observer becomes an active participant in the research setting

participatory action research (PAR): A research strategy in which the population to be studied is included as partners in all aspects of the research process including developing hypotheses, deciding on the best method to obtain data, and interpretation of the results

participatory evaluation: Sometimes known as **empowerment evaluation**; the use of evaluation concepts, methods, and findings to promote program improvement and self or social change through research that creates a partnership between researchers and non-researchers involved in the study

passive consent: A form of informed consent that requires parents or legal guardians to provide written notice only if they refuse to allow their dependants to participate. If no objection is provided, the dependants decide for themselves whether they want to participate at the time the study is conducted

Pearson's r (Pearson's Product Moment Correlation Coefficient): The most common statistical computation of correlation

perceived need: What people say they need

phenomenology: A philosophical position that asserts reality consists of objects and events as they are perceived in human consciousness and not of anything independent of human consciousness

plagiarize: To steal and pass off the ideas or words of another as one's own; use another's production without crediting the source; present as new and original an idea or product derived from an existing source

population: The totality of persons, events, organizational units, etc. on which the research problem is focused

positive correlation: The extent to which two variables co-vary in the same direction

post-hoc analysis: A variety of tests used following ANOVA to compare the means of each of the groups two at a time in order to determine which groups statistically differ

posttest: A measurement conducted following the introduction of the independent variable

posttest-only with comparison group research design: A quasi-experimental research design in which two nonequivalent groups are observed at posttest, with only one group having received the independent variable

posttest only with control group research design: An experimental research design without the use of a pretest; groups are measured only following the introduction of the independent variable

predictive validity: The ability of an instrument to predict a future state on some external criterion

pre-experimental research design: A research design that involves only one group or one round of observation

pretest: A measurement conducted prior to the administration of an independent variable

pretest-posttest with comparison group: A quasiexperimental research design in which two nonequivalent groups are observed at pretest and posttest, with only one group having received the independent variable

pretest-posttest with control group: An experimental research design in which the two groups are formed by random assignment and observations are made at pretest and posttest, with the experimental group subject to the independent variable and the control group not having received the independent variable. Also referred to as the classic experiment

pretreatment equivalency: Also referred to as between-group equivalency; the extent to which the experimental and control group share similar characteristics related to the research question; a condition created by random assignment

primary data: The collection of new data

probability: The odds or chances that something will happen based on the ratio of the number of favorable outcomes to the total number of possible outcomes

probability sampling: A sampling procedure in which every element in the sampling universe has a known probability of selection

process evaluation: An assessment of the activities performed by the organization and the quality with which the organization delivers these activities

process objectives: In program evaluation, objectives that focus on how a program is operating rather than on the results that it produces

program: An organized set of activities designed to reach specific objectives

program evaluation: The use of research methods to answer questions related to planning, evaluating, and improving programs

program monitoring: The ongoing collection and review of data over time as a routine organizational activity in order to monitor and improve organizational functioning

properties: Traits or attributes; distinctive characteristics

proportionate sampling: The proportion of each stratum in the sample corresponds to the respective proportion in the population

prospective research study: Involves the collection of pretest data and observation of the dependent variable as the independent variable is exerting its influence

pure observation: In observational research, the observer remains apart from the group, event, or person being observed

purposive sampling: A nonprobability sample in which selection of elements is intentional and is consistent with the goal of the research

p-value: The probability that a relationship between variables or a mean difference found in a sample is a result of sample error

qualitative content analysis: Systematic observation of text or artifacts (e.g., garbage) to detect patterns and the extent those patterns are represented

qualitative research: Umbrella term for methods of research investigation using an interpretive framework. It is concerned with understanding social conditions through the meaning individuals ascribe to their personal experiences; generally involving in-depth data collection and analysis

quality assurance: Sometimes referred to as the model standards approach; a type of evaluation in which an accrediting body or the organization itself defines the conditions for a quality program. Evaluation assesses the extent to which the program meets the quality standards

quantitative research: A systematic approach to research based on the positivist tradition that relies on quantification in measurement and the analysis of data using descriptive and inferential statistics. Often involves hypothesis testing with large samples

quasi-experimental research design: Design in which there is no random assignment to groups, but there is more than one group or more than one round of measurement

quota sampling: A nonprobability stratified sampling method in which the selection procedure is not random

random assignment: In experimental research, all elements, whether they are people, communities, or organizations, have an equal chance of being assigned to each condition

random digit dialing: In telephone surveys, computers generate phone numbers randomly after a geographic area is selected using the area code and/or first three digits of a telephone number

random error: In measurement, those sources of error that are neither consistent nor patterned, and are expected not to affect the overall distribution of scores

random sampling: A sampling procedure in which there is no purposive inclusion or exclusion of any element in sample selection; elements are drawn at random

range: The lowest and highest possible values on the scale. The spread between the minimum and the maximum values in a distribution, calculated by subtracting the minimum value from the maximum value and adding one

rates under treatment: A method of needs assessment in which need is measured by the needs of populations or communities similar to the one being assessed

ratio measurement: The attributes of a variable have order, equally spaced categories, and a true zero point for the measure

reactivity: A threat to external validity; when the situation of being studied produces different results than would otherwise be found because participants know they are part of an experiment; also known as the "Hawthorne effect." Change in research participants' usual behavior when they know that they are being observed

recoding: Changing one value to another in a database

record: The totality of data for each sampling unit (person or otherwise)

reciprocity: An interest in giving something back in exchange for what was received

refereed: A process used by academic journals to determine whether an article is worthy of publication. A journal is considered refereed when experts in the field review manuscripts and no author information is included when a manuscript is sent to experts for review

reflexivity: The researcher's own reflections on how he or she and the process of data collection may have impacted the research process, including the conclusions

rejection level: In statistics, the level at which the null hypothesis will be rejected. In social science this is typically <.5

relative need: what comparisons with similar populations indicate is a need

reliability: In measurement, the extent to which a measure produces consistent results each time the measure is administered

replication: Conducting a research study two or more times to see if similar results are obtained with different samples

researcher bias: A threat to external validity; when researchers see what they want to see, when they interpret findings toward the positive for the experimental condition and toward the negative for control and comparison groups

research hypothesis: The opposite of the null hypothesis and proposes the existence of a relationship between two or more variables

research manuscript: Describes a completed research study usually with sections that include abstract, introduction, method, results, discussion, conclusion, and bibliography

research methods: The procedures for conducting research studies and gathering and interpreting data so as to get the most valid findings

research process: A method of accumulating knowledge that involves five concrete distinct steps: Identifying a problem, defining that problem in terms of a question that is capable of study, developing a plan to answer the question, gathering data according to prescribed practices and drawing conclusions from the data

research proposal: Describes why a research project should be done and outline of the plan for how the research will be done

resentful demoralization: A threat to internal validity; a reaction to being part of the control group when group members know to which group they were assigned

respondent validation: Checking the results of the data analysis with the participants of the research to see whether they agree with the researcher's interpretations and conclusions. Also known as member checking

response rate: In a survey, the response rate is the percentage of all those selected in a sample who actually respond

retention: The ability to retain participation of the same individuals over time

retrospective baseline: A baseline that is one based on past experience, for example, descriptions of behavior based on memory, notes from a diary or journal, or formal records such as class attendance or homework monitoring from the school system

retrospective research study: Involves designing the research and conducting the analysis after the data have been collected and after the independent variable has already exerted its influence; looks back (versus prospective research which looks ahead)

reversal design: In single subject research, a baseline period is followed by the intervention. This is then followed by a third phase involving withdrawal of the intervention. In the fourth phase, the intervention is again provided

reverse scoring: In creating a scale, the process of coding some items in reverse so that all items indicate high scores as high levels of concept. For example, on a five-point scale, reverse coding would result in: **1= 5, 2 = 4, 3 = 3, 4 = 2, and 5 = 1**

sample: A selected subset of the population

sampling: The process of selecting a subset of the population

sampling bias: The systematic tendency to over- or under-represent some segment of the population

sampling error: The degree of difference between the sample and the population from which it was drawn

sampling frame: A list of all of the elements in a population from which the sample is selected

sampling plan: A plan that outlines where the data will come from and that justifies the choices made in sample selection and method

sampling units: The entities from which the data are gathered

sampling universe: The totality of population elements on the sampling frame

saturate: A term used in qualitative research to indicate when no new information is gained with additional participants

saturation: Collecting data until no new information is obtained

scale: In instrument construction, a score obtained by adding scores assigned to specific responses and also taking advantage of any intensity structure that might exist among the individual items, for instance by weighting the responses to the individual items differently

scattergram or scatterplot: A way to show visually the relationship between two linear variables on a graph in which each data point is plotted at the intersection of the horizontal axis (first variable) and vertical axis (second variable)

scientific method: A systematic method of investigation based on definition of concepts, collection of open and closed questions

secondary data: Data that were previously collected for a purpose other than the research at hand

selection bias: A threat to internal validity; when the groups are not comparable prior to the study, the change observed in the dependent variable could be due to pre-treatment differences between the groups rather than to the independent variable

self-administered questionnaire: A survey that is mailed to potential respondents or that is given in person to be filled out by the respondent without help

semi-structured interview: An interview in which some questions are predetermined but the interviewer also has leeway to follow the interviewee's lead into previously undetermined areas

semi-structured survey: A survey in which the interviewer is free to clarify the questions and follow-up on the participant's responses, although an initial list of questions is predetermined

simple random sampling: Choice of a subset of a population, i.e., the sample, utilizing a method that allows each element to have an equal chance of being chosen. The sampling frame is not subdivided and should not be ordered

simple time series research design: Uses of one group with three or more observations before and/or after the introduction of an independent variable

single subject research (SSR): Also known in the literature as single subject design, single system design, single case experimental design, within subject comparison, and n of 1 research; uses systematic methods to assess the effectiveness of an intervention by using a series of measurements prior to and following the introduction of an intervention with a single case

skewed distribution: Distributions that are not symmetric when plotted

snowball sampling: A nonprobability sample in which selection of elements relies on referrals from the first individuals who are identified for participation in the study; the process of identification continues until the desired sample size is reached

social artifacts: The products of social beings and their behavior

social desirability: A feeling of pressure to respond to research questions in a socially acceptable way regardless of whether or not it is true

social work research: A systematic way of developing knowledge for social work practice that relies on the research process

Solomon four-group research design: An experimental research design that combines the pretest/posttest control group research design and the posttest only with control group research design; allows an assessment of the effects of testing

sparse table: Table in which 30% of the cells have five or fewer elements

split-half reliability: The extent that one half of the items on a standardized measure correlate with the other half when a single concept is measured

split-middle method: A way of analyzing the significance of change over time in a data plot by plotting a trend line through two points, one that represents the mean of the first half of the baseline data points and the second that represents the mean of the second half of the baseline data points

standard deviation: A statistical measure of the amount by which a set of values differs from the arithmetical mean

standard deviation method: A method for determining the success of a single subject research by plotting a line representing one or two standard deviations from the mean of the baseline period and judging the results of the intervention period in relation to this line

standardized instrument: A measurement instrument that has already been developed and has known reliability and validity

standardized open-ended interviews: Interviews in which a standard set of open-ended questions are used to gather data from interviewees

state measures: Measures designed to quantify or describe constructs that are situationally dependent or that vary frequently

static measure: Measure that by its very nature is not amenable to change over time, e.g., number of arrests in 1998

statistical inference: The use of mathematical calculation to estimate the probability that a decision is correct based on probability theory

statistical power: The ability of a statistical test to detect a true relationship when one exists, in other words, to reject the null hypothesis correctly

statistical regression: A threat to internal validity; a tendency of extreme scores to move toward the mean over time

statistical significance testing: The likelihood that the findings from sample data are the result of sample error or chance

statistical success: The intervention has produced changes in target objectives that are greater than would be expected by chance variation, but have not necessarily fully reached all objectives

string data: Consist of letters, words, or numbers for which mathematical operations will not be performed (e.g., zip code)

structured survey: A survey in which the interviewer asks the questions as they are written with the aim of standardizing the administration process as much as possible

summative evaluation: Research to determine whether the program produces positive changes in the quality of people's lives

survey: A systematic way of collecting data from a number of respondents. The use of mailed and Internet questionnaires, telephone and face-to-face interviews to provide information if the sampling method is appropriate, the instrument is valid and reliable, and the response rate is good

systematic error (also nonrandom error): In measurement, those sources of error that have a pattern and will influence the overall distribution of scores

systematic random sampling: The selection of elements within a sample when an ordered list of the population exists; elements are chosen from the list by applying a uniform interval from one another and utilizing a random start point within that interval

systems framework: A way of conceptualizing phenomena as consisting of interrelated and interacting parts that constitute a whole within an environmental context

testing effect: A threat to internal validity in experimental research; involves the danger that observed effects are due not to the independent variable but to the fact that performance on a test is influenced by taking a previous test, i.e, the pretest

test-retest reliability: The extent that a measure produces consistent results when administered twice in a relatively short time frame under similar circumstances

theoretical coding: In qualitative research, coding of data based on concepts relating to a specific theory

therapeutic success: An intervention is considered a therapeutic success when the goals of the client have been reached

time series: Use of three or more observations before and/or after the introduction of the independent variable; often used in single subject research designs to evaluate individual practice

time series with comparison group research design:

trait measures: Measures designed to quantify or describe constructs that are stable and long lasting

treatment contamination: A threat to internal validity; the danger that the effects of the independent variable will also be experienced by the control group due to interaction of the groups or program personnel

treatment fidelity: The extent to which the program is being delivered as intended

trend study: Longitudinal research that compares individuals with the same defining characteristics at different points in time; for example, teens in the 1980s, 1990s, and 2000s

triangulation: Using several different measures or sources to assess progress towards or outcomes of an objective; useful in establishing the validity of findings

trigger: Something that prompts a response

unimodal: A distribution with only one mode

unique case identifier: A unique variable that identifies the sampling unit for each particular record

unit of analysis: The system level that will be studied; for example, the individual, family, group, community, geographic area, artifact, and so forth

univariate analysis: Analysis of data based on examining one variable at a time, typically reporting results such as frequencies and measures of central tendency

unstructured interviews: Open-ended, in-depth questioning for the purpose of understanding complex phenomena without imposing any preexisting notions of categorization

validity: In measurement, the extent to which a measure is measuring what is actually intended to be measured

variable: A concept with attributes that can vary; regardless of whether or not the attributes represent qualitative or numeric differences

variable label: A short description of the variable

variable names: Conventions for naming variables in a database or statistical program

weighting: In sampling or data analysis, emphasizing some aspect or variable by giving it "more weight" or "less weight" in the final result. For example, an ethnic group with few members in the population may be sampled in greater proportion to their actual number in order to ensure a subsample large enough for data analysis

Index